The Last Wesleyan

a life of Donald Soper

The Last Wesleyan

a life of Donald Soper

Mark Peel

First published in 2008 on behalf of the author by
Scotforth Books, Carnegie House,
Chatsworth Road, Lancaster LA1 4SL.

ISBN 13: 978-1-904244-48-6

Printed in the UK by The Cromwell Press, Wiltshire

Contents

Acknowledgements

When Martin Lawrence, Donald Soper's nephew, first approached me about writing a new biography of his uncle in the immediate aftermath of his death, I was immediately taken with the idea and have sought from the very beginning to adhere to his premise of approaching the assignment from a fresh angle. There were three biographies of Donald Soper during his lifetime, all of which had various degrees of co-operation from him, and while all had their value, none of them were able to tell fully the story of a brilliant but highly complex public figure whose shadow continued to loom over them.

It is now nearly a decade since Donald Soper died and easier to see his life in perspective and offer a number of value judgements about his work and the causes to which he held dear. In particular, by drawing on much fresh material, I have tried to focus on his gargantuan personality and explain the paradox of why one of the most eminent figures in Methodist history and a leading member of the Labour Party should remain something of an outsider.

I'm very grateful to Donald Soper's most recent biographer, Brian Frost, for depositing his material in the Soper Archive in the John Rylands Library, the University of Manchester. Some of the information was particularly useful. I'm also much indebted to all those who supplied illustrations for this book.

During my many visits to the John Rylands Library I was much indebted to the help of Dr Gareth Hughes, the Methodist Archivist, and Dr Peter Nockles, the Chief Methodist Librarian, and the support I had from the staff. I also gladly acknowledge the help I received from the National Library of Scotland, New College Library, the University of Edinburgh, the Leslie Weatherhead Archive in the University of Birmingham, Lewisham Libraries, the University of Bristol Library Department of Manuscripts, the British Library National Sound Archive, the British Newspaper Library at Colindale, Cambridge University Library, the State Library of New South Wales, the State Library of Victoria, Queen's College and Ormond College, University of Melbourne.

Others to whom I owe a lot for their help include: Fred Baker, the Archivist of the Methodist Church of New Zealand, Suzanne Griffiths, the Assistant

Librarian, St Catharine's College, Cambridge, Bill Hetherington, Chief Archivist of the Peace Pledge Union, Carl Spadoni and the Research Collections staff of McMaster University, Hamilton, Ontario, Darren Treadwell and the staff of the Labour Museum of History, Manchester, Jeff Walden and the BBC Written Archives Centre, Caversham Park, Reading.

I am indebted to the Soper family for permission to quote from letters of their late father, and to Martin Lawrence for allowing me to quote from testimonials relating to his grandmother.

Transcripts of Crown-copyright records in the Public Record Office are reproduced by permission of the Controller of Her Majesty's Stationery Office.

Extracts from the BBC Archives are reproduced by courtesy of the BBC Written Archives Centre, material from Bristol Penguin Archives is reproduced by courtesy of Helen Fraser and Penguin Books and extracts from the Soper Archive are reproduced by courtesy of the University and Library Directorate, the John Rylands University Library, the University of Manchester and the Archive and History Committee of the Methodist Church.

For permission to quote from material in their possession or of which they own the copyright, I am pleased to thank the following: The Rt Hon Michael Foot, the Revd Graeme Jackson, the Revd David Mason, the Revd Dr John Newton and Lady Sheppard .

Every effort has been made to contact copyholders regarding printed or illustrated material. In some cases this has not been possible. Where any infringement of copyright has been made, the author offers his sincere apologies and will seek to redress this oversight in future editions.

I would like to express my grateful thanks to the following who gave freely of their time to share their reminiscences of Donald Soper: Mrs Ann Horn, Mrs Judith Jenkins, Mrs Bridget Kemmis and Mrs Caroline Soper [daughters], Alan Jenkins [son-in-law] and Martin and Patricia Lawrence [nephew and niece by marriage].

Others to whom I am grateful are: Jean Anderson, Professor Philip Bagwell, the Rt Hon Tony Benn, the Revd Gary Best, the Revd Derek Bibb, Ann Bird, the Rt Hon Lord Callaghan of Cardiff, Kay Calton, Saul Cantor, the Rt Hon Baroness Castle of Blackburn, the Revd David Cruise, Olive Delves, Councillor Arthur Downes, the Revd Brian Duckworth, the Rt Hon Michael Foot, John Grant, the Revd Dr Kenneth Greet, Councillor Illtyd Harrington, the Revd Jeffrey Harris, Judge John Hicks, Mary Hicks, the Revd Paul Hulme, the Revd Graeme Jackson, Bruce Kent, Ian Kiek, Margaret Marshall, the Revd Dr Colin Morris, the Revd David Mullins, the Revd Dr John Newton, Denys

Orchard, Cliff Padgett, the Revd Caroline Pinchbeck, Henry Rutland, Rt Revd Lord Sheppard of Liverpool, Kath Short, the Revd Raymond Short, Alfred Sleep, the Revd David Smith, Peter Terry, the Revd Arthur Valle, the Revd Dr John Vincent, Ron Watts, Len Webb, Dr Pauline Webb, the Revd Derek White, Canon Alan Wilkinson, Renée Willgress, the Rt Hon Baroness Williams of Crosby.

The Revd Kenneth Brown, besides being an invaluable mine of information, was also a constant source of help and encouragement, as was Donald Soper's secretary, Kath Humphreys, who not only put me in touch with various people but provided much useful material. I'm greatly in their debt, as I am to Julie Davidson, Andrew Murray, Frank Pearson, Robert Philp and Ivo Tennant for reading through parts of the script and offering a number of helpful suggestions.

Gavin Lloyd, the Revd David Mason and Owen Dudley Edwards were towers of strength not only for their many illuminating insights but also their time, encouragement, wisdom and support throughout my endeavours. I owe them more than they can imagine, as I do once again to Mrs Sandra Edwards for turning my illegible handwriting into art form. She is the consummate professional. Finally, I would like to thank Anna Goddard and Lucy Day of Carnegie Book Production for all their efforts and good cheer in bringing this project to completion.

Mark Peel
Edinburgh 2008

Prologue

During the closing years of the twentieth century, as churches lay empty all over London, victims of a growing secularisation, a voice from an earlier era continued to ply his trade in a style familiar to those who had listened to his homilies over the decades. Although increasingly decrepit, Donald Soper, esteemed Methodist minister and Labour peer, continued to defy everything nature and old age threw at him by unfailingly appearing every week at his old stamping-grounds, Tower Hill and Hyde Park, to pronounce upon the great issues of the day in what he called the fellowship of controversy. Although lacking the numbers and atmosphere of yesteryear, these encounters still made good copy for the plethora of feature columnists who frequently journeyed to these shrines of evangelism to witness one of the greatest open-air preachers since John Wesley practised his art. And it wasn't simply for show, for behind the repartee and dramatic gestures there was a bewitching intensity to the arguments rehearsed, just as there had been over the previous seventy years since Donald Soper first became a public figure back in the 1920s.

Born into a strict Nonconformist household in South London in 1903, Donald freely imbibed the values of his parents while at the same time developing a zest for life which eluded his austere father. Endowed with good looks, great charm and inestimable gifts, it says much for the profundity of his faith that he forsook easy riches elsewhere for a lifetime's vocation to the Church of his youth.

In his work as Superintendent of the West London Mission, a post he held for forty-two years between 1936 and 1978, Donald stood firmly in the line of eminent Free Church ministers such as Hugh Price Hughes, its founder, such was his domination of the pulpit. Yet it was his aping of another Nonconformist tradition, the platform, that catapulted him to national prominence and shaped the character of his ministry thereafter. Employing his angelic tongue to maximum effect, Donald's weekly encounters in the open air were soon the talk of London as he discoursed on all matters from Christianity to communism, missing few opportunities to see off the hecklers with his erudite wit. To the majority of the vast gatherings he attracted it was unlike anything that they had heard before, since Donald cut through much theological verbiage to offer a practical Christianity directly responsive to everyday needs. Drawing his inspiration from the Sermon on the Mount, he insisted that the kingdom of God on earth wasn't only a personal experience but a social one too, channelled through a Labour Party dedicated to socialism. Such was his support for the underdog and a host of other progressive causes, that it committed him to a life of marches and demonstrations, often in the company of such seasoned campaigners as Michael Foot and Tony Benn. They at least as elected politicians had to consider the vagaries of public opinion on occasions, but for Donald there was no such obligation. He was his own master, responsible only to a higher authority. This meant that to him a cause which was morally right was politically acceptable, a position which made him an uneasy companion in the Labour movement as it repeatedly oscillated between socialist idealism and political pragmatism. When Donald became an alderman on the London County Council (LCC) in 1958, he publicly denounced any attempt to bind him to the party whip. There was then his friendship with Harold Wilson, leader of the Labour Party 1963–76, which earned him the title of Labour's unofficial chaplain, an accolade more apparent than real, since Wilson's Governments were far too cautious for his taste. Nothing would budge him from his unshakeable commitment to Clause IV nationalisation, not even when a later generation of Labour leaders struggled to come to terms with a more affluent society. "Does Soper," pondered Alan Wilkinson, in his book on Christian Socialism, "by bestowing divine blessings upon ideological factionalism and optimistic utopianism, share responsibility for keeping the Labour Party anachronistic and on the margins for so long?"[1] If he did, he never showed any remorse when during his final years he saw his vision of a truly equal society consigned to history, along with the other great cause of his life, pacifism.

Donald's relationship with Methodism was an equally ambivalent one. Although a Methodist through and through in so much of his personal ethos, most notably his extreme aversion to gambling and drinking, his high media profile, political activity and ecumenical contacts separated him from the rather staid, cloistered world of his colleagues, especially since the drudgery of church committee work held little appeal for him. Consequently, he remained something of an outsider within his own ranks, pilloried before the Second World War for being too liberal in theology and afterwards for being too Catholic in his sacramentalism, and always for being too politically divisive. This was especially the case at the Methodist Conference in 1950 when he expressed a preference for a Britain which was red rather than dead, or when as President in 1953–54 he castigated the Queen over horse racing and her Government over the hydrogen bomb. Even the *Methodist Recorder*, the respected mouthpiece of Methodism, felt moved to admonish him that as President his prime task was to speak for his Church rather than himself.

In addition to his unconventional beliefs, many Methodists resented his addiction to the limelight, his seeming exemption from the Methodist itinerant system which should have taken him out of London into the provinces, and his prophetic warnings of a Church in danger. Much as he loved Methodism, he long felt that its only hope in the face of declining numbers was as a preaching order inside the Church of England. It was in this context, and in his desire to become a bishop that he strongly supported Anglican-Methodist reunion. The collapse of these talks in the late 1960s–early 1970s vexed him greatly, leaving him an even more isolated figure within his own denomination. It was only during his twilight years when the passion of former battles had stilled that the *enfant terrible* became the Grand Old Man of Methodism rightly acclaimed for a life of outstanding service to the Church. Had the more emollient side of his character, seen so often in his pastoral work, been employed to some effect in his political campaigning, he might well have achieved more in this field, but then Donald, according to Alan Wilkinson, had always been a restless matador looking out for a bull, his passionate beratings of a fallen society ensuring him a turbulent journey along life's bumpy road.

CHAPTER ONE

Under Orders

Donald Oliver Soper was born on 31 January 1903 into a Britain that was fast changing as the august calm of the nineteenth century was giving way to a new and uncertain era.

When Londoners thronged the streets of their capital in June 1897 to pay homage to Victoria their Queen on the occasion of her Diamond Jubilee, the celebrations seemed suitably appropriate. Not only did large parts of the globe lie under the sovereignty of the British flag, the mother country seemed a byword for economic prosperity and political stability. Yet beneath the surface a darker side existed as industrialisation had created new mass ranks of disillusioned trade unionists, some of whom toyed with ideas of a socialist society. Most debilitating of all was the spectre of primary poverty exposed all too clearly by the exhaustive studies of two respected philanthropists and statisticians, Charles Booth and Seebohm Rowntree in London and York respectively. Not only did they reveal that some 30 per cent of the population lived in poverty, but most of these people were actually in work, data that challenged long-held assumptions about unemployment being linked to defects of character.

If the moral case for government-inspired social reform was overwhelming, then so was the practical one following the abject showing of Britain's troops in the Boer War (1899–1902). At a time when her industrial supremacy was under threat from Germany, Japan and the United States, and her control of the seas from the Kaiser's navy, the need for a physically resilient army and workforce had never been more compelling. The fact that the Conservative Government of Arthur Balfour, representing an establishment still largely landed and Anglican, failed to act decisively enough, helps explain their catastrophic defeat at the 1906 general election. Their victors weren't the newly formed Labour Party, which broadly represented the working man, but the Liberal Party composed of provincial businessmen, artisans and traders desirous of a more open, inclusive society. As the Liberal ranks were swelled with an unprecedented number of Nonconformist MPs, this marked the high-watermark of the Free Churches, and of Wesleyan Methodism, the denominational badge of the Soper family, in particular. Yet, even now, as they savoured their rise towards respectability, there could be no cause for complacency. Aside from the growing scepticism about biblical truth being expressed from Darwinists and others from within the universities, the Churches, Anglican and Nonconformist alike, had rarely penetrated the world of the industrial working class. Church attendance broadly remained the preserve of the middle class, but even here the portents weren't encouraging. For as the strict observance of the Sabbath was no longer sacrosanct following the growth in sporting and leisure opportunities, the continuing allegiance of the younger middle class began to wane even in their outward observance. Such a mood of indifference was one that the Churches increasingly had to confront thereafter, and their uncertain response to this dilemma was greatly to shape the life and ministry of Donald Soper.

His father, Ernest Frankham Soper, born in 1871, was the son of a tailor based in East Hill, Wandsworth in South-West London who later married the daughter (Donald's paternal grandmother) of one of the wardens of the British Museum. If his paternal grandfather's origins were relatively humble, there is no doubt that by the time Donald was born, the family, contrary to his later claims about his own modest origins, had long lost any association with the upper working class.

Starting life as an office boy with the City firm, Charles Cooper and Sons in Leadenhall Street, Ernest Soper worked his way up to a position of considerable authority as an average adjuster in marine insurance. In this erudite field of employment he dealt with complex claims for ships that came to a sorry end, as was very much the case during the First World War. To his staff like C. R. Kelsey, Ernest was a straightforward disciplinarian who gave instructions which he expected to be obeyed, yet was equally disposed to lend a sympathetic ear to those who approached him with a problem.

Away from his work and his involvement with the Police Court Mission, Ernest's life revolved around the Church. A committed Nonconformist, he was, in addition to his duties at the Salvation Army Mission in Earlsfield, a pillar of St John's Hill Methodist Church, Wandsworth. A popular superintendent of its Sunday School, with a preference for lengthy classes, he was also an accomplished open-air speaker and Superintendent of the Union Band of Hope. Founded in 1847 to campaign for teetotalism, especially among the young, this organisation was near the peak of its influence, and Ernest's leadership sparked new life into the weekly meetings, especially the magic lantern evening each month. Greta Reynolds, one of his charges in Forest Hill, later described him as a kind of Old Testament prophet: always kind to them as children, he would inscribe their names beautifully in any prizes won.[1] In 1897 Ernest married Caroline Pilcher, a member of a family of well-known local builders with roots in West Hartlepool, County Durham. Caroline's background was Congregationalist (a form of Protestantism which gives complete self-government to a local congregation or church) but she was happy enough to transfer her allegiances to Methodism, a symbol of the devotion she felt for her husband. A small, intense woman, Caroline, born in 1877, gained a top-class teaching degree which majored in Religious Education before beginning her long and distinguished teaching career as an assistant mistress at Swaffield Road Primary School, Wandsworth, in 1898. Immediately establishing herself as a firm disciplinarian, she was acclaimed for the quality of her teaching in science, needlework, history and drawing as seventy-three scholarships for her girls testified. According to Mrs E. E. Cadley, the headmistress there in June 1914, she had always been a beacon of excellence, especially in her work with older pupils. "Her teaching is thorough, intelligent, methodical and painstaking, and the tone of her class is excellent,"[2] she wrote in Caroline's testimonial. She also commended her inspirational leadership of the choir, which gained the Shield at the South London Music Festival in 1912 and participated in the City of Paris Music Festival, accomplishments which, according to Mrs Cadley, justified Caroline's promotion. In her estimation she would make an efficient and capable headmistress.

The following year Caroline had her reward when she was appointed Headmistress of Stillness Road School, Lewisham – one of the very first women in the London Teachers' Union to reach such a promotion – a post she held for five years. There, her commitment to educational breadth and quality was reflected in the way she encouraged her staff to light the spark in every pupil across a range of academic and extramural activities. Her own interest and enthusiasm were infectious and soon had their desired effect. A record number of scholarships were gained. The sport and music flourished and there were major contributions to the war effort. When Caroline applied for promotion in September 1919, she received a glowing reference from the School Manager, Frank Proul. "From the above particulars," he wrote, "and in view of her remarkable personality, you will agree that I am fully justified in stating that Mrs Soper is eminently suited for a position in a Grade 3 school. I hereby strongly recommend her for any post of that nature which is vacant."[3] It says much for the judgement of the managers of Morden Terrace Girls' School, Greenwich, that they took the hint and appointed her. Again her impact was to be immediate. Not only were up-to-date academic methods introduced, especially in the sixth form, she also maintained sound discipline and encouraged the development of games. During her time there,

Caroline, according to London County Council Inspectors in October 1922, transformed the school from one of average standing and success to one of outstanding merit in every respect. The fact that the girls, mainly from respectable working-class homes, weren't specially fortunate in their circumstances made the high standing of the school all the more remarkable in their eyes. Such achievement reflected enormous credit on the headmistress and her staff, they concluded. Not surprisingly their judgement was endorsed by the Chairman of Managers, M. G. Fearon, who called her "a most excellent Headmistress and an indefatigable worker, liked and respected by pupils, parents and staff alike".[4] One former pupil of Hazelrigge Road School, Clapham, where Caroline was later headmistress, recalled her as strict and dedicated. Girls were not allowed to blink an eyelash when she came into the class to talk to them. When she took Assembly in the hall her eyes would be on every one of them and her parting shot to leavers was, "You all have lovely complexions and hair now, don't spoil them by painting your faces and perming your hair as soon as you leave school. That will come later when you reach my age".

It says much for Caroline's energy and organisational ability that amidst all her teaching commitments she found as much time as she did to devote to her family in their spacious three-storey home at 36, Knoll Road, Wandsworth. In this salubrious environment Donald, his sister Millicent (born in 1905) and brother Meredith Ross (born in 1907 and known as Sos because his sister when young couldn't pronounce the R in his second name), spent their early years. Despite her unrelenting efforts on behalf of her children, Caroline's preoccupation with her work meant that much of the responsibility for the children's upbringing was shouldered by two live-in friends. One was "Aunt Lizzie", alias Miss Woollard, a bridesmaid at her wedding, and the other "Aunt Nellie", alias Miss Watson, a fellow teacher, who also helped Ernest in the running of the Sunday School. Neither brooked any nonsense as Donald discovered on those occasions when he allowed his high spirits to get the better of him. Once when he disobeyed "Aunt Lizzie's" instructions to stop using a carving knife as a sword during some capers with his friends, she reported him to his father, who summarily beat him.

Although a lady of high ideals and good works, sharing Ernest's passion for the Church, Caroline Soper possessed a lighter touch than her more pedestrian husband, providing Donald with much of his zest and humour. Conversation fairly flowed at mealtimes when she was around, as did family musical soirées and when the Sopers entertained young people she proved to be the perfect hostess. She was also a secure haven in distress and someone in whom her children could confide, even though such encounters would lack the intimacy of many a family today. Not surprisingly Donald was closer to his mother than his father, especially since the latter, according to Donald, failed to respond to the more sensitive side of his nature. Nevertheless it was his father who had the greater influence on his career and development, since for all Caroline's female tendencies which made her a strong supporter of the suffragette campaign for votes for women, she was happy enough to defer to her husband on family matters.

A man of austere integrity with severe features lining an otherwise hand-some face, Ernest led his life strictly according to his faith. At breakfast each day he would unfailingly read the Bible to his children, the words inducing a sense of wonder in Donald. Smoking, drinking, gambling, dancing and the theatre were seriously frowned upon. Even on a rare night out to a restaurant his children had to endure the curious glances of the other diners as Ernest insisted, in full shot of everyone's hearing, on saying grace. Diligence, disci-pline and duty were his abiding precepts and woe betide the child who strayed from this narrow path, for justice was severe, as Donald, the most flighty of the three children, frequently discovered when confronted with his whippy cane. Later he recalled that although his father forgave him many times as a boy he couldn't help noticing that contrition in no way impaired the rigour of the penalty. It was this dogged insistence on the highest standards that made Donald feel inadequate, not least in his work ethic, a burden which he had to carry thereafter, and which accounted for the emotional distance between them. That said, there was never any question of him seriously rebelling against this severe upbringing. For apart from respecting his father's saintlike integrity and erudition – he used to boast in the playground that between them his father and he knew everything – he was able to see that he did have his best interests at heart. During his final years when asked by one of his own disciples, Colin Morris, who had been his hero, Donald was unequivocal in his reply. His father. "There was a quality of enduring faith which I'm quite sure I needed then and need still."[5] At this stage it is worth remembering that this faith was more about a sense of moral obligation to do certain things and avoid others on pain of everlasting damnation, rather than a compendium of great theological issues. "I was brought up to believe," Donald later recalled, "that I had to take greatest care or else I was going to hell. And not only that hell was something that was going to happen if I died, but they could make hell for me down here, and somebody of the best intention could get me into a lot of trouble. And in one sense I was very early convinced that religion was what I had to do to escape."[6]

He also unhesitatingly accepted the church-centred world of his child-hood, greatly enjoying the mixture of devotion and entertainment it brought, not least the girls he met there and the prizes he won at Sunday School for either singing or religious knowledge. He later recalled his first Sunday away from home as a fifteen-year-old bayonet-fighting instructor in the Cadet Corps down in Devon, when he ran four miles to church, such was his desire to attend.

In this Donald wasn't entirely unusual because in a more simple, spiritual age, a dynamic church could be the hub of local activity. This was especially the case in Methodist circles with their emphasis on Sunday School, chapel teas, lecture halls and musical soirées. Born in the evangelical revival of the eighteenth century, Methodism under its revered founder, John Wesley (1703–91), revived a stagnant established Church by sending its ministers out into the world to offer salvation to the sinner through God's redeeming power. Shopkeepers, artisans and distinct working communities united by a common interest such as the Durham miners, flocked to the banner enabling it to become the largest of all the Free Churches outside the traditional Anglican–Tory establishment. Although united by a general distaste for a fixed liturgy and episcopal government, alongside its attachment to the spoken word and a simple ethical lifestyle, Methodism steadily descended into a schismatic body, divided over what level of congregational authority was deemed acceptable. Leading this plethora of sects were the Wesleyan Methodists, the most wealthy, Anglican and clerical among them with their emphasis on ministerial authority over lay autonomy, not least in the administration of the sacraments.

By the beginning of the twentieth century they were at the apogee of their influence, especially active in the affluent suburbs of the South and where their churches and Sunday Schools acted as potent recruiters to the faith. "Poor old Wandsworth," confided John Wesley to his Journal in 1790, "I preach once more at poor Wandsworth," something he had done intermittently over the previous forty-two years, since he had been stoned by the rabble. At least three of his visits were to the small chapel erected in the High Street in 1772, the first Methodist chapel to be built in and around London. Then after Methodist ranks began to expand in the middle of the nineteenth century, St John's, a stately Gothic building with an imposing turret, was erected in 1864. It was here amidst this fairly well-to-do congregation, some in top hats, that the Sopers worshipped every Sunday, and where Donald was baptised by the Revd Josiah Flew, a distinguished family name in the annals of Methodism.

Aside from attending Morning and Evening Service, where the great hymns of Charles Wesley were celebrated with true gusto, the Soper children also attended Sunday School twice and sang hymns around the piano before retiring early to bed on pain of yet further biblical study. So sacrosanct was the Sabbath that Ernest, the superintendent of his children's Sunday School, allowed nothing to detract from things spiritual. Reading Sunday newspapers was strictly forbidden, as was gardening, although he was happy enough to stroll around the flower beds whistling a hymn, and planning what he'd do on Monday. Then there were Band of Hope lectures on Monday evenings at which Donald listened to his father rail against the evils of alcohol, using empty bottles with exaggerated labels as props. In addition to the strictures of his faith, Ernest's passion for abstinence was shaped by the unhappy experience of both his mother and father-in-law being alcoholics. One of Donald's earliest traumatic recollections was of his father being summoned out on a Saturday evening to rescue his mother from the pub and clearly his father's campaign had a profound effect upon him. "I was so badly concussed at soccer one day," he recalled, "that my team-mates took me to see the trainer, who said, 'A drop of brandy should pull him through'. Well, the word brandy alone was enough to shock me awake. I sat bolt upright and said, 'I refuse to touch a drop of that stuff'. My father was inordinately proud."[7]

For all the solemnity of the Wesleyan Methodist ethos, which Donald later described as very narrow and middle-class, comparable with the future Prime Minister Margaret Thatcher's upbringing in Grantham, it would be wrong to depict his childhood as devoid of enjoyment. In addition to the traditional childhood preoccupations of charades, sport and cycle rides, music was a particular outlet for their entertainment. All three children, taking after their mother, had exquisite singing voices, and in addition both boys were accomplished instrumentalists. According to Millicent, Donald by the age of thirteen played the trumpet, clarinet, piano, guitar and tin whistle, priding himself on the fact that when receiving a new instrument on Christmas morning he could play any carol by the time they assembled for church. Aside from their informal soirées when the children would sing hymns or Negro spirituals, the family could sustain a complete musical evening with Donald on the piano, Sos the violin, Ernest singing bass, Caroline contralto and Millicent soprano. Donald later recalled how during one holiday at Minehead they heard a pierrot troupe perform on the promenade. As they listened his father would be busy remembering the words while he remembered the tune. They appropriated many songs in that way. Together with Sos they would play Vivaldi and Mendelssohn, making it up as they went along, taking care to avoid wrong notes. "It was a primitive kind of fun but its value lay in bringing us close together."[8]

A shared love of sport was another area which bound him to his brother and sister who was an excellent swimmer-cum athlete. Sport had been in the blood. Donald's paternal grandfather, a friend of Jerome K. Jerome, the celebrated author of *Three Men in a Boat,* was a great Thames man who won many cups for swimming, while his father had been a top-flight athlete and useful cricketer. He organised many an expedition to Wimbledon and Streatham Common to tutor his children in the art of fast bowling and was later a loyal supporter of school teams – on either the touchline or the boundary. Such vigorous activity formed an integral part of the annual family holiday to the seaside, be it Minehead in Somerset, Worthing in Sussex or Heacham in Norfolk, when Ernest (having first established the location of the nearest Wesleyan chapel) ensured that every minute was put to good use. In addition to swimming in all temperatures (although not on Sundays), both boys adored their sporting tussles on the sand, which helped to refine their technical skills, Donald proving especially adept at cricket and tennis, Sos at football. The brothers' close relationship was furthered by their similar inquisitive minds, idiosyncratic sense of humour and well-developed social consciences. This latter trait was shared by Millicent who later became a Sunday School teacher in Streatham prior to her sterling work in the teaching profession.

In 1908 Donald went to his first school, Swaffield Road in Wandsworth, where his mother taught and was acting headmistress during his final year and which almost became a second home to him. He later recalled how, when in pocket, he was able to buy a farthingsworth of old English toffee at the shop close to the entrance to the playground and suck it through scripture and maths. His form master was Mr Pike, whom he regarded with affection, despite the fact that he periodically beat him on the hand with a short cane when he transgressed, although, mercifully, Mr Pike never reported him to his mother. On the whole he found his time at Swaffield Road to be a happy, carefree period in his life, an enjoyable prelude to his seven years at Haberdashers' Aske's School, Hatcham, where he went, on a scholarship awarded by the Haberdashers' Company, in 1914. This was also the year, incidentally, that the family moved to a large semi-detached house at 243, Devonshire Road, Forest Hill, so that Caroline could be closer to her new school in Honor Oak. Later, they moved again to Streatham.

Haberdashers' Aske's School, Hatcham, founded in 1875 and known as Aske's, grew out of a bequest by Robert Aske (1619–89), a wealthy silk merchant and Freeman of the Haberdashers' Company, one of the twelve "great" Livery Companies of the City of London. When the original boys' school in Hoxton was relocated to Hampstead, a new fee-paying school was completed at Hatcham, then a desirable middle-class suburb in South-East London. With a selective intake, boosted by generous scholarships from the Foundation, and a Common Room committed to excellence, the academic credentials of the school were soon assured. Its growing success in public exams and university admissions was officially recognised in 1913, when Aske's was granted the public school status it sought by its admission to the Headmasters' Conference before such neighbouring establishments as Alleyn's, Colfe's and St Dunstan's, and an upbeat School Inspectorate report in March 1914. Three years earlier the school had appointed the Rossall-and-Oxford-educated Ernest Basil Falkner Headmaster at the age of thirty, making him one of the youngest in the country. His wish was to broaden further Aske's academic and sporting horizons as well as inculcating the public school ethos. To this end he developed the school's facilities, founded the CCF and introduced a uniform dress: black coat in the winter terms and blazer in the summer.

It was with some irony that Donald's formative years directly coincided with the First World War, so that his education at Aske's became a learning process geared to a wartime environment. In retrospect, such experiences could well have warped the memories of the future pacifist. The fact that they didn't, we know from Donald's own recollections of himself as a normal outgoing pupil who found his niche in the broad gamut of activities on offer.

Intellectually, he had little trouble complying with the school's challenging expectations reflected in the studious atmosphere in class, although his apparent facility for completing his prep on the train home induced envy in his siblings as they laboured every evening. "A vivacious, pleasant mannered boy. Quite straight and works hard".[9] This was the Lower Fourth form master's assessment of him in his Christmas 1915 report, and "a gentlemanly boy" the following term, "although inclined to resent reproof".[10] Promoted to the Upper Fourth for the summer term, he continued to impress with both his effort and progress although the reference to his restless behaviour in class told of a character trait most evident in later years. After another year of endeavour in the Upper Fifth there was again a mild deviance from accepted norms in the Middle Sixth when his work became a touch erratic, causing his form mistress Mrs Earp some concern, despite her susceptibility to his wit and charm. "Work variable. History very good. Requires watching"[11] was the slightly ominous verdict in July 1918, but thereafter the onset of public exams brought with them their own stimulant for renewed vigour. Come the end of the school year and aside from some reservations about his French, Donald was once again back on track as a model pupil. "Most of the masters taking the Arts set agree that it is one of the best forms there has ever been,"[12] noted his form master Mr F. Richmond-Coggan in July 1919, so for Donald to come first out of thirty-two in his English General School Certificate that summer was no mean achievement. He was also top in Latin, although in a much smaller set, and for all his travails in French, fifth out of thirty-two in the written exam with 65%. In History he was sixth out of fifteen with 69% and acquitted himself respectably in both Arithmetic and Elementary Maths, if not in Advanced Maths where a paltry 5% revealed his Achilles heel.

Placed in the Upper Sixth for his final two years, Donald continued to flourish, developing his great love of literature, especially the works of Shakespeare, Dickens and Robert Louis Stevenson which had been keenly nurtured at home by his father. "An enthusiast, interesting himself in all the activities of the school,"[13] wrote C. A. King, his form master, at the end of his penultimate year. "Has literary power and appreciation of a high order. Sound, sensible and appreciative of good".[14] This was the verdict of E. S. Poole a year later during his final term when he won the School History Prize, and was the proud recipient of an exhibition by the Governors to help him through Cambridge.

Away from the classroom he was prominent in most areas of School life, not least his contributions to the Drama Society, the most memorable of which was his portrayal of Stephano in scenes from *The Tempest*. The fact that Donald enjoyed acting despite his father's abhorrence of the theatre and his later admission that he never went himself until aged twenty-one, says much for his sense of showmanship as well as his participation in Sunday School pageants and charades at family parties. Despite exasperating his music teacher by his tendency to play almost by instinct, he was a valued member of the choir and was invariably a leading fixture in the annual Christmas Concert, when his amusing monologues caused much merriment. "D. O. Soper sang 'Land of Hope and Glory' and 'The Chorister'," reported the *South Eastern Herald* in December 1916. "He is a clear mezzo soprano and his performance deserves much commendation."[15] Three years later his tenor voice duet with Mr Rees, a young master, entertained the capacity audience with renditions of "The Gendarmes" and "The Twins", a prelude to their vocal duets of Lane Wilson the following Christmas when their virtuosity won them a rapturous ovation.

Another of his prominent responsibilities, which was perhaps surprising in light of his subsequent career, was his invaluable role in the School Cadet Corps, the initiative of a headmaster whose attachment to the Royal Naval Air Service meant his absence from Aske's between 1916 and 1919. Despite the occasion when a visiting officer to the School on Inspection Day found his platoon playing indoor football rather than being smartly dressed on parade, Donald greatly enjoyed it. It so happened that his time at Aske's began weeks after the outbreak of the First World War. This was a war which elicited the same kind of patriotic fervour in the Soper household as it did in almost every home in the country, such was their unquestioned acceptance of the rightness of their cause against the Kaiser's Germany. The war fever, fuelled by the patriotic pageant at Sunday School and regular homilies in School Assembly, not least when the deaths of old boys were somberly announced, gave added meaning to Wednesday afternoon drill in the CCF. In common with almost all his contemporaries, Donald soon joined, revelling in the wearing of his uniform and later the right to wear a badge of crossed swords on his hat, his reward for having passed the army gymnastic staff exam with an essay on "The Spirit of the Bayonet". When training as a bayonet instructor, Donald took part in a combined Aske-University College School (UCS) Field Day on Hampstead Heath in May 1920, which featured an attack by Aske's on UCS. "On our right," the school magazine *The Askean* reported, "Sgt. Soper skilfully captured a party of the enemy, whose valour got the better of their discretion."[16] He was promoted to CSM for his pains.

For all his intellectual and cultural exploits, it was in the sporting arena where his star shone brightest. Besides becoming School swimming champion, he was captain of boxing, football and cricket, the latter for two years. In 1919, aged sixteen, he was opening the bowling for the 1st XI, impressing in the two-day fixture against the Common Room with figures of three for 6 in the first innings and three for 8 in the second. The following year he again proved their nemesis, this time taking six for 14 in a match the School narrowly lost, in addition to taking eight for 40 in the two-day fixture against Haberdashers' Aske's, Hampstead. All in all through the season, in which he led by example, he bowled 173 overs, 65 more than anyone else, taking 48 wickets at 6.48, a most impressive return which helped revive the reputation of the cricket after several fallow years. "An excellent captain, and a reliable and enduring bowler," opined *The Askean*. "Rather lacks confidence in batting and is inclined to be slow,"[17] this latter characteristic out of kilter with the rest of his effervescent personality. The next year matters were rectified as the great advance he made with his batting turned him into an all-rounder of genuine quality. Because of his prominence in so many walks of school life, Donald's talents brought him considerable responsibilities at a tender age. A House Prefect and Assistant Instructor in the CCF at fifteen, he was Head of King's House, Secretary of the Football Club and a School Prefect aged sixteen and Captain of Cricket aged seventeen.

Not surprisingly perhaps as a result of this sporting prowess as well as his boundless self-confidence and immense popularity, he was appointed School Captain for his final year. "I don't want to sound arrogant," Donald later recalled, "but I was the type that stood out in a crowd. Normally, older boys would not have anything to do with a much younger boy like me, but because I played the game as well as them, I was an equal. It gave me an experience of leadership not shared by boys of my age."[18] Aske's trust in his leadership potential again proved well founded as he exhibited plenty of character in the football team, not least with his sturdy performances at centre-half and his resolution in overcoming a spate of team injuries to record a creditable set of results. "An excellent captain both on and off the field," enthused *The Askean*. "Tackles accurately and supports his forwards well."[19]

His star was very much in the ascendant but despite his ready absorption with the school's conventional ethos he also proved sympathetic to those outside the fold. On Armistice Day he was confronted with the first of what he later called a series of transforming experiences. The son of a local communist wouldn't observe the Two Minute Silence and walked around the playground. As School Captain it was Donald's job to make him conform. The dissenter wasn't a friend of his, but he was assailed by his peers for his gesture, so Donald stood by him and was glad he did. "Afterwards, I wondered why I had defended him," Donald later recalled. "I knew, I suppose, it was my job and I think, if it isn't too pompous to say so, that it was at that stage that I began to entertain thoughts about those who were in a very different frame of mind to my own; that people believed in quite different things to the ones that I believed in. And I think I learned a certain amount of tolerance."[20]

In March the following year Donald won further kudos by managing to win an exhibition to read History at St Catharine's College, Cambridge. His success helped seal the great affection he had developed for his school, so that in the years to come, he remained a devoted alumnus, returning on many occasions to talk or preach on Founder's Day. His final term captaining the cricket should have been a triumphant recessional as he recorded some outstanding returns, such as seven for 42 against Haberdashers' Aske's, Hampstead, and six for 26 against the Old Boys, but sadly it became clouded in tragedy by an accident which haunted him thereafter. The summer of 1921 happened to be one perpetual heat wave and the drought baked the playing fields dry. By now Donald had turned into an extremely quick bowler and the opening over of a house match on the school field at Nunhead saw him pitted against a batsman with a weak heart. His third ball leapt up at the batsman who, unable to take evasive action, was hit over the heart and collapsed in Donald's arms as he ran down the pitch. He was dead. At the inquest Donald was asked by the coroner whether he possessed any malice towards the batsman, an extremely insensitive question to a schoolboy. Donald replied that he had never met the boy before and was just a cricketer. Clearly the whole affair greatly upset him, but to infer, as some of his earlier biographers did, that it kindled his pacifist faith, is surely to miss the point. For aside from his lifelong fascination with the violent sport of boxing, he resented the fact that he never bowled quick again because he felt that someone should have told him to put the whole trauma behind him and continue as before. Deprived of this show of confidence the element of guilt lingered, affecting him as he went up to Cambridge in a state of some confusion as his childhood certainties came under heavy assault.

The fact that the Cambridge of the post-war era was full of mature war veterans in their mid-twenties made it a daunting experience for someone who, unlike most of his contemporaries, had never been away from home before. Despite his undoubted pedigree, Donald suddenly found himself for the first time in his life a small fish in a big pond, unknown and unloved. He was given a room out of college, since St Catharine's had scarce accommodation facilities, and had to endure a landlady who lacked maternal instincts, and a tutor in no hurry to make his acquaintance. The fact that he was also in some pain from boils on his face and neck which prevented him from playing his sport, only compounded his misery. It was in this fragile state that he was lent a copy of J. B. Bury's *History of the Freedom of Thought,* a book he later described as a somewhat naïve and implausible document. At the time, however, by drawing attention to inconsistencies in the Bible, not least in light of scientific discovery, it asked searching questions about his faith which his simplistic Methodist upbringing proved ill-equipped to cope with. "I assumed Christianity was true," he later recalled, "because it was obviously true for my parents and it had given me such a happy life. Here, all alone for the first time, I found intellectual problems I had not anticipated and which threatened all my religious values. No mother, no father, no church, it was a critical time for me. Suddenly, I found I didn't believe anything."[21]

In this turbulent state, which in reality was part of the normal process of adolescence bordering on adulthood, he found himself going to the Superintendent of Wesley Church, Christ's Pieces, where he had been contracted to teach at Sunday School and informed him of his atheistic tendencies. The superintendent, sensing Donald's pain at suddenly finding himself spiritually shipwrecked, proved very understanding. When he asked whether he could remain inside the fellowship of the Church to play the piano at Sunday School, he was more than accommodating. The superintendent's wisdom proved critical in the long term, but it did little to alleviate Donald's misery over the coming weeks. So lonely and depressed was his condition, and so physically afflicted was he by his painful boils that he took a razor-blade in the dark and cut off part of his chin.

Fortunately, beams of daylight were soon to enter his dark cell and aside from the support of his church, Donald had his musical expertise to thank for his rehabilitation. As William Purcell, one of his previous biographers, wrote, "There was a freshers' concert at which he was a brilliant success. He played the piano and was enthusiastically received. The Captain of Boats invited him to tea the next day, and he had arrived."[22]

St Catharine's, founded in 1473, was one of the smaller, less well-endowed Cambridge colleges, public school, conformist and athletic in outlook. At this stage it was a curious mixture of eighteen-year-olds and ex-servicemen up to ten years their senior but what might have been an uneasy combination blended quite harmoniously owing to sensitivity on both sides. With his passion for sport, Donald was soon in his element, winning College colours in cricket, football, tennis, swimming and hockey, and playing the occasional match for the University hockey team, but it was his music which established him as a person of substance. He became an active member of the Midnight Howlers, a college concert party which enlivened the Saturday evening smoking concerts, and he won rave reviews for his performances with the tin whistle and his glorious baritone voice. He also played jazz duets, and had the facility to bring home hit songs from the music hall and effortlessly repeat them in his friends' rooms note perfect. His great sense of humour found an outlet in College Smokers, a social occasion for mild indulgences, while the Sunday afternoon teas opened to Methodists at the university featured Donald at the heart of an admiring circle, captivated by his scintillating conversation. "He remains the life and soul of Cats," reported a fellow Old Askean in July 1924, "and the prohibitionist interest in Cambridge;"[23] this at a time when Prohibition in America had given a timely boost to the sagging Temperance Movement in a Britain where public drunkenness tempered by the demands of the First World War, appeared to be on the wane. According to Walter Strachan, an exact college contemporary and later a revered schoolmaster at Bishop's Stortford College, he was ebullient and popular. Yet for all his charisma and sense of fun, which included him getting a ducking from Eric Baker, later Secretary of the Methodist Conference, when out punting on the River Cam, he was a man with few close friends. He did holiday in Italy with his room-mate "Tar" Morrison, another public school master in the making, but contrived to lose touch with him and other college contemporaries once he had left. He made slightly more effort with close acquaintants in the Student Christian Movement (SCM) yet even with fellow Christians on retreat he rarely mixed with them outside meetings, a trait, he later acknowledged, which often caused him much loneliness in his contact with other people. Consequently, he cherished the few really close friends he made, one of whom was Joe Webb, a South African he met at Wesley House, who later attained prominence back in his native land by thrice becoming President of the Methodist Church. With music and Methodism in common, they became virtually inseparable, and Webb spent many a vacation at the Soper home. They continued to remain close after Webb returned home, even though their views on South African politics and pacifism somewhat conflicted.

By his second year Donald had undergone a genuine religious experience, bolstered by his continuing fellowship of the Church, which provided him with much of his social life with its choirs and dramatic performances. The fact that he wanted to remain within its confines wasn't lost upon him and taught him through its mutual fellowship and support a reality about religion just as basic as his desire to confide in its teaching. Later, he was to write, "We are bidden to love God with heart and mind. The inability fully to obey that invitation with the mind does not prevent the obedience of the heart ... The fellowship of a Church can make the love of God real for those who share its life and gather at the table of its Lord, and it is a gratuitous insult to claim that they are the victims either of a pipe-dream or a conspiracy."[24] Within this climate of trust Donald began to view his agnosticism about certain doctrinal statements with a new sense of perspective. By accepting many of the doubts that had caused him to lose his faith, he gradually put his atheism behind him and returned to the fold. The faith, though, to which he returned was a pilgrimage of trust as he no longer believed that Christianity could answer all problems, especially those to do with pain and suffering. What he had increasingly come to see was that atheism had to be dealt with through faith and action, believing that to see the world through Jesus Christ was the way to good.

Relishing his new won freedom to make his own decisions he became an active member of the Cambridge branch of the SCM, a genuinely interdenominational body then at the height of its fame. Founded in 1905 out of the British College Christian Union of 1894, it embraced the winds of change blowing out of continental theology which had become fashionable in a university like Cambridge, then at the forefront of scientific thought and modernist theology. This meant parting company with the Christian fundamentalists of the Cambridge Inter-Collegiate Christian Union (CICCU) by stressing a more rational approach to the Bible which acknowledged only those parts which were intellectually acceptable.

The First World War with its shattering of old certainties had only hastened the advance of this liberal theology with its tenuous belief in biblical truth and divine conscience. The upshot of this was that ideas such as the virgin birth, atonement and physical resurrection increasingly gave way to the "Jesus of History", who was a moral exemplar and social crusader on behalf of the poor.

In 1924 Donald attended a mission to the university and listened to William Temple, later Archbishop of Canterbury, who made a great impression on him, especially his claim that of all the religions, Christianity was the most materialistic. Through the auspices of the SCM he was able to hear such eminent divines as G. A. Studdert-Kennedy, the famous First World War chaplain with his clarity, resonance and apt illustrations, and Dean Inge, formerly the Lady Margaret Professor of Divinity at Cambridge. That same year Donald was a Methodist delegate to COPEC (Conference on

Christian Politics, Economics and Citizenship) in Birmingham organised jointly by the Church of England and Free Churches and presided over by Temple. The actual conference for all its commissions and reports produced little of actual substance, but its effect on Donald was quite considerable, not least in its idealistic thrust towards a social gospel based on extensive welfare reform. This religious awakening brought with it a profound development in his political convictions as he came to see that the world was much larger than a London suburb. "I had no consciousness of changing from liberalism to socialism," Donald later recalled. "What I had was a deep and increasing consciousness that I hadn't any base in the traditional Methodism of my childhood and here was something which was filling it."[25] He went on to say that his Liberal background was totally inadequate in expressing what he was increasingly coming to see as the essence of the social gospel. Even more of a mentor to Donald than Temple was the eminent historian and educationalist R. H. Tawney, who ironically had been a close friend of Temple's since their time at Rugby and Balliol, Oxford together. In later years Donald went as far as to credit Tawney with a revolution in his thinking and converting him politically. Having read his book *The Acquisitive Society* decrying the evil of inequality, Donald persuaded himself that the naked competition of the capitalist system was incompatible with the principles of the Christian faith. Later he was to be further influenced by Tawney's second great work, *Religion and the Rise of Capitalism*, in which he urged the Church to return to a more collective role in economic and social affairs.

Donald's eyes were to be further opened through his work for the SCM thanks to his friendship with Edward Woods, the charismatic vicar of Holy Trinity, Cambridge, who helped to organise the open-air evangelical campaigns in the vacation. It was on one of these to Derby in 1924 that Donald, along with two others, played Gilbert & Sullivan on the tin whistle to attract support from the female workforce at Britannia Mills for a lunchtime meeting in the marketplace. From that moment he never doubted his call to preach. Later that week he was offered the opportunity of visiting the old LMS engine works, one of the principal local industries, and the immediate effect of visiting a factory working at full blast was dramatic, as he later recalled. "The experience had all the ingredients and power of a religious conversion. It was a 'second birth', since I became vividly aware of a life of which previously I had known nothing. It was a 'revelation', incomplete of course, but self-authenticating in the sense that it seemed to preclude any doubt. In that brief excursion into the world of industry, I had a direct experience of a truth vouchsafed to me for the first time, which demanded a radical change of mental and moral direction."[26] Donald went on to say that that revelation in Derby was the sudden recognition of the lawyer's question prior to the Parable of the Good Samaritan: Who is my neighbour? "Like the Jew and the Samaritan, those factory workers and we undergraduates belonged to two, almost entirely different, economic and political and probably social worlds."[27] The following year in St Helens, Lancashire, on another SCM camp, that gulf was again vividly exposed as Donald stood on an improvised platform next to the cinema preaching to a motley crowd of drunkards, prostitutes and unemployed. He later recalled learning very quickly that the way of Jesus couldn't be the way these people were living in the so-called enlightened capitalist West. At the same time he couldn't advocate that way until he walked it himself. If these unprecedented experiences gave Donald some cause for reflection, then his exposure to domestic events such as the General Strike of 1926, in which his sympathies lay unreservedly with the workers in their struggle against the coal owners and Stanley Baldwin's Conservative Government, added further weight to his burgeoning socialist convictions. In common with many radical Nonconformists in the bitter aftermath of the First World War, he abandoned the Liberal Party of his parents and joined the Labour Party.

The Labour Party was largely the product of an ever-changing society driven by mass industrialisation and urbanisation and reflected in the expansion of the trade union movement, especially in unskilled industries such as the mines and the railways.

Ever since the legalisation of the trade unions in 1825 their ranks had been imbued with the zeal of Primitive Methodist preachers who, fired by their communal ethos nurtured in the chapel, took a leading role in their activities. Foremost among them was Joseph Arch, the pioneering union organiser for agricultural workers, and Peter Lee of the Miners' Association who gave his name to a new town in County Durham. Most trade unionists were traditionally Liberal in their political allegiance, especially the old craft ones, but the failure of the party to respond to the new working-class consciousness of the late-nineteenth century created a void readily filled by those of a more radical disposition.

It fell to the Scottish Free Churchman Keir Hardie to assume responsibility for the formation of a new party in 1893 dedicated to ameliorating the lot of the working class. Chapel and Temperance Society provided much of the spiritual impetus for the new Independent Labour Party based around the textile town of Bradford in the West Riding of Yorkshire. Then when the Labour Party was established in 1900 out of the mass ranks of the trade unions, Nonconformist influence remained strong. Two of its leading lights, Arthur Henderson and Philip Snowden, were committed Methodists and teetotallers, so that when Donald joined the party as a probationer Methodist minister he was following in a proud tradition.

If Cambridge made Donald a socialist it also converted him to pacifism, although his conversion to the latter was less dramatic. When he began there in 1921 he was little different from many patriotic flag-waving eighteen-year-olds, whose schooling in the shadow of the war had given their military training a greater significance than otherwise might have been the case. Donald had accepted the premise behind it, and had excelled in the various activities, but mixing with war veterans in college changed all that, as he heard at first hand the grim reality of trench life. "The very reticence of those who spoke to me about it, was revealing. The so-called 'martial exercise' that I had enjoyed became part of an obscenity of which I was ashamed."[28]

Donald recalled how during a vacation he met the husband of one of the teachers at his mother's school. "I can see him now, with a collapsed and useless lung and a look of resignation, and indeed of bewilderment, in his eyes, as I prised out of him something of what it had been like to rot in the trenches. I was terrified at the thought that what he had done and what had happened to him might happen to me. That fear must have concentrated my mind and it cannot be excluded from the dominant agents which contributed to my renunciation of war, and my confidence that such a renunciation could be universally successful."[29] For, like many of his contemporaries in the post-war era, Donald felt that in the spirit of American idealism that had spawned the League of Nations at the Treaty of Versailles in 1919, there was an opportunity to begin anew.

Alongside the development of his religious faith, Donald's pacifism (in time) owed something to the influence of books such as G.J.Heering's *The Fall of Christianity* and Garth Macgregor's *The New Testament Basis of Pacifism* which helped convince him that the early Church was pacifist. There were also two other formative influences. First, there was his friendship with Alex Wood, the dedicated socialist Fellow of Emmanuel College, leading Quaker, and later Chairman of the Peace Pledge Union (PPU). His serenity and depth of grace made a deep impression, as did his homilies on the subject. More important, there was his association with the Methodist minister, Henry Carter. An outspoken critic of the First World War and later founder of the Methodist Peace Fellowship (MPF), Carter's awkward personality saw him shunned by fellow Methodists, but his influence on the young Donald was incalculable, not least in supporting his inclination to use the Church as a platform for his political convictions.

Having graduated in 1924 in the History Tripos with a 2.2 for the first part and a 2.1 for the second part, it seemed a logical enough step for Donald to enrol at the recently opened Wesley House to begin his two-year training as a Methodist minister. Captivated by the spirit of Jesus from the time he learnt children's hymns on his mother's knee, Donald used to trace his commitment to a life in the Church to a particular breakfast aged thirteen. When his mother quizzed him about possible plans for a future career his father told him that God's son had become a minister and he would like him to do likewise, a request to which Donald was only too happy to accede. The fact that it suited him later to dramatize this defining moment in his life doesn't necessarily invalidate it, given his total absorption with the life of the Church at every stage, even when temporarily afflicted by doubt. Not averse to taking services in the family home, as a boy, he was a Sunday School teacher in Forest Hill before going up to Cambridge. Then once in residence, he used to slip away to London on occasions to address temperance meetings, a practice he had first instigated as a thirteen-year-old. Yet, despite this, he had taken precious few steps to prepare himself for the plunge. It needed his friend Eric Baker to stir him into action towards the end of his second year at St Catharine's by getting him accepted as a local preacher by the superintendent minister of the local Wesleyan circuit.

Donald's entry into the ministry came at a time when there was growing pressure within the Methodist Church, especially among laymen who had been denied a good education, to establish training ministries at Oxbridge to participate fully in the Christian academic tradition. One of the prime movers in such a scheme was Michael Gutteridge, a prosperous Wesleyan businessman and local preacher who submitted a resolution at the Methodist Conference in 1911 that it consider the establishment of a college at Cambridge. Helped by his offer of £5,000, Conference the next year accepted his resolution, and then, after the war years had stymied the initiative, a major breakthrough came in 1919. First, a further report proposed a postgraduate college of up to thirty Wesleyan students. Second, a trust fund set up almost immediately, received a huge fillip when William Greenhalgh, a self-educated weaver from Southport, left an endowment of £20,000 in his will to help found a new college. That same year, 1920, Gutteridge travelled to Cambridge to put his enterprise into practice and although initially it had to make do with a rented house belonging to Cheshunt Congregational College, help was at hand. A suitable site in Jesus Lane, opposite Jesus College, soon became available, containing student rooms, a dining hall and a common room. In April 1925, as the first students, including Donald, moved in, an inaugural dinner was held for students and staff. Then, when it was formally opened that October, it was to be in the style to which Wesleyan Methodism was accustomed, such was its preoccupation with social status.

By then Wesley House had experienced fluctuating fortunes during the first four years of its existence. The first six students, which included three future Presidents of Conference, Eric Baker, Harold Roberts and Russell Shearer, were of the highest possible calibre. However, when two of the four entrants in the subsequent year dropped out, one due to a serious illness, the other because of a change in allegiance to the Baptists, the credibility of Wesley House was called into question. For, according to Paul Glass, the college's historian, there was a slightly disconcerting tradition within the Nonconformist denomination whereby students failed to complete their studies. So when this trait began to undermine Wesley House in 1922–23 and again in 1926, critics of the new college weren't slow in coming forward. The fact that Wesley House's Principal, Dr Maldwyn Hughes, could withstand this pressure by pointing to the success of Donald Soper as an example of a Wesley House education, was not inconsequential to the morale and reputation of the fledgling college.

When Donald entered Wesley House in 1924 he was one of fifteen students there, some living like him in Cheshunt College, others in lodgings. It was here while in residence at Cheshunt that he wrote his name into college folk-lore by confronting the indomitable Bertha Johnson, wife of the residential tutor E. S. Johnson, over the scarcity of food available. The fact that Donald was kept – in contrast to many of his colleagues – on a very tight financial leash by his father and had to account for all his expenses, might well have had something to do with his actions. Certainly, in the true Nonconformist tradition, thrift was a virtue to be practised at all costs as far as Ernest Soper was concerned. When he used to accompany his son to Tower Hill during the 1930s, the convention grew up that father and son took it in turns to pay for each other's lunch in the local café afterwards. One week Donald was short of money when it was his turn to pay and asked his father to help out. His father obliged only on the condition that Donald repaid him the following week.

Since its foundation, Wesley House had been under the leadership of Dr Maldwyn Hughes, Welsh scholar and a kindly, honest figure who together with his wife did much to create a family atmosphere. He was, though, a rather turgid lecturer, bitterly hurt when Donald's passion for sport took precedence over attendance at his lectures. A much greater intellectual influence was the esteemed F. R. Tennant who lectured in the Philosophy of Religion, the subject which Donald, like most Wesley House students, was now reading. Tennant was a scholar and theologian of some repute. He was extremely lucid in his teaching, and his precision of thought, choice of words and theological content left their mark on Donald thereafter, not least in his ability to give his pupils' faith a firm intellectual backing. For one of the lessons Tennant always stressed was the need to postpone a conclusion about the existence and nature of God until all the evidence had been checked for its validity. A second concerned the danger of rejecting wholesale any belief cherished by men however many fallacies were attached to it, since in the desire to eradicate errors there existed the probability of overlooking something that was true. Another influence was the renowned Scottish theologian, Dr John Oman of Westminster Theological College. He used to advise his students, "Take large texts gentlemen and when they persecute you in one city, flee into the next," the implication being that it was far more preferable to consider the big issues of life, however difficult they might be, than to concentrate upon the more day-to-day requirements of living. A third port of call was Harold Roberts, then Assistant Tutor at Wesley House. Donald, apart from enjoying his company socially, was impressed by his sacramentalism and the rigorous way in which he presented the Gospel, although he made little headway in his tutorials with him on the Greek New Testament.

Despite those mentors, Donald later affected indifference to much of the biblical theology he came across, claiming that he didn't remember much of what his tutors at Wesley House had taught him. "I am a sacramentalist," he once said, "because I find in the doing of the sacrament a compensation for what I cannot find ultimately in the recitation of the words." More important to him were the writings of Temple, R. H. Tawney and Charles Gore, the High-Church Bishop of Oxford (1911–19). Gore's social gospel was based specifically on the Fatherhood of God in the divine family, language which Donald frequently employed. Come his final year, Donald's studies were badly interrupted by a severe nervous strain to the eyes which caused him to be absent for some time. As speculation over his future mounted, he found succour in Joe Webb who read texts to him, and pre-exam conversations with his tutors, so that few of the questions set caused him much surprise. Thanks to the scale of his photographic memory and powerful intellect which enabled him to follow even the most erudite lectures without taking notes, he did what few people taking up the Philosophy of Religion do at university, and that was to gain a first. His success in this most demanding of subjects did much to boost the prestige of Wesley House, and helps explain the reverence with which Donald was always held at the college thereafter, especially after becoming the first of its alumni to be elected President of Conference.

Away from his studies, Donald played an active part in developing the close bonds that existed in this small tightly-run college where discipline was strict and expectations high. As one of the Cambridge graduates at Wesley House, Donald was invaluable in continuing the task of successfully integrating this new pioneering Methodist establishment into the university as a whole. It was probably with this in mind that as a leading participant at the Wesley House Committee, the college's student body, he opened a discussion about the length of the college term, which was a week longer than the university one. On his prompting, a resolution was passed unanimously, asking the Principal to shorten their term on the grounds that the extra week had a demoralizing effect on the students and diminished the standing of Wesley House within the university. He was to the fore in the monthly House meetings, proposing that Eric Baker should be their representative to the Cambridge SCM and leading Wesley House's support for a Cambridge General Retreat. In May 1925, in recognition of his leadership prowess, he was narrowly elected Chairman of Wesley House students by six votes to five for the forthcoming year over L. A. Parsons, a former Jesus graduate.

The following October, with numbers up to seventeen, Donald welcomed the new men and assured them that "they would find the rest of us very genial folk".[30] He organised a social for them and provided much of the entertainment himself, invariably bringing the house down either with his singing or his virtuosity on the piano. According to his contemporary Maldwyn Edwards, later a distinguished church historian and President of Conference in 1961, there was no escape from the full blast of his personality, especially in such select company. Captivated by Donald's effortless authority, Edwards felt him to be a born leader who wore his crown by right. Either in committee or in conversation, his fluency was such that he simply assumed that his listeners saw the logic of his position, a confidence which ensured he was rarely angry or nonplussed. Yet for all his outward gaiety and vitality, he never lost sight of his religious vocation. He instituted a quiet half-hour in college at 6.30 each Wednesday evening, thinking it a spiritual necessity as well as supporting the Fellowship of the Kingdom (FOK) study circle. For the second consecutive year he was one of the seven Wesley House students elected to go on the FOK retreat for young Methodist ministers to Swanwick in Derbyshire for discussion and mutual support, a connection he maintained post-Cambridge. It was here that he fell under the influence of the inspirational Russell Maltby, Warden of the Wesley Deaconess Order, who, according to the Methodist historian Rupert Davies, possessed an uncanny knowledge of the human heart. At a time when major social changes enhanced by the First World War had exposed the aridity and complacency of much traditional evangelism, Maltby's liberal theology emphasised a very personal Gospel based on a close relationship with the Jesus of the New Testament. It was a message which greatly appealed to Donald, as it did to his friend Leslie Weatherhead, a future giant of the Methodist Church, whom he first encountered at these retreats.

From what we can glean from the records there were no major contretemps during Donald's year as chairman, and at his final meeting in June he thanked the House for its support. He had proved popular and effective in the discharge of his duties, even if his views hadn't always commanded total allegiance.

While at Wesley House, Donald continued to hone his skills at the more practical side of the ministry. He later recalled the lacklustre performance of his first effort to put that role into effect when preaching. It took place at the tiny village of Stow-cum-Quy on the Newmarket road and lasted twelve and a half minutes. It was on the text "What lack I yet?" and a farmer who heard it commented that Donald had a good singing voice. Realising that he lacked something worthwhile to express, he was more than receptive to ministerial advice that when required to give his testimony he should repeat a genuine religious experience.

As an active member of the Wesleyan Church and a trainee minister, Donald was asked to take an occasional service, and often a number of college friends went to hear him. According to St Catharine's contemporary, Frank Marston, Donald, after one such service, asked for their comments on his performance. Marston replied that, as a prospective schoolmaster, he had been particularly impressed by his address to the younger members of the congregation. "That's damning with faint praise," exclaimed Donald, but Marston retorted that if he could so grip the younger members of the congregation, he would have no problem in future dominating adult crowds. It was a discerning comment. Ever since Donald first spoke in public at the Band of Hope aged thirteen, he possessed a flair for impromptu speaking and now he increasingly put it to good effect even though it could land him in trouble with the fundamentalists in the CICCU.

On one occasion at some Christian function he, along with several others, was asked to speak for three minutes on a biblical passage unknown to him. Donald's assignment was taken from Psalm 147: "He taketh no pleasure in the legs of a man". He rose with the utmost gravity and gave a fluent exposition of the words, much to the delight of his audience even though he might not have uncovered the Psalmist's mind. His versatility was evident on other occasions. When he went to preach in little country chapels he often ended up playing the piano and organ, turning any current dance into the most solemn voluntary without any of the congregation realising. During the General Strike, he and Joe Webb entertained local strikers at Romsey Town on the outskirts of Cambridge with Webb on the piano and Donald the penny whistle.

With his facility for relating the Gospel in simple, contemporary terms, Donald's attributes as a preacher were soon in demand in and around

Cambridge. During his final term he preached at Sutton, Ely and The Leys School, a Methodist institution, earning 15/- (75p) each for the first two of these assignments, from which he would have to pay some 5/- (25p) in expenses. All this experience in preaching and evangelism would be invaluable for his subsequent career. His first appointment was due to be as a probationer minister at the Methodist Mission House, which somehow didn't accord with his adventurous instincts. He later recalled how on the very day he was sitting his final examination he was told that the appointment had fallen through. Instead, a month later, he found himself posted to a church in the South London Mission in an alien environment very different from his privileged upbringing. It would be another big step on the spiritual and political pilgrimage he had embarked upon at Cambridge, and a pilgrimage from which there would be no turning back.

And yet, despite a lifetime marching to the drumbeat of socialism, Donald in manner and mores remained something of an establishment figure. In contrast to many middle-class radicals whose iconoclasm was shaped by unsettled childhoods, Donald's was gilded by comparison. So much so that his formative influences remained very much with him thereafter, as they did with the future Labour Prime Minister Clement Attlee, whose earlier upbringing in neighbouring Putney was on a grander scale than the Soper household in Wandsworth. Their mutual attachment to family and institutional structures from Oxbridge to the House of Lords not only provided a ballast when they were engulfed in the storms of controversy, it also helped explain their elitist tendencies in their respective vocations. Certainly Donald never lacked self-confidence in exerting leadership, a trait he shared with other left-wing privately educated clerics such as George MacLeod, Trevor Huddleston and Mervyn Stockwood, which helped enhance his aura of gravitas. Like them he was a traditionalist in worship, sparing no expense to achieve beauty in holiness and conventional in lifestyle. Shunning futile gestures towards inverted snobbery, he was a stickler for old-fashioned proprieties, not least in his gallantry towards women, and while popular with working-class congregations, he was equally at home in a more rarefied ambience extolling the virtues of a Gilbert and Sullivan operetta or his Cambridge college. Indeed, as time went on, his social conservatism became ever more apparent, so that his later membership of the House of Lords was less momentous than it appeared at the time.

CHAPTER TWO

The Soapbox Socialist

Donald Soper was a creature of habit in much of his public ministry and private lifestyle. The same could be said of his theology. The ideas he fashioned in the Cambridge of the 1920s broadly remained with him thereafter. Unlike some Methodist ministers, he seldom read or discussed the works of leading theologians such as Rudolph Bultmann or Karl Barth – "best forgotten", he used to say – although he was later an enthusiastic follower of Professor Hans Kung, the radical Roman Catholic theologian. Consequently he rarely kept abreast of new thinking and was unfazed by periodic theological controversy. Thus when John Robinson, Bishop of Woolwich, caused ructions with his *Honest to God* in 1963, in which he questioned traditional beliefs about prayer and God, he hardly viewed it as groundbreaking stuff. Two decades later, when David Jenkins, the Bishop of Durham, aroused controversy with his scepticism over the virgin birth and the physical resurrection, Donald claimed that he had been saying something similar for fifty years, despite the fact that Jenkins went much further than anything that he had ever uttered. And when Donald, on a trip to the United States in 1971, was asked about the "Death of God" debate which was then all the rage, he answered somewhat flippantly that he didn't know God was ill, only later to confess his ignorance about the jargon behind the question. He also admitted to travelling light theologically, believing that in a world of innumerable languages and new words, religion placed too much emphasis on doctrinal precision rather than human experience. He was, however, an outstanding theological philosopher, as evident by the profundity of his discourses in the open air, and, as Brian Frost, one of his biographers, has asserted, he endeavoured to preach Christianity in the context of a scientific revolution which had led to philosophers questioning the nature of faith itself. He was helped in this challenge by his own brief lapse into atheism at Cambridge, since the experience had taught him that belief in God was a hazardous intellectual and moral adventure, not a foregone conclusion. Thereafter, he felt liberated from the burden of living on creeds imposed upon him by the Church, since for all their importance they were, in his estimation, secondary to Christian action, and felt under no compulsion to come to a full understanding of God which in reality remained beyond him. For whatever new beliefs or scientific discoveries might have come to light, he felt sustained in the knowledge that, however vast the universe with the possibility of its limitless planets, it was but part of God's creation, which in itself was a force for good. "Because this is God's world, through and through," he wrote in *Aflame with Faith*, "and if there are other planets, well, God is the Father and the Master, and the Lord is there too. And God is the Lord of eternity, as well as of time, and, whatever men may do to us in this life, nothing can separate us from His love."[1] Years later he was to write in his autobiography *Calling for Action*, "I find it immensely encouraging that in the minds of some of the most distinguished scientists and philosophers of our time, Christianity not only can bear the scrutiny of scientific discovery but thrives on it."[2] Then referring to Hans Kung's celebrated book, *Does God Exist?*, he continued, "I find him unanswerable, not only in his presentation of the basic case for the existence of God, but equally so in his defence of this Christian belief as being the more credible as our general knowledge increases."[3]

This new-found freedom was evident in Donald's attitude towards the Bible as he retrod the path back to faith. He considered it to be the most important document ever written, replete with insight into human nature and linguistic beauty, revealing God the creator, the world as his creation and the after-life. He regarded it as a reputable record, but not a final and infallible authority, especially since certain passages couldn't be accepted at their face value. Like most of his contemporaries he found the Old Testament difficult, not least its picture of Jehovah as the God of Hosts, and the record of wars eked out with almost interminable detail. Its supreme value he felt lay in providing a necessary historical and ecclesiastical background for the New Testament, especially the expectation and hope of Jesus Christ, the one unifying pattern of the Bible.

The New Testament was much more to Donald's liking, especially St John's Gospel which he thought contained the highest spiritual appreciation of the Christian faith, although even here he had his reservations. Much of the Book of Revelation he found to be lacking in credibility and the Synoptic Gospels baffled him with their historical inconsistencies. Whether these difficulties originated from the fewer opportunities he had for academic biblical study compared to most Methodist ministers because his main preoccupation at Wesley House had been with the philosophy of religion, is a moot point. If so, it was rarely evident in his preaching, since he often displayed great insight and sensitivity in the way he explored and developed the Gospel for the Day.

Dismissive of traditional teachings concerning the Holy Trinity and other cardinal doctrines, Donald opted instead for a simple minimalist faith centred around three basic beliefs. First, God the loving father, the creator of his children and the one supreme authority whose family lived an ethic of giving and sharing. Second, Jesus Christ, the human photograph of God, the one man who made his vision of giving and sharing possible. Third, the Cross, the meaning of everything Jesus taught about suffering love and the fulfilment of God's purpose for humanity. And in defending these core beliefs, Donald was granite-like in his conviction that the character of Jesus was unassailable and that all his claims must be accepted. Some inkling of his paradoxical approach to biblical criticism can be gleaned in his book *Popular Fallacies about the Christian Faith* when he wrote: "... if I may give my own experience, these difficult passages in the Gospels perplexed me very much until I realized that the Christian life means ultimately a personal experience of the Saviour of the World with whom we can find fellowship through all those who know and love Him; and when He indwells the humble and contrite heart, we possess an inward witness which dare not ignore the historical records where first we met Him but does transcend them ... Where the records are ambiguous or conflicting I am content to await further light which will be thrown upon them."[4] This passage is revealing since it reinforces Donald's deep spiritual tendencies which often were overshadowed by his political pronouncements. David Sheppard, later Bishop of Liverpool, recalled how Donald came to his theological college, Ridley Hall, Cambridge, during the early 1950s for two sessions, staying overnight in between them. "In the first one he emphasised the place of social justice in the Christian calling. There was a good deal of consternation among the most evangelical of the students. Did this man really believe in the Gospel of personal salvation? In the morning he said, 'I want you to know that I firmly believe in the need to know our Lord Jesus Christ personally and His forgiveness. But I didn't think it would do you any harm to have to wait a little to find out!'"[5]

Spurning the opportunity to heap metaphysical terms on him, Donald focused instead on the human Jesus, believing that his supreme example in the day-to-day things of life was the gateway to personal allegiance and eternal life. Drawing on the historical knowledge available, Donald depicted Jesus as the Arab Jew, a dark swarthy medium-built type with an aquiline face, whose life was set in the midst of an ordinary family. Although hailing from humble surroundings, he became an inspired teacher who attracted a mass following, a political revolutionary who died a Roman death for being a resistance leader, and a man who rose from the dead by returning to his friends, although not with the same physical body. In accordance with this humanity associated with liberal theologians, Donald's Jesus wasn't all-powerful, but a man of moral excellence forced to compromise with the world as he found it. Consequently, he walked along Roman roads built by slave labour, advocated paying tax to Caesar, accepted hospitality from sinners and parried the leading questions as to his prophetic mission in the early stages, sacrificing himself only when it would have the maximum effect. The only area which was non-negotiable was his attachment to non-violence, prompting Donald to do likewise. For whatever other compromises Donald himself was prepared to make, he wasn't prepared to be bought on this since by refusing to compromise with the supreme evil of violence, he believed it would be easier to create social justice.

As to his teaching, Donald claimed that Jesus wasn't a moral propagandist laying down a set of rules of conduct. Rather he was preaching the good news of salvation and pointing to a path of individual and social fulfilment. At the core of his message was the command to seek first the kingdom of God and its righteousness, the expression of all Jesus' teaching in the Sermon on the Mount, where he laid down an ethical lifestyle by which God would have his children live, both here and in eternity. Donald stressed that, contrary to the interpretation of many fundamentalists, he wasn't simply talking about some future bliss in which people could live in private happiness and joy. Why, he asked, would the Romans have bothered to crucify someone if his sole intention was to edify the private habits of individual citizens of their empire? Rather he was exhorting his listeners to build a new society on earth in the spirit of God's family through the creation of peace and material fulfilment for all.

In order to build that kingdom in the world, Donald recognised that in the tradition of Tawney and contrary to the view of popular evangelists, the Christian needed to get involved in the political process. For, as Donald often acknowledged, if one believes Jesus is the Lord of all life, He is the one by whose Grace we are redeemed from the bane of evil. Later he was to write: "It is plain to me that war and poverty and unemployment arise out of a failure to understand the meaning of the world in which we live. Because of that failure, society is maladjusted; out of that maladjustment friction and disaster inevitably emerge. The true meaning of your life and mine is found in the God who as our Father bids us come to the Family table and be satisfied there, and then go out into His world to build that cultural and spiritual fellowship which is life indeed. That is why, not in the interests of materialism at all, not from the determinist promises, but as a simple understanding of the Christian Gospel, I want the Church to enter the economic sphere ... We are brothers because God is the Father. We can find material satisfaction because God wills it. We can live at peace because peace is in the plan of things. We shall be perfect because God our Father is perfect. Therefore, to feed the hungry as Jesus fed the five thousand, not because they were good but because they were hungry, is not to demoralize them, but to begin to clear the way for them to enter life."[6]

Christianity then was revolutionary change. The political ideology most applicable to Donald's theology was socialism, since he saw in Acts 2 and 4 the new Christian Church born at Pentecost through the coming of the Holy Spirit, carrying out God's will in his kingdom. Central to this was renouncing the idea of property and individual possessions and distributing according to need in the spirit of the family, so that nobody was excluded. The fact that this ideal didn't last, he argued, was not that it lacked validity, rather it was because of the Church's concordat with the Roman Empire which exposed it to secular forces.

From the time of F. D. Maurice and Charles Kingsley in the mid-nineteenth century, through to Tawney in the early twentieth, Christian socialism became a viable force in Britain, and Donald one of its more formidable proponents thereafter, consistently supporting an equal society and world government. He recognised that there was no such thing as the perfect party, but the Labour Party, for all its flaws, was the best instrument by which to build Jerusalem. He wasn't totally dismissive of the Liberal Party, not least its dissenting roots, but felt its attachment to individual responsibility inadequate to reflect the social gospel. Conservatism, in contrast, he held completely in contempt, since its emphasis on private profit rather than public service he felt ran counter to the central tenets of Christianity. The only way a Tory could get to heaven he used to say, tongue in cheek, was by a circuitous route, although he would fully admit that many of them were better people than their precepts.

The second part of the Gospel, according to Donald, revealed a God who not only blessed the search for the kingdom but had shown the way to accomplish it through the non-violence of his son. This was especially so at the supreme moment of his life when confronted by the brute force of the Roman army. By dying in love on a cross he had broken the power of Rome and unleashed a new redemptive power through the world. Donald accepted that in a fallen world, where the doctrine of original sin couldn't be ignored, no one was free to act in absolute obedience to his enlightened conscience. Ultimately, non-violence could only be achieved when the kingdom of God was realised. Nevertheless, they were free to renounce most forms of violence, even though such an approach, he appreciated, was fraught with risk. Yet deriving strength from the Sermon on the Mount about God bestowing care on those who followed his commandments, he wasn't to be deterred. In *Peace*

News in April 1947 he outlined the expectation placed on the Christian. "…
his first duty is to obey God's laws, not to alter them, and he has the example
of Jesus Christ whose triumph was that He went on obeying God when everybody else thought He was an idealistic fool and a practical failure. I can't argue
all this out, and it's so easy to put difficulties in the way and say yes, but 'what
would happen if, … but it seems to me that this is the way of the Cross and
somebody – and who can but the Christian – has got to take it before the
world can rise to a new and tranquil life."[7] This new life incidentally not only
renounced war but force of any kind be it capital punishment, blood sports
and boxing. Beyond this, a total rejection of violence, lay the recognition that
human beings of whatever race, class or creed, were members of one family.
Thus world government through the United Nations (UN) could replace the
self-serving nation state, and that every member of that family should be entitled to a place at that table. "Christian pacifism is the revolutionary principle,"
wrote Donald in the autumn 1958 edition of *Kingsway*, the magazine of the
West London Mission, "that men, women and children everywhere should be
given the food, clothing and education they need."[8] Only with God's reign in
the world as well as in the heart, would true progress be made. In practice this
required a church which was spiritually renewed, politically engaged and
related to the ordinary man in the street. Too often Donald felt that it was
found wanting, either in its failure to practise what it preached or its remoteness from day-to-day needs. It was a theme he returned to consistently
throughout his career and although his barbs wounded many of his colleagues,
it helped concentrate his mind in getting through to ordinary people. Such
people would form the majority of his congregations at the South and Central
London Missions together with his audiences at Tower Hill or Hyde Park.

Little geographically separated some of the more prosperous parts of
London from the more deprived ones, but despite the close proximity of the
Sopers' home in Streatham to his new appointment in 1926, nothing could
have prepared Donald for what he found. The dockland community of
Bermondsey, situated on the south bank of the Thames downstream from
Tower Bridge, was something of a backwater in the capital, blighted by unemployment, poverty and chronic overcrowding. The image of rat-infested
tenements in dilapidated terraced houses overhanging dank, narrow streets
teeming with undernourished children devoid of hope or purpose, told its
own desolate story. Not surprisingly, in this climate, violence, alcohol and
prostitution abounded, as did the activities of the local Communist Party.

It was his exposure to the unforgiving world of Bermondsey that helped
form the background to the Revd Andrew Mearns's *The Bitter Cry of Outcast
London* in 1883, a pamphlet which, once published in the *Pall Mall Gazette*,

aroused the national conscience. At the heart of that response were the Wesleyan Methodists, who for some time had been trying to reach out to the poor of the inner cities. Now in 1889, Conference approved the establishment of the South London Mission. Thanks to the work of the Revd Henry J. Meakin, money was raised for a Central Hall in Bermondsey which opened in 1900. It became the leading light in the Mission which at various times comprised nineteen other churches and social centres. One of these was Oakley Place Methodist Church just off the Old Kent Road, and it became Donald's new home.

Opened in 1874, with 1,000 seats, it experienced conflicting fortunes in its history, with the years before Donald's accession being some of its less auspicious ones, given the declining numbers and the dilapidated building. One of his tasks on taking up residence in September 1926 was to seek out his superintendent, Roderick Kedward, to request a renovation programme costing £300, but the resources simply weren't available. Not to be defeated, Donald told his predominantly female working-class congregation of his intentions to carry out the programme himself and appealed for volunteers to decorate. To his astonishment, twenty not in church the day before, turned up to help him wash the ceiling, and although a number of them soon fell by the wayside, others stayed to be regulars in the Church, one becoming a lay preacher.

At Oakley Place, Donald conducted the services with a pleasant mixture of order and enthusiasm, leading the singing at a pace which countered the tendency of the congregation to drag. His sermons were crisp and relevant, proving that the Christian message could relate to everyday life, his illustrations often suffused with anecdotes. In addition to vibrant worship, Donald looked to increase the range of church activity. The Sunday School was given a new lease of life with outings organised to Riddlesdown and Hayes Common in Kent. Bible classes and Band of Hope took place with greater regularity and Women's Meetings were held on Monday, giving poor people the opportunity to buy various necessities.

In such a deprived environment the need for enterprising people with a sensitive touch was paramount, and Donald, shocked by the depth of poverty and degradation he encountered, never shirked going the extra mile for those in need. Arthur Kelsey recalled how his father died within days of Donald's arrival and when he heard the news he was round immediately to console his mother. Not only that, he gave her £1, which to a widow with two growing sons was in those days a handy sum. Kelsey also remembered how when his cousin was dying of cancer, Donald used to go to his aunt's house and play the piano to cheer her up, a gesture which the family never forgot.

On another occasion, according to Hilda Gent who played the piano at the

Sunday School, a woman who attended the open-air service came to the church to ask Donald to accompany her home. He readily agreed and with Hilda set off only to find the woman's husband, their daughter and her boyfriend all very drunk, as well as the daughter in an advanced state of pregnancy. The woman, by now a Christian, wanted them married before the baby arrived to avoid social stigmatisation in what was then a much more censorious society. Donald consented and officiated at the ceremony, although worried that the baby would arrive during the service.

Poverty not only bred sadness and immorality, it also bred violence. Previous biographers related the incident when Donald was quickly summoned from a Women's Meeting to a house in rundown Rivet Street where a man was threatening to cut his throat. He arrived to find the man brandishing a razor in front of his petrified family. He offered to shake hands with him and as the man put down his razor to oblige, one of his children grabbed the razor and ran off with it. On another occasion in the same street, Donald recalled a man walking up to a policeman and announcing that he had just killed his wife. His children were distraught. Donald managed to get them into the National Children's Home, which explained his lifelong links with this Methodist institution thereafter, most notably at its annual meeting in Conference week. He ministered to their father until he was hung for murder. It was during these conversations that he discovered the essential good in a man that one moment of madness had obscured.

It wasn't all gloom and doom, however. About this time the Charleston came over from the United States and Arthur Kelsey has recollections of a little girl asking Donald at the Choral Society if he would do the dance with her. He gracefully assented, much to her delight, although his version of the dance was rather more stately. Similar gallantry was on display when Donald took the part of Frederick in a highly acclaimed production of *The Pirates of Penzance* weeks before his wedding in 1929. Dilys Rouse recalled how as a little girl she presented him with an Easter egg with a bride and groom on it. Donald lifted her up and thanked her with a kiss.

In general, the women and children loved this suave, handsome minister in their midst and many girls had his signed photograph hanging in their bedrooms. "That's my Donald," they used to say. Donald, for his part, never exploited this adulation, but when singing he would often fix a piercing gaze upon a particular girl who would blush accordingly, while he himself kept a serious face.

But if Donald's charisma impressed South London, so did his humility, as the following story illustrates. He received a phone call one day to say that a substantial amount of clothing had been collected at the Central Hall and had been allocated to Oakley Place, although Donald would have to arrange for its collection. To hire a car would have been expensive, but he knew where he could borrow a coster barrow and thus transport the clothing free. He asked his church caretaker to push the barrow to the Central Hall, load up and bring it back. "Sir, I couldn't be seen in the Old Kent Road pushing a coster barrow. I have my reputation to consider." "Oh, couldn't you?" replied Donald, "Well, I can. I haven't got any reputation to consider." At which point he set off down the Old Kent Road in his clerical collar, past a row of pubs, loaded up and came back the same route, pushing his barrow with great insouciance.

For all his dynamism and good works, there were those in the congregation less enchanted by their new minister. Aside from his brash exterior which was apparent on organisational matters, Donald's liberal theology on such issues as the virgin birth and physical resurrection offended Methodists of a more fundamental bent. Within a couple of months, some of the more orthodox office-holders felt that it would be in everyone's interest if he were to leave at the end of the year. Musing over the dilemma with his father, Donald took his advice and alerted his superintendent, the popular Roderick Kedward, a person to whom he grew very attached. William Purcell recalled how when Donald apprised Kedward of his troubles, Kedward appreciated his openness without appearing too flustered by the gathering storm. But at the next Quarterly Meeting when Donald was just about to introduce it with a prayer, the door opened and Kedward came in, announcing that he would take the chair. Thereupon he dealt with the situation, ensuring that there was no more trouble.

There was one other activity which preoccupied Donald during his time in South London. Shocked by the desperate hand fate had dealt many of his congregation, he sought out the well-known socialist intellectual Harold Laski at the London School of Economics to see if he could pursue a PhD in the causes of poverty. Laski was unconvinced by the idea, seeing that Donald knew next to nothing about economics. He did, however, turn to him as he was about to leave and asked him: "Are you as a clergyman naturally interested in political and religious matters?" Donald replied that he hoped he was. "There was a syndicalist in the Sorbonne in seventeenth-century France, Edmond Richer," Laski continued. "He had a lot to do with the current issue in France of Gallicanism and Ultramontanism. If you could do it, that would not be an unacceptable thesis."

"Will you help me?" Donald enquired, to which Laski assented. Donald found him a very kindly, erudite tutor if a rather childish name-dropper, and stood in awe of him over his thesis. At one point Laski felt he was giving him too easy a ride, so he intimated that he should rewrite one particular part of it because it wasn't satisfactory. Donald forgot about what he said and took the same treatise back to him. In time the thesis "Edmond Richer and the Revival of Gallicanism from 1600 to 1630" which discussed the ongoing struggle within the Roman Catholic Church in France between autonomy and centrifugalism, was completed. It not only gained him a doctorate, thereby adding to his stature, but helped him to gain further insights into the baleful effects of doctrinal disputes – a theme which preoccupied him thereafter – as well as the ongoing tensions between Church and State. His studies, however, nearly cost him in the short run as he neglected his probationer studies and spectacularly failed his exams. His explanation failed to impress the formidable Dr John Scott Lidgett, Warden of the Bermondsey Settlement 1891–1949, Chairman of the District and the Grand Old Man of Methodism, but no father figure to the young probationer. Unsettled by Scott Lidgett's fierce line of questioning, Donald's brazen ripostes won him few favours since he came across as impertinent. "Justice first, charity later" was the Warden's terse rejoinder to Roderick Kedward who tried to intercede on Donald's behalf. Then having rebuked the young man for his failings, Scott Lidgett, in recognition of his intellectual faculties which he secretly admired, changed tack to, "Charity will prevail. He may go forward to ordination". Ordination duly followed at the Wesleyan Methodist ministry in Plymouth on 30 July 1929, the prelude to a move to the Central London Mission where he would become the first minister of the new Islington Central Hall.

In retrospect, although Donald galvanised the life of Oakley Place Church and brought succour to many in this part of the metropolis, he rarely reminisced about his time there and formed few lasting bonds. He did speak at the centenary of Oakley Place in 1974, seven years before its final closure in 1981, but his foreword to the history of the South London Mission in 1989 was brief to the point of terseness. Nevertheless, valuable lessons were learnt, not least an insight into the precarious life of the working classes. He later recalled how little children afflicted by tuberculosis and with scant hope of a cure would come home to die. Placed in the downstairs parlour facing the street, they would hold court in summer to passers-by who came to talk, bear gifts and bid their farewells, a scene as poignant as it was macabre. He also had recollections of the day when he noticed one of the healthier-looking members of the congregation limping. On asking him what the matter was, the man showed him his leg, ulcerated from knee to ankle. He said that his doctor had ordered him to bed, but if he complied with his order, he would lose his job and the source of all his income. "That was burnt into my memory," Donald later wrote. "There was the supreme evil of the Capitalist society, which made people work because otherwise they would starve. It is this terribly disproportionate amount of trouble, or of difficulty, or indeed of suffering that is endured by those who are under the constant threat of insecurity, which struck me."[9] He felt that the Methodist Church of his youth had prepared him inadequately for this type of ministry since it was too narrow and remote. The Old Kent Road soon cured him of any such lingering sentiment, reinforcing in his mind the inescapable link between socialism and Christianity.

It was during his time in South London that a chance conversation in February 1927 led to one of the most defining experiences of his life and which made him a household name. Will Thomas, a young man in his congregation who worked in the City, mentioned to him one day that every lunchtime he went to Tower Hill to listen to a variety of speakers, and that in contrast to the persuasive advocacy of the Roman Catholics, the Protestant case lacked conviction. Would Donald consider trying his hand? Thomas had come to the right person, especially since Donald, disappointed by the rows of empty pews at his church, was looking to alternative ways of spreading the Gospel. By now well versed in the great Methodist tradition of public speaking, both from his mother who taught him how to project his voice and his evangelical campaigns at Cambridge, he was confident that he had a Gospel to proclaim that might find a response in the street. He was thus willing to give it a try.

Clad in Oxford bags, he turned up at Tower Hill the following Tuesday at 12.30 p.m. and asked a friendly-looking bystander with more than a touch of anxiety how best to start a meeting. "Get up on the wall. They'll come," responded the man. Donald accepted the advice but little happened, so he sought out his friend again. This time he was told to clap his hands, which he did, and having enjoined others to do the same, a crowd soon gathered. Liking what they heard, they reappeared the following week for more. A new institution had begun, and soon Donald, conspicuous by his sturdy frame and batsman's forearms, was regularly attracting crowds of anywhere between one and two thousand. One of them was the future Prime Minister, Jim Callaghan, who first came across him in the early 1930s, when working in Seething Lane near the Tower of London. He would take his sandwiches and listen to him with interest, marvelling at his quick wit. Soon, he became something of an inspiration to him and one that Callaghan never forgot.[10]

Tower Hill, the Mars Hill of the nation's capital, first became a centre for open-air meetings in December 1666, attracting especially large crowds during the London Dock Strike of 1889. It was a 300-square-yard area, populated by speakers and fish merchants, surrounded by office blocks and a wall three feet high with a large drop onto the street closest to the Tower of London. It was upon this wall that speakers of all persuasions took up their positions, normally on wooden boxes, to speak to the assortment of city workers and dockers who comprised the bulk of the crowd during the 1920s. The leading figures were Father Vincent McNab of the Dominican Order whose evangelistic gifts and personal integrity were of the highest order, Wal Hannington, the communist leader of the National Unemployed Workers' Movement and Bonar Thompson, the author of *Hyde Park Orator*. By unwritten law the man who could control the biggest crowd took the best position on the wall. Soon, that position on a Wednesday was Donald's as many a docker preferred to miss his lunch than miss him.

A lean, tanned face with distinguished black hair and penetrating blue eyes – invariably dressed in a smart suit and bow tie – Donald cut a debonair figure as he spoke with such power that his voice resonated across the Thames to Greenwich. Believing that he was engaged in a great Christian enterprise, he took pains to ensure that, like the great actor polishing his craft to entertain his secular audience, his performance was a class act. Hence his emphasis on a rich vocabulary, command of language, beautifully balanced sentences and animated gestures reminiscent of a flamboyant QC. He also tried to spice his homilies with wit and controversy to maintain interest and stimulate thought. He didn't expect immediate conversions but hoped that having liked what they heard, non-Christians would return for more, thus paving the way for new disciples over a period of time.

Taking his cue from Jesus, who told simple stories to which ordinary people could relate, Donald wanted to present a religion which wasn't prescriptive but rather one which was liberating and relevant. This meant meeting people's needs and answering their questions, some of which he admitted he couldn't do with complete conviction, be it on the absolute veracity of the Bible, or the Christian response to suffering. He would certainly do the next best thing and provide intelligent explanations to mysteries beyond human understanding, such as why an all-powerful God would allow his world to be polluted by evil. To Donald, the idea of active divine omnipotence was seriously flawed since logically this led to a God acting against the wishes of his people. Such a failure to do so would lead them to think of him either as all-powerful but unloving, or loving but impotent. The truth according to Donald, lay in a God whose voluntary abnegation of divine power enabled his people to enjoy a measure of freedom over their lives. The fact that man had forsaken his ways helped explain the existence of both evil and suffering in the world. Not least there was the scandal that two thirds of its people went hungry in a land of plenty, or that unlimited resources were wasted fighting wars of conquest rather than a war against poverty. While accepting that only in the world to come could the perfect answer be found for such vicissitudes, Donald would point to the supreme example of Christ crucified as the Christian's refuge in times of trial and ultimately his future hope over all things temporal. It was a theme he would return to again and again as much in the open air as he would in the pulpit.

Having read up on the day's main stories, Donald liked to begin every week by introducing a contemporary topic of universal interest, placing a controversial slant on it and expressing what ought to be done. As he laid out his store he surveyed the crowd with an eagle eye to see from which corner the predator might pounce. It wasn't long before a protagonist normally appeared and at that point battle was joined, more often than not on the subject of Church failings or religious scepticism. Whilst understanding the risks involved if caught out by his ignorance or obscurity, Donald, unlike many speakers, wasn't fazed by interruptions. They gave him the opportunity to expose the fallacy behind the premise of his opponent's argument, especially in light of Christian truth or political theory. It helped of course that he was such a quick thinker and a repository of knowledge on many religious and political matters, albeit slanted towards his own particular perspective. He also relied on his razor-sharp humour which enabled him to see off an opponent without having necessarily answered the points raised in their entirety. A very small man once ridiculed his pacifism. "If I'm attacked, shouldn't I defend myself?" "In your case," retorted Donald, "I wouldn't bother." On the subject of pacifism he carefully parried the frequent question posed to him, "What would happen if someone attacked your wife?" with the stock answer, "You don't know my wife". Fully aware of the need to stop the hecklers railroading the meeting, he reckoned that one should hit them as hard as one could, preferably above the belt, although the severity of some of his answers could shock even his father. One favourite put-down was, "My friend, if I may say so in all humility, you have a cesspool of a mind". Another priceless gem was, "Our friend says that the unrighteous won't inhabit the kingdom of God and I want to tell him that the unintelligent won't get very near to it either".

Interrupted once when he was in full flow – about loving your neighbour with all your heart – by an atheist who questioned this concept, since the heart was a pump, Donald asked him whether he was married. When he replied he wasn't, Donald affected no surprise. "Fancy proposing to your girl, saying, 'my darling will you be mine, I love you with all my pump.'" The crowd erupted.

Not that he always got the best of the exchanges. Donald recalled the Wednesday they were discussing Prohibition. A heckler was describing with some lucidity the dreadful effects of the Eighteenth Amendment in which the United States had banned alcohol. Donald asked him, "Have you been to America?" "No." "Then," said Donald rather truculently, "don't talk of things you know nothing about." Whereupon a well-known atheist said, "Have you

ever been to heaven?" and when Donald confessed to the obvious, he countered with: "Then don't you talk of things you know nothing about." On
another occasion someone asked whether God controlled the elements.
Donald said he did, to which the questioner, eyes lighting up, replied, "Then
why put lightning-conductors on churches?" Perhaps the best put-down he
was subjected to was the time he was asked to prove that parsons weren't mad.
He found it difficult and procrastinated by asking: "Well, can you prove that
you are not mad?" He said, "I can," and he did by producing his discharge
certificate from a mental institution.

In the battle for ideas, Donald found that he always saw off the atheists,
fundamentalists and Roman Catholics, their humourless respective claims
for authority in the case of the last two no match for his wit. A more effective challenge emanated from the communists because of the greater
coherence of their ideas. However, once Donald had read up on his Marx,
which until then was foreign territory, he could make a convincing case for
Christianity over communism, without ever denying the validity of some of
its arguments. Wit and erudition weren't always able to see off the latent
hostility which lurked among some of the more troublesome personalities
who frequented Tower Hill. A deranged seaman, always threatening Donald
with violence, one week became unduly hysterical and at the end of the
meeting as he climbed down from the wall, rushed towards him brandishing
a knife. "Don't be a damn fool," (the nearest he ever came to swearing)
Donald uttered as he turned his back and walked away. A couple of weeks
later, he heard his potential assailant had been sent to an asylum for knifing
a woman.

In 1931, at the height of the political crisis which brought about the down-
fall of the second Labour Government as it failed to grapple with the spiralling
debt caused by mass unemployment, peaceful argument gave way to rancorous
bickering. One afternoon when a massive demonstration organised by the
communist-backed National Minority Movement engulfed the Hill, Donald,
although assuring them that he was on their side, refused to vacate his position on the wall, whereupon he was pushed off by a large man carrying a
banner with "Liberty" attached to it. In the melée that followed, the atmosphere became heated, until wiser counsels prevailed. It was agreed that
Donald, nursing a few bruises, would speak for another ten minutes and at the
end of this period, his new audience, riveted by his radical Christian message,
shouted, "You should be with us."

Thereafter, Tower Hill remained tense and "The Red Flag" often rang out.
Later, in the mid-1930s, he was occasionally roughed up by Oswald Mosley's
fascist thugs, but despite the extreme rhetoric of other malcontents, the British

tradition of constitutional fair play invariably held the wilder fringe in check, and the police were never summoned.

In general Donald found that some of the most vociferous opponents in the crowd with their profound antipathy to Christianity were people of integrity and geniality in their personal lives, sometimes in need of his charity when their world caved in around them. He did his best to oblige, be it with a small gift, a private visit or a reference to a potential employer. He was sometimes called upon to officiate at their weddings, baptise their children and comfort them on their deathbeds. "I only want Donald Soper," said one, and Donald was there in even time. And then of course there was the silent majority who admired his humour, courage and Christian convictions. Some would ring in after a rowdy meeting to express their support, others might have a word on the spot and a number were inspired to go and do likewise. Once, after one of his talks, a man came up to Donald and asked him if he could possibly shorten the meeting by fifteen minutes as he ran a printing firm and on Wednesdays his whole staff arrived back fifteen minutes late. Donald suggested that the man should listen to him one day. He did and afterwards he gave his staff an extra fifteen minutes lunch break on Wednesdays. Others didn't have such sympathetic employers and some were threatened with dismissal unless they became more punctual. This didn't stop many from discussing his views back at work, quoting animatedly some of the more spirited exchanges which had taken place. "Londoners realise," reported the Nonconformist journal the *British Weekly* in 1936, "that the City possesses an open-air preacher whose gifts have probably not been equalled since Hugh Latimer, in the reign of Henry VIII, addressed the crowds at St Paul's Cross."[11]

Many years later, one of Donald's foremost disciples, the Revd George Dolbey, recalled the occasion back in 1937 when, after surveying a building due for alteration near Tower Hill, he emerged for lunch and heard a stentorian voice. Drawn to it he saw a large crowd listening to a vigorous dark-haired man standing on a wall arguing the case for Christ. Until then he had never appreciated the fact that there was such a case to be made. He returned there on Wednesdays time and again, and when ten years later he offered for the ministry he realised that one of the formative influences behind his decision had been the man behind the voice.[12]

In the summer of 1929 the crowds had their chance to show their appreciation. One Wednesday in early July they were discussing Christian marriage and Donald was asked whether he was married. He replied that he wasn't but was about to rectify this situation in several weeks time. He thought nothing more of the exchange until the following Wednesday one of the crowd presented him with a silver teapot as a wedding present from the assembled company, but not before it was passed around to enable those who hadn't previously contributed, to fill it with silver. As the contents were handed to him, Donald, deeply moved by this generous gesture, remarked that its contents couldn't have come at a better time as at the end of the meeting he and his fiancée were off to choose carpets for the new manse.

Despite Donald's later fame as an open-air orator resting largely on his exploits at Speakers' Corner, it was Tower Hill which throughout his long life remained his greatest love. The fact that he continued to turn out in all weathers and often at some personal discomfort till literally the very end to preach God's saving power was a triumph of valour and perseverance in the best traditions of Bunyan and his faithful pilgrim.

CHAPTER THREE

Faith and Good Works

Before Donald took up his post in Islington there was the small matter of his marriage and the beginning of a special union which was to last an incredible sixty-five years. Although attracted to the opposite sex from an early age, Donald had never had a serious girlfriend until one evening in 1924, aged twenty-one, he met this "blazingly beautiful and graceful girl" at a party to which he had been invited to meet her elder sister. In his own words, he was instantly smitten and couldn't take his eyes off her. Donald arranged to meet her the following day and was astounded to find her in a gym frock coming out of school. Her name was Marie Dean and she was only sixteen years old. Unperturbed, he courted her with walks, dances, games of charades and visits to the cinema. He wasn't alone in his affections, however. Donald later recalled how he was impetuous enough to ask his brother Sos to keep an eye on Marie when he returned to Cambridge. He kept a very possessive eye on her and for four years she couldn't decide between the brothers. At one point Donald had to send Joe Webb on a mission to London from Cambridge to iron out some complications in the relationship and keep it on track. Eventually, Marie succumbed and in 1929 they became engaged, the wedding to take place once Donald had been ordained, which under Methodist edicts was the earliest a minister could marry.

Marie Dean, born in 1908 into a prosperous Anglican family but educated at a Catholic convent, was the fourth of eight children, five boys and three girls, living in Pollards Hill, Norbury, South London. Her father, Arthur Dean, was an electrical engineer, and the idea of his convent-educated daughter marrying a Methodist minister quite appalled him, but in the face of Donald's determination to win her hand he put his reservations to one side. They were married by Roderick Kedward at West Streatham Wesleyan Chapel on 3 August 1929, three days after Donald's ordination [not the day after as he used to say]. The reception at The Grandison Hall in Norbury was a sumptuous affair, but probably in deference to Methodist sensitivities, especially in the groom's family, a separate room was discreetly set aside for those who wished to consume alcohol.

After the honeymoon, the Sopers began married life in a quaint little house in Kelross Road, Highbury, North London, which for Marie was like moving to the other side of the world. She came from a large, outward-going family where culture and entertainment were very much the norm, and her brothers had been educated at the prestigious Dulwich College. Now, not yet twenty-one, she was suddenly transported into an alien environment where not everyone was well disposed towards her, perhaps because of her privileged background. Chairing meetings of the Women's Committee, with all the stalwarts eyeing her every move was quite an ordeal, but in the end her strength of character saw her through and she became an accomplished speaker. She also, as a devotee of all things elegant, proved the ideal homemaker, embellishing it with style, as well as becoming the perfect foil for Donald when at the end of a long, hard day, he could come home to relax. Within two years they had started a family and with Donald soon away for long periods of evangelism, it fell to his wife to bear the brunt of their children's upbringing. It was a major undertaking on her part, calling for painful sacrifices, something she performed with great stoicism.

If the years 1931 and 1933 were replete with joy at the birth of their first two daughters, Ann and Bridget, then 1934 was a year of profound sadness following the sudden death of Sos, aged twenty-six, from diabetes. Having followed his brother as School Captain *en route* to St Catharine's, Cambridge, to read History, he had for the previous five years been a committed and popular schoolmaster at King's College School, Wimbledon, and a good enough tennis player to win three amateur championships in 1933. He was also a conscientious Sunday School superintendent at Streatham Methodist Church and had, unbeknown to Donald, begun speaking in the open air at Tooting Bec. Now he was gone, and the effect on Donald was quite devastating. He later recalled the evening Sos died, walking along a crowded street, thinking it wrong that people should be talking away, and that his brother wasn't there. Marie aside, his friendship with Sos was the deepest he ever forged and even the passing of the years barely cushioned the blow of what he later called "the greatest sorrow of my life".[1]

Donald's seven years at the Central London Mission were crucial to the development of his career, as the success he achieved there made him a household name, yet like his time in South London, this was a time he rarely referred to thereafter. On assuming the responsibilities of the new Islington Central Hall, formed out of two Methodist churches, Liverpool Road and Drayton Park, Donald's first priority was to try and make the merger work. This was no easy undertaking since it had caused considerable bitterness, especially from the former, which effectively moved to the latter, but it was to Donald's credit that he very quickly soothed these ruffled feathers by refusing to take sides.

In line with the Church's desire to reach out to the working classes, both spiritually and materially, the concept of the Central Halls took shape in the 1890–1930 era, thanks to the work of the wealthy industrialist Joseph Rank who was converted to Methodism in his youth. Constructed as auditoria with tip-up seats and surrounded by a complex of rooms and offices, they were noted for their functional rather than aesthetic features which disappointed a confirmed aesthete such as Donald. The Islington Hall, costing £44,000, was round, with a gallery shaped like a horse-shoe and had a capacity for some 1,300 people. In those days Evening Services tended to draw larger congregations than in the morning, including Sir Jack Hobbs, the famous England cricketer, so electrifying was Donald's appeal, with his easy conversational style of preaching and his ability to relate to their individual needs. Soon it became common practice to close the doors before the start of a service. Services were highly charged with a sense that God's love was being expressed and many in the congregation, which comprised a significant proportion of young people, soon found that Donald, as he paced up and down the platform, had the capacity to change their lives. When somebody mentioned to him that he talked over the heads of his predominantly working-class congregation he tartly replied, "I'd rather be over their heads, than under their feet."

Regular worship aside, Donald wasted no time in establishing a very live mission, with evangelising permeating all its activities. Holy Communion took place in the big hall beneath the main one, and rooms were set aside for devotionals, a consulting hour and other meetings like the Men's Group. The Sunday School and the Band of Hope flourished, as did the Children's Play Hour, the Youth Orchestra, the Music School, the Church Dramatic Society and the Scouts. Young people were encouraged to make the Mission their home during the week when a variety of games and activities were provided. In general the congregation was exhorted to help in visiting and to go to Highbury Corner, where Donald spoke every Monday evening, to give him its support.

In order to realise his vision for Islington, and the extra numbers flocking to the Mission, Donald demanded a secretary, two full-time deaconesses and fifteen stewards to man the gallery every Sunday. He also appealed for voluntary workers to help in the weekly activities. The writer Angela Rodaway was one of those who responded positively as she recalled in her autobiography *A London Childhood*. "Donald Soper, at the Islington Central Hall, was running a canteen for the unemployed. Marjory Denotkin and I wanted to help and went to see him. He said he would like us to serve in his canteen providing our parents knew all about it. They did not. When I told my father he was furious. He said that the men who went there were the scum of the earth and no daughter of his was going to serve teas to them. He said all the things about the unemployed that everyone else had been saying for years."[2]

A chance encounter helped Donald make giant strides with the music. On 25 January 1930, he was playing the piano at a concert in Finsbury Park Wesleyan Church, and on hearing the quality of the Ladies' Choir he asked George Irons, their conductor, whether he would consider accepting the post of musical director at Islington. Despite his other teaching and concert commitments, Irons, a musician of some calibre, was happy enough to oblige, and a week later the Special Meeting of the Islington Trustees unanimously agreed to Donald's request. "We would like you to begin as soon as you can," he subsequently wrote to Irons, "it cannot be too soon for us."[3] So began a most harmonious and productive partnership between Minister and Musical Director.

Irons very quickly revolutionised the singing of the seventy capped and gowned choir – a rarity in Methodism – teaching them the modern methods in choral training, and established a young orchestra. The first Saturday evening concert was held in September 1930. In London during the inter-war period it was common in the big Methodist Central Halls to hold popular concerts, mainly composed of light entertainment interspersed with comedy and conjuring. On one occasion Islington played host to the celebrated comedians Arthur Askey and Tommy Handley. Leslie Irons, George's son, recalled how on another occasion a performance of Rossini's *Stabat Mater* replaced the Saturday night concert. George Irons had engaged four eminent opera singers to take the solo parts. They were able to command high fees and Irons, despite offering good money, had difficulty in getting two of them to perform with a church choir of amateurs.

After the performance when Irons entered the dressing room to pay the artists, one of them told him that they were all overwhelmed by the amazing atmosphere they had just encountered. He didn't claim to be a religious man but that evening he had felt a true spiritual presence and an incredible bond with the conductor, choir and audience, something which he couldn't really explain but all four of them had felt it. They had discussed all this and decided that if Donald was amenable, they would be prepared to give their services free for another performance at the Evening Service on the following day. Needless to say Donald willingly assented and the encore was a great success.

Children formed a crucial part of Donald's ministry. According to Len Webb, then a small boy in the congregation, he was very good with the young, always giving a children's address in the main Morning Service, which he made up on the way to church. One popular innovation begun in 1930 was the Saturday afternoon film shows when over 1,000 flocked to the hall to see films for 2d (1p). To get the films either cheap or for free, Donald used to descend on Wardour Street, one of the centres of the British cinema, and procure them by what he called a process of unsanctioned blackmail. He obtained some good films but still felt the need to censor their content, disliking anything sexual or violent, especially Cowboys and Indians, although he later admitted the impracticality of producing pacifist Westerns!

His dilemma was graphically illustrated one afternoon by Angela Rodaway, who grew up in working-class Islington during the 1920s–30s. "On the occasion which I remember so well the supporting film was suddenly switched off and Donald Soper came on to the stage to address us. He said that he had only just realised that the film was unsuitable and we must all go home. We were a rough lot and many were much older and bigger than my brother and I. There must have been several hundreds of us and we could not have our money back, but we went and nobody seemed to mind very much having had a moral lecture instead of the show we had come for. I remembered this when, years later, I saw Soper pulled from a wall on Tower Hill where he was preaching pacifism during the war."[4]

Donald also showed films after Evening Services at Islington on a screen which was lowered in front of the pulpit, but only to those who had attended the service. In 1931 he became Chairman of the Children's Cinema Association to organise cinema exhibitions and, writing four years later, he felt that his church could claim a leadership in using film in particular Methodist missions.

Altogether 2,000 children were touched each week by Mission activities at Islington. Donald was always strict with them but his kindness shone through, making him popular and well respected in turn. When the children came out of Sunday School and he escorted them to the Holloway Road to see them safely across it, they would push and shove to be one of the two lucky ones to hold his hand. To some from difficult homes, "Doc" as he was invariably known, was the one person to provide them with a sense of security. Many of them formed part of the 500 underprivileged children who were given breakfast every Christmas by the Mission. They were supposed to arrive at 8 a.m., but most were there by 6.30 and Donald needed a whistle to organise them. The effort, however, was worth it when he saw the pleasure generated.

Further contact with the children came through games of table tennis and the Scouts. The Liverpool Road Church brought with it a strong Scout group and Donald, given his later ban of all uniformed organisations when he went to Kingsway, surprisingly agreed to become Rover Scout Leader, wearing uniform, attending regular meetings and going to camp whenever possible. To all members of the Rover Crew, "Doc" was renowned for his insatiable energy and his great sense of fun. At camp he would sometimes take everyone out for a meal and insist on paying. On another occasion on camp in Devon when the Scouts were being taunted by local youths on a bridge, Donald threatened to throw them into the river unless they desisted.

It should be recalled that Donald's tenure at Islington very much coincided with the worst effects of the Great Depression, especially the traumatic years 1931–34 when there were approximately three million unemployed, 7,000 of whom were in Islington. Donald was present at the National Unemployed Workers' Movement demonstration in Hyde Park in 1931 and he later recalled it as the most dynamic he ever attended. Memories of a visit to a mining community in the Welsh valleys ravaged by unemployment, also left a profound impression on him. With his growing conviction that the Church must stand shoulder to shoulder with the "have nots", Donald set up in 1932–33 a great community centre in the Hall for the unemployed, comprising a soup kitchen, a boot repair centre, a library, a darts club and other amenities. Men who drifted into church premises to while away the pointless hours were encouraged to take up simple crafts to keep them from excessive brooding. In order to help people to deal with their problems, Donald or one of his two deaconesses was available daily in attendance. He always respected the dignity of those seeking help, and treated them with great courtesy. His sympathetic approach induced great loyalty in return and a number actually became Christians. At the same time he could be disarmingly blunt to those who he felt were being unduly feckless. One old lag leaving an interview with Donald was overheard to say, "That bloke doesn't mince his words. He told me exactly what I've got to do and what will happen if I don't. Anyway, he's right. I've got no choice."

This uncompromising straight-talking was put to good effect on another occasion when Donald was sitting in one of the smaller rooms at the Hall. Suddenly, the door gently opened and a tall young man with a cap pulled down over his eyes entered. Not noticing Donald who was seated right behind the door, he whispered the all-clear to his accomplice, ordering him to stay there and keep watch. At that point, Donald made himself known to the intruders and ordered them – both armed – to sit down, while he admonished them about the perils of prison. He didn't call the police, but let them go once they had promised to renounce their life of crime. Later, when defending pacifism in all forms, Donald used to refer to this incident as an example of how he put his faith in moral exhortation over the merits of physical force.

For all his popularity at Islington, Donald had his detractors, as he did in

South London, over his grandiose ideas for the Mission. Much of that opposition came down to cost. Donald was unapologetic, stating that one couldn't have champagne at beer prices, and he clashed with his trustees over his personal expenses. It was unusual at that time for a minister to have a car, let alone a new one at regular intervals, and when Donald wished to move the manse from Highbury to the more salubrious East Finchley, despite its more distant location from the church, he insisted on the purchase going ahead. There were also ructions about the contents. David Mason, later a member of the Notting Hill Group Ministry in the West London Mission, recalled Donald saying to his wife years later when discussing their new home there, "You buy what you want, darling. Don't put up with the rubbish furniture that the Circuit Stewards tried to put in our manse in Islington."

Alfred Sleep, one of Donald's congregation in Islington, and a leader in the Scouts, recalled him arriving at camp at Rottingdean in Sussex and causing offence by exclaiming, "Why do you come to a place like this? It's like a London suburb." He also proved less than tactful when Sleep, drawing on his links with the shoe trade, provided him with a new pair, on the grounds that they were too cheap. To Sleep, Donald was a magnetic figure capable of moving mountains, but prone to high-handedness when dealing with others in an official capacity. For all his egalitarian tendencies he relished his status and could be quite dismissive of those who were his intellectual inferiors. For instance, when Ernie Higgins, the organ-blower from Liverpool Road, developed a tendency to go to sleep during his sermons, Donald, bristling with indignation, wanted him dismissed, and only relented under pressure from a colleague. His intolerance of crass stupidity, so evident in the open air, was no passing phase. It stayed with him thereafter. Sleep remembered another occasion years later when Donald came to open St John's Methodist Church in Potter's Bar, and preach. After the service, Sleep informed him that the local reporter had mentioned in passing that he hadn't understood the sermon. Donald asked Sleep to point him out. Taking one look at him, he replied, "I'm not surprised." Even those to whom he was attached could suddenly find their grammar being corrected, while a spark of intelligence from a poorly educated person could elicit admiration and surprise in equal measure. One of Donald's favourite sayings when officiating at the funerals of his congregation was that they too had served the Church in their capacity as doorkeepers or flower arrangers. It was meant as a compliment, even though such comments sounded faintly patronising towards lesser mortals. The truth was that although he understood better than many the plight of the destitute, he was less *au fait* with the day-to-day drudgery of Mission staff or ordinary families, not least the concept of a working mother. One loyal member of the

West London Mission to which he moved in 1936, was somewhat affronted when Donald organised the Women's Committee to meet at 4 p.m., little realising that some people like her would be unable to attend because of work commitments.

Endowed as he was with such compelling personal and intellectual attributes, it was hardly surprising that Donald's great confidence should incline towards vanity, quaintly expressed in his case through a tendency to preen himself whenever in sight of a mirror. Always a great competitor who liked to dominate at whatever activity he pursued, and used to running his own outfit, the prospect of being even *primus inter pares* didn't greatly appeal. Thus sharing platforms with others, unless he greatly respected them, or listening to them in committee, was to be avoided if at all possible. Hence his infrequent appearances within Methodist power structures, or other ecumenical bodies, leaving one with the paradox that a person so able to bring people together under his own leadership could rarely co-operate when under the leadership of others. Douglas Thompson, Donald's first biographer, shed further light on this paradox when referring to the concept of God's grace which informed so much of his teaching and preaching. The danger of the doctrine of the Holy Spirit choosing his man and working through him, Thompson declared, arose when human will became conveniently shrouded in the divine, so that truth gave way to inflexibility. History is of course littered with good men undone by their fanaticism, and although Donald loved to engage in what he called the fellowship of controversy, he was rarely receptive to new ideas in these exchanges, not least in that partisan atmosphere of Tower Hill when beating off the hecklers was everything. Such resolution made him admirably consistent in his beliefs, but investing his political principles in moral absolutes not only made him eager to cast out the philosophical beam in his brother's eye, it made him blind to the beam in his own. Even Tony Benn, a fellow Christian socialist and good friend, rather parted company with him on his contention that socialism was indissolubly linked to Christian morality in comparison with other political ideologies or parties. This flaw in Donald's make-up in many ways cost him dear, as he later acknowledged when regretting his isolation in both the Church and the Labour Party. "Partly my fault," he confessed, "I was very arrogant and I thought I knew better than most other people."[5] This stubbornness operated at a more personal level. Even his wife was often at a loss to get him to change his mind, recognising that he had a strong ego and always did his own thing. David Smith, later Donald's deputy at the West London Mission, recalled Marie being driven to fury when her husband insisted on taking an Evening Service despite being far from well. The result was a two-week spell in bed. Later on he kept ignoring surgical advice to have an operation on his shoulder but ultimately was forced to bow to nature as the pain became debilitating.

And yet for all those streaks of hubris this was a man whose own personal lifestyle, elegant home aside, was anything but sumptuous – a point reflected in his shabby office at the West London Mission which, apart from a bust of John Wesley, was almost devoid of furniture. Aside from his most basic of tastes in eating and drinking and increasingly in his austere mode of dress, he endured much pain and discomfort from phlebitis during many a march or mission, especially in bad weather. Perhaps most commendable was the way in which he shunned privileged treatment on Order of Christian Witness (OCW) campaigns when it came to accommodation. That such an eminent personality, as he was by then, was willing to share the most spartan amenities of a church hall with his young followers was a fact that didn't go unnoticed. Those however who engaged in adulation were quickly given short shrift. Away from the platform it was his humility which normally shone through and won him many friends amongst the downtrodden. For a man who could have made his fortune as a leading barrister or possibly even a professional musician, the fact that becoming a Methodist minister was the acme of his ambition perhaps best brings out his unworldliness. David Mason has recollections of going to see him as a young man with some doubts as to his continuing vocation. Donald stared at him in some astonishment and refused to discuss it. He loved being a minister and couldn't understand anyone having reservations about such a fulfilling vocation.

A similar point was made by Colin Morris, President of the Methodist Conference in 1976, many years later when preaching the sermon at Donald's Service of Thanksgiving. He affirmed that beneath all the layers of his personality he was at heart a very simple man. Morris recalled his surprise when his choice of hymns for the *Songs of Praise* programme in celebration of his ninetieth birthday, included, "I think when I read that sweet story of Old", the one he had sung as a very young boy. "One might of expected Donald the English stylist to raise an eyebrow at such Victorian versifying, but Donald the child-like believer bellowed his lungs out singing it. He had the drawing power of holy simplicity."[6]

Simplicity was also the hallmark of his holiday arrangements, which invariably comprised several weeks in rented accommodation on the beach with the family in Cornwall, first at Newquay long before it became fashionable, and then at Mullion. Always a glutton for the sea and the surf, whatever the vagaries of the weather, Donald was equally happy indulging his love of ball games, and entertaining his children with his facility for telling stories or humorous asides. On Sundays when visiting the local church to preach, they would eagerly speculate as to how he would bring some cricketing score into his sermon. So committed, incidentally, was he to the outdoors, that he confessed to wearing his trunks under his cassock to accommodate a quick return to the beach. This then to Donald was the royal life, and so entranced was he by the beauty of its surroundings, that Cornwall in August remained his earthly paradise for the rest of his days.

It was during his time at Islington that Donald's experiences were further deepened by his appointment as a Methodist Chaplain to Holloway and Pentonville Prisons, since it taught him how little he knew about the culture of prison. He used to observe what remarkable headway the Nonconformist conscience made in Pentonville when the inmates discovered they could get an extra hour out of their cells by attending worship. He expected sullen, unresponsive types, but was surprised how alert and responsive they were at the Saturday services. As he visited a number in their desolate cells, including the chilling experience of ministering to those on death row, Donald came to realise the unforgiving environment which many prisoners were born into, and how each one had their own desperate story to tell.

In his book *Christ and Tower Hill*, Donald recalled one such incident. "I was visiting prisoners in Pentonville Prison one Saturday after taking the weekly service for Nonconformists. I unlocked the door of C 3 21. A rather pleasant and cultured-looking prisoner faced me.

'I know your face, don't I?'

'You ought to – before I got this packet I used to be up on the Hill in your crowd most Wednesdays.'

'What are you in for?'

'Picking pockets.'

'How many previous convictions?'

'Nine.'"[7]

The conversation was the beginning of many and he admitted that the sort of religion Donald was offering had its attractions. Donald wanted him to promise to keep in touch once he was released. He simply said that he would continue to come to Tower Hill spasmodically. Sure enough he returned, and some time afterwards wrote to Donald that he had become a Christian and was working at a boys' club connected with the local Baptist church.

Aside from the respect with which Donald was held by the prisoners because of the candid yet humane way he related to them, and the friendships he formed with people such as Wal Hannington, these visits left a lasting impact on him. Essentially he felt prison wrong because it was an escape by society from responsibility for the problems which bred crime, and that it was an imperfect corrective for recidivists, since its brutal conditions did little to promote faith and penitence. As far as Donald was concerned, the earlier a prisoner could be released, the nearer he could be brought to the personal effect of his crime and the greater chance of remorse. Four years he felt was the longest anyone should be incarcerated, even for murderers, a view which seemed absurdly lenient, especially when history has shown that many released back into the community had reoffended.

Aside from his mission work, prison-visiting and membership of an unemployment committee in Islington, Donald was beginning to spread his wings as his exploits at Tower Hill raised his national profile. This was reflected in his first appearance in *Who's Who* in 1932, the year he first spoke at Methodist Conference. All of a sudden the invitations began to flood in, and Donald, being Donald, found them hard to resist. There was his pacifist work for the Methodist Peace Fellowship (MPF) which included a visit to Canada and the United States in 1935, there were his contributions to local Labour Party rallies in Islington, his membership of the Society of Socialist Clergy and Ministers and his participation in London Mission rallies. In 1929 he was uncharacteristically late for a rally at the Lycett Methodist Church in Bethnal Green, by which time all members of the Stepney Circuit staff were in their allotted places. Apologising profusely, his explanation that his late arrival was due to being heckled at a political meeting was greeted with mirth all round. There was little mirth, however, when Donald tried to articulate opposition to Oswald Mosley's British Union of Fascists at various open-air meetings in Ridley Road, Hackney, during the mid-1930s. We have only his own account of these bruising encounters, but not surprisingly the experience left him so disenchanted, especially with the brutality of the stewards, that his contempt for all types of totalitarianism remained absolute thereafter.

Donald also spoke in schools, including his old one, and on Empire Day every year he visited Hazelrigge Road School in Clapham, where his mother was now the headmistress. After his well-received talk, his final announcement was always to inform the girls that they would be having a half-holiday in the afternoon, with the approval of the headmistress, of course. Consent would be given whereupon he would be clapped and cheered by the whole assembly.

There was also Donald's baptism on radio, a partnership which, apart from his ban during the war years, was to endure happily for the rest of his life as he found the ideal outlet for his love of the limelight. His chance to shine had much to do with him meeting, in 1932, H. R. L. "Dick" Sheppard, a communicator of genius whose church at St Martin-in-the-Fields in Trafalgar Square had pioneered religious broadcasting in 1924 and had become the setting for regular ecumenical Sunday evening broadcasts.

Sheppard, a cricketing buff like Donald, took an instant liking to him, as did the Director of Religious Broadcasting, F. A. Iremonger, a protégé of the BBC Director General, Sir John Reith, who heard him at Tower Hill at the end of 1933. He was so impressed that he invited him to broadcast a series of fifteen-minute talks for which he would be paid five guineas each, good money for that time but well earned all the same, for Iremonger was a hard taskmaster. Not only did he insist that all texts were submitted to him well in advance for his perusal, he wasn't averse to voicing reservations where appropriate. "This is quite excellent and I have only one or two suggestions to make. First of all, I am quite certain that it is impossible to say that war is a result of capitalism. I am sure you will think I am very old-fashioned in this, but I cannot help saying it when the most bellicose nation in the world today is a nation which is trying to shed capitalism and start a Utopia of its own. I seriously doubt whether you ought to make a statement of that kind in a talk where you cannot amplify it. ... There is another sentence in which you say, 'the arguments for drink all come from the barrack room'. I don't quite know what this means, but if it means that only sergeant-majors like their beer, it seems to me perhaps rather too generalised a statement."[8] On 10 June 1934, Donald made his radio debut at St Martin's. Several weeks later he followed it up with the first of a series of talks about his evangelistic experiences in the open air called *Question Time on Tower Hill,* adapting nicely to an intimate conversational style very different from his fiery rhetoric on the soapbox. When a second series appeared the following year the quality was such that the Revd R. B. Shapland in the *Methodist Recorder* marked him down as one of the two outstanding Methodist broadcasters, the other being Leslie Weatherhead. Twice in 1935 and 1936 the BBC paid him the compliment of broadcasting live services from his church – "my listening millions" as Donald proudly proclaimed – and in November 1936 his Sunday afternoon talks *Christianity and Its Critics* won him further acclaim. The *Methodist Recorder* reckoned that the case for Jesus Christ had never been more reasonably or conclusively put, while Iremonger expressed his gratitude for a "really fine bit of work".[9] At a time when the uneven quality of religious broadcasting was causing him some concern, especially the tedium and remoteness of many preachers, he, an ordained Anglican, wanted to attract the very best whatever their denomination, and saw Donald as his ideal type. He, along with Weatherhead, the Congregationalist J. S. Whale and the Church of Scotland minister George MacLeod, quickly became an important ally in his quest to attain excellence by making the Gospel more intelligible to the man in the street.

Iremonger was again to the fore the following year with his support for

Donald and his six talks entitled *Popular Fallacies about the Christian Faith* but continued to temper his praise with admonishment whenever Donald sailed too close to the political wind. "This is very good. I have only two criticisms to make. I am afraid that you must knock out that bit about capitalism a few lines from the bottom of page 7. It rather assumes that any money which is made in a capitalist system is tainted and this, I think, is a little too tendentious (good word) for a Sunday afternoon talk."[10] A month later he wrote in similar vein. "I think your last talk is quite the best you have done yet, if I may say so, but there are one or two suggestions I feel bound to make. Page 5, line 7 – surely not all the money made on the Stock Exchange is gambling. There is a very large number of people who hate gambling just as much as you and I do and who deliberately invest their money in such stocks as war loans, provincial corporations and others. The real scum – if you can get at them, which you can't – are the Greeks, Armenians and Jews who sit in large and expensive offices in Paris and rig the international market."[11]

Owing to serious illness Donald was unable to broadcast in 1938, but returned in style the following year with *Will Christianity Work?*, which elicited many letters of appreciation from Christians and non-Christians alike, and *After Tea on Sunday*. By the time war broke out his success behind the microphone had made him a household name, and his professionalism under Iremonger's tutelage a ready accessory to his natural eloquence, which made him such an accomplished media performer for the rest of his life.

In July 1936 Donald left Islington behind for the West London Mission. Perhaps the clue to his reticence in future years about his time there was his later admission that it was there that he had made his mistakes; and it is true that his style of leadership didn't appeal to everyone. That said, his failures were miniscule compared to his success in giving the Islington Central Hall the best possible start, not least in clearing it of all debt. Any successor would have had an unenviable task following in Donald's shoes, but it was unfortunate that the man chosen so lacked any warmth or inspiration that numbers rapidly declined, with some accompanying him to Kingsway Hall. After Islington had been badly bombed during the Second World War, the days of the Central Hall were numbered and sadly it was forced to close in 1946, another victim of a more secular age.

CHAPTER FOUR

Towards the Precipice

Because of his exceptional talents and his success at Tower Hill and Islington, Donald Soper was clearly a man destined for great things. In February 1929 the *Methodist Times* had referred to him as the livest wire in London and in December 1931 the *News Chronicle* depicted him as a worthy successor to General William Booth, founder of the Salvation Army. What's more, C. Ensor Walters, sometime Superintendent of the West London Mission, London Mission Secretary and President of Conference in 1936, had had his eye on him since hearing him at Tower Hill. In November 1935 he went to Islington to pay homage in person, saying that there were few chapters of history more impressive in Methodism than the success of Dr Soper at Islington. Thereafter he nominated him for the superintendency of the West London Mission, in succession to Ira Goldhawk, convinced that he had the courage and sense of adventure suitable for the job. When Donald was informed of Conference's endorsement he was delighted. Not only was Kingsway Hall a living example of the social gospel he so passionately believed in, it was close to Tower Hill and to his family. For a Londoner keen to stay in the capital, Donald was extremely fortunate to spend all his working life there, so avoiding the traditional Methodist itinerant system which invariably meant a spell in the provinces.

In September 1936 Donald, aged thirty-three, became the youngest super-intendent of a Central Mission. The general rule stated that a superintendent minister in a Methodist Circuit should have travelled for twenty years. He had done half that time but the Stationing Committee at Conference waived this stipulation. At his induction service at Kingsway, accompanied by glorious music, a congregation of some 2,000 comprising many friends and associates, gave him a rousing reception when he rose to speak. He drove home the argument that Christianity had at its heart a loyalty to a person, not a subscription to a creed. The one consuming passion in his life, he declared, was the knowl-edge of what God had given him in Jesus Christ, that every single person regardless of caste or colour was of supreme, eternal value.

Donald's words won him glowing reviews in the press as he began his ministry at one of the great city Missions, born out of a concern in 1887 to help the urban poor. The great force behind this Mission was its first superintendent, Hugh Price Hughes, the eminent Welsh evangelist and social reformer, and while it had changed home four times before settling at Kingsway Hall in 1912, its ethos remained very firmly intact. The Kingsway Hall, designed by the architect Josiah Gunton, was situated on one of the city's main north-south thoroughfares close to Holborn Underground station. It was an unprepossessing building of seven floors, containing various social and educational amenities as well as accommodation for its workers and a hall which could hold 2,000 for worship, mainly in tip-up seats upholstered in red velvet. Over the years it had been home to a number of famous names in Methodism including J. E. Rattenbury and C. Ensor Walters and possessed a proud musical tradition, but above all, its commitment to social outreach was unrivalled in the country.

Determined to continue where he had left off in Islington, Donald immediately took the place by storm, creating a great sense of purpose and fellowship as he lifted the eyes of his flock to the hills. New members were recruited, teams of volunteers were expanded and money for additional projects sought. Monthly prayer-meetings sprang up, a weekly devotional group called the Guild was established and the excellent *Kingsway Messenger* detailing the life and ethos of the Mission came into being. There was much to report.

In January 1937 Haile Selassie, the Emperor of Abyssinia, then living in exile in England, opened an exhibition at Kingsway called "Conquest of Healing". It ran for five days and was seen by 4,000 and sought support for the medical missions of all the Churches. In March the Sopers were presented to George VI and Queen Elizabeth at Buckingham Palace; then in May Donald celebrated ten years preaching at Tower Hill by leading a congregation of nearly 1,000 in community singing from the piano.

George Lansbury, the leader of the Labour Party 1931–35, present on this occasion, was one of many to pay tribute to his evangelistic gifts. He observed that Donald had brought a view of life appropriate to the needs of London and his Gospel on Tower Hill was altogether more uplifting than the austere one presented to him as a boy. Convinced that Christianity needed to be rescued from the yoke of outworn doctrinal absolutism and its narrow judgmentalism, which to his mind bred popular alienation, Donald, like Leslie Weatherhead at the City Temple, was unapologetic in his scepticism towards biblical infallibility. In his vision of the human Jesus forged out of life's struggles and who forgave rather than reproached, he preached a faith that was personal, inclusive, optimistic and relevant. "The Reverend Donald Soper MA PhD," wrote

Free Churchman, in the *Western Evening Herald*, "is a Methodist whose fame at the early age of 34 has spread far beyond the limits of his denomination.

"It has spread indeed far beyond the limits of the Christian Church, for there are thousands of people who never darken the doors of a church who are interested, cautious, critical and admiring hearers of the young preacher at Tower Hill. A keen brain, a well-equipped mind, and an apostolic courage and ardour make Dr Soper's ministry one of the most valuable assets of present day evangelism in England."[1]

The *Evening News*, the *Evening Standard* and *Methodist Recorder* were similarly complimentary, and Muswell Hill Methodist Church in North London unveiled a stained-glass window depicting him on Tower Hill, making him one of the very few to appear in a stained-glass window during his lifetime.

Later that summer Donald, accompanied by Marie and his young family, set off for South Africa at the invitation of Joe Webb for an arduous five-week tour. The visit left him with a conflicting set of emotions as he and his family savoured the fulsome hospitality accorded to them. Warming to the indescribable beauty of the countryside, the near perfect climate and the wonder of the game reserves, he later told of the most thrilling moment of his life when shooting a rampaging lion, an ironic admission given his subsequent commitment to the anti-bloodsport cause. But behind its sunny exterior there lay a darker side to South Africa which a man of Donald's radical temperament quickly discerned as he witnessed the inadequacies of the leading Dutch Reformed Church. For not only was he profoundly troubled by the plight of the despised coloured population, the most pitiable he had ever encountered, but also he felt ashamed at the intolerable way Christian people treated their black servants. Such concerns he shared with the large crowds he addressed in Wesleyan churches in Pretoria, Cape Town and Johannesburg and in the Town Hall in Durban. Not surprisingly his core themes of socialism and pacifism didn't endear themselves to his all-white audiences reared on a rugged frontier mentality, and he wasn't invited back. More serious than his politics was the plight of his family. On the eve of their departure, Ann, then aged six, contracted pneumonia, forcing Donald to leave her with Marie in hospital in Cape Town while he and Bridget sailed for home. Within minutes of their departure, Bridget, too, fell prey to pneumonia, leaving Donald to nurse her through the tropics on the boat, not knowing whether Ann would survive. Fortunately, both girls fully recovered.

On his return there was no let-up in the rash of commitments he undertook. In September he was the principal speaker for Youth Week at the Liverpool Civic Hall, which attracted record crowds. In October he preached every Friday lunchtime at St Martin-in-the-Fields, and besides attending countless other missionary events in London, he was in constant demand further afield. Birmingham, Brighton, Bromley, Cardiff, Clacton-on-Sea, Huddersfield, Ilminster, Oxford, Portsmouth, Sheffield, Sittingbourne, Sunderland, Tavistock and York are just some of the names which feature on his list of engagements for 1937. And, dwarfing all this, there were the Jubilee celebrations of the Mission to organise. To mark the occasion, some major new initiatives were launched. A new home for girls on probation called the Katherine Price Hughes Hostel was opened in Doughty Street, a club for needy young men in Drury Lane started in June 1938, and most ambitious of all, Donald, following his work in Pentonville, planned a hostel for ex-prisoners. The project had its detractors, but he persisted, and a generous donation of £1,000 helped bring it to fruition in 1939. He recalled how for fifteen days no one appeared, then a criminal sentenced to death in Utah turned up. He stayed three weeks, the first of many for whom a spell in the hostel helped them readjust to normal life and find work. No wonder that *Christian World* referred to the West London Mission as one of the lights of London in July 1939 – a lesson of hope and renewal in the very midst of the capital.

Aside from his pastoral and pacifist activities Donald continued on his busy way throughout 1938. He rarely disappointed as the *British Weekly* correspondent discovered after attending worship at Kingsway. "The first thing that strikes one about Dr Donald Soper is his vigour. He is surprisingly youthful to be so well-known. When he read the passages from the Bible his voice gave the impression of a power under control. In the words and gestures of his speech the power was more open, but still natural and unforced. He spoke to his youthful congregation as one who shared their problems, but with the authority of one who had found an answer. He spoke of knowing God through material things, as music must be played to be heard … . It was a good sermon, the sort of sermon one remembers with satisfaction, and his audience drank it in."[2]

Several months later the *Church Times* called him one of the shining lights of English Methodism today, and when invited to give the one hundred-and-seventy-seventh Heckmondwicke lecture series that June, hundreds had to be turned away from Westgate Congregational Chapel in the Spen Valley. In his talk, Donald, quoting John Wesley, stated that the first duty of a Methodist preacher was to save souls. Christianity wasn't good advice, but good news of the salvation which God had provided for all humanity through the sacrificial Christ on the Cross of Calvary. God was stronger than sin. That July he made headlines with his support for women ministers to "stop the rot in Methodism". His long illness from a potentially dangerous thrombosis then put him out of action until December. As he lay restless and frustrated on his bed, his long absence had the one consolation of confirming him in his vocation. To be one of John Wesley's travelling preachers was to him the ultimate reward. It was a sentiment from which he never departed.

During his absence Donald's replacement for much of the time was a twenty-six-year-old Methodist trainee from Sydney called Alan Walker, who was on a six-month tour of leading British mission centres. Walker never understood how it was that Donald entrusted such a task to a young, untried and virtually unknown Australian, a decision about which Donald could offer no satisfactory answer when quizzed about it in old age. His hunch, however, proved a shrewd one since Walker's experience of preaching in front of 2,000 people held him in good stead for his later eminence as Superintendent of the Sydney Central Mission and Director of World Evangelism for the World Methodist Council. In years to come he always looked back on this time in Britain with special gratitude and the lessons Donald taught him. Although recognising his tendency to be harsh in his judgements and a little intolerant, Walker felt that Donald was a magnetic figure blessed with supreme self-assurance, charm and ability, which helped explain the quality of his leadership, not least at Tower Hill. The fact that he simply stood up there and spoke without the singing testimonies and other distractions so often associated with the Christian open-air tradition, marked him out in Walker's eyes as an evangelist of very rare calibre. As with the case of W. E. Sangster, the celebrated Superintendent of the Central Hall, Westminster, Donald was very generous with his time, challenging Walker to look beyond the personal deprivations of the Sydney he had witnessed to the structures which caused and perpetuated them. "Soper's point of view wasn't the important thing as far as Alan's preparation for later ministry was concerned," wrote Walker's first biographer, Harold Henderson. "What was important was the realisation that the Gospel is both the personal and social, that the prophetic is as much part of the biblical tradition as the evangelical and pastoral and that the Gospel relates to the whole of life."[3]

In addition to Donald's strong social conscience, which later influenced other distinguished clerics such as David Sheppard, Bishop of Liverpool, and Robin Eames, Archbishop of Armagh and Primate of All Ireland, Walker was much taken with his internationalism and pacifism. As Europe hovered on the brink of destruction their discussion assumed a certain intensity. "Well, Alan, you'll soon return to Australia," Donald said to him. "What are you going to be – a pirate, a policeman or a pacifist?" Walker thought long and hard about Donald's parting shot and finally converted to pacifism on board the boat home as it neared its destination.

While Donald made his mark during the 1930s as a dynamic minister with special talents, he was increasingly active in foreign affairs amid the gathering gloom. As a pacifist minister he stood in a proud Free Church tradition, especially among the Quakers, and had seen his sentiments strengthened by listening to Mahatma Gandhi's talk about passive resistance when the mystical Indian leader was in London in 1931 to discuss his country's struggle against British rule. Pacifism as a movement, although dating back to the mid-nineteenth century, had lacked popular support in Britain, especially in Anglican circles, and even most Nonconformists rallied to the war effort in 1914. Thereafter, despite the revulsion against war following the slaughter in the trenches, and the backlash against the punitive Versailles peace treaty, seen as unduly harsh on Germany, it remained becalmed through most of the 1920s. The catalyst for change came with the publication of the war poetry of Wilfred Owen and Siegfried Sassoon and R. C. Sherriff's play, *Journey's End*, which, combined with the fear of aerial bombardment in a future war, brought many new converts to the pacifist cause. The liberal theology of the time with its rational, optimistic assumptions also played its part, as did a mainstream Anglican priest.

Dick Sheppard, formerly of St Martin-in-the-Fields and Canon of St Paul's at the time of his death in 1937, probably became the best-known cleric of that era, greatly loved for his warmth, compassion and humility. Nothing seemed too much trouble for this complex figure whose unhappy childhood and appalling memories of trench life when serving as a war chaplain, fomented his idealistic tendencies. It was this infectious warmth and enthusiasm, coupled with a deep-seated piety, that gave him an iconic status in Donald's eyes, as he, like countless others, fell under his spell. He used to recall his pride at becoming one of the first recruits to the Peace Army dreamt up in February 1932 by Sheppard, Maude Royden, the greatest woman preacher he ever heard, and Herbert Gray, a senior Presbyterian minister and former army chaplain. Eight hundred signatories applied to join, but the famous trip the three of them and Donald made to Tilbury, supposedly to board a ship to Chopei in China to mediate in the Sino-Japanese War, and mentioned by previous biographers, didn't actually occur, according to the historian Martin Ceadel. His view is supported by Donald's evasiveness in later years when questioned about this rather bizarre episode in his life which, in any case, seemed more than a little far-fetched.

Several months later in June, Sheppard's Peace Army, with Donald in the vanguard, travelled to the West India Dock to protest against the sailing of the steamship *Ben Alder*, replete with arms to Japan. Denied entry to the port they resorted to making their presence felt by the gates. It gained some publicity but little practical result and by 1934 the Peace Army had been disbanded. Its demise was but a small reverse at a time when the rise of the Nazis in Germany and the collapse of the International Disarmament Conference in Geneva further galvanised the politics of peace.

In November 1933, thanks to the efforts of Henry Carter, the MPF was born as an offshoot of the Fellowship of Reconciliation (FOR), a predominantly Nonconformist Quaker pacifist organisation founded in 1914, as 500 ministers accepted its covenant of peace and reconciliation. Carter became its first president, Donald and Eric Baker joint secretaries and the Islington Central Hall played host to many of its meetings. That same year the Methodist Conference – without fully adopting the pacifist position – had committed itself to disarmament, and declaring that war was a crime against humanity, repudiated it as a method of settling international disputes. Then in October 1934 there came a crucial moment when Sheppard, in a famous letter to *The Times*, attempted to discover the full extent of the desire for peace. Within a few weeks, 50,000 had answered in the affirmative and the origins of the Peace Pledge Union (PPU) were born.

Sheppard, as was his wont, for he was a man of painful indecisiveness, didn't follow up his letter for another nine months until a crowded rally of 7,000 at the Albert Hall in July 1935 gave some shape to his plans. By now the cause for peace had been further undermined, since fascist Italy under Mussolini stood poised to invade the backward African state of Abyssinia. The failure of the League of Nations to take effective action once Mussolini invaded that October (a failure due chiefly to the reluctance of the British and French to give a meaningful lead) meant that, by the time the PPU was officially launched on 22 May 1936, the League's authority lay in tatters. Donald joined the novelist Storm Jameson, the politicians George Lansbury and Arthur Ponsonby, the Anglican cleric Charles Raven, the Regius Professor of Divinity at Cambridge, and Brigadier-General Frank Crozier, a veteran of the First World War, as one of its initial Sponsors. Later, its ranks were swelled by a talented collection of political and intellectual heavyweights such as John Middleton Murry, Siegfried Sassoon, Aldous Huxley, Rose Macaulay, Bertrand Russell and Ellen Wilkinson, although the turmoil of their personal lives caused Donald to label them a pretty odd lot. Because of Sheppard's dependence on his early Sponsors, Donald, despite his youth, exerted quite an influence on the policy pursued. This policy centred on the effectiveness of passive resistance of the type advocated by Gandhi to an invading German army. According to Ceadel, in light of the failure of economic sanctions to stop Mussolini invading Abyssinia, Donald wanted to face the worst scenario. "Perhaps," he wrote in the May 1936 edition of *Reconciliation*, "the nation which renounces violence will suffer crucifixion: that is a possibility, though I think today a small one. But though there is little chance that its women and children will be butchered, the people of a country might have their lives seriously restricted and their outward freedom denied them. That I think is a real prospect if such an invasion were to come from a so-called civilised power."[4] He didn't believe, however, that it would entail any loss of life.

The following month Donald, using the same periodical, drafted a spirited response to a savage critique of Christian pacifism by Alfred Duff Cooper, the Secretary of State for War. Such a creed, according to Duff Cooper, was unpatriotic, not to say heretical, in the eyes of many. "Our refusal to co-operate in recruitment, our rejection of the claim that we ought to assist in the defence by armed force of our country is," Donald declared, "rooted in the teaching of our Lord. We seek to co-operate in every way that is possible for us with the civilian authorities, but finally our loyalty is to Jesus Christ; and whatever pressure you may bring to bear upon the place of armed violence, war or national defence in the Christian life, we say No."[5]

On Saturday 20 June, in what he later called one of the most remarkable meetings he ever attended, Donald, Dick Sheppard, George Lansbury and the novelist Vera Brittain of *Testament of Youth* fame, addressed the sweltering thousands on the Roman amphitheatre at Maumbury on the outskirts of Dorchester. The crux of Donald's speech lay in its warning that the next war would threaten women and children at home, an accurate enough prediction given the intense bombardment of the German Luftwaffe on British cities during the Second World War. In God's world, he continued, man could only assure peace by undeterred faith with strength received from the Almighty. The exhilaration of that meeting and the journey back to London afterwards by train with her fellow speakers, especially their slant on Christian pacifism, made such an impression on Vera Brittain that it soon led her to become not only a pacifist, but also a committed Sponsor of this new movement. This commitment was never more so than during the war years when, teaming up with Donald in a spirit of friendship, she often traversed the country to put the case for peace. The fact that there was a considerable cost to be borne not only in the long absences from her family but also the deep unpopularity incurred, made a strong impression on her daughter, the crusading politician Shirley Williams.

With Sheppard anxious to broaden the base of his organisation by recruiting left-wing intellectuals and non-Christians, the PPU under the umbrella of his own extraordinary magnetism was able to embrace a wide coalition of supporters. Such diversity also contained the seeds of its own destruction, as illustrated in Raymond Jones's biography of Arthur Ponsonby, who happened to be Donald's introduction to the world of high politics. Ponsonby, the former Labour leader in the House of Lords, regarded the Albert Hall Rally in November 1936 as more or less a religious gathering. He felt uncomfortable speaking under the protection of an odour of sanctity, although was prepared to concede that Donald could bring the house down with God and Jesus Christ. In the PPU, Ceadel argued that Sheppard exhibited the unresolved pacifist tension between preaching it as a faith derived from spiritual beliefs about God and constructing it as a practical political programme which would commend itself to all men of goodwill. Or as Adrian Hastings put it in *A History of English Christianity 1920–1990*, "The trouble with 1930s Pacifism was that it had moved the context of its protest from a Free Church to an Anglican milieu. Sheppard, Raven and the like were not Nonconformists. They really did want 'to stop the next bloody war'."[6] Consequently they looked to convert the dictators and their armies to the cause of peace by following a reasonable policy which, in the light of events, made them appear to underestimate the threat from this quarter. This nebulous approach not only failed to convince the general public, it failed to convince many left-wing intellectuals who found their resistance to fascism more important than their opposition to violence, a fact underlined by the 12,000 volunteers who fought for the Republican Government in the Spanish Civil War. It also found little favour with renowned Christian theologians such as Karl Barth, Professor of New Testament Theology at Basel University, and Reinhold Niebuhr, Professor of Christian Ethics at Union Theological Seminary in New York City. Both Barth and Niebuhr felt that in light of 1914–18, the liberal optimism of many pacifists was dangerously sentimental.

Cracks were already beginning to appear in the edifice of the peace movement, when it suffered a crushing blow in November 1937 with the death of Sheppard, who had been sick for some time. As London mourned his passing by turning out in huge numbers for his funeral, the mood was distinctly sombre at a pacifist gathering in the Albert Hall, where an empty chair on the platform with a wreath on it marked a silent tribute to a lost leader. Whether consumed by the emotion of the occasion, Donald as he appealed for more money, allowed himself to make the fanciful prediction that Europe was on the verge of a pacifist landslide just as Hitler's Germany was preparing for a major onslaught on Central Europe (preferably without war). In the atmosphere of dissension and disarray that now permeated the PPU, Canon Stuart Morris, a former Chaplain to the Royal Flying Corps, lacking Sheppard's charismatic personality, was appointed its new leader and Donald his deputy at the first Annual General Meeting in April 1938. With more defections from the political and intellectual wing of the movement, the PPU at least now shed much of its ambivalence and carried a more precise message of peace at any price. In June Donald was reported as saying that there was something of God in everyone including Hitler and Mussolini. Then, as tensions between the Germans and Czechs over the future of the German-speaking Sudetenland were deliberately exacerbated by Hitler, he along with most churchmen supported the Prime Minister Neville Chamberlain's efforts to act as a peace-maker.

After a fortnight of extreme brinkmanship during which war remained a distinct probability, a deal was hatched at Munich on 29 September whereby the Sudetenland was ceded by Czechoslovakia to Germany. Chamberlain returned to Britain a national hero for having averted war and secured "peace in our time". Although acknowledging the political differences between them since Chamberlain was a Conservative, Donald commended the Prime Minister for his statesmanship. "I am thoroughly in favour of umbrellas," he later commented on Tower Hill, referring to Chamberlain's much caricatured mascot, "for I think they have done more in the last few months than battle-ships could have done."[7] He continued to stand by him as the national euphoria quickly evaporated as the true nature of the Nazi beast became more evident, especially its barbaric treatment of the Jews in the "Night of Broken Glass" that November.

This support came from the sidelines because for much of this time Donald, so physically robust until then, was out of action, incapacitated by a near fatal illness following complications from an appendix operation at St Mary's Hospital, Paddington, in July 1938. Clots developed in both his legs and later his lungs, forcing him to take warfarin thereafter, and consigning him to six months of painful recuperation, much of it on his back. After a month in hospital and a period of convalescence in Kent he returned to Kingsway on 15 December to sympathetic murmurs as he painfully shuffled up the steps to the pulpit, despite all his efforts to play down his illness. By January 1939 he reappeared at Tower Hill, delighted to be reunited with his flock. "I cannot tell you," he wrote in the *Methodist Recorder*, "how bitterly I felt it – to be silent when it seemed I ought to have been looking into the faces of those who for so many years have looked to me for a sort of leadership."[8] Once back he detected a visible hardening of opposition to the dictators among the crowd, especially once Hitler grabbed the rest of Czechoslovakia on 15 March, confounding his previous claims to be simply a Versailles revisionist, since Slovakia had never been part of Germany. As the country clamoured for action, Donald counselled caution and understanding. At Northampton the following week, he said that Christians had to think of Hitler and Mussolini as children of God, so that while their aggression was worthy of denunciation, they were called to love them as Jesus loved those who crucified him. Predictably his words had little effect as rearmament was hastily accelerated and peacetime conscription introduced for the first time. In this bellicose climate Donald continued to fight his corner, railing against conscription at a PPU rally in the West End on 4 May and berating the failure of many Nonconformists to oppose it, several weeks later in Barnstaple. In a *cri de coeur* he depicted the world drifting into intolerance because people were neither strong nor united enough to withstand its imperfections. The nineteenth-century Church had been wrong to talk of the world as a garden when the scandal of mass poverty had shown that the wages of sin hadn't decreased. Turning to the immediacy of war, he reiterated his belief that one couldn't be a good Christian and kill. It was inexcusable to place the responsibility of the coming reckoning on men of twenty when it was their elders who were to blame. Lord Ponsonby had said that Winston Churchill should be the first to be interned, and he agreed. He concluded with this fervent observation: "I believe honestly and sincerely that if the Christian Church said that war was against the will of God, and it was against the law of the Church to engage in this murderous thing, the Christian Church could lead us out of war for ever."[9] He received firm support from Vera Brittain for his utterances, but amidst defections within its ranks, the pacifist movement was also being undermined by careless talk from within. As early as 3 March, at a Sponsors' Meeting, Donald, alive to growing disenchantment with the PPU, warned that its central message was becoming obscured by peripheral issues, and now as spring gave way to summer his concerns were amply vindicated. For in their understandable desire to avoid war, elements of the PPU became too accommodating to German demands on Poland, the country whose independence Britain and France were now committed to defending. With Hitler in no mood for further serious discussions, hostilities commenced on 3 September when Britain and France declared war on Germany following its invasion of Poland. The day before Chamberlain's fateful announcement, PPU groups from all over the country came to Kingsway Hall to pray and reaffirm their opposition to war, as Donald and Morris asserted that circumstances couldn't be allowed to alter principles. It was a brave line to take when fewer and fewer people were listening. The next few years were destined to be lonely ones for Donald and his pacifist friends as Britain fought for her very survival against a genocidal tyranny, the like of which the world hadn't seen before. Even Donald accepted that in these circumstances Britain had no choice but to fight. Later he was to write in *Peace News* in December 1944: "The utilitarian arguments for non-violence break down under the overwhelming pressure of brute fact." Admitting that many of the arguments he had used to denounce war had lost much of their force when confronted by such an evil, he went on: "I am alone sustained by the Christian faith which assures me that what is morally right carries with it the ultimate resources of the universe."[10]

Looking back on the peace movement in the pre-war era, Donald reckoned that it lacked numbers because the Church didn't get out into the open air and attract the working classes in a campaign of non-violent manoeuvres which could outmatch the processes of corporate violence. "The truth is," he wrote in his autobiography, "that we never found the equivalent in the war against war that the Salvation Army found in the war against the devil. By 1939 the anti-war movement of the previous eight years or so had demonstrated that if nothing succeeds like success, nothing fails like failure."[11] He also concluded that they had fought too shy of the moral argument as the dilemma of how best to oppose the iniquities of the dictators grew ever more intense. "More and more often, the question was posed as to whether a certain situation may not become so morally intolerable as to justify armed violence as the only method of dealing with it. Those of us who … may have rather too easily declared ourselves opposed to war, made little attempt to answer this question." When he did, he increasingly found that the moral case, buttressed by a Christian faith which opposed violence without exception, ruled supreme. "Armed violence against evil, however comprehensive and dastardly that evil may be, is not the way to overthrow it. The history book as well as the ethical argument confirms the pacifist case."[12]

Casting aspersions on St Thomas Aquinas's concept of a just war, he lambasted the Church for continuing to propagate it, since war by its very nature wreaked havoc on the innocent. Had Britain lost the Second World War, Donald used to say, it would have been Air Marshal Sir Arthur Harris on trial at Nuremberg as opposed to his German counterparts, for masterminding the indiscriminate destruction of German cities with the resulting mass casualties. If airmen saw the damage they caused from 25,000 feet, he felt sure that they would refrain from acting in such a monstrous fashion.

Donald also questioned the efficacy of war since the victors rarely profited in a way they imagined. The First World War and the Versailles treaty of 1919 didn't prevent 1939, and if the Jews were the intended beneficiaries of the Allied war against Nazism then such a strategy badly backfired. Later he was to write: "I've been to Auschwitz – I've seen the whole thing, and I still keep the moral stench of it in my nostrils. But to me the answer to this terrible violence never appeared to be the necessity for more violence. I felt Auschwitz was produced by the war. The persecutions of the Jews were not produced by the war; they were there before it. But the actual enormity of mass genocide was the result of going to save the Jews, if people were going to save them.

They did not save them, and this is an argument which I think is perfectly sound: if you employ violence, even under the most terrible conditions, you may in fact increase it. I think the war did."[13]

Even if we accept the validity of Donald's assertion that success in war invariably comes at a huge cost, the question of how best to protect the just from the unjust still had to be faced. At the heart of his various statements between 1933 and 1939 was his assumption that pacifism was winning the battle to deter the dictators, little appreciating their complete indifference to spiritual forces, not least in the treatment of Christians and Jews in Germany. Even before the war Reinhold Niebuhr, who left FOR in 1931, cast doubt on the validity of pacifist theology in his book *Moral Man and Immoral Society* because of its flawed belief in man's inherent goodness and the ideal of a universal brotherhood. He developed these points in his *Christianity and Power Politics*, published in 1940, arguing that there was no simple way, as pacifists believed, out of the sinfulness of human history. Neglecting its power was to deny the central importance of God's redeeming love through the Cross.

And then writing afterwards, Ulrich Simon, a Jewish refugee from Germany turned Christian, denounced the concept of non-resistance, calling it wholly discreditable to those who were victims or survivors of the Nazi terror. Had these people forcibly resisted arrest they would have helped to reduce the number of those murdered.

"It is clearly impossible," he wrote in *The Cross and the Bomb*, "to return to the ethical foundations which prevailed before institutional terrorism became a tool of government. Hence an all-embracing pacifism cannot be acquitted and must be branded immoral, for it is an evil act which condones evil intentions ...

"No one has the right to 'sacrifice' groups of human beings to naked power, to yield to terroristic threats on behalf of others. Appeasement isn't only a farce but a sin."[14]

The debate was set to continue with ever greater fervour in the nuclear age.

CHAPTER FIVE

A Prophet Without Honour

On Sunday 3 September 1939, Donald was leading worship at Kingsway Hall when suddenly war sirens interrupted the service and on the advice of a police officer in the congregation, everyone moved downstairs to finish the proceedings. It was, Donald later recalled, an electrifying occasion, the first of many false alarms during the "phoney war", but once Hitler swung fully into action in May 1940 with a devastating assault in Western Europe, it would only be a matter of time before London itself was in the firing line. For fifty-seven nights from September 1940 and on a regular basis till May 1941, the nation's capital felt the full force of the Nazi war-machine as bombs rained down on its citizens.

It was a source of great fortune that Kingsway, despite one or two near misses, escaped unscathed from the onslaught, enabling the Mission, with its deep basement, to provide sanctuary for both staff and those living in the vicinity. Sister Lotty Hudd, one of the three deaconesses at Kingsway during the war, later recalled how after one particularly punitive raid on the Theobald's Road area, over 400 people flocked to the Hall at a time when it was without gas and water. Undeterred, Donald had a tap set up in the middle of the road and directed a human chain until services could be restored. On another occasion when a bomb landed on a neighbouring block of flats, he led a rescue party to pull people from the wreckage. He later confessed that the bombing raids used to frighten him, but that although his bed was once showered with glass, he never felt he was going to die. Ironically, his one near brush with mortality came in entirely different circumstances. On holiday in Newquay, in August 1943, Donald's bad leg gave out while swimming in heavy seas and as he battled unavailingly with the conditions, he had to be rescued by a female life-saver. Back on shore he collapsed and an ambulance had to be summoned to take him home. Fortunately for him his recovery was rapid and the experience left him with no ill effects.

As a pacifist minister in wartime, Donald recognised that pacifism did not nullify his communal responsibilities to a city under siege. He thus willingly took his turn roof-watching for fire bombs. Another invaluable service he offered at Kingsway was the provision of two feeding centres. One was in the Community Centre providing meals for the girls evacuated from the Mission hostels, neighbouring firefighters and volunteers in the Hall; the other, set up in the Lecture Hall in October 1940 and continuing until December 1944, when neighbouring cafes took over, offered a daily breakfast service from 6.30 a.m. for the hungry and dishevelled who emerged, often carrying their sleeping-bags, from the tenements in Drury Lane or from the Holborn Underground station shelter across the street. For 1/3d (6 ½p), they could enjoy a slap-up meal, waited on by Donald and Marie amongst others. One morning when Donald, dressed in mufti, was at the cash desk, a wordly-wise customer, leaning over to him with a knowing wink, said, "I bet the minister is making a packet out of this." According to Professor Philip Bagwell, the historian of the West London Mission, it acquired such an enviable reputation for the provision of meals that the Ministry of Food contacted Donald in September 1942 to see whether some of his staff would be able to help distribute surplus vegetables stored in Covent Garden to people who needed them, as the bombing had dislocated their deliveries. Donald agreed, but he needed some vans to transport the goods to Kingsway. He rang the Ministry of Transport for help. The official was sympathetic but couldn't promise anything. He asked him his name again and when Donald told him, the official enquired whether he had been at Aske's School. On discovering that they had both been pupils there, they chatted about old times before the official eventually said, "Now, about those lorries. How many did you say you wanted?"

Although the number of worshippers at Kingsway dropped during the Blitz, and in the Little Blitz between January and April 1944, this decline was the exception rather than the rule. Indeed, Donald, who moved into the Mission with his family for much of the war, was able to sound upbeat in the April 1942 edition of the *Kingsway Messenger*. "We were able," he wrote, "to say a year ago that despite bombs, blackouts and all kinds of wartime difficulties, we were holding on, full of work and in excellent heart. We thank God that we can say it again and more. This year we have gone forward."[1] Weeknight gatherings were scaled down, but Donald organised a devotional meeting at which all sorts of plans were discussed and people were asked to sign up for various duties. Up to eighty helped out with breakfast alone. Arriving the night before, they slept in the basement in fitted bunks. Leslie Gore has recollections of how Donald would read night prayers with great sensitivity and how, in a situation often fraught with danger, his was a voice of calm certainty in the love and providence of God.[2] Others assisted with the Youth Club, which under laxer supervision in wartime, was bedevilled by drunkenness and destruction, while Donald was a welcome visitor at the Katherine Price Hughes Hostel each Monday to answer questions from the girls. He also held three services on Sunday as usual at Kingsway, in addition to holding one in an air-raid shelter every Sunday evening in Woburn Place. An exceedingly busy day would end when Donald, clad in his black cassock, would visit the Holborn Underground station shelter to help care for the people seeking refuge from the air raids. These missions of mercy he was always willing to perform, even when called out in the middle of the night, feats of endurance which failed to diminish his unfailing welcome to all those who used his premises during the day. To many jaded workers and families without a home, Donald Soper was a rare light in the darkness, lighting their pathway of hope to a better future.

Politically, his war began in some embarrassment when it was revealed in October 1939 that he and Maude Royden had given their support to a pacifist organisation tainted by fascist and Marxist sympathies. When the full list of the twenty-eight signatories of the British Council for Christian Settlement in Europe, formed to stop the war, was made public, he and Dr Royden resigned, claiming that they had not been aware of the identity of their co-signatories.

Their explanation caused some bemusement to John Beckett, the Secretary of the British Council for Christian Settlement, and a close associate of Oswald Mosley. In a letter to the *Manchester Guardian* he let slip the fact that his name as Secretary of the Council was on the notepaper asking them to sign, and they had also been supplied with a list of all those invited to sign, including Mosley and James Maxton, the left-wing Labour MP. He also disclosed that Maude Royden's signature was the result of personal correspondence – copies of which he possessed – and that she was well aware of his own associations with Mosley. Donald was on firmer ground when he intervened at the Methodist Conference in 1942 to oppose the sending of a resolution of goodwill to Marshal Pétain, the puppet leader of German-occupied France. He was not, however, averse to a similar message going to General de Gaulle, the leader of the Free French, since in Donald's estimation he represented the true aspirations of the French people. His words caught the mood of Conference and as a result, de Gaulle became the sole recipient of the motion.

Despite the defection in May 1940 of many leading pacifists from the PPU, including three Sponsors, Storm Jameson, Bertrand Russell and Philip Mumford, in the face of the growing Nazi peril, Donald stood firm in his beliefs. His steadfastness won him yet further respect from Vera Brittain, whose religious commitment was ever increasing. "I went to the PPU Council yesterday," she wrote to Storm Jameson on 18 May, "and nothing could have been saner than the attitude that most people (led by Ponsonby, Donald Soper and John Middleton Murry) are now taking. Since the war can't be stopped, all propaganda of a Government-opposing kind is being abandoned, and their object is to become a sort of religious fellowship, a nucleus of sanity, to help prepare people for what is coming."[3]

Donald, in his opposition to the war, was joined by Henry Carter and Henry Bett within Methodism, which otherwise conformed to official Church thinking in finding the war both inevitable and just. Other notable pacifists included Dr Edward Barnes, the Bishop of Birmingham, Garth Macgregor, the Professor of Biblical Criticism at Glasgow University, Dr J. S. Whale, the President of Cheshunt College, Cambridge, Charles Raven, George MacLeod and the actress Sybil Thorndike. Not surprisingly Donald was much in demand as a speaker among his fellow dissidents. At the Armistice Meeting of Christian Pacifist Groups in November 1940 held at Kingsway, he reminded his listeners that the Gospel of divine power was available to all those disposed to accept it as a way of overcoming earthly difficulties. Fifteen months later at the Christian Pacifist Council at Friends House in a talk entitled "The Christian Alternative", he expressed the conviction that perplexity was the price to be paid for the sin of the world. Such perplexity, he contended, couldn't be resolved by reasoning. Rather, the most practical activity for the Christian was in his endeavour to win others to faith in Jesus Christ by evangelism and example. Never one for shirking hard choices, Donald adopted an uncompromising line when he again addressed the Armistice Meeting in November 1943. Talking from experience, he explained how the pacifist faith must of necessity create a tension in the heart of the believer as he became separated from his fellow countrymen. Emotional neutrality towards the war wasn't a realistic option for pacifists as they faced up to the dilemma of obeying God's will when their weakened humanity craved to do something else. The answer to such a predicament was to express their love and peace in fellow-suffering with the sorrow of others.

Donald's unflinching opposition to war brought him into conflict with the State. Prior to the war, the BBC had been proud of its autonomy, and in June 1939 the new Director of Religious Broadcasting, the Revd James Welch, having consulted a number of associates including Donald, decided that the Sunday broadcasts in wartime should offer a fuller exposition of the kingdom of God in relation to all other aspects of life. He, unlike Iremonger, wanted debate regarding the practical relevance of Christian principles, but not in a debilitating manner which undermined the corporation's presentation of an ecumenical Christian faith. Even this mild innovation in breadth was placed in some jeopardy, since once the war began, the corporation became increasingly subject to Government control. During the early months, Donald and

MacLeod had both preached on the radio, and by playing down their pacifist convictions had attracted little comment. All this now changed in the wake of a trenchant pacifist talk by the celebrated Birmingham Congregationalist minister, Leyton Richards, on 11 February 1940. In the face of furious criticism from the press and parents whose sons were serving in the armed forces, the BBC's Board of Governors, despite Welch's support for Richards, felt compelled to reconsider their position. Their hand was finally tied by the dramatic events of May 1940, when the devastating German thrust through Western Europe left Britain standing alone and in peril. Consequently, on 6 June, they issued a directive putting severe restraints on freedom of speech from which no Christian minister could be given special exemption. Furthermore they decreed that religious broadcasts should be in full accordance with the national effort, and no individual or member of an organisation unsympathetic to this viewpoint would in future be invited. In effect this edict forced Donald, Raven and MacLeod off the air. Reflecting the deep unease within the Church, Welch, although no pacifist himself, sympathised with their plight and fought their corner with the corporation. In a memorandum dated 2 August, he argued that if the Churches didn't prohibit pacifist clergy from preaching, and if the BBC hadn't claimed official control over the clergy, it couldn't do so now. He fully accepted the corporation's stance that pacifism shouldn't be directly broadcast, but this, he insisted, should not exclude these three. For not only were they among the pick of his broadcasters, they also provided interesting material not directly out of the pacifist stable. Welch received little joy. In upholding their ban of 6 June, the Governors on 9 August made it clear that war negated complete freedom of speech, since protecting the nation was the overwhelming priority of the broadcasters, a view supported (if not indeed demanded) by the Government.

Despite private assurances to the contrary by Frederick Ogilvie, the Director General, Welch continued to harbour reservations about the BBC having pandered to political interference. His views were broadly in line with those of the Central Religious Advisory Committee, which was responsible for relaying mainstream Church opinion to the BBC religious department. When they met on 2 November, its hackles were raised by the proposed bans on Archie Craig, a Church of Scotland minister, and Sir Hugh Robertson, Conductor of the Glasgow Orpheus Choir, on account of their pacifist beliefs, although neither belonged to an active pacifist organisation. The Governors again stood firm, but opposition to the ban was growing in informed circles. By the beginning of the following year, the press, some Labour backbenchers and the National Council for Civil Liberties all spoke out, and William Temple, soon to be Archbishop of Canterbury, weighed in too. In a letter to Sir Allan

Powell, the Chairman of the BBC, he said that no man should be excluded from the privilege of broadcasting the message of the Gospel on the grounds that he was a known pacifist, provided that he undertook not to use this occasion to advocate the pacifist position.

Although Duff Cooper, the Minister of Information, refused to establish an inquiry into the BBC's line on pacifism, on the premise that no individual possessed the right to use the BBC as a forum for the exercise of free speech, help seemed at hand. On 20 March the Prime Minister in a statement in the House of Commons appeared to accept the fact that when it came to hampering the war effort, the case of Sir Hugh Robertson was very different from that of a speaker like Donald, since Robertson was merely exercising the artistic freedom of an individual. Churchill's words pulled the rug from under the feet of the BBC. In April 1941 the Governors relented to the extent that from now on the ban would apply only to those who opposed the war effort and were renowned for their stand. This enabled MacLeod and Craig to resume broadcasting because they had not actually voiced their opposition to the present war. Donald, as an active member of the PPU, and Raven had. They therefore remained excluded from the airwaves, and although Welch continued to plead their case, not least in 1944, in light of the diminishing Nazi threat, the Governors refused to budge, insisting that to do so would be construed as the BBC favouring pacifism. It was a decision that Donald accepted with greater equanimity than Raven, who to his dying day remained bitter about his pariah status during the war years.

Donald was also a marked man at Tower Hill. He learnt from W. E. Sangster that the authorities had sent an official every Wednesday to take down everything he was saying, in case they needed to prosecute him for misbehaviour. The official made himself known to Donald and together they established a good rapport, Donald on occasions stopping and checking that he wasn't going too fast. If he was, he would gladly repeat himself.

Aside from providing a base at Kingsway for Henry Carter's Christian Pacifist Forestry and Land Units, Donald's public witness to pacifism made him a friend in need to many conscientious objectors, one of whom was the young Donald Swann, the composer and entertainer. After the unsavoury atmosphere which pervaded the CO tribunals in the First World War there was a more honest attempt to respect conscientious objectors this time round, helped by the fact that there were too few of them to constitute a real threat. Only 3 per cent of the total of 62,300 went to prison, compared to 30 per cent between 1914 and 1918, even if the tribunals knew little about the Christianity underpinning their pacifism. Donald, along with Henry Carter and Vera Brittain, provided the main support to the conscientious objectors – not that

Donald always helped their cause since he had enemies on the tribunals and clashes weren't unknown. William Purcell recalled the occasion at Fulham Town Hall when Donald was asked as a witness whether he had told his friend what Jesus had said about fighting. He said he had. He was then asked if he remembered telling him that soldiers were bidden to be content with their wages. Donald said he had not done so for the very obvious reason that it was not Jesus who said this, but John the Baptist, who also went on to say, "and do violence to no man". This he thought was excellent advice to any soldier. The applicant got off, which is more than happened to Henry Rutland, Donald's lifelong friend from the Central and West London Missions. Rutland had become a pacifist when at Islington and Donald accompanied him to the tribunal to speak before him. He said that he didn't take the extreme position of opting out of civic duties altogether, unlike Rutland, who was imprisoned for nine months in Wormwood Scrubs and Wandsworth Prisons. He found the experience to be quite dreadful, alleviated only by Donald's weekly visits, when he expressed his pride in his principled stance.

Another to experience the Fulham Tribunal – one of the most unsympathetic in the country – was David Mason, later a distinguished Methodist minister but then a callow sixth-form boy attending Kingsway. His fate was to appear before the acerbic Judge Hargreaves, who served as chairman of the three-man panel. Mason was told by those who knew him that it would be fatal to call Donald as a character witness. Hargreaves detested him and invariably those who invited him to speak for them ended up in prison.

"Undeterred, I asked Donald to be there," he recalled. "His eyes twinkled, 'You know what you are doing, boy, don't you?' I said 'yes'. 'Then, of course, I will come'.

"The expected encounter took place. After I had given my testimony and answered some hostile, but not impossible questions, the clerk asked if there were any character witnesses. Donald strode cheerfully into the witness box. Judge Hargreaves glowered at him in obvious detestation. Before he could open his mouth, Hargreaves said in a voice of shocked condemnation, 'Dr Soper – you have profoundly influenced this young man. Is that not true?'

"The experienced open-air orator exercised his craft. 'Of course I have influenced him, my Lord. That is my vocation – to influence people. I should be ashamed of myself if I had not influenced him'. There was a long silence. And the Tribunal accepted my plea and I went to scrub floors and wash dishes at University College Hospital."[4]

For all the hostility he aroused, Donald continued to preach pacifism at Tower Hill every Wednesday during the war, where, according to Caroline Moorehead, he would phlegmatically stare out from behind his glasses as he paced up and down before large crowds. On one occasion Ian Kiek, a friend of his, was listening as a doodlebug complete with its rasping noise hovered overhead. Donald looked up and immediately remarked, "There you are, another example of spiritual wickedness in high places." Joking aside, he was particularly contemptuous of those who talked about servicemen sacrificing their lives. "Their job isn't to sacrifice life," he protested, "their job is to take someone else's in hate or indifference." For the most part, the crowd was reasonably tolerant, but there were several extremely tense moments. George Dubock has recollections of Donald making a point about pacifism when a tough-looking person at the front of the gathering engaged him in serious disagreement. Finally he challenged Donald to turn the other cheek, at which point Donald climbed down from the wall and stood facing his adversary. It was a frightening moment. As Dubock hurried down below the wall just in case Donald was pushed off, the preacher continued to stare down the man before offering him the hand of friendship and resuming his position on the wall. Mason recalled a similar incident at Staines in 1943 when an airman lost his temper and threatened to hit Donald on the nose. The whole crowd went silent before the airman walked away. Looking back on the war years in old age, Donald recalled being rescued twice by mounted police from the furore of the crowd, an experience which he had found to be very alarming. What had sustained him during these awkward encounters was the added conviction he had derived from the declaration of his pacifist beliefs. Equally, he confessed to lacking the requisite sensitivity, such as the occasion when he ridiculed an incoherent questioner at Tower Hill until the questioner abandoned his stridency and said, "I wonder how you would feel if your brother had been killed in the desert as mine was last week?" The pathos of his comment haunted Donald for a long time, reminding him that reality was more important than thought.

Not that he always lacked tact, as his eloquent tributes to the fallen on Remembrance Sunday would testify. Often his controversial utterings such as his condemnation of the air raids on Dresden, could be softened with the necessary sensitivity to avoid an undue ruffling of the crowd. Cliff Padgett, a good friend from a services background, recalled him comforting a man whose son had been killed in action over Germany, and Raymond Short, later a BBC Religious Affairs producer but then a young airman, went to see Donald to talk through his moral dilemma about the justification of the war. Essentially he had wanted Donald, as a confirmed pacifist, to convince him of the merits of pacifism, but Donald would not oblige. In line with his private convictions that in practice the doctrine was not foolproof, he fully recognised the scale of Short's dilemma and knew it was something that he must work out for himself.

During the war, Kingsway became a haven for pacifists and conscientious objectors. A number slept, worked, debated and worshipped there, and from the autumn of 1941 at a series of meetings, Donald spent time with some of the younger ones discussing key points of the Gospel. At the last of these meetings he suggested that it was time for them to proclaim their faith and that he would take his stand in Hyde Park on Passion Sunday 1942. One motive prompting the new initiative, according to Professor Bagwell, was to compensate for his exclusion from national broadcasting for the duration of the war.

And so began another proud chapter in Donald's life which lasted right until the end as he built upon his previous experience at Tower Hill. The early stages, of course, weren't easy, as the abuse which he had suffered elsewhere was also evident in Hyde Park, and his voice was temporarily impaired as he tried to combat the heckling. With his health already the cause of some alarm back in 1940 when the President of Conference, Dr Henry Bett, implored him to scale down on his labours, Donald's Hyde Park activity was yet another burden to bear, but he was oblivious to such concerns. He saw Hyde Park as a duty and it warmed his heart when a number of hecklers became worshippers at Kingsway. It was also a pleasure providing another outlet for his talents, as Leslie Weatherhead recognised in his tribute in the *Methodist Recorder* in January 1943.

"On getting off a bus at Marble Arch, the ringing tones of a fine, strong voice came to me from the direction of Hyde Park. I found my friend Donald Soper addressing by far the largest crowd in the park ... For over an hour on a raw, foggy December afternoon, he spoke magnificently, answering questions with that vivacious humour and imperturbable good temper which has endeared him to us all ... It is a long time since I myself had such a spiritual tonic. I went away physically and spiritually renewed, and proud to think that through a brother Methodist such a ministry was being offered to men who never enter a church. Visitors to London shouldn't miss this arresting example of Christian witness. Methodism must be proud indeed that on active service in the front line of battle is this stalwart soldier of the Cross."[5]

Once war had become a reality and his worst fears realised, Donald took refuge in a deep spirituality which offered an alternative vision to the madness then engulfing him and his fellow countrymen.

On 4 February 1940 he told his congregation at Kingsway that the earth belonged to God. "I want a world in which the gifts which God has given to us are shared, and they must be shared in a common responsibility which we all owe, and which we never break."[6]

On 12 May, as Britain stood ready to face the Nazi menace alone, he cautioned that the only answer to accumulating violence and bitterness lay in a fellowship bigger and stronger than the world had ever known. "I find perhaps the greatest comfort and strength on the day called Whit Sunday is in the certainty that this is a miraculous world."[7]

Two weeks later, as the row about whether his pacifist convictions should be broadcast simmered away, Donald remained unrepentant, finding strength in being a child of God. "Other people may take away my goods, may sneer at me, but if I am loyal to what I believe to be the truth, if I can see the footmarks of the Master and set my feet to follow in them, I know what happens." He ended with an appeal to "look beyond these present days and see the new world. We will go out into the world to redeem not as master, but as servants",[8] a turn of events which could only come about when every man or woman had been renewed in spirit. In his eyes to build this new creation placed an awesome responsibility on the Church. Far from hiding its light under a bushel while hostilities raged, it should show its face by revitalising Sunday School, filling the empty family pews at worship and giving more responsibility to laymen. Above all, the Church had to put its former divisions to one side and rediscover a fellowship which could be expressed in a practical way through feeding the hungry and helping the oppressed.

As Hitler's bombs helped to promote an unprecedented egalitarianism in the country as rich and poor stood side by side in their suffering and stoicism, moves began to build a better world at home as well as on the continent of Europe. The Beveridge Report of November 1942, recommending a massive expansion of the welfare state, was received to near universal acclaim, while Temple, the "People's Archbishop", talked of the need for a new social order. Such sentiments naturally had Donald's blessing. He had been a great admirer of Temple since Cambridge and later shared a platform with him at his final public meeting in London on 5 September 1944, weeks before he died. For most of the war Donald travelled the country calling for an end to hostilities and outlining his Christian vision of the future. At St Stephen's Roman Catholic Church, Walthamstow, in June 1941, a remarkable example of early ecumenism, he dismissed the communist concept of a new order, asserting that there were many passages in the New Testament, such as the Magnificat, which were more radical than the *Communist Manifesto*. At Haywards Heath in July, he reminded his audience that the Christian concept of economics was the just sharing of things which God had provided on earth. If Middle Europe had been fed and clothed adequately from 1928 there would have been no war. He went on to extol the onset of rationing and made the pertinent point that free food was given in prisons, and if it were given there, it could be given to a Welsh miner whose only crime lay in the fact that he wasn't wanted in the workplace.

At St John's Methodist Church, Southampton, in June 1942, the concept of fellowship was again uppermost in Donald's mind. War had created that true fellowship which the Christian progressive had to turn into something permanent. The need to prepare a new material order as well as a spiritual one had to be recognised. "What is the good of talking about a new world order," he wondered, "if when the opportunity for such an order comes, we are still back in the ruts of the past?"[9]

Much of Donald's preaching was, as ever, uncompromisingly political, but he learnt to exercise tact when necessary. Stanley Frost, one of his congregation at the South London Mission, recalled the occasion at a large Birmingham Mission rally when he was asked what he thought of the Royal Family. He paused, looked all around the hall and asked politely, "Is there any member of the Royal Family present this evening? No. Then we can discuss this matter" – which he proceeded to do very fairly. He recognised that monarchy might have a social function to fulfil, but class distinctions certainly did not and on the whole he was not a good royalist. Monarchy, he averred, tended to reinforce class distinctions and he proceeded to spend the time talking about the evils of class rather than royalty as such. Donald's answer, with its sensitive handling of a delicate question in wartime Britain, impressed Frost, especially since the post-Abdication monarchy was still vulnerable. He demonstrated responsibility in matters of a more serious nature. For all his commitment to pacifism and his position as Vice-Chairman of the PPU, Donald appears to have played an increasingly passive role within the movement, rarely attending its meetings or trumpeting its policies. Why this was the case remains a matter for some conjecture, but we have several important leads to go on. First, there was his traditional dislike of committees. The PPU was more turgid than most. Second, there was his lack of rapport with many of his colleagues, a number of whom led lifestyles rather different from his own, and third, there was his unease about its anti-Government propaganda. Not only did he oppose Morris, by now the PPU's General Secretary, standing as a pacifist candidate in the King's Norton by-election in the autumn of 1941, he also strongly disapproved of his antics the following year. With confidential information supplied by a civil servant, Morris had been compiling a dossier about the Government's contingency plans for a Gandhi-inspired rebellion in India. His action, deemed illegal under the Official Secrets Act, led to his conviction in January 1943 and imprisonment for nine months.

The case, hushed up at the time, caused major dissension within the PPU. There were those like Vera Brittain who thought Morris's method of collecting information reckless but no more reprehensible than the manner in which Government agents acted. Others such as the Chairman, Alex Wood, and

Middleton Murry were less tolerant. Leaving aside the fact that Morris hadn't consulted his chairman about the action he was taking on behalf of the organisation, he considered it morally wrong and politically crass. Vera Brittain recalled how at a meeting of the National Council (the PPU's new governing body) on 20 February, Wood made them aware of representations he had received from Donald urging him to resign to maintain his own integrity. The Council voted by 16–11 to suspend judgement on Morris until he could meet them at a later date. Wood and Donald, however, weren't going to let the matter rest, resigning as Chairman and Sponsor respectively.

Their decision threw the movement into turmoil, sowing dissension within the ranks. The issue was vigorously debated as resolutions from the various branches poured into PPU headquarters. A minority, sympathetic to Morris, felt that Wood and Donald had been unduly provocative in their stance, but a clear majority supported them, believing that their objectives had been entirely justified. The pressure had its desired effect. At a meeting of the Council on 10 April, a resolution was overwhelmingly passed that, in view of Wood and Donald's resignation and the deep cleavage within the movement, Morris's position as General Secretary had become untenable. In addition to this, Wood and Donald were asked to resubmit themselves for nomination to their former positions, a request with which they were willing to comply, although Donald's faith in PPU had been badly shaken.

As Donald traversed the country preaching to full houses, he found it difficult not to compare his own dynamism with the lethargy of his denomination as a whole. "The fact is that at present," he lamented in the *Methodist Recorder* on 28 September 1944, "Methodism, with some notable exceptions, isn't capturing the imagination of the people."[10] He felt something much more dramatic and imaginative needed to be done to win new recruits, and it was in this context that he lent his support to the idea of a Gothic-designed Methodist cathedral near Hyde Park Corner. Aesthetically he thought that this would appeal much more to people than soulless mission halls, and it would also be a powerful symbol of the Church Universal – open to the socially diverse crowds that flocked to Hyde Park. Proposed plans for the unusual architectural design were published in the press; however the cost would have been a prohibitive £0.5 million, and this alone was enough to stymie this most ambitious of projects.

Another of Donald's wartime initiatives was his contribution to food relief for starving populations in Nazi-occupied Europe as the Allied blockade bit deep. The main instigator behind the enterprise was Vera Brittain, who, appalled by the suffering especially in Greece and Belgium, two former Allied countries, became Chairman of the PPU Europe Food Relief Campaign.

Hoping to persuade the Government to ease the plight of the undernourished by relaxing its European embargo, she toured the country to stir the nation's conscience. At a mass rally in Trafalgar Square on 25 July 1942, Donald was instrumental in helping to win near unanimous support for their cause. Later, on 30 and 31 December 1943, as news of starving bodies piling up in lorries emanated from Greece, he joined Vera, Muriel Lester, Charles Raven, Alfred Salter and Alex Wood in a FOR-inspired two-day fast to draw attention to the gravity of the situation. Eventually, early in 1944, some good wheat was allowed into Greece, but by and large the pleas that the Government should lift its blockade fell on deaf ears, especially until such time as Europe was liberated later that year.

That Christmas Donald was in uncompromising mood as he looked back on the previous five years. "All honour to those who have worked and planned together in these days of violence and are still doing so. But let us learn the lesson from the events through which we have passed." The renunciation of war and the refusal to take part in it was not enough. Thinking of the Christmas message and the chance to begin anew he wrote, "First – pacifism can only be a point, even if a focal point, in a compass which looks in every direction. There is a false simplicity in the idea that we can concentrate upon the renunciation of war without at the same time concentrating on the abolition of capitalism and nationalism and power-politics … . Non-violence must go hand-in-hand with economic security for all, a common government to secure the welfare of all, and a comprehensive justice that can be indifferently administered in the interests of all … . The second thing is this. Pacifism can only become a strategy if it is first a philosophy or, better still, a religion. The only answer to the question 'Will it work?' is to be able to say 'It must because it is in the nature of things that it should.'"[11]

On the eve of war, Donald had told his congregation at Kingsway that paradoxically a world crumbling into chaos gave the Church immense opportunities for leading a spiritual revival. Yet for all the heroic relief work in wartime London and other cities, it wasn't to be. Six years of carnage and sixty million dead helped put paid to that, and his earlier optimism gave way to something much more fatalistic. Days before the armistice, Donald deplored the decline of Church attendance, apportioning blame equally between the inadequacies of organised religion and a more worldly generation. Increasingly he referred to the pagan society in which man acted without God and few acknowledged the reality of sin. Was he being unduly alarmist? Perhaps, in the sense that he was prone to alternate between hope and despair at the state of the world, and this particular perspective was a pacifist one set against the backdrop of war.

Yet equally, his pessimism has been borne out since, for, even allowing for a modest rise in churchgoing in the years after 1945, the decline of Christian Britain has continued long term.

Such higher thoughts failed to preoccupy the majority of Donald's countrymen during the closing weeks of the war. When the inevitable Allied victory came on 8 May 1945, Donald's attitude was one of relief rather than euphoria. He marked the historic occasion with a service at Kingsway, at which, according to Vera Brittain, he gave a really inspirational address on thanksgiving, penitence and dedication.

The war had taught Donald much, as it had everyone else, about the ability to stand firm under the heaviest of emotional pressure. One lesson he had learnt was that feelings never completely tally with convictions and that short of totally opting out of society, there had to be some compromise along the way. One minor one had been to preach at RAF stations and to avoid full-blown pacifism in his addresses. Another was the giving of 1/-[5p] to his daughter for the School Spitfire Fund so as to avoid embarrassing her with her peer group. Above all, he listened avidly to the news and recalled the sense of satisfaction whenever the Allies gained a significant victory. Furthermore, as a gifted military historian he entertained a sneaking regard for the whole blood-thirsty practice of the martial arts, something for which he reproached himself many times thereafter, as his quest for Peace on Earth became ever more passionate.

CHAPTER SIX

The Good Shepherd

The war had been a difficult few years for Donald. At a time when the fight for national survival against the forces of evil was paramount it was an awesome task to preach the Gospel of loving your neighbour. The cost to his reputation was considerable, as the white feathers sent to him by some members of the public would attest, and even at Kingsway, a number left the Church in disgust. Yet among his own followers he was a beacon of courage and principle and with war turning to peace and despair to hope, with Labour's overwhelming victory in 1945, Kingsway remained a fortress of idealism for the better world they wished to build.

Donald's renown made him part of a celebrated triumvirate within London Methodism (all detached from the normal circuit system) incorporating W. E.Sangster at Central Hall, Westminster, Leslie Weatherhead at the City Temple and himself at Kingsway. For nearly twenty years, in an age when great preaching was still in vogue, these three illustrious ministers held sway, with some worshippers travelling to London on a Sunday to listen to Weatherhead in the morning, Donald at Hyde Park in the afternoon and Sangster in the evening. Sometimes they resolved to speak on the same theme and later enjoyed hearing how Methodism spoke with one voice. It wasn't always thus. For although all three were scholars, preachers and pastors of high repute, they were reared in different stables so that their monthly meetings often descended into amicable disagreement as they discussed their work. Sangster, with his powerful dramatic gestures, was a traditional Wesleyan evangelical who stood in the Old Testament prophetic tradition with his vision of the kingdom of God within. Weatherhead, in contrast, had a quieter, more disarming style, and as a pioneer of psychology helped people to understand themselves through preaching and counselling, whereas Donald, the junior partner of the three in age and experience, was the political partisan. Or, as irreverent theological students used to say, "Sangster loves God, Weatherhead loves the people and Soper loves an argument."

Sangster, a nineteenth-century style puritan like himself, had, in Donald's estimation, a powerful influence on a certain religious type with the intensity of personal belief, but his rotund oratory was a bar to clear exposition. Weatherhead, in contrast, he felt was a brilliant communicator with a bewitching voice whose path of faith through doubt was similar to the road he had travelled. His book *The Transforming Friendship* had a considerable influence on him. At the same time, he felt Weatherhead, like Sangster, had an imperfect concept of the kingdom of God, since to them a personal faith was the overwhelming requirement of all teaching, whereas to Donald this kingdom was but the gateway to something fuller.

Weatherhead, who lived near the Sopers in North London, was also closer to Donald in character. They engaged in regular bouts of badinage when speaking together at meetings and even after their heated altercations they'd both descend into laughter. Paul Sangster, author of *Dr Sangster*, recalled how they used to joke over his father's complete indifference to female beauty. Once, when the two were left together for a few minutes, they concocted a question to test him. On his return, he was asked who he would rather interview, a pretty girl with a short skirt, a frilly blouse and a low neckline, or an old hideous black-toothed hag. After due reflection and serious consideration of the question, for they carefully concealed their amusement, Sangster answered, "On the whole I'd rather interview the senior lady. She would have more experience of life." After that they gave up on him, at least as far as pretty girls were concerned. He was clearly a hopeless case.

At that time when these three princes of the Methodist pulpit were all preaching within twenty minutes walk of each other, Sangster and Weatherhead had a built-in advantage because they appealed to the more conventional, respectable London Methodist. Donald, in contrast, pitched his wares at the unconventional, the Catholics, the pacifists, the agnostics and ethnic minorities, one of whom was Jomo Kenyatta, later President of Kenya, and they came, as did a number of tourists, despite Kingsway's inconvenient location compared with the Central Hall and City Temple. He never quite matched the number of his more established colleagues, but he was remarkably close – 1,500/1,700 to their 2,000. At Kingsway in those post-war days, and during the Suez crisis in 1956 to hear Donald's homilies on peace, worshippers had to arrive early to get a seat in the gallery, and latecomers spilled over into the choir stalls. The sense of expectation with its animated atmosphere pervaded the hall prior to a service, before a reverent hush descended as Donald swept in in his cassock and academic robes to lead worship with great dignity. He was helped by the superb acoustics which enabled him to speak unaided to all and sundry. The quality of the music and the choir, to which he attached such importance, also drew inspirational strength from the surroundings, as great hymns such as Isaac Watts's "When I Survey the Wondrous Cross", and Charles Wesley's "Love Divine all Loves Excelling" and "O Thou who camest from Above", frequently resounded across the hall.

Given Donald's autocratic tendencies, the order of service, printed each Sunday, very much bore his imprint since he chose all the hymns and prayers, read the lessons and preached the sermon. In addition his powerful baritone voice could often be heard soaring above the choir, and once, when the organist was unaccountably absent, Donald stepped into the breach coping with everything except one verse in the penultimate hymn when his feet became entangled with the pedals.

Morning Services tended to be more liturgical, based on the majestic language of Thomas Cranmer's *Book of Common Prayer*, with its psalms and canticles, whereas the Evening Service was more Nonconformist. For his choice of prayers, Donald, contrary to Methodist tradition, opted for short, simple ones, and a period of silence concluded his intercession and prayers for the coming of the kingdom. Just before he mounted the stand to preach, he'd clasp his hands appearing very nervous. He started quietly, but as he progressed he warmed to his theme and he would pace up and down the platform in his enthusiasm, using his hands to help emphasise a point as he went. Shunning emotionalism, his sermons were notable for their consistency of thought, the quality of their language and arresting style. Such was the power of his words that not only did they transfix his audience they fuelled intense discussion afterwards, not least between strangers. According to Peggy Dring, Donald, despite the length of his sermons, could hold the attention of a congregation longer than anyone she had ever known such was their interest and value.[1] Morning talks tended to be more devotional when Donald might preach the Gospel for the day or expound on a hymn or a theme. Evening ones were likely to be more political, often relating to something which he had recently read or discussed in Hyde Park that afternoon, but all were in the context of an unchanging Christian faith ever pertinent to the needs of the world.

Donald wasn't a great theologian – although he knew his Bible well enough – but then his sermons weren't primarily theological discourses. Rather they were a call for action, a means for transformation through the person and teaching of Jesus Christ. Clifford Austin, later a medical missionary in China, recalled the overwhelming feeling that mere prayer and meditation weren't enough; rather it was imperative to translate Sunday worship into the world beyond Kingsway, whether it be international diplomacy or tending to social outcasts, so that Christ could be found in the hostels for the down-and-outs, the unmarried mothers and the ex-prisoners.[2] If his lack of awareness in the development of theological thinking or his lack of preparation made him prone to repetition in the morning, Donald's thirst for current affairs made him invariably fresh in the evening. "Sunday night after Sunday night," recalled Len Barnett, a future minister himself and National Secretary of the Methodist Association of Youth Clubs 1949–58, "I sat there spellbound; no other word for it. He gave me a vision of what the kingdom of God was all about both personal and social and it was the sheer force of the man's personality. You couldn't help but be gripped by it. The abiding memories are of a man who made the Christian religion intellectually not only acceptable but enormously satisfying."[3]

Another to recall those Evening Services was Alex Lyon, later a Labour MP who first came under Donald's influence in 1950. He used to marvel at the difference between the ruthless conquest of hecklers in Hyde Park on Sunday afternoon and the submissive preaching on Sunday evening at the foot of the Cross. This was the Donald Soper that many never witnessed as was his memorable contribution to the Three Hour Service on Good Friday when, standing throughout, he spoke with great profundity on the "Seven Words from the Cross". By coming to terms with the inner meanings of the Christian faith, Donald really drew together all the main themes which informed his ministry. First, the love of God as our heavenly Father and the kingdom which he prepared for our enjoyment. Second, the sanctity of the family with Jesus' words on the Cross, "Woman, behold thy son", "Son, behold thy mother" as a command to each member of his family to accept their mutual responsibility in the political as well as the moral field. Third, the problem of pain and suffering which Jesus wasn't immune to. Fourth, the need to be penitent. Fifth, the central importance of salvation by faith. Sixth, obedience to God's will and God's power as the architect of the future and lastly, the primacy of hope.

His devotional tendencies were also apparent at the 10 a.m. Holy Communion in the Little Chapel with the candles on the altar and the common chalice, not the holy inkwells as he disparagingly called the individual communion cups. Donald's propensity for regular Communion placed him absolutely in the tradition of John Wesley as did the use of Charles Wesley's hymns, since he felt that it was the basis of Christian life and the best possible way to start the week. When Donald, draped in the appropriate stole for the day, pointed to the table as the alpha and omega of all worship, communicants gained a real sense of divine presence.

The spirit of Kingsway was equally on show outside worship, its various missionary activities exhibiting a real communal flavour evident in its slick monthly magazine and the popular socials at which Marie was the belle of the ball as people queued up to dance with her. Under Allan Brown, Fela Sowande a Nigerian pilot in the RAF who used to play Memphis style duets with Donald, and Donald Cashmore, the music retained its own distinct quality. The Kingsway Choral Society attracted sizeable audiences for their Saturday evening concerts and their Christmas innovation of singing carols on the steps of St Martin-in-the-Fields grew so popular with other churches that it was soon held in Trafalgar Square. There was also the revenue-raising Christmas fair, the popular Christmas dinner for the homeless, a Sunday evening open forum and the internal mission each January, which Donald normally led.

Underpinning all this was the Guild, attended by many of Donald's closest followers, especially the young. This became the hub of the Mission. At these meetings, held on a Tuesday evening post-war, Donald would sit on an old Bible playing his favourite hymns on the piano, before giving a series of erudite talks on anything from Old Testament prophets to the meaning behind modern Russian writers. Then, after a session for prayer and reflection, they would break up into discussion classes. This, especially with OCW in mind, was Donald's opportunity to mould the evangelists of the future. In order to further this process, he would set them assignments on preaching, which he then proceeded to correct, paying particular attention to the quality of the prose and grammar. He would also encourage his laity to draw in new members and make them feel welcome; a habit he practised himself. Donald Rotherham recalled an occasion when he was in London on business some forty years ago, staying in a hotel near Kingsway. Given the close proximity, he decided to pay a visit to see if there was anything happening that evening. "There was a meeting, a normal mid-week one held there. I went and crept in and sat at the back. Donald Soper was leading the meeting and I was astonished to see that he also played the piano for the hymns. After the meeting, which was pretty full, he made a beeline for me and introduced himself, and after asking who I was etc., took me to a couple and asked them to look after me, which they did. I marvelled that a VIP of Methodism, busy with all sorts of things and his mind full of the meeting, … should notice me at the back and seek to make me feel at home."[4]

Another to be attracted by the warm embrace of the West London Mission was David Lange, the Prime Minister of New Zealand 1984–89, during his year's sabbatical in London in 1967–68. Having listened to Donald speak with great authority and insight on the subject of turning the other cheek, Lange went for tea in the hall afterwards. It was the beginning of a productive year at Kingsway during which he participated fully in Mission activities and met his future wife, Naomi, in the process. He also developed his political philosophy under Donald's tutelage. As a lifelong Methodist disillusioned with its narrow horizons back home, Lange was struck by Donald's contention that the key to making good the Christian socialist ethic of helping the underprivileged lay in the political arena with a socialist party committed to an extensive programme of practical reform. It was advice he followed to good effect in future and for the rest of his life Donald remained one of Lange's great mentors.

The West London Mission from its earliest days had dedicated itself to those who were most in need and had begun its social work by caring for prostitutes in the West End. By Donald's time, the full scope of its work made it the single largest unit in the Methodist Church. Its crèche, founded in 1888, catering for sixty children, was the oldest of its kind in the country. The Men's Hostel for discharged prisoners proved a highly effective means for rehabilitation. The Clothing Centre served several hundred people a week. The Kingsway Youth Club kept young reprobates out of trouble and the Katherine Price Hughes Hostel for delinquent girls in need of care, under the tutelage of the exceptionally gifted Sheila Townson, a woman much loved by her charges, was a model of its kind.

It was an enviable record, but now even as the welfare state took root, there was no question of Donald's Kingsway resting on its laurels. He was always looking to expand and adapt as new priorities emerged. There was the Hungerford Club dating back to 1941 when a shelter for vagrants was established under Hungerford Bridge by the FOR and the Anglican Pacifist Fellowship. By 1944 the arch was no longer available so the West London Mission, with help from the LCC, took over the lease of the old Casual Ward at 25a, Wincott Street, Lambeth, catering for forty men and thirty-six women. The place was given a facelift; then, when the need arose, it became a home for discharged prisoners. That in turn gave way to perhaps the most inspiring project of the lot – St Luke's and St Mary's Rehabilitation Home for Alcoholics, soon to become the finest of its kind in the country, opened in May 1961, the costs being met by Kingsway and the LCC. The hostel under an experienced warden and project director was family-based but exacting in its standards. No one was allowed into the house if they had been drinking, and although there were many violent altercations, the policy remained firm to good effect, with many of the occupants managing to put their problems behind them. Indeed, so productive was their work on alcohol rehabilitation that the West London Mission was invited by the new Greater London Council in 1965 to consider opening a hostel for methylated spirit drinkers.

Other ventures initiated were a lunch club under the expertise of Olive Delves, the chief cook, for the benefit of staff and nearby workers, and the Young Wives Club which visited mothers of Sunday School children who didn't go to church, and homes for the elderly. There was also the restored Emerson Bainbridge Hostel for Ex-Young Offenders and the opening of Gertrude Owen House in Drury Lane in 1948 with its five staff to provide accommodation and care for seventeen unmarried mothers and their children for anything up to two years. This was only the second of its kind. In 1960 Grove House, caring for fourteen young unmarried girls expecting babies, came into being, and in 1957 the Katherine Price Hughes Hostel moved into more suitable premises in Highbury, later catering for men as well as women. One of the more go-ahead institutions of its type, its climate of protective care was balanced by a culture of self-reliance so that residents learned to earn as well as save. By no means all of them could bridge the divide from their previous existence and Donald for one was quick to understand this; yet for the more enterprising the lifebelt was there to grasp.

As evident by his regular attendance at the monthly in-house committees, Donald involved himself closely in the work of all the hostels getting to know both the staff and the students. According to Peggy Dring, a Kingsway stalwart in the 1950s who had responded to his appeal for volunteer helpers in the hostels, his visits were eagerly awaited by the girls, who warmed to his sympathetic approach. Sometimes he came to lunch; at other times he would call in one evening during the week when he would sit in the lounge while they sat on the floor at his feet asking him questions and chatting enthusiastically. He also joined in their parties at Christmas, playing games and dancing. Mixing with the girls was the more rewarding side of Mission work. Developing similar contacts, say at the Hungerford, was much more taxing, since the people housed there were the real outcasts of society, and often, according to Donald, for good reason. Under no illusions about their character or lack of gratitude towards the Mission staff, he once described them as mentally warped, personally unattractive and often verminous. To like such caricatures of what God intended men to be, he said, was well nigh impossible. Yet by loving the unloved and by attending to their needs, the wardens and the voluntary workers to his mind demonstrated the true meaning of Christian discipleship. Their commitment certainly appealed to Raymond Short, who in June 1968 made a television documentary on Donald and the West London Mission and recorded his experiences in *Kingsway*. "Frankly, I was impressed. I had not expected to find the work being tackled so professionally. I had not expected the various hostels to look so attractive – not luxurious but cheerfully decorated, spick and span. Clearly some of the work is right at the front in its field, pioneering methods for professional and voluntary bodies alike. There's a great deal of co-operation and some integration with the statutory social work run by local government and state. This is good. The bridge between amateur and professional is not always easy to cross." [5]

Presiding over this vast array of projects was clearly an arduous business, especially as money and volunteers were often in short supply. The truth of the matter was that Donald relied enormously on the dedication of his staff, a number of whom, like Sheila Townson, had been attracted to the Mission by his personality and who served him faithfully for years. Although ignorant of some of the domestic pressures under which they laboured, such as the preparation of meals in antiquated kitchens, and the undue level of commitment they gave to the Mission, he repaid their loyalty in kind with the quality of his leadership. To listen to "Dr" as they called him, elucidating the scriptures was a privilege, to count him as a friend a pleasure. Such was the devotion he generated, that staff would compete with each other to look after him, be it taking up his lunch or carrying his stand to Hyde Park. Every Wednesday morning a meeting of leading officers would be held at Kingsway to discuss the Mission in its entirety. Priding himself on his ability to remain on top of his brief, Donald placed great store on this gathering, and attendance was obligatory.

As with his Circuit Quarterly Meetings, Donald was renowned for being the quickest chairman in London, brusque, efficient and to the point. Invariably committed to a particular line, he used the fertility of his mind and the force of his personality to push through the policies he wanted, merely pausing to see whether there might be dissension. Not many did take him on, but if they did, he respected them for it. When in trouble he would look to a friendly face to speak up on his behalf before coming in himself. David Mason recalled how he used to say to him, "Always get to a meeting early, and seek out potential allies." The tactics invariably paid off.

For all his autocratic tendencies and prominence in major new initiatives such as acquiring new premises, Donald rarely meddled in day-to-day details and indeed was happy to defer to his subordinates on the financial committees, not least his chief fundraiser Frank McCarthy, a pioneer of modern fundraising, whom he greatly respected. He offered advice when required and was quite content to let his staff launch their own initiatives, accepting that they wouldn't always work to perfection. In general he was a solid shoulder to lean on, not least for the wardens of the more exposed hostels where vandalism, malfeasance and theft were often rife. If there were problems with an employee's attitude, he rarely criticised in public, reserving his admonishment for private. Although not that interested in his own personal finances – he rarely carried money around with him and never signed cheques – Donald could be an astute businessman, proving a formidable negotiator over the sale of Kingsway to British Land. He was a past master at squeezing money out of the LCC for his Missionary projects, even at times resorting to writing in distinct red ink to help attract attention.

Aside from the time spent officiating at weddings and funerals of family and friends, when his words invariably captured the mood of the occasion, Donald gave a high priority to his pastoral work. This was a mammoth undertaking given the number of letters he received from strangers, stimulated by his radio broadcasts, or listening to him in the open air. All of them were answered and sometimes such correspondence could lead to something more personal. One Supernumerary Methodist minister recalled the heartbreak he felt back in August 1963 after losing his son in a cycling accident. Requesting a meeting with Donald, he found him so gentle and understanding when they met weeks later at Kingsway. Comforting the bereaved was something he excelled at, enhanced no doubt by the loss of his brother at such an early age. In line with one of his favourite sayings about religion being what a man did with his loneliness, he would try and find some useful role for those at a loose end to keep them preoccupied. When he renewed acquaintance with such people he would quickly ascertain how they were bearing up and continue to offer solid moral support.

In addition to his surgeries at Kingsway on Sunday and Tuesday evenings, he was willing to see others, including those in the armed services, by appointment, although he would never arrange meetings in the open air. If he came across a down-and-out demanding money or wanting a job, he would get him to the Mission to talk through his particular predicament. To regulate the queue which formed outside his office before Evening Service, he relied on his secretary, the formidable Muriel Place, and Circuit Stewards such as Cliff Padgett or Jean Anderson. Only known troublemakers would be denied an audience. Once inside the vestry Donald, seated on a long settee, would listen intently to a number of problems, invariably showing much patience and sympathy, even when exhausted himself, a far cry from the fractious image he liked to promote. As people laid bare their inner fears and darker secrets, they found he was quite unfazed, indeed tolerant of those who faced stigmatisation in that more repressive age. Cliff Padgett remembered how Donald used to tell the story of a couple with a little boy who came to church but never stayed for Holy Communion. When he asked why, the man confessed they weren't married and that his real wife was in a mental hospital. Confronted with this situation, Donald said that that constituted grounds for divorce, and when the man felt unable to go through with it, he persuaded him to take Communion anyway. At the same time he wouldn't hesitate to give blunt advice to those he felt had been barking up the wrong alley, while self-indulgent cranks who wasted his time were given short shrift, and told not to bother him again.

As a man in a perpetual hurry with a disconcerting habit of looking at his watch when conversing with others, Donald's patience had its limits which could detract from his counselling skills. His natural reserve also counted against him, especially with people he knew well. Denys Orchard, one of his Circuit Stewards, has recollections of writing to him about a particular problem. When Donald later asked to see him, he confessed to having burnt the letter because he reckoned he had opened up too much. Controversy and intimate problems, incidentally, were topics in which he hated becoming embroiled. It is one reason why his own missives tended to be brief and rather formal. For a man who loved the limelight and who could positively sparkle in company, Donald was essentially a very private person, more interested as he once put it, in causes rather than people, so that even after the Guild he was quite capable of peremptorily disappearing without even as much as a word to his flock. David Mason recalled the case of McEwan Lawson, a Congregationalist minister of great ability and charm and a fellow pacifist quite captivated by him, whose efforts to form a closer relationship were, much to his dismay, tersely brushed aside. Another to experience this remoteness was Frank Jarvis, the leader of the West London Mission hostel in Norland Square, Notting Hill. He was in hospital when Donald turned up to visit him. "I'm glad that Marie reminded you to come and see me," Jarvis remarked, bringing a wry grin to Donald's face. Hospital visiting was never one of his priorities nor was social glad-handing. Ever ultra-punctual when visiting local churches, he nevertheless remained ensconced in his car as long as possible to avoid undue felicitations with the dignitaries gathered to greet him.

Such reticence, it has been suggested, can be attributed to his lack of interests, but this is surely to misunderstand the man. Aside from his fascination with history, politics and philosophy (which he later read in French), he was a talented musician and a devotee of most sports and *The Times* crossword which took him some ten minutes to complete. Add in the countries visited, luminaries encountered and issues discussed and he could hold his own with almost anyone. Where he did struggle was in his ability to engage with the more mundane aspects of daily living, especially of people he barely knew. Consequently, although capable on public occasions of instant acts of recognition, even of occasional churchgoers, the names and accomplishments of colleagues' families rather passed him by.

Part of the clue to this introspection lies in his upbringing, where in a self-contained family which displayed scant outward emotion, the Sopers mixed little outside the narrow confines of their church. Part relates to his position. As a natural leader set apart from his flock, he expended so much effort on things spiritual that he found it difficult to summon up the energy to engage in social pleasantries, especially with people who weren't *au fait* with his vocation. What spare time he had, he naturally wanted to spend with the family he loved and rarely saw. To Donald, his home was his castle and few outsiders rarely crossed the drawbridge. His telephone number was ex-directory and when called to speak he didn't tarry. Even good friends rarely saw him off duty, so that while dinners with Michael Foot and his wife weren't unknown, it wasn't until the occasion of Donald's ninetieth birthday that Tony Benn, a friend of over forty years standing, first met Marie.

When officiating at weddings, he took a cursory interest in the reception and left as soon as possible. Invitations, smart or humble, made little impression upon him. David Mason remembered how repeated efforts by colleagues to get him to socialise came to nothing. The only time he succumbed was during the war when a group of young men persuaded him to go to a restaurant, and even then he kept looking at his watch.

There was also a wariness in Donald about developing emotional relationships with people, especially men, however much he admired them. Consequently really close friends such as Joe Webb, Eric Baker and Bill Weston, who ran the Youth Club at Kingsway for many years, could be counted on one hand. In a rather fraught radio interview entitled *Friendship* in March 1981, Donald, under interrogation from his former protégé, Harry Morton, sometime General Secretary of the British Council of Churches, found himself admitting that this wariness was partly a reluctance to get involved in areas where his writ didn't run large. Morton went on to recall that at the height of their friendship when he sought advice from Donald in confidence, they would have a meaningful discussion until there came the moment when Donald rather abruptly terminated the meeting. Both would then part without as much as a word of affection for each other. Such standoffishness probably accounts for Morton's view of Donald as a fire at which many people were allowed to warm themselves, but none were admitted to real intimacy.

Another clue to Donald's elusive personality came in this same broadcast when he accepted Morton's contention that when he, Morton, was President of Conference in 1972, Donald made his presence felt in such a way so as not to feel overshadowed by one of his protégés. Used to his own show at Tower Hill, Hyde Park and Kingsway or star billing elsewhere, Donald wasn't somebody voluntarily to share the stage with the rest of the support cast. David Smith, his assistant at Kingsway and good friend, recalled how Donald liked to take the credit for the ingenious ideas of his subordinates, while Brian Duckworth, sometime Superintendent of Hinde Street Church, upset him by insisting he spoke last in a discussion on Anglican-Methodist reunion. He also resented criticism from those in the ranks. David Mason incurred his wrath when deigning to comment on a shoddily prepared talk to the MPF in Birmingham, and John Vincent, Director of the Urban Centre Unit, Sheffield, even more so for openly disagreeing with him in a series of articles in the *Methodist Recorder*, in which he described a number of Donald's prize shibboleths as spiritually obsolete. Fortunately with Vincent the storm soon passed, but with Morton the rift never quite healed.

In 1939, after three uncomfortable years in a cramped flat with no garden in Hyde Park Mansions off the Edgware Road, the Sopers moved to Wildwood Road in Hampstead Garden Suburb. There they stayed, when not based in the Mission, until 1946, the year they moved to Radlett in Hertfordshire, a time when it was still a genuine rural idyll. They were only there three years. It was too isolated for Marie, especially with only one car; so in 1949 they moved back into London and Hampstead Garden Suburb, an enclave founded by Dame Henrietta Barnett in 1906 to provide decent housing for all classes. There Donald, amidst many intellectuals and socialists, remained for the rest of his life. For much of that time he lived in Willifield Way, in a large detached mock-Tudor house with an attractive garden, owned by the West London Mission. In this agreeable corner of North London, close to large open spaces and golf courses, Donald, although rarely at home, was able to find some respite from the pressures of his job. To his more uncharitable critics the sight of a socialist minister living in a certain style beyond the means of his congregation smacked of hypocrisy, yet during one memorable encounter in Hyde Park, Donald was unsparing in his contempt for such carping. Having established that his female accuser shared his commitment to eradicating poverty he then, to general merriment, asked her why in that case she would consign him to live in it. Such hollow gestures, he contended, would ultimately do little to help the very people who needed it most. To burden a preacher with the anxieties of economic insecurity would only dissipate his powers, and impoverish his ministry.

When Donald married Marie he made it clear that he didn't expect his wife to become an unpaid curate. Yet despite her continuing lukewarm attitude to Methodism which owed something to its spartan image, she was soon playing her part at Kingsway, attending church every Sunday and immersing herself in committee work. Easing the plight of unmarried mothers became one particular interest, aiding boys on the loose another. During part of the war she had lived in some discomfort with the girls in the Mission and given a hand with the waitressing, much to general approval. Afterwards, with an ever growing family (Judith was born in 1942 and Caroline in 1946), she adopted a somewhat lower profile but helped run the Mission's much valued second-hand clothing shop, played a leading part in fundraising events and organised a number of popular pilgrimages.

In all these various activities her natural warmth and glamour, her soft seductive voice and great interest in others, made her an ideal ambassador for Methodism, although playing Calpurnia to Donald's Caesar had its frustrations when people treated her as a mere appendage rather than as an intelligent person in her own right. Aside from her sporting prowess, especially on the golf course where she won a number of trophies, she was artistic to the core with the most discerning eye for beauty. Consequently, all her homes were tastefully furnished and decorated, each room having its own individual touch, while the garden which she lovingly tended without any help, radiated colour and bloom. A stylish dresser herself, complete with her stunning hats, her creativity extended to making clothes and collages, a number of which she donated to the Mission. Her artistry was particularly on show at Christmas time, her decoration of the tree and arrangement of the stockings creating a real aura of magic for the children.

With Donald away so much it naturally fell to Marie to provide a haven of security for the children, shielding them whenever possible from public intrusions, especially at those times when controversy engulfed their father. In this she succeeded admirably. Aside from her gifts as a homemaker and organiser, Marie brought a loving touch to the concerns of each of her four daughters, avoiding criticism whenever possible. (Later, when they in turn became parents, she and Donald, according to their eldest daughter Ann, proved model grandparents taking a great interest in their grandchildren, yet never interfering in their upbringing.)

Alive to her husband's great vocation and sensitive to his labours on behalf of others, Marie accepted his need for silent contemplation rather than conversation at home even though there might be much she wanted to discuss. Although a consummate hostess of genial dinner parties, she also kept their socialising within bounds and removed from him the chores of the household, as well as much of the responsibility for the girls' upbringing, including their education at Queenswood, a boarding school for the children of Methodist ministers in Hertfordshire. It would be a rare thing indeed for any of them to receive a letter or a phone call from their father, let alone a visit, especially if that meant missing a service at Kingsway, a *faux pas* which upset Marie. She was also irritated by his obsession with Tower Hill, to the exclusion of anything else, especially the occasion when he opted for his soapbox rather than to take her to Harley Street to see a specialist. "I only hope I don't die on a Wednesday," she used to joke to a friend. "Donald will be at Tower Hill." She did, however, secure a rare triumph when she forced him to cancel an anti-nuclear rally at Epping in order to attend her sister's eightieth birthday. Although she was happy to fall in with many of his views, she wasn't afraid to speak her mind on such issues as bloodsports, abortion or pacifism if she detected a flaw in his argument or in his judgement on people. More often than not she hit the nail on the head and acted as a restraining influence on some of his more impetuous designs.

Knowing Marie to be an excellent mother, Donald was happy to defer to her in the household, very rarely answering her back, even on those few occasions when she reproached him. Because of the limited time he spent with the children, his influence over them was considerably less than that of their mother. Although naturally proud of their accomplishments, not least in the academic field with all of them going to university [Ann to Nottingham to read Zoology, Bridget to Hornsey School of Art, Judith to Reading to read Botany, Zoology and Psychology and Caroline to Exeter to read Politics and Economics], he didn't harbour undue expectations of them. Piety was one thing as children of the ministry they were spared, although they were expected to attend church. Always a stickler for punctuality, he expected the curfew of 10 p.m. to be met if they had been out for the evening and he would be out in the drive looking for them if late. Otherwise, he wasn't the judgmental type. If one of the girls stepped out of line he tended to affect shock that they could behave in such a manner, rather than issue strict reprimands. For their part, they admired his business acumen (never sign a cheque on your own, always have a witness, was one piece of advice he gave), his virtuosity on the piano, his sharpness of eye, his ready wit and his acceptance of their friends. What they perhaps found hard to understand was the level of his Christian commitment, while Donald in turn, although regretting the sacrifices to family life, not least his absence on Christmas Day or at the weekend, saw it as the price that had to be paid for his vocation. One of the reasons why few clerics measured up to his estimation was their lack of total commitment, and certainly Donald, with his restless energy, was somehow destined for a life permanently in the public eye rather than tending to domestic chores.

It was during these years that one of Donald's great wartime adventures, begun with a faithful few, mushroomed into something greater, as hundreds flocked to his banner. So it was with OCW, one of the most satisfying things he ever did. Jean Anderson, one of the leading members, recalled how during the spring of 1942, eight young people sat in the library at Kingsway. The conversation turned to open-air speaking. The question was, could they do it? Donald promised to help. One Sunday in June they took the plunge at Marble Arch. It proved a daunting experience, but, undeterred, they looked forward to their first major challenge.

It so happened that the Surrey commuter town of Dorking had a strong interdenominational Christian youth movement which wanted to hold a week of mission there but had no team to help them. The local minister relayed the news to Donald who gladly assented to a team visit in August. On the day after the Germans reached Stalingrad, the team took up their respective places in Dorking High Street to begin their mission in the open air. Despite some indifferent weather and becoming embroiled in a local defence exercise, a great camaraderie grew up among all those who participated. This augured well for future campaigns.

The next year the Kingsway Preachers – as they became known – were invited down to Liskeard in Cornwall by the Financial Secretary of the Methodist Missionary Society. They stayed in a local church and spoke to congregations and committees in the surrounding area. Douglas Thompson related how one afternoon Donald arrived in the main square in Launceston ready to preach, only to find the open-air cinema van of the War Savings Movement parked on his site. The two campaigns, both well advertised, had collided. The War Savings Chief, however, offered to give Donald first use of the van's amplification system to speak to a large crowd, which Donald willingly took, prompting headlines in the local press of "After You, Padre".

In 1944 the Kingsway Preachers returned to the West Country, to Barnstaple in Devon, in a somewhat different guise. This was mainly due to the influence of a young Canadian firefighter with pacifist leanings called Keith Woollard, who had been attracted to Kingsway the previous year when his role in the Canadian Fire Service had taken him to Wimbledon. He took on much of the managerial responsibilities for the campaign, introducing the format of team preachers for Barnstaple, and over the course of the following year provided as much professional training as possible for those speaking.

Following the success at Barnstaple, Donald wrote to all London Methodist districts, asking if they were interested in this kind of campaign, and inviting them to Kingsway on 24 February 1945. Nervous about what to expect, David Mason recalled that he was disappointed with the turn-out, but those present contained many of the brightest and best in Methodist youth. At the meeting, Donald talked about those in his Kingsway congregation who could speak in the open air. Others could be effective, he declared, in seeking ways of proclaiming the Christian message to those outside its walls. Sold on the idea, those in attendance agreed to visit Salisbury that August under the banner of The London Christian Campaigners. One hundred and forty duly went and took it in turns to man the stands in the crowded marketplace, while others hovered on the fringes, introducing themselves to small groups to explain the purpose of their mission. The response was most positive as crowds lingered in groups some time after the speakers had left the platform. During the week the campaigns followed a routine, which more or less became the norm thereafter.

The group would arrive at their destination on Saturday and spend the Sunday in as many church services as possible. The campaigners divided into smaller units, living in a local church, men on the floor, women on camp beds, and responsible for their own catering. After breakfast everyone was assigned to various groups and given duties for the day, before heading off into the city to engage with those in the crowds listening to a speaker and encouraging them to come to a private meeting. Donald sometimes spoke of sanctified flirtation, through which members of the female sex might be more able to induce a response. After a day of preaching and conversing, proceedings would conclude with evening prayers, and this schedule would be repeated daily (aside from their day-off) until the final rally on the Friday when Donald's farewell address would inevitably be a *tour de force*. The week's expenses, mainly for food and travel, which came to about £4 was paid for by the individuals themselves, although those who could afford more helped subsidise those who had less. One year Jeffrey Harris, sometime Secretary of the London Mission, recalled that the expenses were significantly more than they had budgeted for and Donald in a private meeting said, "We must be honourable and foot the bill ourselves." They did.

After Salisbury, Donald received an invitation from the Plymouth Free Church Federal Council to bring a bigger team the following summer. The weather was dismal, the catering arrangements taxing and the response better in the villages than the towns. Nevertheless, a crowd of 2,000, of whom a number were from outside the ranks of Methodism, crammed into Plymouth Town Hall for the final uplifting rally. It was here that Donald celebrated the Eucharist, establishing a precedent for all future OCW meetings. For, by always finishing with the Eucharist, it became in the Revd Gordon Wakefield's words, "a converting ordinance which those who had been won for Christ pledged themselves along with the campaigners". In 1947 OCW (as they had now become) broke new ground not only by visiting an industrial area but also with the introduction of a "commandant", a deputy in charge of a group of thirty campaigners, to try and establish a more intimate feel to the occasion. Over 100 churches in the Huddersfield vicinity opened their pulpits on the Sunday and loyally supported the plethora of activities which comprised the usual open-air meetings, as well as visits to factory canteens and clubs throughout the district. It was here that the campaigners soon discovered that casual talks with little groups or individuals outside the works proved better tactics than talks in the canteen at mealtimes. The week ended in triumph on the Friday evening with six well-attended rallies – one for each area – with Donald speaking at each.

He was at the heart of all the great OCW campaigns, marshalling his troops like a seasoned officer, his morning meeting resembling a military-style briefing, an irony given his pacifist principles. Having led the singing and recited some of the great prayers, he then outlined the plans for the day ahead, stressing the need for punctuality, for anything less he asserted, demonstrated a lack of urgency for Christ's sake. As for the talks themselves, he insisted that they were written out three times, focused on the big questions, were devoid of undue piety, included concrete experiences and ended with an appeal. He would then accompany different groups to their respective destinations, sometimes speaking but just as likely acting as a confidant for those coping with the challenge of addressing large crowds for the first time. To those debutants, he was a reassuring presence, while his commitment to the spartan sleeping arrangements and his ebullience off-duty as he entertained on the piano, only raised his stature in the eyes of his followers. Many, subconsciously or not, imitated him in their own declamatory style, and fully embraced the essence of his social gospel.

For the next few years beginning with Cannock Chase in 1948, OCW continued to attract the imagination of the communities it visited. At Cardiff in 1951 massive crowds saw Donald demolish a local communist in a brilliant speech, demonstrating a better grasp of Marx than his opponent. Then at Exeter in 1953 the large hall used for public meetings was packed to capacity on two consecutive nights for the first time in its history. Douglas Cock, a young reporter, found the whole experience most edifying as his account in the *Methodist Recorder* indicated. "As might be expected of a movement founded by this year's President, open-air speaking has played a large part in their strategy. Much of this has been of a high quality, and it is perhaps the OCW's chief significance that large numbers of young Christians of several denominations are being trained in this exacting art. There have been no highly emotional appeals, no open-air collections and no 'bronchial harmoniums'. Instead, the Christian case, and its relevance to the contemporary situation, has been forcefully and intelligently presented."[6]

The Rhondda visit of 1957, supported by Churches of different denominations, was another memorable experience, a view endorsed by the BBC who were filming the campaign. They left impressed with what they had seen, most notably with Donald's common touch as he discoursed with miners and teenagers alike. By then he and Kingsway were gradually reducing their links with OCW just when the momentum of the post-war years was beginning to fade. In 1960, the year of the last big campaign in Birmingham, Donald was forced to conclude that the expectations of Salisbury, Plymouth and Huddersfield hadn't been realised, partly because the crowds had been disappointing and partly because the support of the local churches had never been wholehearted. "What I do feel ought to be said," he wrote in the 1960 OCW Yearbook, "after all these years ... is that it is the silliest of fallacies to think that those who are embedded in a secular civilisation and quite outside the Church can easily be influenced towards Christian thinking, let alone brought to the feet of the Master."[7] The last point was surely the crux of the matter. In a more affluent society which was becoming more godless and cynical, the age of mass rallies was drawing to a close (indeed OCW adapted more to house-to-house and small-group meetings). The fact also that OCW failed broadly to penetrate the Church of England was another reason, as was its lack of a national organisation such as George MacLeod's Iona Community which kept a strong guiding hand on its scattered membership. Left to the local churches, seeds planted in August tended to fall by the wayside.

When OCW was officially wound up in 1996 its demise could be seen as an overall failure, but this shouldn't blind us to its achievements. It helped mould a generation of able young ministers such as Harry Morton, its one time secretary, Jeffrey Harris, David Mason, John Vincent and John Stacey, as well as a number of Labour politicians such as Peter Archer. It also provided the most effective method of lay training ever seen within the Church and inspired a number of its members into a life of public service or inner-city projects such as the ones in Honor Oak in South-East London and Tiger Bay in Cardiff. Indeed, fifty years on from its heyday, it goes without saying that many of the willing foot soldiers of OCW remain Donald's most fervent disciples.

CHAPTER SEVEN

Into the World

Ever since John Wesley's travels in North America during the late 1730s, Methodism had the makings of a world Church. Methodist Societies there, the work of Irish immigrants, were in existence by 1768, and from 1784 the Methodist Episcopal Church was a reality. It continued to grow rapidly throughout the nineteenth century in numbers, wealth and evangelistic mission, the latter an activity central to British Methodism. Through the missionary zeal of Thomas Coke in the West Indies, where strong Methodist roots were put down, the Wesleyan Methodist Missionary Society was set up in 1813. In time, it became the established vehicle for spreading the word to many parts of the British Empire, especially Australia, Canada, South Africa and West Africa, giving credibility to John Wesley's celebrated dictum about the world being his parish. For much of the twentieth century mission work remained a sacrosanct part of British Methodism, synonymous with the words "To the friendship of the English-speaking world" which were displayed outside Kingsway Hall. Given Donald's renown as an evangelist with international contacts, it should come as no surprise that demand for his services should soon extend outside Britain. He did his best to oblige, and certainly for most of his professional life he was a seasoned traveller, especially in the United States and Canada, where he was active on behalf of FOR. The years 1947–52 were the heyday of his missionary activity, when he cut an imposing sight in the pulpit and lecture hall, or on his soapbox, but the results weren't altogether to his satisfaction, not least in Australia, where the open-air culture appeared to him to be more conducive to recreation than evangelism.

In 1947 Donald made his first trip to Asia. The background to the visit lay in the growing attraction to Marxism among the students in the University of Ceylon at a time when the country was clamouring for independence from Britain. The situation was perilous enough to alarm Basil Jackson, who as Chairman of the South Ceylon District of the Methodist Church, was helping to minister to a Christian population of some half million there. He wrote to the Methodist Missionary Society, asking that Donald be approached to see if he would visit Ceylon (now Sri Lanka) for six weeks to conduct a special mission among the young, educated people there. "The present political situation in Ceylon together with what might be called 'normal' post-war unrest, are creating many problems for our young people," he wrote, "and we are convinced that the Church should take immediate steps to help our young people to combat anti-Christian tendencies of thought. The only way of doing that is to help them come to a full Christian experience and a real conversion, but this can only be done by someone who is fully alive to modern political and intellectual tendencies. An evangelist of the older type would fail to cut any ice at all. Even a man like Dr Stanley Jones is losing his grip on the younger generation in Ceylon today. Our need is for a man of outstanding intellectual qualities and deep Christian convictions. The person we have in mind is Dr Donald Soper."[1]

Helped by the fact that the Revd G. E. Hickman Johnson, the secretary in Methodist Mission House for that area, was a friend of Donald's, Jackson, six months later in September, found himself greeting his man. It was the start of an arduous tour of the island comprising some sixty rallies and meetings before he moved on to Australia. Donald soon discovered that he brought with him great expectations, as he recorded in his diary days after his arrival. This diary and several of his missives survive, giving us a fresh insight into his character. They often reveal a man under some pressure, suffering from migraine, exhaustion and homesickness, which might well account for many of the acerbic comments, especially about the competence of a number of his hosts, or the parlous state of Methodism in foreign parts.

Having endured a five-day flight via Cairo, "a city to break the evangelist's heart", Bahrain, Karachi, Bombay, "a wonderful sight", and Madras, the Sopers crossed by boat to Jaffna, the northern city in Ceylon. Donald's first impressions were favourable. The Sinhalese, he thought, looked more intelligent than the Indians, and Colombo was a beautiful city, although somewhat surprisingly he compared its seafront to Clacton-on-Sea, an unfashionable resort in Essex. After a brief period to recuperate, he was off with Basil Jackson to Galle, an attractive town on the southern tip of the island, for an agreeable weekend of worship and lectures. Staying at the old Dutch Governor's House, where he was royally entertained, Donald revelled in the size of the audiences which gathered to hear him, and in the quality of their questions, not least from the Buddhists. After a day out to Matara, he returned to Colombo content. His major priority for the first full week was the Wesleyan College for Ministers' Convention, where aside from entertaining them on the piano and "teaching the Ceylonese to sing better", he spoke to them about evangelism.

Using OCW as his model he encouraged them not only to address people in everyday language, but also to relate the mighty works of God to an economic and political setting.

Throughout their trip, the Sopers attracted huge crowds in a country that they soon found to be in some ferment, where the racial-religious cleavages between the Sinhalese Buddhists and Tamil Hindus were all too clear. Anti-imperial sentiments too were evident, not least the time when Donald saw people trooping out of the cinema during the rendition of the National Anthem. Only on the cricket field did he detect proper co-operation between the Europeans and the natives.

As he undertook a hectic round of visits to schools, universities and churches, he found the island to be a tropical paradise comprising polite menfolk, beautiful women and happy, plump children, but also gripped by poverty, squalor and class distinctions. What particularly shocked him was the lot of the rickshaw coolie – a poor, undernourished Indian, who eked out a precarious existence by getting in between the shafts of a small cart to drag visitors behind him through the streets of Colombo. It was conditions such as this that had helped breed political extremism. Donald later recalled how one communist said to him, "You Christians talk about the value of human life. We intend to get rid of rickshaws." Such exchanges simply reinforced his belief that clerics like himself had to engage with the contemporary scene as well as putting their message across simply. "There is a great chance for political leadership," he wrote during his first week, "and it is being missed by the Church which is out of touch with youth."[2]

Shocked that so many of its leaders were politically ignorant, not least about the names and policies of the left-wing parties at the recent election, he told the mission staff in no uncertain terms that this was something he aimed to rectify. In Colombo, he addressed 5,000 (with the help of loud-speakers) on the fashionable Galle Face promenade and intrigued them with his contention that Christianity's own concept of the classless society was more revolutionary than communism because it levelled up not down. He also dissected the deficiencies of the latter, pointing out its divisions and irrelevancies, a telling point in a country where the Communist Party, for all its potential support, was riven to the core. He continued to make a stir, as Buddhists, communists and Christians alike clamoured for his presence; and, when he wasn't preaching, teaching, or answering questions, he was giving interviews on the radio. Attracting the largest crowd at the university, he found many of the students to be lively, intelligent and on the march, and he compared the uproarious meetings in Colombo's Town Hall to Tower Hill. At the final one, the crowds were so vast that they thronged the surrounding verandas and corridors in what Philip Penning of the *Methodist Recorder* called the largest gathering of its kind in the capital. With hundreds hanging on his every word, Donald again stressed the value of the three C's – Communication, Community and Communion – and implored the young to sign up to the Christian faith, or at least to make further inquiries by joining a group. Similar tumultuous receptions awaited him in Kandy, the ancient capital in the heart of the island, where he and Marie were shown the famous Temple of the Tooth by a saintly Buddhist abbot. As the trip had progressed, he had warmed to many aspects of Buddhism, especially its pacifist element, but ultimately concluded that for all its sanctity and piety, only a world-embracing religion like Christianity could overcome suffering through the Cross. This was a view he continued to sustain in an age when other religions became more fashionable. Despite his admission that Christianity had no monopoly of virtue, he still felt that, for all the proud traditions of Judaism, Hinduism and Islam, they lacked the depth of human insights and wisdom comparable with the leadership of Jesus.

Despite atrocious weather in Kandy where intense flooding had wreaked havoc, the mood remained very upbeat as the mission caught the imagination of the local community. Donald approved of their spiritual curiosity but was less taken with their singing; at the end of one meeting at Trinity College he made them sing properly. Word of his tuition must have spread for at Kingswood College the following evening the students were insistent that he break into song. Initially he was reluctant to oblige, pleading a hoarse voice caused by his onerous speaking schedule. Eventually he succumbed, and accompanying himself on the piano he treated them to a moving rendition of the Negro spiritual "Deep River", before playing a syncopated version of "Onward Christian Soldiers" – much to everyone's amusement. After a brief respite on the Central Plain of Ceylon, Donald and Marie returned to Colombo where they were accorded a rousing farewell at Methodist College. "These Ceylonese are gentle and kindly people," Donald confided to his diary. He went on to say that Marie had had a most successful trip, "looks fit and obviously enjoyed herself".[3] While she had captivated her hosts by her poise and articulate talks to women's groups, he had experienced one of his most fulfilling missions, enhancing his credentials as a biblical authority of some repute. He had also left his hosts well pleased. According to the Revd Hickman Johnson, his visit made an impression on the mind of the community such as no other Christian had ever made. In the estimation of Basil Jackson, Donald stemmed the tide of Marxism in the university. "Soper's visit has been a success beyond our highest expectations great though those were. His meeting in Colombo gained new heights in size and quality as the campaign proceeded, and he left an indelible impression upon the mind of the Church and upon the lives of individuals. The real significance of his message at this point has been in the influence it has had upon the thinking of many of our young people who have been strongly attracted by the social programme of the left-wing politicians. Dr Soper's contribution has been to bring these young people together in a desire to find a Christian socialist solution for the ills of capitalist society."[4]

After the fascination with Asia, it was on to Australia for a further six weeks, which, with no Marie to accompany him, proved much less satisfying, especially since the country was simply too conservative and insular for someone of his taste. His presentiments were aroused at a Methodist reception on arrival in Brisbane, predominated by old people, very British, patriotic and pious who sang "God Save the King". "Where were the youngsters?" he wondered in his diary. "I hope Australia isn't going to be polite and pointless."[5] Brisbane he found to be a bourgeois community with houses looking like cricket pavilions, and possessing an unhealthy preoccupation with England. After repeated questions about life back home at various stodgy receptions, Donald had had his fill of patriotic sentiment. "This love for the old country continues to get under my skin,"[6] he fulminated.

As the leading attraction for the various celebrations marking the centenary of Methodism in Queensland, Donald took Brisbane by storm. All his meetings were well attended, especially his final one in the Albert Hall, where he waxed lyrical on "Christianity and Communism", a theme he constantly revisited over the next decade. Both Christianity and communism stood for the classless society, Donald told his capacity audience, and the right of people to enjoy a full life, but communism denied human liberty which should belong in any worthwhile society. Referring to the evils of imperialism and exploitation, he declared that mankind had to solve its difficulties without resorting to war. "Let us by all means hit men as hard as we can above the belt, but with words of truth and not violence. We should show communists that by Christianity we can obtain the same results they desire but without the violence of their programme."[7] Then after two "thoroughly boring" visits to girls' schools and a civic reception with the Lord Mayor, he headed out of town into the hinterland.

His peregrinations in a Chevrolet took him via Ipswich, Toowoomba, "a lovely setting", Maryborough (whose comic chairman of the district synod reminded him of the comedian George Formby) and Gympie. Aside from the sumptuous hospitality, which found him reluctantly eating to excess, the abiding impression he continued to hold of Australia was a land of plenty with little understanding of the values he espoused. On arrival in Sydney he met up with Alan Walker, and together they visited the sights. He fell for the magnificence of the harbour and the bathing beaches but again wondered whether the lazy open air and non-communal life civilised, as he contemplated the hedonistic culture of the "lucky country". Then it was down to business, beginning with a service at Walker's church. Having browbeaten a meeting of ministers one day and visited four synods the next, all of which received the same address, Donald made for Newcastle, the second largest city in the state. At a crowded synod he was grateful to find more youngsters than hitherto, but the low intelligence of Australian Methodists continued to bother him.

After a hectic round of engagements back in Sydney and an exhausting surf on Bondi Beach, Donald left for Melbourne with his stock ever rising, as the following encomium in the *Methodist*, the New South Wales equivalent of the *Methodist Recorder*, testified.

"The recent visit of the Reverend Donald Soper, MA BD, of London, will not soon be forgotten by anyone who had the privilege and satisfaction of hearing him. During the few days in which he was in our midst he was almost literally whirled from one assembly to another, but he seemed to be able to adjust himself to each new situation immediately and his addresses, even those which were obviously given quite off-hand, were of such a quality that they made and left a profound impression upon all his hearers."

Having paid tribute to his brilliant mind and fluency of speech and capacity to entertain, the writer went on to applaud his determination to avoid shallowness of thought and superficial observation. Rather, it was his intellectual depth and religious conviction which stood out.

He is still a comparatively young man, but has clearly read widely and to good purpose, and his reading, so far from cluttering up his mind with other people's ideas, seems rather to have been done to acquire knowledge not otherwise obtainable, and to provide a spur for his own thoughts. Years of hard study undoubtedly lie behind his dicta, and whether all his views are shared by his hearers or not, it is impossible to treat them other than with respect.

Clearly he knows what he believes; and his convictions have all been thoroughly tested out. In the course of his address to the ministers of Sydney on Monday morning of last week he stated that when he began his work he held out to almost a hundred things; now he held three, or rather three held him. He did not say precisely what they were, but the impression he gave by all that he said was that they were the reality of God as He has revealed Himself in the universe and in human history, the centrality and supremacy of Christ for the Christian faith, and the imperishable worth and salvation of man. He made it unmistakably clear that he regarded the Gospel of Christ in all its fullness and power as the one and only hope of the world. The acceptance and rejection of that Gospel is, beyond denial, a life and death matter for all men and for the ceaseless and passionate proclamation of it the Church everywhere is responsible.

Few men, we imagine, can more readily adjust themselves to an audience than the Doctor. His long experience as an open-air speaker – he has been haranguing people on Tower Hill week by week for twenty years – has probably helped him more than anything else to put himself easily *en rapport* with hearers of varying mental capacity and moral status. At all events he is quickly at home with a congregation, and, what is equally important, a congregation is equally at home with him. He is a master of the telling phrase and if any demonstration of the fact were needed that the polished shaft flies faster and with greater precision than the unpolished, it may be seen in his cultural use of the English language. It is a sheer delight to watch the workings of his nimble and coruscating mind, and to hear him use his mother tongue with such freedom and felicity and seemingly with such spontaneity and unstudied emphasis. Altogether he is an unusually gifted and able man and is proof positive that all the really great men are not dead – yet.[8]

Donald liked Melbourne with its English setting of parks, but Geelong, "flat marshland like Romney Marsh", an hour or so to the south, he didn't. "Talked to parsons for two hours (mostly moronic), then tea with the ugly sisters and evening meeting poorly planned and badly attended. Victorian Methodism is stuffed with reaction"[9] was his damning indictment. A game performance on the golf course at plush Royal Melbourne raised his spirits, as did purposeful outings to Methodist Ladies' College Junior School and Wesley College – two of the city's most elite schools – where he met some Kingsway stalwarts afterwards. A trip to the Victorian gold towns of Ballarat and Bendigo through lovely scenery also afforded much pleasure, but again the empty pews forced him to conclude that "Methodism in these parts has had it".[10]

Things were little better in Tasmania, a paradise island with a strongly English feel to it as he picnicked in hedgerows and played cricket with his hosts. It was precisely because of the stunning scenery, not least the southern coastline which he thought one of the most beautiful in the world, and the absence of anxiety that contributed to the slothful state of Methodism on the island. Even in Devonport, "a Cornish Padstow", where the crowds were respectable in size, Donald derided them as "very conservative and low mentality. Everything too easy in Tasmania".[11]

Beginning to feel the strain of such a sapping itinerary, he found a new lease of life back in Melbourne as the advent of some hecklers injected a touch of brio into the exchanges. On his trip to Adelaide, "an excellent planned city", he stayed with Frank Hambley, a preacher of some repute and the most able minister he had yet encountered, which helped strike the right note for the duration of his stay. Although unimpressed by the amateurish atmosphere of South Australian politics when shown around their Parliament by the Speaker, and the conference of ministers over which he presided, his meetings on "Christianity and Communism" exceeded expectation. The same was true of the centenary rally of the Home Mission Department, chiefly because of the quality of the singing. On his final day there, he made three broadcasts, all ad lib, met representatives of the Aboriginal Society of Pacifists, sang Negro spirituals at a women's meeting, was received by the Mayor and Aldermen at the Town Hall and held a successful rally at the Mission. Buoyed up by Adelaide, he departed for Perth, a pleasant open city whose climate he compared to California. Although rather critical of the Methodist Church in Western Australia for its lack of drive and vision, the crowds turned out to hear him. This was particularly the case in the goldmining town of Kalgoorlie where some people had travelled up to 150 miles, and at his final service at Perth's Wesley Church where hundreds had to be turned away. "Everyone professes great sorrow at my departure,"[12] Donald confided somewhat sceptically to his diary, feeling that the reaction to his mission had for the most part been distinctly underwhelming.

Only Adelaide with its large, enthusiastic crowds did he deem a success. He departed the country, appreciative of the warmth of the hospitality, but disconsolate with what he saw as the narrow horizons of the Methodists, too steeped in their middle-class ways and their fundamentalist prejudices. He also reproached himself for his own failure to ignite the flames of faith. On both counts his judgements were too harsh. Certainly his hosts were happy enough with his performance as formally expressed at their 1948 Conference, and as for his impact, one story suffices. It centres around his visit to Queen's College, University of Melbourne. Having spoken to the students in the Common Room, two Indians who had been upsetting their Christian colleagues with their vehement Hinduism, began to question him aggressively. In his reply, Donald, by showing a deeper knowledge of their religion than they themselves possessed, crushed them so completely that, much to their fellow students' satisfaction, they never again caused trouble.

In November 1949 Donald headed to Canada, a country he had briefly visited in 1935, for a mission lasting some five weeks. He flew via Iceland to Toronto, gaining a magnificent view of the St Lawrence estuary *en route*. His venue there was the Royal York Hotel, which he deemed to be full of local spivs. Never one to defer judgement, he was soon forming his impressions of Canada. "Compared with Australia, the level of scholarship is high, and there is universal prosperity. Everyone frightened of the Roman Catholics."[13] His final remark referred to the recent elevation of the Archbishop of Toronto, James McGuigan, to the position of cardinal, a development which Donald dismissed as inconsequential. The background to the growth of anti-Catholic sentiment lay in a bitter labour dispute which had convulsed the country for much of that year. Between February and July, 5,000 asbestos miners in Quebec Province, concerned about health dangers caused by asbestos, and in search of better wages, had opted for strike action. Their decision was fiercely condemned by the anti-union Premier of Quebec, Maurice Duplessis, who repeatedly declared the strike to be illegal. A fierce showdown ensued between the provincial police and the workers, leading to bitter allegations on either side. In contrast to its Protestant counterparts whose sympathy lay broadly with the authorities, the Roman Catholic Church in Quebec, as was its wont, publicly condemned the police for their undue aggression and in tandem with Maurice Roy, the Archbishop of Quebec City, organised church collections in support of striking families. Eventually, thanks to Roy's mediating presence, the dispute was finally resolved in July; yet sectarian tensions continued to fester as Donald discovered throughout his visit. His natural tendency to side with the underdog found him not for the first time to be out of step with his hosts. After only one day in Toronto, he was flying over prairie country to Edmonton, a city of great wealth and wooden houses at the end of the Alaska Highway, which he thought comparable with Brisbane. Acclimatising didn't come easily. Soon he was complaining that his host Angus McQueen, the local pastor, "bored him to tears" (his wife was even worse), the city lacked beauty and the local culture was superficial. His disillusionment was to some extent assuaged by the enthusiasm of the locals to his presence and the positive spirit in which his talks were received, even though he recognised that they were "too revolutionary for most". One particularly memorable encounter came at the University of Alberta when "a horse faced woman" asked a question about Christian Science. "After flattening her out I found to my horror that she was the wife of the president of the university, but most unpopular, so I am on solid ground with the students,"[14] he wrote. On his penultimate day he rose at 5a.m. to go duck-shooting with a prominent dental surgeon. After a forty-mile journey they encamped in some weeds and stayed there till 3 p.m., presumably to no good purpose in Donald's case. "I aimed at no duck and shot no duck," he remarked with some satisfaction, "but it was cold."[15] Another full meeting that evening elicited a heartening response. "Everybody appeared well pleased but with what results?"[16] he wondered. His parting engagement in Edmonton was a dinner at the McQueens replete with local ministers all attacking Roman Catholics. Donald responded in kind by defending the Pope.

From Edmonton, it was off by train to Saskatoon, a new town on the edge of the prairies. He was met by his old friend Keith Woollard, whom he felt hadn't changed a bit, and some others who, as he mischievously put it, "needed to change a lot". Woollard was to act as his minder throughout his week there, and his guide around the city. His company and a spate of activity, which prompted him to write half way through the week that "they are working me pretty hard" would suggest the need for a touch of solitude to renew himself. Apparently not. The next day, having dined by himself in his hotel between two large rallies, he reached the rather startling conclusion that he had never been alone so much during his entire life. The claim seems surprising given his early experiences at Cambridge, but that aside, it sheds interesting light on his character. For despite his aversion to socialising, especially the contrived bonhomie of Rotary, which greeted him at every stage of his travels, and his intolerance of unintelligent and bigoted people, he still yearned for fellowship. His life after all had been nurtured on the collective culture of institutions be they family, school, university, the Church, the Mission and the Labour Party, and his gospel was very much a social one based on co-operation. As a man of rare calibre, equipped with a real missionary purpose, the public stage was his natural habitat and the one where the spark was truly kindled. Solo pursuits such as sustained reading, writing and research, not to mention silent spiritual retreats, were much less his niche; for as he told Colin Morris years later, he always looked at life in terms of personality not abstract thinking. He found comfort and assurance in people, especially those in the same kind of milieu, dealing with the same type of problems. Given this natural quest for companionship which grew ever greater throughout his life, it does seem strangely ironic that someone with such a winsome personality as Donald should struggle to form close bonds. It was a fact which he readily came to accept, not least as a major cause behind the moroseness to which he was periodically prone, but which was never fully explained.

Private doubts aside, Donald's week in Saskatoon was characterised by large, enthusiastic rallies, countless questions not all of which he had time to answer, and late nights as the locals mulled over his words. The one rather deflating experience concerned his talk on evangelism to the local churches, a number of whom remained unreconciled to his message. "Not particularly inspiring," he concluded, "ministers themselves need to be evangelised."[17] Despite this, he left satisfied in the knowledge that overall his words hadn't fallen on stony ground and that according to Woollard, many ministers had gone home with a new conception of what their job entailed.

His next destination was Hamilton, a steel town close to the Niagara Falls. Here he was introduced to curling, which as with all sports, he proved quite adroit at mastering. (In Edmonton he had beaten the local champion at table tennis.) By now winter with its plunging temperatures had firmly set in, but the crowds continued to turn out in droves to hear him, especially at McMaster University. The buoyant atmosphere there was in marked contrast to the interminable Rotary lunches where "the undergraduate humour of ageing tycoons of industry" somewhat taxed him. At one meeting the chairman barred the discussion of politics, only for him to denounce socialism as he discoursed on the railways.

In Ottawa, "a lovely city", the momentum continued apace, though Donald by his own admission won few adherents to the socialist cause. He did however admire the common sense of the old ladies ("it's the forty and fifty group who are the trouble") and found the students at Glebe High School splendid to talk to. Afterwards he swapped limericks with the headmaster. Having been shown around the Canadian Parliament which he considered very inferior to Westminster, he headed for Moreton, a typical American-looking small town full of Rotary, apple pie and curling club suppers; the latter he dismissed as "another of those adolescent affairs with horseplay and singsong". It was while he was here that he ran into a group of fundamentalists; attempting to provoke them, they refused to rise to his bait.

His visit ended in Newfoundland where he dined with the Prime Minister, was heckled at a women's rally over his views on smoking and was intrigued to discover that the parsons met every Monday for a skittles evening. Newfoundland he felt was Canada's poor relation although he was pleased to come across the first working-class congregation in a land where politics, to his regret, verged on indifference. He had found his hosts kind enough, but felt that their comfortable standard of living had blunted their spirituality.

As he prepared to depart, the weather was inclement enough to warrant the cancellation of all flights from Gander Airport. It needed some gentle cajoling from someone in the ministry to make an exception for Donald's flight, so that after a delay he was airborne taking off in a howling blizzard. They had been going some twenty-five minutes when over the most desolate part of the island, a terrifying noise caused shock and alarm in equal measure. It transpired that the antenna had broken, forcing an immediate return and in the midst of an infernal racket they returned to Gander at midnight. Once they had landed attendants tried to hustle him out, but Donald, pointing to his gammy leg, the legacy of his 1938 blood clot, wasn't to be stampeded into an emergency evacuation. Soon they were airborne again and this time the homeward flight passed off without incident.

He was back across the Atlantic the following March for a brief trip, this time focusing on the United States, a country with eleven million Methodists, the largest of its kind in the world. He began in the rarefied atmosphere of Stanford University, California, which reminded him of Cambridge except more opulent. The informal service featured "gushing females and overfed males" he observed, "but very receptive". Buffalo, his next stop, was a large unprepossessing steel town where he derived much pleasure from addressing some left-wing activists. At Cincinnati at a "Religion and Labor" conference at which Elliott Roosevelt, son of the former President FDR, received an award on behalf of his mother Eleanor, Donald harangued them and "they lapped it up". His tone was rather subtler at Northwestern University campus in Evanston near Chicago and Wooster College, Ohio, but still met with approval, and although Lynbrook on Long Island was more controversial, Donald wasn't complaining. From Lynbrook he travelled to New Haven, Connecticut, by train, beset by a lachrymose Italian in the throes of lost love. Yale University turned out to be a sprawling mass of campuses, but he was much taken by the colonial setting of the Divinity School where he conversed with the students in the Common Room. It was a relaxing end to an agreeable few days, despite the unnecessarily taxing itinerary which owed everything to enthusiasm and very little to logistics.

In addition to his work at the West London Mission, OCW and in foreign parts, Donald had remained politically active in the post-war era. An avid supporter of the Attlee Labour Government, with its commitment to the universal welfare state, he defended it at a Methodist Anniversary gathering in Coventry in 1948 when he spoke on "Marxism or Christianity".

His support, however, wasn't unconditional, for when the dockers went on strike in the summer of 1949, placing national food supplies in jeopardy, he defended them at a large rally at Tower Hill, one of the few to do so, as the Government reasserted its authority.

More important was his work for peace, which in no way was diminished by the end of European hostilities in May 1945 – the month incidentally when he became Chairman of the MPF. In *Calling for Action* Donald related how he was on the beach in Cornwall when he heard about the dropping of the atomic bomb on Hiroshima on 6 August 1945, a cataclysmic event which shaped much of his activity over the rest of his life.

Now that the nightmare of nuclear obliteration hung over the whole world, Donald grew ever more convinced that the old argument that war could achieve certain objectives lacked all credibility. He was equally dismissive of the contemporary one which justified the proliferation of nuclear weapons on the grounds that they acted as a powerful deterrent from their being deployed. On the contrary, he countered, escalating stockpiles only strengthened the considerable barriers of mistrust which already existed between East and West rather than creating the climate of goodwill necessary to build lasting peace. In March 1946 he chaired a huge nationwide protest against atomic war at Central Hall, Westminster, organised in conjunction with FOR and PPU. Yet, for all their efforts, warnings of nuclear holocaust struck little resonance with a nation keen to erase war from its memory and get back to normality.

With PPU/FOR membership and finances in decline the mood assumed an air of desperation at the 1947 General Meeting. There a motion was passed requesting that the National Council take the lead in destroying completely the National Service Act introducing peace-time conscription rather than obtaining an exemption from its provisions for objectors. When the Council met, it found itself sharply divided about the legitimacy of such an extreme motion. While opponents were happy to support the right of an individual to oppose the Act, they felt unable to commit the organisation to such tactics. The fact that the motion passed led to six of the original Sponsors of the PPU, including Donald, Charles Raven, Middleton Murry and Alex Wood resigning from the Council. "You probably know that I have been fairly unhappy about PPU for a long while," Donald observed in his resignation letter. "In my judgement the founding nature and purpose of PPU is now different and to me unacceptable."[18] He did conclude by reaffirming his commitment to the sense of pacifist fellowship and returned as a Sponsor in 1967.

The departure of the six found support from many who were not present, so that at an Extraordinary Meeting the original resolution advocating civil disobedience was overturned. Undeterred by this confusion, Donald, in company with Vera Brittain, kept ploughing a lonely furrow, addressing large FOR/PPU meetings at Caxton Hall and Hyde Park in April 1948. He also spoke out against conscription when the growing tension in Europe persuaded the Government in December that year to extend the period of military service from twelve to eighteen months. In the shadow of a general election FOR organised an anti-conscription week between 4 and 11 February 1950, the highlight of which was a "Church and Conscription" meeting at Holborn Hall at which Donald spoke. People were often reminded of lost liberties elsewhere, he remarked, yet how seldom was conscription with its totalitarian tendencies condemned. The fact that this was the year when boys without active service were being sent as National Servicemen to the Malayan jungle only added to his indignation. Much of it was to boil over at the Methodist Conference that year in a blaze of publicity as his pacifist convictions exposed rifts within his Church.

Donald Soper was a committed Methodist but not an orthodox one. His views were too eclectic and unpredictable, the result being that his relationship with his denomination was always strangely ambivalent. It so happened that his rise within Methodist ranks coincided with a steady erosion in the prominence of the Free Churches on the English national landscape. Not only had Nonconformity lost its political clout with the decline of the Liberal Party, its spiritual spark had been doused by growing consumerism and affluence. By the 1940s, Methodism in common with other Free Churches, found that its northern heartlands were in retreat as it experienced declining congregations and a diminishing hold on the local community. As its powerbase continued to shift southwards and many of its members found a home in the Conservative Party, so the Church lost something of its élan and audacity. Hence the intriguing paradox presented itself whereby someone of Donald's dynamic radicalism was, according to Adrian Hastings, increasingly out of kilter with the more conventional sentiments of a staid elderly church. Thus, while he was greatly respected for his social work at the West London Mission and his expertise in the open air, his liberal theology, socialism and pacifism raised many hackles among clerics and laymen alike. This was especially the case amongst the latter, since of the two they tended to be the more conservative. There was also the personal factor. Donald was a maverick and his outspoken comments lamenting the malaise within provincial Methodism, or the deficiencies of his colleagues naturally upset many who were unable to measure up to his standards. His success at Tower Hill and on radio had given him a more elevated position in the national consciousness than anyone else in Methodism, but for all the favourable headlines he generated, he appeared at Conference as something of an outsider. This was mainly by choice since he rarely participated in Methodist structures, disdaining committees which deliberated instead of acting. (Kenneth Greet, later Secretary of Conference, has recollections of him whiling away the time on one by composing his signature 500 times.) He also appeared a somewhat detached figure at Conference as he sat there, ear-plug tucked into his cassock, listening to the cricket, suggesting that his priorities lay elsewhere. He rarely participated at length in debate, but when he did he had the uncanny knack of timing his intervention to perfection and commanding the greatest effect. Often his words, delivered with compelling power, found an immediate echo, and many a motion of his was carried unanimously, yet equally on occasions they could spark a furore. This was never more the case than in his intervention in the world peace debate at Bradford in 1950.

The debate came at a particularly tense moment in the Cold War following the establishment of NATO in 1949 in reaction to Soviet consolidation of power in Eastern Europe, the fall of China to the communists the same year and the impending war in Korea between the two sides of the ideological divide. Donald had never been a communist – a point he was forever stressing – but he was prepared to view communism and the Soviet Union more objectively than the vast majority of his compatriots, not least because of her military accomplishments during the Second World War. Back in 1934 he was to write that "whatever the history book of the future will think of Marxism, it cannot but record the monumental activities and successes of the USSR. Multitudes have been given hope and status. Millions have been inspired to fresh vigour and belief. If the standard of the worker today in Russia is not so high as it was in 1928, it is much higher than it was in 1914. If the cultural achievements are slender in many fields of art, they are at least provocative in architecture and epoch-making in photography, the film and the ballet. And so one might go on. Surely it is sufficient to remind ourselves that Russia in 1917 produced one of the great men of all time, Nicolai Lenin. We ought to be big enough to recognise all this and to understand that it is a vindication of the human soul rather than a justification of the Communist position. We can accept all this freely and even gladly, and still go on to the most rigorous criticism and demolition of the Marxist 'credo'."[19]

Having thoroughly analysed much of Marxist thought (which he admired more for its discernment into the way economic forces shaped communities than for its flawed sense of prophesy), he was quite prepared to admit that it was a closely articulated secular religion with much in common with Christianity in the commitment to a revolutionary society in which the humble and meek were exalted. This enabled him to equate the goings-on in the Soviet Union as closer to the kingdom of God than a great deal in the atomised society of the so-called Christian West. He also felt that the planned economy would be a more efficient creator of wealth than the capitalist alternative. In his eyes, capitalism had had its day with the countries of the eastern bloc, and would never return there. At the same time, he unreservedly denounced communism for its godless materialism, its totalitarian oppression, its violence (although he made little reference to the Stalinist purges of the 1930s and 40s) and its underestimation of the human spirit. People weren't simply pawns in the economic game he asserted, but masters of their own destiny with their ideals and visions. The fact that he had recited these reservations over many years, not least to communists themselves, counted for little in the feverish atmosphere of the time, making it easy for his enemies to brand him a fellow-traveller.

At Bradford, Donald's greater concern was pacifism. In the discussion of the Church's attitude to world peace, he supported a resolution passed unanimously, calling for the banning of the bomb. When called to speak, Donald, taking issue with the "just war" theory, drew a distinction between the use of the hydrogen bomb and a bayonet, not so much in the realm of ethics as in the realm of the incalculable results which would follow the use of terrorising forms of war. Mr Unwin, the General Secretary of the Department of Christian Citizenship and sponsor of the motion, had invited them to believe that the real issue was the division of the world into two camps. He, Donald, would rather see a world temporarily overrun by communism than be plunged into a Third World War. Ignoring shouts of "No", he went on to say "that the intransigence of Russia has been referred to but it seems to me that there were violent concepts on the other side which are ethically just as disreputable".[20] As he walked back to his seat to a few disapproving murmurs, Leslie Weatherhead feared that his speech might have proved the death knell of his presidential chances. Within an hour a member of Conference asked the President, W. E. Sangster, that it be made clear that Donald's view was very much a minority one and didn't reflect that of his colleagues. The President obliged. Outside the hall there was mayhem, as ministers opposed to Donald besieged the Press Information Office to try and stop him hijacking the Conference with unfavourable headlines. Some hope. The *Bradford Telegraph and Argus* had the story on the streets in minutes, and the other papers soon followed.

As the ecclesiastical crockery crashed around him Donald remained unfazed, repeating his contention at Tower Hill, days later, to a very large crowd. He didn't support communism he said, but supported many communists because a great many of them were very good people and a great many of their beliefs came out of the New Testament. "Dr Soper," according to "Cassandra", alias William Connor, in the *Daily Mirror* on 20 July, "speaks softly and from the heart, and although he says he would rather see the whole world overrun by Communism than risk it being plunged into war, one must recognise the sincerity of his mind as well as the blazing idiocy of his head."[21] Undeterred, Donald expressed similar sentiments to MPF in Bradford days later. "Certain people said last week I was guilty of an hysterical outburst and that I didn't mean what I said. I have tried to say this for many years."[22] This of course was absolutely true. He wanted his fellow countrymen to face the terrible fact of war and cosmic obliteration and if that nightmare scenario ever came to pass he felt that a temporary occupation by the Russians would be preferable to nuclear war since the former at least offered the chance to deal with the problem. Not that he regarded the prospect of a bloodthirsty Russian invasion as remotely serious. "It is one thing to enter a town where there is resistance and fighting," he said, "but another thing to emerge into Kingsway, for example, with the West London Mission arranging tea for them." None of this impressed an editorial in the Independent Labour *Socialist Leader*. "It is this sort of twaddle that is damning pacifism and the anti-war movement among ordinary folk and which is making our work more difficult than it should be. We would remind Dr Soper that Communist forces do not come to power temporarily; if they come, they come to stay. Second, Dr Soper and his friends would quickly discover that pacifism is not included in the vocabulary of Communism. The commissars would make short shrift of Dr Soper and his propaganda."[23]

There were other unpalatable repercussions to face from the speech. When informed that the Mayor of Cheltenham and the Rector of St Matthew's Church wouldn't attend the OCW rally in their town if he spoke, Donald, concerned that OCW shouldn't be sidetracked, reluctantly decided to stay away. He also had to contend with the resignation of his good friend, Sir Malcolm Perks, as Senior Circuit Steward of the West London Mission and one of its leading benefactors, a departure which he deeply regretted. For all that, he continued to speak his mind. At the PPU rally in Trafalgar Square on 6 August to mark the fifth anniversary of the bombing of Hiroshima, Donald remarked that if Moscow was bombed with food parcels, then ordinary people would think that a new spirit was abroad in the world. Weeks later in Newcastle upon Tyne during the OCW campaign, he condemned those who talked glibly about the next world war and rearmament. His defiance continued to damage his credibility severely in some quarters, with Dr Eric Waterhouse in *Christian World* regretting the fact that Donald's comments had overshadowed the wiser and weightier things discussed at Conference. In all the acreage of print devoted to Donald's speech at Bradford few matched the balance and wisdom of the editorial in the *British Weekly*. "It is the merciless reality of Dr Soper's antithesis that has shocked. We all know in our hearts that it is only too likely to prove the true one. The mass of people benumbed by the horror of the potentialities of our day do not like to have the cushions so unceremoniously removed any more than they liked to be told that Mr Neville Chamberlain's 'peace with honour' would all too probably turn out a rather shabby illusion. Dr Soper is a Christian. Having a clearer head than the Dean of Canterbury he does not try to be a Christian Marxist communist. He has no more illusion about the men in the Kremlin than Mr Chamberlain. But he believes that it is not the way of Christ to resist evil by the way of war and the painful drama of his statement is really in the simple faithfulness and utter obedience of his choice. He bids us count at least what may be the cost whatever way we take."[24]

In the same year, Donald became President of the Methodist Sacramental Fellowship (MSF) founded in 1935 to revive sacramental devotion in Methodism, on the retirement of J.Ernest Rattenbury, one of his predecessors at Kingsway. It was a recognition of his transition during the war, when he had begun, according to Adrian Hastings, to reinvent himself as a priest. Increasingly the smart suits and red ties were replaced by his cassock, and Kingsway was transformed in appearance from mission hall to church as the Eucharist became the centre of worship. It was a far cry from his youth when Communion was taken once a month, but both a desire for the beauty of holiness and his political involvement helped bring him to sacramentalism. There was also the profound influence of Rattenbury, author of many eucharistic hymns and one of the few people in whom Donald confided. In his talks at Kingsway in Holy Week and in private discussions, Rattenbury taught him that this lost art of Nonconformity was the centre of the devotion and spirit of Christian living since it revealed the ultimate faith. "Like his predecessor at Kingsway Hall, Hugh Price Hughes, and like the Wesleys," wrote William Purcell, "Donald said he had found in the Eucharist a converting ordinance, the mainspring of the Church's mission to individual sinners and to mankind."[25] Those in his congregation at Kingsway used to remark that once Donald pointed to the table and invited everyone to participate, he created that real sense of presence. "In the Sacrament of Christ's broken body and shed blood," wrote Dr John Newton, "the way of sacrifice, which underlaid Donald's pacifism, is clearly set forth. The material elements of bread and wine highlight the importance of created things, matter, the body, the day-to-day stuff of human living, which inspired his social and political concerns."[26] He repeatedly said that he couldn't go into Hyde Park on a Sunday afternoon unless he had presided at the Lord's Table.

By the end of 1949 MSF London was meeting regularly at Kingsway and Donald, on his accession to the presidency, aimed to enhance the importance of Holy Communion by celebrating it more frequently, raising the fear among some of his colleagues that Methodism was becoming too priest-ridden. What particularly provoked disquiet was a letter in the *Methodist Recorder* on 29 March 1951 from him and the Secretary of MSF, Dr Donald Sharp, denouncing certain aspects of contemporary Methodism, especially the neglect of administering the sacraments. Not only did this give rise to irrelevance, drabness and even squalor in worship, they contended, it deprived evangelism of the opportunity to flourish. "Further we assert that the sacramental basis of evangelism is Methodist as well as apostolic, and only such a basis can protect evangelism from mere emotionalism on the one hand and arid morality on the other." Equally crucial was the prospect of Christian reunion. "Yet it is of the utmost importance that our place in the Catholic tradition be recovered, while our place in the Protestant succession continues to be stressed. Proper and essential to both these roles is the sacramental nature of the Christian Church and its worship, the treasuring of its historic creeds, the maintenance of its liturgical glories – in short, a zealous care for those characteristics of the Catholic Church which still offer the only sure foundation upon which to build the United Church of Christ which is to be. With this spirit and temper our people must join forces with all movements towards one united Body of Christ!"[27]

If lacking the drama of Luther nailing his ninety-five theses to Wittenberg Cathedral door, Donald's letter still aroused the strongest of emotions as the *Methodist Recorder* became embroiled in heated debate over the course of the next month. There were those like David Mason who fully supported his depiction of contemporary Methodism. He lamented the fact that those of his vintage drawn to the Church by inspirational ministers during the war years, had been disillusioned by the insularity they had found. "We thought we were joining a communion of the catholic Church," he wrote, "and instead discovered a sect."[28]

The vast majority thought otherwise, believing that MSF was over emphasising the sacraments. On 24 May Donald and Sharp responded to these concerns by rightly placing their sacramentalism within the tradition of the Wesleys, and reassuring their critics that they weren't belittling the importance of preaching and extempore prayer. They finished by once again stressing the importance of both Holy Communion and Methodism in the quest for reunion between the Church of England on the one hand and the Free Churches on the other.

Donald's deep personal commitment to sacramental worship, which grew ever greater as he grew older, carried with it a certain subsidiary doctrine. Unlike many of his colleagues, he never doubted the reality of sin either at personal or community level. Indeed, his conviction of its reality became more profound. Not only did the social blight of war and poverty remain unresolved, he also witnessed the baleful effects of the permissive society with many parents failing to give an adequate moral lead to their children, not least in their responsibility to others. To him, sin was the second most powerful force in the universe after the love of God and it needed to be confronted by the Church, for to talk about religion without sin was like discussing gardening without mentioning weeds. This then placed a special onus on penitential prayer (a particular discipline which many contemporary Christians find difficult to practise), since only through prayer could one secure forgiveness and find the strength to serve God.

This need for penitence and forgiveness became ever more important to Donald during his final years when looking back with regret over past imperfections in his character, and realising that he had little time left to do anything about it. Throughout his career he commended the power of forgiveness for many a miscreant so they could be free to begin anew, a conviction which had informed his attitude to penal reform. He also practised what he preached in his personal life, since it was rare for his anger towards others to be more than a passing phase. So it was with some irony that just at a time when society was casting aside the act of penitence, not least with the abandonment of the traditional Sabbath, he increasingly came to lean on it as the gateway to hope. "We need God's help," he remarked during the last year of his life, "and penitence is the opening of the door to the required power whereby the Kingdom of God comes and at the same time there comes the determination to take up the Cross in faith."[29] It was in this context that the Three Hour Service on Good Friday meant so much to him – the opportunity to look on that "dear disfigured face".

In May 1951 Donald joined forces with Geoffrey Fisher, the Archbishop of Canterbury, to address 6,000 at the Festival of Britain United Christian Rally of Anglican and Free Churches; a cause close to his heart. In June he became President of MPF following the death of Henry Carter and in August he led a highly successful OCW trip to Cardiff, teaming up with the Labour MP George Thomas, himself a well-known Methodist lay preacher.

At the end of August Donald set off on his most lengthy mission ever, with a three-and-a-half-month tour of the United States, Canada and Australia. His first engagement was the National Convocation of Methodist Youth at Purdue University, Indiana, presided over by an African-American pacifist in an enormous concert hall similar to the Rockefeller Centre. In stifling heat, his talk was well received and he later enhanced his reputation by trouncing a local chaplain in a debate on pacifism. As he surveyed the full array of mission activities, not least the splendour of the folk festival, he was astounded by the wealth and initiative on display and much taken with the quality of the young Methodist leaders. He continued his tour of the American Midwest with visits to Detroit, where a speaking engagement at an English-style school at Cranbrook left him impressed, Chicago, Evanston and Wooster "as pleasant to revisit as to see the first time". His audience, however, containing many students, failed to match the quality of the surroundings. "How these middle-class Americans love to play at religion," he wrote acidly, "how superficial is their thinking on it."[30] After lunch the next day at the Southville Inn in Wooster, "a phoney reproduction of an old English pub", he motored the considerable distance to Delaware, finding it difficult as a notoriously quick driver to keep to the sixty-mile per hour speed limit. Once again, he was damning about his audience at the Pastors School, stating unreservedly that "many of these middle aged pastors are quite unequal to the job they are having to do".[31]

Donald was complimentary about his time at the FOR International Conference at Lakeside, Ohio, where he enjoyed swimming in the lake and lecturing to good effect on "The Pacifist Message for Today". His final port of call on the North American continent was Vancouver to stay with the Wool-lards for an intensive three-day mission during which he barely paused to draw breath. Having opened to a packed meeting at the Anglican cathedral, he drew another capacity crowd in New Westminster, the old capital of British Columbia, as well as recording five Evening Services straight off at the broadcasting station. An interview with a dissolute reporter with a hangover was the only minor blemish to an otherwise highly successful trip in which many people were led to a clearer understanding of their lives. Nearly 2,000 attended the final meeting in the Domain and the fruits of these labours were later harvested with the establishment of an OCW branch in Vancouver, the first of its kind in Canada.

From Vancouver, Donald journeyed to Australia to participate in the Crusade for Christ, spending much of the time in conversation with an Australian farmer who refused to believe that he was a cleric. He dismissed Honolulu as cheap, commercial and pagan, the playground of the American lounger. Fiji, in contrast, he thought a very beautiful English crown colony. "Very restful after the United States," he confided. It was the calm before the storm, since his arrival in Sydney saw him step straight into the fiery furnace on an issue then polarising his hosts.

The Crusade for Christ was the brainchild of J. W. Burton, the President-General of Australian Methodism in the immediate aftermath of the Second World War. Inspired by the eager involvement of the Methodist Church of America (previously the Methodist Episcopal Church) in evangelism, Burton found support from his colleagues for a three-year crusade beginning in 1949 to get people back to church, train up Sunday School teachers and increase giving to charities. It was to give the crusade a fitting climax that Donald was invited by the Council to undertake a three-month tour with the express hope of galvanising the local churches into supporting the venture. Sadly, such hopes, as Donald was soon to discover, were misplaced as many stood idly by. Their apathy was mainly self-induced, coupled with considerable resentment at his political maladroitness.

In the wake of the fall of China to the communists in 1949 and the ideological struggle then raging in Korea, the right-wing-inclined Government of Robert Menzies had exploited the fear of communism in the region to declare war on the Australian Communist Party. A referendum seeking public support to amend the constitution so that Parliament in future could dissolve the party was scheduled for 27 September – twelve days after Donald's arrival.

Even allowing for splits within the Australian Labor Party caused by the Roman Catholic Archbishop of Melbourne Daniel Mannix's fervent opposition to communism, the referendum had broadly divided the country along left-right lines, with the Labor Opposition under Dr Herbert Evatt claiming that they were defending democracy against a police state. Consequently, with feelings running high, it appeared an inopportune moment for someone of Donald's divisive temperament to be appearing on the scene. Whether the media anticipated trouble or not is unclear, but they turned out in force at Sydney Airport for his arrival to hear him out. He kept his replies commendably general. He had no fear of communist interjectors when preaching, he informed them. They were very vulnerable once you understood them. "I find communists easy to handle if you get them face to face instead of shouting at them from a distance. When they talk they make more heat than light."[32] After the press conference, he was welcomed by the Federal Crusade Director, the Revd Norman Pardey, and entertained by his Sydney hosts who prayed that his visit would bring a great spiritual revival. Donald in turn thanked them for their welcome and informed them of the deep sense of responsibility he bore. That evening, before he went to bed, he read the papers to acquaint himself with the main facts about the referendum. Then, having convinced himself that the ban was an offence to freedom, he decided to declare his hand.

With much advance publicity given to his leadership of Sydney Methodist Week, Donald was rarely short of an audience as he began an onerous schedule the next day at Lindfield Church by talking about the Church being the body of Christ. The official launch came that afternoon in the Domain, the Sydney equivalent of Speakers' Corner, where in front of an expectant crowd of 3,000, boosted by a few communists from a nearby meeting, he talked about "Christianity and Chaos". Heckled from the beginning, he was asked about ministers standing up for a "No" vote in the referendum. Making clear that he was speaking for himself and not his Church, he said he supported such a move, since there was ample provision in the Crimes Act to deal with subversive groups.

His words met with a mixed response. Some cheered loudly, others objected. One minister shouted out, "This is your view," and as a group of his colleagues went into an anxious huddle to discuss this turn of events, another suggested turning off his microphone, something which subsequently happened, although the organisers later claimed that it was a mere accident. Undeterred, Donald continued to speak without power, and warming to his theme, exclaimed that if they were going to outlaw communism they would have to do it by Christian methods as opposed to political ones. "The more you drive communists underground the more they increase and start underground movements. They are the movements that have changed the world. That is what frightens me about chasing the communists underground. I believe in British justice and not in the legislature and executive taking over the powers of the judiciary."[33] Cautioning against the use of similar methods to the ones employed by the Pharisees against Jesus, Donald concluded his homily by urging his audience to show communists a better way of life.

Coming at such a sensitive time in the referendum debate, Donald's comments were headlines the next day, much to the embarrassment of his hosts. The President of New South Wales Conference, Dr A. M. Sanders, denied that Donald was voicing the opinions of the Methodist Church in the state. "I, as president, am the only one who can give the Church's view on the referendum," he declared gruffly, "and we refuse to do that. No church has the right to dictate to people on how they should vote." Equally strenuous in his reaction was the Prime Minister, who at a large rally at Hurtsville two days later, bitterly attacked Labor's allegations that Government powers would be used against non-communists, quoting the legal opinions of two eminent New South Wales KCs to support his case. Then in sardonic mode he continued, "It is true that these KCs did not have the advantage a reverend gentleman had yesterday of arriving in the country for the first time and then in one hour mastering the constitution, the Statute Law of the Commonwealth Parliament and a knowledge of our circumstances. He must be a brilliant if conceited man to learn all these things in one hour. I devoted twenty years of my life to learning them. Let me say at once on behalf of all the people of Australia," he continued to loud applause, "we are quite competent to deal with our problems and we propose to do so."[34]

The political tornado unleashed by Donald's comments caused consternation among his hosts on the Welcoming Committee, some of whom began to have second thoughts about his visit. Any initial plans of inviting Marie out to join him were quickly shelved. "My speech cooked that goose," he admitted.

What's more the Church, as he soon recognised, became less receptive to his message as the controversy continued to dog his meetings and raise his ire. This disillusionment, his diary entry for 19 September, his fourth day, makes clear. "Arose early to speak at Methodist Ladies' College. [the Sydney equivalent of the Melbourne school]. Regaled the little brats with a story or two. Then argued the 'No' case in the referendum."[35] That evening he spoke at Sydney Town Hall. "Town Hall Meeting by no means full and I am feeling the strain of almost continual talking. Not a good meeting. The controversy of the referendum has divided the Church."[36]

After a week in Sydney the highlight of which, aside from a brilliant talk to the Student Christian Movement at Sydney University, was his second meeting in the Domain, he journeyed west to Bathurst. "A month gone and it seems a year," he sighed. His spirits were raised by an invigorating drive into the Blue Mountains, some of the most enticing scenery he had ever seen, and in this enchanting atmosphere he found himself pondering the character of Australia. His verdict displayed a certain ambivalence which already existed and remained with him thereafter. "The crude are very crude," he wrote. "There are a great many lazy people, but it is a good land and a promising one."[37]

As the quintessential public performer Donald came alive when surrounded by large crowds, taxing questions and a buoyant atmosphere. He found anything less debilitating, yet now as he explored Australia his discovery of a prolonged indifference to his Christian message weighed heavily on him. Some of his frustration could be attributed to natural fatigue and loneliness. The rest, according to David Mason, could be explained by the fact that he had never been an ordinary Circuit Minister working outside London. This quirk of fate had sheltered him from much of the mediocrity which afflicted his Church. "He spoke of Circuit Rallies and Mass Anniversaries," Mason recollected, "and knew nothing of an ordinary Sunday service in provincial Methodism."[38]

The first real signs of his black mood came in Wollongong, an industrial town south of Sydney, where, after a surfeit of poor crowds and meaningless speeches, he wrote dejectedly, "This Crusade for Christ doesn't exist. I feel I'm here under false pretences."[39] A couple of days later in Cessnock, a mining town in the Hunter Valley some way to the north of Sydney, he was equally downbeat, lamenting the curse of fundamentalism "which isn't Christianity at all but another religion", and the demoralizing lack of support from the local churches. His melancholia, enhanced by the gravity of the dispute between Britain and Persia over the latter's nationalisation of the Anglo-Iranian oil company, could well have also been related to the continuing furore within Methodist circles over his diatribes on the referendum. The letters column of the *Methodist* was totally preoccupied by the affair. Most not only disapproved of his views but also his undermining of a specifically Methodist celebration by talking about Caesar rather than God. These views were echoed by an unusually astringent editorial in the *Methodist* on 29 September.

"The week of special witness would, we believe, have been much more influential for good if the Doctor had stayed clear of current political controversies, had been more expository in his preaching and teaching, and had either ruled out questions altogether at the end of his addresses, or had decided to answer only such questions as arose out of the subject-matter with which he had been dealing. As things were, many good people were grievously and some needlessly hurt by statements, which, though made in all sincerity, had only a very remote bearing upon the objectives the General Conference had in view when the Crusade for Christ was launched."[40]

Such was the strength of feeling that Norman Pardey felt compelled to come to the aid of his guest in a letter to the *Methodist* in that same edition. He had been brought to Australia, he explained, to reach principally secular people who were asking questions not being answered by the Church. "Dr Soper answered fearlessly many of these questions on Sunday the 16th, but central in his address was Christ, whom he exalted in a soul-stirring utterance."[41] While the row rumbled on, Donald, in low spirits, journeyed to Newcastle, convinced that his message was failing to ignite the locals as he surveyed more empty seats. Whatever his private consternation about the poor attendance in some of the country areas it didn't prevent him turning in his usual polished performances. According to J. W. Staines, the Deputy Principal of Newcastle Training College, many agnostic teachers who went to hear him found him compellingly interesting, witty, provocative and relevant. "Dr Soper," declared Russell Gibson, the Chairman of the Newcastle District, in the *Methodist*, "proved himself a champion of Christianity, capable of defeating in spirit and thought the Goliaths of communism, capitalism and humanism. His courage at question time was only equalled by the completeness of his Gospel message and challenge to follow Christ."[42] In presenting a clearer vision of Jesus Christ for the locals, Donald made a convincing case for Christianity outliving all isms.

He also sparkled on the final leg of his tour of New South Wales after a relaxing weekend back in Sydney savouring the delights of the harbour and surf. At Armidale he managed to fulfil five engagements in one day, including a major speech on evangelism in a packed town hall. Drawing on his frustration with what he saw as the fundamentalist obsession with individual salvation, Donald declared that the current crusade could only be made relevant if the Gospel was translated into the present tense. "I get a bit tired of

Christians who have their coats and hats on waiting for the next world. To make Christianity relevant we have to believe that we can embody Christian hopes in this world. We have to take Christianity and put it into plain clothes."[43]

Condemning a lust for power, be it political extremism or war, he asserted that the basic question above all others was whether an individual life reflected the characteristics of Jesus. The Christian Church could never fulfil its mission until the ordinary rank and file won converts for Jesus. At the local university, Russell Bell, Chairman of the Armidale Circuit, recalled students commenting afterwards on the unprecedented quality of his speech. His visit won universal commendation.

At neighbouring Lismore, the next day, it was a similar story, with even Donald satisfied with his reception. Every minister in the district was present at his School of Evangelism and at a large District rally in Lismore Church, he again attacked fundamentalism. Religion based on fear, he claimed, held out little appeal. The Bible of Christ shouldn't be emasculated by confining it to a string of negatives such as the condemnation of smoking, drinking and gambling. Instead, the positive benefits of life after conversion should be stressed.

If Donald hoped Queensland would be an improvement on New South Wales, he was soon to be disappointed, not least by the number of inebriated Aborigines he encountered, a condition he attributed to their callous treatment by white settlers throughout the ages. His verdict at Townsville on the Great Barrier Reef was one of half-empty churches, conceited hosts and small, dull crowds where once again he was left to make his own entertainment. To one so used to the red carpet treatment, this was all very demoralizing. "Something wrong with Townsville and Methodism," he growled, "or I'm slipping – perhaps both."[44]

Rockhampton *en route* to Brisbane was better as he spoke to trade unionists at the local meat factory and attracted the largest religious gathering in the city since the celebrated American evangelists Moody and Sankey eighty years earlier. Although their form of emotional Christianity wasn't entirely to his taste, Donald was a worthy follower in their footsteps. He concluded his stay with a sermon described by the Revd Richard Pope, the organiser of his trip to Queensland, as one of the best evangelical addresses he had ever heard. The upsurge in his morale was only temporary as he journeyed to Brisbane. "Evening paper has a very dirty letter about me," he wrote in his diary that night, and the Brisbane Rotary withdrew their invitation to him because of his stance on the referendum. Despite attracting similar size crowds compared to his previous visit, he poured scorn on both the abject state of the Church and the decadence of Australian city life. As a keen cricketer, his only consolation was going to the Woolloongabba, the Brisbane cricket ground, to watch the legendary Ray Lindwall take seven for 61 for Queensland against New South Wales. In retrospect, Donald's downbeat assessment of his time in Queensland was to some degree borne out by the Methodist Church of Australia's monthly journal for February 1952. "Dr Soper had a mixed reception," the correspondent wrote. "His forthright utterances were met by disapproval by some, with strong opposition by others. Some of our own church people refused to support his meetings. However, quite a few of his critics changed their attitudes after hearing him. Many who are still critical would have changed their attitude had they given him a hearing."[45]

On his way to Tasmania, Donald discovered that after six and a half years in opposition, the Conservatives, under Winston Churchill, had returned to power with a narrow majority. Not rating the Government's chances of longevity high, he would have been appalled to think that they would be in power for the next thirteen years. As on his previous trip four years earlier, he enjoyed the Tasmanian countryside and polished off a Baptist heckler in Hobart to the delight of the crowd. In Launceston, he met up after Sunday worship with a fellow student from Cambridge, a former member of the Kingsway choir and a Tower Hill heckler, all yearning for the mother country. He left the island feeling that the local churches were mired in indifference and conservatism.

Port Pirie in South Australia where the attendance at the Men's Meeting was a paltry nineteen, did little to disabuse him of this view, but brighter skies dawned at last in Adelaide, the city of churches. Here, as on his previous trip, the response was distinctly more forthcoming, as was a flying visit to the silver-mining town of Broken Hill, where an open-air meeting on its dusty streets attracted much local interest. Content to be staying again with the Hambleys, Donald mixed work with leisure and derived much satisfaction from the size and quality of his audiences. The meeting of the Student Christian Union at the University was particularly memorable since it stimulated activity of an unprecedented type; while a visit to the Adelaide Oval, "the loveliest cricket ground in the world", was an additional bonus.

From Adelaide, Donald flew to Perth over the interminable sandy wastes of the Nullarbor Plain. The journey left him jaded and once again plagued by migraine, while a trip into the hinterland left him distinctly unimpressed. At Colley, a town of 7,000, he counted twelve bookmakers and five pubs, and complained about fielding "the same old questions". Perth, in contrast, he found as beautiful as ever, and a trip on an Admiral's barge of the Australian Navy up the magnificent Swan River helped revive him. "All very proper," he chortled – "little did they know I was a pacifist."

Although the itinerary remained too arduous for his liking, and one open-air meeting was undermined by the churlish demeanour of some drunks, Donald pronounced himself satisfied with the quality of the meetings and the warmth of his reception. The final leg of his tour took him to Melbourne, which he considered a much statelier city than Sydney, and better planned. He received a generous welcome from the Anglican Archbishop at a lunch given in his honour at the Grosvenor Hotel and indulged in some relaxing golf which convinced him that with practice he could become quite a good player, before heading into the state's interior. At Horsham and Ballarat he enjoyed squaring up to the fundamentalists; in Bendigo he was prevailed upon to play jazz on a "shocking Methodist piano" and in Geelong he addressed an "earnest and ineffectual crowd". As he counted down the days to his departure, the mixed reception to his visit continued to bother him. "Hecklers galore and very silly and persistent ones" was his verdict of his final meeting at Yarra Bank. It had been a similar story two days earlier. After a meeting at Wesley Church he felt that he had spoken quite well, "but there is a great indifference to the whole crusade, and it is very depressing".[46] He was being unduly pessimistic since at least in all of the state capitals large crowds had turned out to hear him – with 4,000 in Adelaide's Elder Park leading the way. Certainly his Methodist hosts, while recognising his mixed reception, were extremely appreciative of his efforts as they assembled *en masse* at the airport to bid him farewell. They reckoned that his mission was the most remarkable and fruitful of their generation. Not only had it rescued evangelism from the rut of discredited traditionalism, it had reached out to unbelievers and shaken many churchgoers out of their complacency. "It was a costly mission for Donald Soper," wrote the editor of *Crusade for Christ News Sheet*. "Many did not hear him gladly neither inside nor outside the Church, yet he spent himself unreservedly in the proclamation of the Gospel. We thank God for Dr Donald Soper and take courage."[47]

With hindsight, Donald accepted that his early problems over the referendum, which ironically the Government lost, were largely of his own making. Yet while recognising the difficulty of holding open-air meetings in a hot climate, he once again highlighted the need for a more dynamic Australian Church in touch with the people through a clear message they could understand. Having dispensed his advice, it was now up to others to act on his words because he never again underwent a major tour of Australia. The time away had been too long and taxing and from now on he was rarely absent for more than a month. Even these trips, especially when Marie was absent, were quite an undertaking given the mixed emotions they aroused. The fact that he continued to travel at all could be attributed to his profound sense of Christian witness.

After his exertions in Australia, 1952 began slightly more sedately. In February he was in Belfast to commemorate the sixty-second anniversary of the Central Mission, and his twenty-five years on Tower Hill were marked in appropriate fashion by the *Methodist Recorder*.

"One may agree or disagree with Dr Soper's pronouncements," its correspondent wrote, "but it is impossible not to admire the masterly way in which he preaches the Gospel on the basis, more often than not, of the most unpromising question from the crowd. With a great gift of repartee, he sends them into roars of laughter, and then in the same breath, drives home the point – the more effectively for that lighter touch."[48]

Addressing Durham Methodists at the end of June, Donald was advocating a British evacuation from Korea, insisting that there was more to fear from the immediate revival of fascism than communism. Then it was on to the Methodist Conference in Preston for a possible triumph or humiliation as the question of the Presidency loomed large.

The election of the President of Conference is notable for its open simplicity. At the beginning of Conference representatives are requested to provide their nominees for President. Names are submitted and printed, then voted on with no speeches or bartering accompanying the procedure. Because the first ballot rarely produced a minister with an overall majority, a second ballot was invariably required, at which point the minor candidates dropped out. Although being President was but a brief interlude in the sun, since its writ lasted only for a year, the office lacked nothing in prestige, and even for someone of Donald's iconoclastic temperament, the honour wasn't one to be despised. "At least I'm on that list," he told a friend as he left Bradford in 1950, and after finishing third in 1951 he found himself pitted the following year against the Revd Russell Shearer, a popular Chairman of the Birmingham District. The vote split Conference asunder, but by the narrowest of majorities (279–261), Donald was elected President for 1953–54 and much to the delight of the President, Dr Colin Roberts, who saw him as his natural successor. In a departure from precedent, Donald, in a brief reply, thanked Conference for according him such an honour and implied that Church unity rather than political partisanship would be his priority during his year in office. It wasn't quite to turn out that way.

Days later, still floating along on a cloud, he had a triumph at the Durham Miners' Gala. On a day of interminable speeches, it was Donald's lot to be last in the queue and he began his address to a handful of distracted miners, yet within ten minutes his audience was almost as big as it had been for Aneurin Bevan earlier. Attracted by the sound of loud laughter, the crowds flocked around in their hundreds. There as a rule they would stay until he finished, even in the driving rain.

Creating a sense of atmosphere was one of Donald's abiding qualities, and it explains why he was in such demand as a speaker. William Smith, a Lancashire Methodist, recalled how at a rally in Wigan, after the local deacon rambled on introducing Donald, he stood up, smiled, picked up his hymnbook and said, "What about singing another one of our old favourites?" The lusty singing transformed the meeting and the congregation sat down in great excitement.

David Mason reckoned that this gift, or acquired skill, as he called it, was seen at its best in the open air. "We were on an OCW Campaign in Risca and Cross Keys in South Wales. Donald got up to speak, his platform the back of a lorry... He looked at the size of the crowd with real appreciation. Then his face fell for, even after five or ten minutes, there were no hecklers. And an open-air meeting without questions is like a Methodist Sunday Service without hymns-flat and insipid. So Donald trailed his coat. Nobody jumped on it. He tried ploy after ploy. Silence. Then he noticed an old coal miner in the midst of the crowd, whose face grew redder and redder as the oratory continued. Donald deliberately pitched the full force of his powerful voice directly at this man. Suddenly there was a shriek of protest.

'Sea-green incorruptible!'

'Who?' retorted Donald.

'Harry Pollitt and the Communist Party' came the answer.

And he lived off that interruption for the next twenty minutes."[49]

In September 1952 Donald was back in the United States for a fortnight, lecturing for FOR International. He began his trip this time in the South trav-elling through the Carolinas and Georgia, observing that all the towns looked the same. Big crowds attended his meetings, but he confessed to feeling puzzled about the state of the Church amid such wealth. At Asheville in North Carolina, he ran into trouble at a Baptist college for attacking Billy Graham, the popular young American evangelist, for his authoritarian fundamen-talism. A similar fate awaited him at a Baptist university in Greenville. At Shaw University in Raleigh (an all African-American university) in contrast, he was greatly touched by the singing, while in Atlanta the university was crammed for a productive question-and-answer session. Moving on to the Midwest and Evansville, Illinois, he revelled in the stream of questions from the foreign students whom he considered more intelligent than the locals. The next few days in Chicago and Cleveland, Ohio, left him feeling very tired; plagued by headaches, he found it impossible to sleep. The fact that he hadn't heard from Marie only compounded the gloom. In Toledo he predicted that socialism was imminent in America – a comment which caused some stir back home. Then, on returning east via Rochester where he conducted an open-air meeting in Franklin Square, and Syracuse, his spirits were raised by a beautiful drive through the Appalachian Mountains and the elegance of Baltimore, which he compared to Melbourne. The tour finished on an upbeat note with a magnificent African-American choir in Morgan College Chapel.

The year 1953 was Coronation Year and depicted as the dawning of a new Elizabethan age when the country could line up behind its glamorous young Queen to celebrate growing prosperity. It began in rather acrimonious fashion for Donald in Hyde Park, a place always liable for potential trouble. There had been one particularly toxic occasion in January 1948 when the Communist Party, in retaliation for being denied a room at Kingsway for a meeting, tried to grab hold of his stand. Now in a contretemps with several hecklers, a scrimmage developed, during which the platform was overturned and Donald was knocked from his rostrum. Fortunately, he was unhurt and when two Irishmen were fined £1 each for a breach of the peace, he turned up in court to plead on their behalf. "One heckler out of doors is worth a thousand saints" was one of his favourite sayings, and for all the embarrassment of this episode, it failed to diminish his enthusiasm for the soapbox. How he coped for so long on the front line, preaching Christ against the agnostic hordes, was a matter of wonder. One of Donald's devotees, the Revd Kenneth Brown, a Supernumerary Minister on the Glasgow Circuit, believed that he was called of God and equipped for this witness, which was beyond the reach of any other person. Certainly Donald felt divine providence at work, which gave him the confidence to overcome many of the challenges that confronted him.

Speakers' Corner at the northern end of Hyde Park had been a famous venue for robust debate on every Sunday since 1855. Donald had sometimes joined students from Richmond College there during the 1920s and 30s, but it was the Second World War which established him as a regular fixture. From the spring of 1942 at 3 p.m. every Sunday in all weathers (aside from the occasions when he was away) Donald walked diagonally from Marble Arch towards the West London Mission stand under the trees at the back of the arena. John Gittings, formerly of the Combined Universities CND in the late 1950s, soon discovered that pitching a platform in his vicinity was unquestionably a mistake as he was impossible to compete with, given the size of his audience and the scale of recurring laughter. When he wound up for the afternoon, he invariably received an ovation. The true force of his personality is best gauged by the void left on those occasions when he was absent. John Vincent recalled being made to feel an unwelcome guest by one regular when he first stood in for him in 1952. His experience taught him that Hyde Park only worked by resorting to theatrical crudities to keep the crowd's attention. Leslie Griffiths, the Superintendent Minister of Wesley's Chapel and Leysian Centre, was another who had a searing experience the first time he deputised. "We haven't come to hear you, young man," cried one. "Where's Soper?" "What have you done with the old buffer?" shouted another. "Shot him?"

Because of its more fashionable location than Tower Hill, Hyde Park tended to attract a rather different type of crowd, more female, elitist and cosmopolitan as tourists and casual passers-by mingled with the regulars. The heckling fraternity might have been more disruptive than the dockers (the result Donald thought of men trying to impress the women), but overall they lacked their wit and intelligence, so that the exchanges on Sunday afternoon invariably lacked the elevating tone of Wednesday lunchtime.

Donald's tactics would be very similar to Tower Hill. Having carefully digested the main contents of all the leading Sunday newspapers, he would introduce a topical issue and speak about it with passionate conviction, yet allowing himself to be interrupted, so that the cut and thrust of debate then ensued. Many of the missiles thrown in his direction related either to biblical quotations from the fundamentalists or to the shortcomings of the Church from those of an agnostic temperament. On this latter point, Donald would often find himself in sympathy with some of their reservations, especially over issues such as war and poverty, although commending the fellowship of believers as superior to any secular alternative. More important, he would draw a distinction between the limitations of the Church as an institution compared to the all-embracing power of Jesus, before relating the relevance of the Gospel to modern man in simple but striking terms which would live in the memory.

So consummate was his skill as a communicator in engaging his audience that he became a byword for those aspiring to prominence in the public domain. The Conservative Party, during the 1950s, paid this staunch socialist the great compliment of sending fledgling candidates down to Speakers' Corner to study his craft. Actors and foreign broadcasters were others who took an interest, and even during his final years when he lacked the vitality of old, columnists sent to profile this ageing British institution at work rarely left dissatisfied. Of particular interest to one and all was Donald's handling of the crowd which became more raucous with the passing of the years, especially with the rise of the professional heckler in the mid-1960s and the black fundamentalist preachers. Aware that many of them were of low intelligence, Donald was authority personified, one minute the benign schoolmaster trying to make errant pupils see sense, the next the combative politician trading insults with his opponents in parliamentary jousts. In whichever guise he presented himself, humour was rarely far from the surface. To the man who, in the middle of a discussion on science and religion, butted in with, "Yes, and what about flying saucers?" Donald responded with, "I'm sorry, I haven't the time to deal with your matrimonial problems at this moment." To the Tory who commented, "How has capitalism survived if it is so awful?" he countered with, "Well, sin has survived." To the dishevelled-looking atheist who claimed that Christianity had been around for a long time without doing much good, Donald retorted, while barely looking up, that soap and water had also been around for a long time, and they hadn't seemed to have done much good either.

When a cockney asked whether Jonah was swallowed by a whale, Donald replied testily that he didn't know, but when he got to heaven he would ask. "But suppose," persisted the questioner, "he didn't go to heaven but went to hell?" "In that case," Donald assured him, "you'll be able to ask him yourself."

There were the longer, more heated duels too. Kenneth Brown has recollections of listening to Donald one Sunday afternoon when a little man with a moustache and a silver knobbed stick pushed through the crowd in anger.

"Take that back, you've insulted the Welsh miners," he exclaimed. "I will not take back anything I believe to be true," retorted Donald. At which point the man began to brandish his stick with aggressive intent. "Don't wag that toga in my face," Donald continued, "and listen." "I won't listen, unless it's good stuff," said the little man. "How will you know if it is good stuff or not unless you listen? Where do you come from?" Donald asked him. The man named some place in North Wales. "Oh, do you know Dr Barber, a notable Methodist minister there?" Donald asked. The man said he did and agreed he preached good stuff. Donald then delivered a powerful statement which had the man jumping in anguish. "But," exclaimed Donald with that seraphic smile, "Dr Barber said that." After further bluster the man calmed down and withdrew with a heartfelt invitation to come to Kingsway that evening. And that was entirely in keeping with Donald's style since he liked to close his meetings by bringing his audience back to the central reality of Jesus Christ as the means of securing the cleansed heart and the new life.

For all his mental agility and witty repartee, the key to Donald's dominance in the open air was the perfect voice which resonated across the park, so that during the war it could be heard at Marble Arch Underground station. In order to reach full volume Donald stood very carefully to get an even flow of breadth and speak in a low tone, which is why he rarely got hoarse. In order to relax he would lean over his stand to get the crowd nearer and if his voice began to tire, he would take the heckler from the front. He enjoyed the banter, and admitted to developing a low cunning over the years, not least in evading challenging questions, either by getting the questioner to repeat the question, so that he could think up an answer, or by inferring it was part of another question which he would subsequently proceed to explain. Above all, there were the witty one-liners to act as useful escape routes. An example of this dexterity came not in Hyde Park but in the marketplace at Newcastle-under-Lyme during the 1962 Methodist Conference. The Revd Arthur Valle recalled a man in the crowd determined to ask him if one could be a Christian and a freemason. Donald was reluctant to answer but under persistent pressure he eventually faced up to the question. "Of course you can," he replied, "you can even be a Christian and a Conservative. Next question."

This approach threw up two problems. The first was a personal one. Donald later regretted his facility for making people look foolish, admitting that in winning the argument, he did sometimes lose the man. The second was a more profound one with critics accusing him of possessing a superficial theology which tended to circumvent the truth. There was substance to these allegations, but as Colin Morris has asserted, the open-air speaker must of necessity simplify complex ideas or risk losing the crowd. The fact that they continued to turn up in large numbers for many years was testimony to Donald's greatness as an evangelist, and while for many Christianity continued to pass them by, for others it proved to be the first step along the road to Damascus.

In April 1953 OCW broke new ground with a week on the Isle of Man. After an exceedingly rough passage across the Irish Sea, the sight of Donald on the quayside ready to greet them proved a massive lift to his beleaguered team. The Bishop of Sodor and Man addressed a large opening rally at Victoria Street Church in the capital, Douglas. The Mayor gave a reception at which he thanked his guests for coming to defend the Christian faith. In his reply, Donald sought tactfully to correct him, declaring that their object wasn't to defend the faith as much as to proclaim it.

In a week of hectic activity the campaigners toured schools, hospitals and youth clubs on all parts of the island as well as the new housing estates in Douglas. A particular highlight was the visit to the Gas, Light and Coke Company, which created such interest that similar requests came from other firms which had hitherto refused meetings on their premises.

A most successful week concluded with eight closing rallies numbering some 1,600 helping to give Donald a fair wind at his back as he prepared for his year in John Wesley's Chair.

The Presidency representing the Methodist Conference, the supreme authority for the Methodist Church, still then carried considerable weight and Donald's accession one month after the Coronation was keenly anticipated, not least by the media. They recognised a star performer when they saw one and certainly they weren't to be short of copy as Donald ensured that his year in office would be no sinecure. He wanted to reconnect the Church with the wider world and he would spare no effort in accomplishing this.

CHAPTER EIGHT

The Battle for God

On Friday 10 July 1953 Donald Soper assumed the highest honour in Methodism by becoming President of Conference. Appropriately enough, the year was the two hundred and fiftieth anniversary of John Wesley's birth, since Donald, born exactly two hundred years later, was in so many ways his natural successor, not least in his sacramentalism and ecumenism as well as his commitment to the open air. The retiring President, Colin Roberts, identified another similarity in his induction speech. "Like our founder, you have not hesitated to be controversial when occasion offered." Having invested him with the presidential gown and given him the symbol of his office, John Wesley's Bible, Donald replied in typical vein. "In trying, sir, to thank you very inadequately on behalf of us all, I found some words in the Conference Agenda which I propose to read. They are, 'At 3.15, 214 for three'." (This was the then score in the Test match.) There was more laughter when Donald, with his mother listening in the audience, told Conference, "...you will recognise, I think, the sincerity of my feelings when I say that this office comes to me with a great sense of surprise – a sense of surprise shared by many others.Somewhat presumptuously, sir, a little while ago, I was reminded of the frailty of human wishes when I bought my Presidential suit. Within a week the house was burgled and the suit was taken. I have looked carefully around Conference and, as far as I can see, it is not here, although I have not yet scrutinised the platform."[1]

In his uncompromising Presidential address – one of those rare occasions when he read from a script – Donald painted a picture of a Church and world separated by a ravine. This he attributed to the ever declining number accepting the tenets of Christianity in an age of scientific doubt, as well as the double standards of so-called Christian ethics on matters of peace and welfare. In a world of war and the stockpiling of nuclear weapons, he insisted that the Church should give a clear lead to the Government by renouncing all compromises regarding armaments. In a country still scarred by poverty, he thanked God for the welfare state and treated with contempt the argument that because it was abused by the few, it should be denied to the many. At the same time, he accepted the need for such a state to have a moral and spiritual foundation to function effectively. The answer lay not in individual piety, he contended, but in recreating the kingdom of God. As he looked forward to his year in office, he aimed to take Methodism back into the open air in the steps of Wesley and his celebrated companion George Whitefield, holding meetings on church steps, in marketplaces, or best of all, next to a communist meeting. "Come with me," he said, "and we will have fun in the name of the Lord. No seedy decorum, no truck with bronchial harmoniums, no elaborate programmes, no divisive items by united choirs, but a sanctified 'free for all' – our liturgy the responsive pattern of worship in the cut and thrust of controversy, a true Christian Mass challenging men and women to see the kingdom which is here, though hidden, and to become Christ's men and women, that together with Him, that kingdom may be manifest and become our common inheritance in time, and eternity."[2] The address was longer than most and in the opinion of the *British Weekly* correspondent a remarkable performance, while according to J. E. Rattenbury, "it was the ablest analysis yet given of the mentality of pagan England".[3]

On Sunday, the Moseley Road Methodist Church was packed for the Official Service of Conference, the first time it had been broadcast, to hear Donald preach about the quality of service indispensable to the kingdom of God, a service which, according to Jesus, must spring from love. Jesus gave his time, service, healing, and finally he had nothing more to give except his hands, which were pierced on the Cross. Jesus had further said that those who were to be the inheritors of his kingdom must take up a cross.[4] That evening, with extra police called out for Sunday duty to clear the traffic, 1,000 turned up to see him take on the city's most hard-bitten hecklers under their leader W. J. Harris in the Bullring, the Birmingham site for open-air preaching. The much anticipated confrontation never took place. Harris was so captivated by Donald's opening remarks and his initial response to other hecklers that he was soon doing his best to keep order, shouting to a fellow heckler, "Now he's given you your answer. So buzz off home." When Conference reassembled the following morning, Donald won its unanimous backing for his protest against a poll conducted by the *Daily Mirror* on whether Princess Margaret should be allowed to marry Group Captain Peter Townsend, a favoured equerry to the Queen but tarnished by his divorced status. He called the poll "an unwarranted and disgusting intrusion into the affairs of that royal personage". Conversely, in a separate debate, he insisted that the Church must try to work even closer with the press, which from his experience, had honestly if not always accurately reported him over the years. Other initiatives saw him calling for closer relations with the Church of England, for parents to encourage their children to enter the ministry and condemning commercial television. In a letter to *The Times* that week he, along with two other Free Church leaders, dubbed it as unnecessary, unwanted and unwise, and called on the Government to permit a free vote when the Commons debated it that autumn. Donald made one other major intervention in the debate on the Strategy of Evangelism, warning of the need to amalgamate churches and find ready substitutes for the decline of Evening Service as congregations spent Sunday evenings at home. Above all, he stressed the need for caring rather than correction, believing that they should "find a place in the porch for those who are not ready to come into the pew". Turning to the revolutionary power of the Lord Jesus Christ as the means to bring about change, he ended with an appeal to Conference that it follow him down the royal road towards God's kingdom. Away from the main proceedings, he was heavily in demand, addressing the OCW in Smethwick, signing autographs in the open air in Walsall and delighting 2,000 at the National Children's Home Conference Rally with his rendition on the tin whistle of "The Girl I left Behind Me". So rapturous was the applause that he did an encore on the piano with "Annie Laurie".

"Prophecy," stated the *British Weekly* on 23 July, "is a hazardous business. Though the prediction that this would be Donald Soper's Conference has been well maintained, the fulfilment has been manifested on unexpected lines. This many-sided personality has revealed a genius for chairmanship reminiscent of old Jolyon Forsyte's way with shareholders. The platform has been in control, with the result that business was finished on Thursday evening – a modern record for celerity."[5] To all those acquainted with Donald's committee work at the West London Mission, these compliments wouldn't have come as a surprise. Not only did he display a thorough grasp of even the most intimate procedures, his chairmanship brooked no tolerance for prolixity, as Dr E. Benson Perkins, one of the great Conference characters inclined to garrulity, discovered. "Mr President, I must admit I don't know much about this issue," he began. "Thank you very much, Dr Benson Perkins," replied Donald beckoning him to sit down again.

And so began an extraordinary year full of incidents and controversy during which the *Methodist Recorder* received 500 letters per week on issues raised by the President or about the President himself. One of his main responsibilities was to deal with the volume of correspondence requesting visits, photographs, autographs and forewords to unknown publications in addition to sorting out personal problems and mediating in local disputes. Donald, according to Presidential tradition, visited as many parts of the country as possible; his novel stipulation being that each visit should include a service of Holy Communion and an open-air meeting.

Being a stickler for perfection, he liked to be fully involved in the drawing up of his itinerary and the order of service, not least the appropriate choice of hymns. As one of the biggest names in the Church and a public controversialist in his own right, it didn't need his Presidential status to ensure widespread interest in his visit. Not surprisingly local ministers, savouring the prospect of their church filled to overflowing, felt much in his debt and most bent over backwards to give their eminent guest an effusive welcome, although occasionally this was tempered by reference to his uncompromising views. "We always like to hear Dr Soper," one remarked, "although we cannot agree with his views. Before he speaks to us, the choir will sing the anthem 'Surrounded by a Host of Foes'," an ironic choice that caused Donald much merriment when he recited the story thereafter.

During his sallies to different parts, Donald would often stay with local ministers and prove highly popular with his hosts, especially since he was a man of few demands. Kenneth Greet recalled how on one occasion he was the guest of a nervous superintendent, who told him that his young colleague was thinking of going over to the Anglicans. Would he be kind enough to have a word with him? The next morning at 11 a.m. Donald called at the manse. The door was opened by the minister's wife. "And who might you be?" she enquired. "Well, I might be the King of Siam," came the instant reply, "but I happen to be President of Conference." "Oh," she said, "my husband isn't up yet." Donald assured the superintendent on his return that he had encouraged the young man to join the Anglicans as soon as conveniently possible.[6]

Despite all his Presidential commitments, he was determined that Kingsway, Tower Hill and Hyde Park weren't left out in the cold, and that OCW, which was running four camps that summer, wasn't neglected. Consequently he spent two days each at Oldham, Exeter, Settle and Bentham. Wherever he went large crowds gathered to hear him, and the caretaker of the large public hall in Oldham who dubbed the decision to put out so many chairs as stupid, was forced to eat humble pie when the hall was filled to overflowing. In a debate with Tom Rowlandson, the communist parliamentary candidate for Wigan, Donald placed his hopes for peace in Jesus Christ because he was the only practical revolutionary who knew how to conduct a revolution. Other revolutionaries in comparison couldn't run a whelk stall. His speech won a warm hand, but Rowlandson too drew applause when he observed that a wider gulf existed between Donald and a Christian such as Senator Joseph McCarthy, the leading influence behind the anti-communist purges in the United States at that time, as opposed to between Donald and himself.

In Exeter, the Civic Hall used for all kinds of political and recreational activities had never before been filled for two consecutive nights as Donald took questions for ninety minutes. On the second evening, he was in a trenchant mood when he squared up to some fundamentalists, some of whom were out to test his orthodoxy. Asked by a voluble questioner if it would be better for those engaged in Christian witness to concentrate on the saving truths of the Gospel and not the things of this world, Donald, eyes blazing, was scathing in his reply. "It is arrogant rubbish, and I'm not prepared to listen to it any more when a well-dressed young man tells me we should have nothing to do with the things of this world. I take it that he has a ration book?" He ended: "Now I love you, but I don't like you at this moment."

That wasn't the only fundamentalist to get his come-uppance. To a truculent heckler who was monopolising the questions Donald said sharply, "Now we've had enough of you; one more question, and then shut up." "All right," the heckler replied. "Tell me, Dr Soper, is your name written in the Lamb's Book of Life?" "Written in it?" replied Donald, "It's printed on the cover!"

On 10 September, prior to conducting a broadcast service from Kingsway on the first Sunday of the new Methodist year, a plaque commemorating his Presidency was unveiled in the foyer. In his sermon, Donald pronounced upon the need to evangelise in the tradition of Jesus, emphasising its social righteousness. Later that month, when addressing the annual valedictory service for Methodist missionaries, he said that knowing something about the problems of evangelising to a secular society, he wanted to offer them experience rather than advice. He felt he knew more about the truth when responding to a heckler than reading a book or sometimes saying his prayers. Evangelising could take its personal toll, he readily acknowledged, but commended the vitality, excitement and joy in aggressive Christianity.

That month saw him back in the political domain. Responding to a Government Royal Commission on Capital Punishment, Donald wanted to raise the basic question of whether the death penalty could be completely abolished. As far as he was concerned, the Church should condemn it as an archaic and unchristian example of barbarism. Later, he also wanted a long overdue Royal Commission to enquire into homosexuality, promoting tabloid headlines of "Dr Soper calls for probe into vice", and a gentle admonishment from the *Methodist Recorder*. It worried that his statement would be seen as unduly gratuitous, especially his observation that "a mixture of paganism and national conscription has weakened the resistance of many young people to temptations they would otherwise have resisted".

October began with Donald, at the invitation of Clement Attlee, preaching to the Labour Conference at Margate and defending political intervention by the Church to establish the kingdom of God in the world as the only means of achieving real progress. He then embarked on profitable trips to South

Yorkshire and the Potteries where the only discordant note came in an open-air meeting in Bradford when a firework exploded in front of him. "That was the action of an idiot," he commented.

November engulfed his Presidency in controversy, when in response to a question in the open air at Deansgate in Manchester, Donald reprimanded the Queen for going to the races. "She would be very much wiser if she kept away from the sport of kings. It is very obviously a household of racketeers. You know it, and I know it."[7] He repeated his remarks on the Mound in Edinburgh the following Sunday as he made a rare foray north of the border. Such comments nowadays would barely raise a flicker of interest but then, in a much more deferential age, this attack on the newly-crowned monarch sent everyone into convulsions. Donald tried to place his criticisms in context by saying that, although he admired the Queen, her subjects couldn't afford to be gambling on horses, comments which upset Fleet Street and prompted a headline in the *Daily Sketch* of "Stop Nagging the Queen". Others rushed into the fray. The Mayor of Berwick-upon-Tweed called off a reception for him on his forthcoming visit to the town (this didn't stop Donald cheekily holding a meeting on the steps of the Town Hall), Taunton School withdrew an invitation to lead a mission there, and the *Methodist Recorder* published scores of letters from irate readers criticising him for his republicanism. It needed support from an unlikely quarter to redress the balance. An editorial in the *British Weekly* declared that Donald was one of the few men to get a hearing for the Christian Church. "Jesus hit the headlines of his day … We have to learn all over again the 'necessity for mixing it', as our American friends might say. Soper 'mixes it'. Not always can all Christians agree with him. What does this matter? Life is better than agreement."[8]

No sooner had he reprimanded the Queen than he turned his attention to her husband. Having implored him in Manchester to give a lead to young people by telling them about God, he kept him in his sights with an article in the *Daily Herald*. Having paid tribute to Prince Philip as a sportsman and a family man, he denounced him for playing polo on Sunday, declaring that as a Royal he should set an example to others. And this, despite a recent admission that he himself often swam on Sunday when on holiday, even admitting to concealing his trunks under his cassock as he worshipped. Again, the vultures gathered. First to plunge the knife in was the *South Wales Echo and Evening Express*. "Dr Soper knows the Royal Family cannot answer back," opined its Monday Miscellany columnist. "He hits them. He allows himself to bathe in the sea but condemns a young man for riding a horse on Sunday. This is the sort of headline Christianity that drives youth out of churches."[9] Next, there arose an unusually astringent editorial in the *Methodist Recorder*, a periodical whose establishment tones so riled Donald that he frequently derided it in front of his followers. "Twice recently in making pronouncements," it counselled, "Dr Soper has said that he was speaking only for himself, and not necessarily for the Methodist Church. With great respect, that is impossible. Whatever disclaimers he makes, the President of Conference is, for the time being, the appointed leader and chief officer of the Church, and he cannot make statements on matters of national importance or on public affairs without involving the Church .... As a private citizen, he may be a socialist, a pacifist, and a republican, as he has made plain, even if his arguments are far from commanding universal assent. But when he assumed the Presidential office he stepped in a peculiar sense into the public arena, and it might fairly be asked whether some of the advice so freely offered to the Duke of Edinburgh might not be applicable nearer home."[10] The editorial went on to voice regret that on the eve of a major Commonwealth tour when the Royal Family needed the prayers of their subjects, there should be one discordant voice.

The *Methodist Recorder* in turn came under fire from a number of readers who expressed concern that its columns had been the outlet for an unprecedented attack on a President. Behind the scenes in a personal show of support, J.E.Rattenbury was positively scathing in his criticism of the *Recorder*, adamant that it should never have published such offensive material, not least the case of the Sheffield minister who publicly took Donald to task for his views on the monarchy. As far as Rattenbury was concerned, Donald spoke for many regarding the growth of a new culture of emperor worship with the Mayor of Berwick as its high priest. Several weeks later, he wrote to Donald again to say that the *Recorder* had in his opinion acted disgracefully in the matter.[12] In two separate replies thanking Rattenbury for his support, which he very much appreciated, Donald alluded to the unpleasant time he had endured and his desire for the row to blow over as soon as possible.

It was in this spirit that his discordant voice turned mellifluous, when he helped to host the visit of Princess Alice, Countess of Athlone, granddaughter of Queen Victoria, to Southlands Training College for women teachers in Wimbledon – one of the two Methodist teacher training colleges – to open the new assembly hall. Before she dedicated the building, Donald assured her that he conveyed the gratitude of Methodists up and down the country for her presence on this occasion. But any hopes that these gracious words had put an end to the lingering controversy were thwarted by Donald's apparent pique at his omission from the vote of thanks from the Chairman of the Governors of Southlands, Harold Roberts. Roberts, of course, was an old friend from Cambridge, but subsequently had become rather envious of his success, especially given the awe in which Donald was held by his students at Richmond College where he was Tutor in Theology. Whether Donald did feel slighted or not is unknown. Word, however, reached Roberts to this effect, prompting him to write a somewhat defensive missive to set the record straight. On the specific question of the vote of thanks, he explained that having no written record of his remarks, he couldn't verify for sure whether he had mentioned him or not; he certainly assumed that he had. If he had failed to do so, would he please accept his sincere apologies. Turning to the wider question of his reference to the Royal Family which he assured Donald that he would have made in any circumstances, Roberts contended that his support for the monarchy on grounds of efficiency was neither here nor there. Of much greater concern to him was the assumption that they should be in agreement about royalty's desire to serve the country, and that was the point that he had been trying to make. Of course he had realised at the time that some would regard the reference as a veiled criticism. The only alternative open to him was to have made no reference at all to the Royal Family, but that, he felt, would have been open to misunderstanding. Equally, there was no attack on him, he assured Donald. He hoped that he would have refrained from choosing such an occasion to express disagreement with his views when he, Donald, was unable to reply. If, as sometimes happened, he was asked whether he agreed with some views that Donald had expressed, he didn't hesitate to give his reaction whether it be favourable or unfavourable. But students and others were left in no manner of doubt as to his unqualified admiration for his gifts, courage and consecration.[13] Whether this reply was enough to appease Donald, had he actually felt aggrieved, history does not relate, but there is no doubting that all this kerfuffle on top of his many other commitments had added to his burden, especially as there were lurking in the background fears concerning the well-being of his daughter Judith. She was forced to spend Christmas in hospital with a mystery illness, later diagnosed as appendicitis, and it was only afterwards that she was able to make a full recovery. Back at Kingsway for the second half of Advent, much to the delight of his congregation, Donald had the satisfaction of having his Christmas Morning Service televised and his New Year's Eve Watchnight Service broadcast on the Overseas Programme of the BBC.

With the dawning of 1954, Donald met Methodist chaplains serving in the forces, assuring them that, despite his pacifist convictions, his ministry was to all men, whether in uniform or civilian clothing. His message struck a chord and several who met him for the first time found him very different from the fractious figure portrayed in the media. His stock was high too in Essex when he completed his traditional Presidential programme despite the lights failing in the middle of the service. After a trip to South Wales, he began February in the West Country, where in freezing temperatures he continued to hold his evening meetings in the open air. In Plymouth, he attacked the Mau Mau insurgency campaign in Kenya against the British as wicked and dangerous, but called for the withdrawal of all the whites in the disputed areas so as to avoid a racial bloodbath. He also called upon all Christian people to renounce war by doing away with the armed services and when someone bawled out that this left the country wide open to attack Donald was ready with his response. "We are wide open to attack now. We are harbouring by agreement a large number of American bombers. These bombers, in the event of war, would be directed against the East. What these wicked Russians would do would be to try to stop them getting off the ground. In the event of another war, people in Lincoln would be in more danger than those in New York. The best defence, if one is talking of bombing, is not to fight."[14] Once again his approach won warm support from Douglas Cock. "The President is using 'the fellowship of controversy' most effectively to commend the Gospel,"[15] he wrote.

The compliments weren't to last. Soon he was again courting controversy when, at the annual dinner of the London branch of the Methodist Laymen's Missionary Society, Donald railed against the use of totalitarian methods in presenting the claims of the Gospel, equating the evils of religious fascism on the same level as political fascism. His principal target was Billy Graham, America's leading evangelist who had enjoyed a meteoric rise since his 1949 Los Angeles campaign, on the eve of his first major mission to Britain. Despite having attacked him when last in the United States, Donald's imprecise knowledge of him was such that he felt compelled to make further enquiries. He wrote on 21 January to the Chairman of the Greater London Crusade to ask about the tenets of his faith at the same time as writing to Keith Woollard in Vancouver requesting "unassailable facts about him". The chairman sent him a copy of Billy Graham's latest book *Peace with God* and Woollard replied on 27 January. He admitted to having only a passing knowledge of Graham himself, having listened to his half-hour weekly broadcasts *Hour of Decision* for the previous year. Drawing on the help of others, however, he was able to confirm Donald's suspicions that he was right-wing, obscurantist and financed to some degree by big business.

Given these characteristics, Woollard fully supported his refusal to lend any encouragement to Billy Graham. He gave an emotional rinse to people already on the inside of the Church but his rigid literalism, his oversimplification of issues and his neglect of social witness made it impossible for him to relate properly to the people Donald referred to as being in the porch.[16]

Armed with this evidence from Canada, and having acquainted himself with the contents of *Peace with God*, Donald went on to the offensive, describing parts of his book as "intellectual rubbish and emotional escapism". It was a charge he was to return to time after time, the passing of the years barely assuaging the wrath he directed against a fellow evangelist whose campaigns brought much succour to large sections of the Christian community, including many Methodists. His war of words on Billy Graham was ironic because Donald unwittingly was one of the former's great tutors in the art of evangelism, since Graham used to go and study him at Speakers' Corner in 1946, before getting his own soapbox. Now, as Donald continued to launch salvoes in his direction, refusing suggestions that he should meet him (and helping to keep him off television), Graham paid him a great compliment. Anxious to learn further at the feet of the master, he returned to Donald's great spiritual home in Hyde Park heavily disguised in large hat and dark glasses to avoid embarrassing his arch-critic. Initially, the response of the media and some clergy to the 1954 Crusade was hostile, but as huge crowds flocked joyously to the Harringay Arena in North London night after night, the critics were gradually won round by Graham's sincerity and humility. His final two gatherings on 22 May at White City and Wembley attracted capacity crowds of 65,000 and 121,000 respectively, with Leslie Weatherhead for one admiring his way of reaching out to ordinary people by simple, challenging preaching. As Graham now basked in the approval of Geoffrey Fisher, the Archbishop of Canterbury (previously a sceptic), the Prime Minister Winston Churchill and Queen Elizabeth the Queen Mother, only Donald remained unreconciled. "There is not a single reputable theologian in the Churches who agrees with what is being promulgated at Harringay," he insisted. His strident tones, which once again upset the *Methodist Recorder*, seem somewhat irrational, but then he was never a man to compromise if he felt a fundamental principle was at stake. What irked him was Graham's simplistic methods which set store by biblical literalism and sudden mass conversions to a religion based on rules that largely ignored the social setting in which man resided. Consequently, he felt his brand of religion tended to be narrow, exclusive, conceited and intolerant, with strong political leanings to the right. "It is much easier to crawl back into the cradle than live in the real world" was one of Donald's favourite sayings when discussing their respective types of evangelism, and certainly it is true to say that Graham rarely engaged his audience in a way comparable with Donald. It would have been rather like St Paul inviting the Corinthians to talk back to him on the theme of love. Donald was also on firm ground when he questioned the culture of mass conversion, since there was a tendency for new recruits to fall away once the initial euphoria of a revivalist campaign had faded. Whether there was an element of envy towards a rival evangelist stealing his thunder is a moot point. When a defender of Billy Graham complimented him on his ability to draw large crowds (over 1,800,000 in his three months in 1954), Donald replied that the same could be said of Hitler. Whatever the case, the spectre of the American evangelist continued to haunt him thereafter, so that even during the 1980s in the open air, the mere mention of his name (and it cropped up frequently) caused Donald to see red.

As he continued his own ongoing battle with fundamentalists, he also became embroiled in a row with Moral Rearmament (MRA), a conservative evangelical movement under the Swiss-American revivalist leader, Frank Buchman, which rose to prominence in the post-war era, partly because of its staunch anti-communist connotations.

What sparked the controversy was a recent statement by MRA declaring that in India it had been able to have fellowship with other faiths, saying the Lord's Prayer together. When it was decided in the interests of greater fellow-ship to eschew the doctrinal centrality of salvation through Christ in favour of the four moral absolutes, Donald was appalled. As far as he was concerned, you couldn't have the spirit of Christianity unless you had the teaching of Jesus and that teaching had to be based on his Deity and atoning blood. Thus, taking his stand on the Cross of Christ as outlined in the Nicene creed, he denounced MRA both in *Tribune* and at the Methodist Laymen's Missionary Society dinner for preferring clichés to theology. "I have no stomach for attacking any group of sincere people, as I believe MRA to be," he wrote in *Tribune*, "but Christians must at all costs defend their faith from becoming a spineless organism without creed or programme ... They are not going to be palmed off today with the Kingdom of God as a refined brand of the 'American way of life.'" He concluded in the same uncompromising vein. "I appeal to my fellow-Christians – let us not despise or run away from the social Gospel as if it were the poor relation of personal piety. They are the obverse and reverse of the same medal."[17] His words touched a raw nerve. MRA was nothing if not voluble in its own defence as it masterminded a propaganda campaign against Donald, and once again he was inundated with complaints from irritated members. Some objected to him using the pages of *Tribune*, a periodical not noted for its spiritual beliefs, to launch his attack on fellow Christians. The majority disputed his claims about Jesus and testified to the comfort they had derived from the movement. The level of hostility directed towards him in the *Methodist Recorder* again concerned Rattenbury who felt that his Presidential authority might be undermined. This time he went public with his concerns. The row dragged on during Donald's tour to Devon several weeks later. At Barnstaple, ill-tempered fundamentalists bawled out, "Don't clap him, pray for him, he's not regenerate yet," when answering questions about the virgin birth and the humanity of Jesus. At Okehampton, he urged his audience not to rush to the Billy Graham jamboree at Harringay. Rather they should come together in worship locally and ensure that their pulpits were filled with Methodist preachers as opposed to any old figure in the Protestant underworld. His words made good sense to the town's Congregationalist Mayor who described Donald not as a detergent but a good old-fashioned cleanser with a lot of spirit in it.

Before this, Donald had visited Sheffield in the snow and a crowd of 1,000 braved the elements to attend the open-air meeting. The locals liked what they saw, but he managed to upset the leader writers with his desire to see Britain leave the Canal Zone in Egypt and Gibraltar. Foreign and defence issues continued to preoccupy him for the rest of his Presidency. On 1 March, two years after their first effort, the Americans detonated their second hydrogen bomb and when the British Government announced its decision to manufacture one of its own, the anti-nuclear lobby decided it was time to fight back. Intent on registering their disapproval they convened a meeting of 300 at the Commons on 7 April to which Donald and John Collins, Canon of St Paul's, among others, were invited. The object was to launch an action group in the Albert Hall on 30 April to mobilise the country against the hydrogen bomb by collecting one million signatures for a disarmament conference. George Thomas recalled in his memoirs how at the meeting the task of appointing a chairman turned into a vanity contest, as both Lord Beveridge, father of the welfare state, and Collins vigorously pressed their claims. Led by Thomas, the meeting thought otherwise, and elected Donald as Chairman of the Hydrogen Bomb National Campaign instead. Days earlier, on Passion Sunday, he had conducted Morning Service at RAF Cranwell, the first President to do so, an experience shot with poignancy. "I looked at their bright and eager faces," he later told his Kingsway congregation, "I listened to the lusty singing – just young boys – and my heart was turned because even if they go on training, some will die and if a war comes, most will die."[18] To make his point, he was soon walking twelve times around Piccadilly Circus during one of its busiest periods, bearing a massive placard demanding the banning of the bomb – a gesture which upset some. A six-day trip to Cornwall began with a minor embarrassment when the Truro branch of the British Legion refused to accompany the Mayor and Corporation to the service at St Mary's Methodist Church because of Donald's pacifist beliefs. They were obviously in the minority, because every one of the 1,500 seats was full. Despite the wet conditions, and a recrudescence of what he considered to be an unhealthy kind of Cornish fundamentalism, the trip, featuring twenty separate engagements, was deemed a success. During a torrential downpour at an open-air meeting in St Austell, Donald observed that bad weather wouldn't deter the sporting fraternity from watching their team. Why therefore should Christians be afraid of something similar?

There was no let-up, not least in the potential for trouble. In the middle of April, Donald paid a brief visit to Belfast, which he dubbed the city of a hundred religious nightclubs. It was while he was addressing the crowds on Belfast High Street that he first clashed with the Revd Ian Paisley, a staunch anti-Catholic who stood under the banner "Dr Soper denies the Virgin Birth of Christ". Reminding Paisley that Ireland was the home of the woodpecker, Donald advised him to keep his hat on. Then come May, he spoke to hundreds from the back of a lorry in Hull, warning them that Christianity must be relevant, so that it was no good talking to people about fellowship without mentioning wages. He also persuaded Doncaster and Barnsley to turn out in unprecedented numbers to take Communion. At the latter, he made a lifelong disciple of Colin Welland, the well-known playwright, then at college in the town. He later recalled how, having just lost his father and sister, he was rather in the doldrums when a socialist friend of his persuaded him to come and listen to Donald in the marketplace. Having deigned to come, Welland discovered this man with iron grey hair, horn-rimmed glasses with a leather belt around his black cassock and a voice like a foghorn speaking from a coal cart. What immediately struck Welland was the sheer sense of Donald's utterances and his ability to enunciate what he thought. He also spoke about God with such straightforward familiarity without any piety and sentiment. From that moment on, Donald became Welland's man. Next, at Kingsway, he addressed his largest congregation since 1939 on the great cause of the time. "I don't believe war is inevitable," he thundered, "only God is inevitable ... Let us witness in the streets... Placards are more important than leaflets. We must become human placards and if need be a fool for peace's sake."[19] Afterwards, he led many of them through the West End, including the choir in their robes, to collect signatures for his petition to promote disarmament. Even one of the policemen signed. Perhaps his most memorable undertaking that month was squaring up to Oswald Mosley, the discredited leader of the British Union of Fascists, at the Cambridge Union. The Union was criticised in some quarters for inviting Mosley, but before a full house Donald was more than a match for him as he, in a *tour de force*, lambasted his opponent's authoritarian view of the world. He dismissed his burly bodyguards standing round the chamber as men "with thighs like hams and brains like biscuit weavels", before going on to suggest that a new way back for his opponent might be as a Methodist lay preacher. His audience lapped it up and when the vote came, Mosley's advocacy of a motion proposing a legitimate but complete change in the system of government was resoundingly defeated by 704–54.

In June Donald won gratitude for his skilful chairmanship of the Irish Methodist Conference in Dublin, attracted the multitudes in Central Wales and preached to 300 at Wallington, his parents' church in Surrey. At a retreat of the Boys' Brigade at High Leigh in Hertfordshire, he returned to the spectre of religious totalitarianism. For three months, he said that he had been browbeaten by young fundamentalists about the need to get converted. "They have been to heaven," he observed. "I liked them much better before it happened." He remained in a slightly downbeat mood when addressing the Annual General Meeting of London FOR. Reviewing his Presidential year, Donald detected a growing public interest in religious matters, but no strengthening of the true Christian Church. On the political scene, he said that they were getting to the end of their tether. Excessive expenditure on armaments had threatened the stability of the welfare state. In an end-of-Presidential year interview in the *Methodist Recorder*, he warned against the inadequacies of Methodist administration. His recommendation was fewer and bigger districts with Super Chairmen serving for five years and a large monthly assembly presided over by a five-year President to provide greater continuity in policy. His final duty was to introduce his successor at Conference. In reply, Russell Shearer paid tribute to Donald's great chairmanship, comparing him, as his predecessor had, with John Wesley shorn of his toryism and his horse.

And so ended a year which had been eventful, controversial and never dull. Through his multifarious statements, Donald had strained the loyalty of many within Methodism in a role which had traditionally been a unifying one. Equally, by his exertions and witness he had given hope to thousands and placed his Church at the centre of the life of the nation at a time when the World Methodist Year of Evangelism had failed to take off. J.E.Rattenbury, writing in the *British Weekly*, certainly judged Donald's Presidency in a favourable light, he too paying him the highest accolade in Methodism. "Dr Soper has discharged his presidential duties with dignity and distinction. He showed himself at the Birmingham Conference a master of Assemblies; his guidance and grip of the great connexional committees has won great admiration, but the outstanding work of the year has been his Presidential Campaign of unprecedented scope and colossal labour. His open-air activity can be compared with nothing more recent than the like activities of John Wesley."[20]

Aside from his efforts on behalf of impoverished ministers' widows, there was one other way in which Donald's Presidency should be remembered. He paid special attention to groups of ordinands, talking to them in a very moving, intimate way about the ministry in a private session from which everyone else was excluded. Aside from commending the sacrament as some-thing to cherish and encouraging a preaching ministry in as many places as possible, he offered specific advice on pastoral matters, warning about the perils of sexual indiscretion, especially peering down a woman's cleavage when dispensing Communion. Listening to people's problems was draining, he contended, but crucial as it helped to understand them better. Nobody was better qualified to judge given his lifetime of service in such an area and it was very much to his credit that during an extremely busy year in a highly prestig-ious position, he never lost the common touch.

CHAPTER NINE

In His Pomp

During the 1950s Donald was at the height of his powers and his Presidency merely served to stir him to yet more activity as he found fresh fields to conquer. It was a decade during which his media appearances became more commonplace, and his political involvement more intense. Needless to say, such activity brought fresh controversy in its wake as Donald, now the leading Christian socialist of his generation, chafed under a decade of Conservative rule in an era when the Cold War kept the Government's hand close to the trigger.

Having seen his budding career in the media rudely cut off by the war, Donald was soon back in action. In 1945 he contributed to a series on the newly established Light Programme on Sunday evenings called *Talking with You*. His five-minute talks, intensely practical and pertinent, provoked a prolific number of questions from his three-and-a-half-million listeners as they tried to find Christ in their everyday lives. He answered as many as he could, although he kept his advice brief. In January 1947 he led another series, this time late on a Wednesday evening for thirteen consecutive weeks which drew warm words of approbation from James Welch. There was, however, one awkward moment in March when a proposed talk on pacifism reawakened old fears among his superiors. "I feel very doubtful about letting it be broadcast," wrote Kenneth Grayston, the Assistant Director of BBC Religious Broadcasting, "because I think it irresponsible to treat a highly contentious subject in this one-sided way and in so short a time ... Soper would argue that he has maintained fair speech, and that people all know he stands for this kind of thing, which we ought not to suppress."[1]

The next day the Controller, Talks Division, R. A. Rendall, replied to Grayston in measured terms.

"As discussed in the circumstances this can be broadcast. But it must not be allowed to develop into a pacifist campaign as a result of answering letters in the remaining talks of his series. An incident of this sort makes it necessary that in any future invitation to Soper, the terms of reference should be considered very carefully. If the terms of reference are general or vague, we must be prepared to receive pacifist scripts from him. Such scripts may be permissible or desirable but there must be decision on that point at the time of the invitation, and if it is thought to be undesirable the terms of reference must be such as to exclude them without any doubts on either side."[2]

Aside from introducing *Time for Worship*, he frequently led *Lift Up Your Hearts* between 1947 and 1952, the most popular daily religious broadcast, which he had previously introduced in 1940. Then in 1949 he was voted the most popular radio preacher ahead of W. H. Elliott, Vicar of St Mary's Warwick, and Ronald Selby Wright, Minister of the historic parish of the Canongate, Edinburgh. By then he was a frequent performer on television having given the first televised religious talk on New Year's Eve in 1947. Despite a tendency to resort to the smart riposte, he was an instant success, his telegenic looks aiding his multifarious skills as a communicator, not least his ability to speak precisely for the time required. After his contribution to a series from Bristol called *Christian Forum* in 1955, the *Methodist Recorder* was moved to rhapsody. "That man of many reputations, Dr Donald Soper, is rapidly winning fresh fame as a television controversialist. There is a saying by an old Parliamentary master that the House of Commons always loves a man who shows it sport, and, by this token, Dr Soper will never lack an audience, because the one attribute he lacks is a capacity for being dull. That in some ways he is partisan and individual in approach is irrelevant .... He believes in what he says and presents his argument in a way that challenges the listener, either to violent disagreement or enthusiastic championship. He is prepared to do battle with all comers, and on this new field his success is remarkable ... May there be many more opportunities of letting the nation share the privilege of Tower Hill."[3] There were, with regular appearances on television programmes such as *Late Night Final* and *Meeting Point,* alongside guest appearances on many others, either those featuring current affairs or those of a more philosophical bent. Well aware of the benefits that television could bring to religion in creating interest and reaching a wider audience even if this helped bring about the demise of the Evening Service, Donald enjoyed participating and accepted any invitation whenever possible. Happiest on a one-to-one deliberation since this afforded more opportunity to give a comprehensive answer, he nevertheless will be chiefly remembered for his consummate performances as a panellist, most notably his fifty appearances on Radio 4's *Any Questions* between 1953 and 1987, where he was adept at putting the Christian view. Fortified by years of gladiatorial combat in the open air, Donald was instantly at home in the cut and thrust of spontaneous debate, his lack of preparation never placing him at a disadvantage. In the opinion of Raymond Short, he was one of the few natural broadcasters with his capacity to talk to individuals in a conversational tone and look at things in a particular way. The brilliant choice of words, memorable turn of phrase, the good-tempered humour and the wonderfully rich voice, were all powerful weapons in his armoury, and when he delivered a statement it had that air of finality about it. According to Colin Morris, sometime Head of BBC Religious Broadcasting, he also created the quintessential "Thought for the Day" long before it had been officially invented – his starting point always being the leading controversy in the newspapers. He knew how to make headlines, and although his propensity for brutal honesty was apt to land him in trouble, especially when he deliberated on some topic outside his ken, he never complained about his treatment by the media. For he recognised them for what they were: sometimes good, sometimes irresponsible but an unavoidable entity in the modern world. The fact that he used them better than most not only broadly enhanced his reputation, it provided greater legitimacy to some of the causes he advocated, such as his support in 1958 for the development of artificial insemination by a donor[AID] as a way of helping spinsters to become mothers. Another example of his media savvy came in 1960 with the setting up of the Notting Hill Team Ministry. David Mason was surprised to read a favourable piece about it in the Londoner's Diary Column of the *Evening Standard*, only later to discover that it had Donald's hand behind it. "If you're looking for publicity, attack the brewers," he used to tell Mason, and certainly Donald was very adept at getting his opinions across in crisp bullet phrases, which were a journalist's dream. Knowing that they would always get an eye-catching quote, or an interesting new slant on a controversial story which had just surfaced, reporters were quick to beat a path to his door. Invariably he would oblige (although not on a Sunday), but on his own terms by providing a considered reply and making the reporter read it back to him. Consequently, for all the furore that his words might arouse, he was rarely the victim of press manipulation. With all his charismatic gifts it isn't surprising that almost without exception the plethora of personal profiles which occurred throughout his career should be so unfailingly upbeat. Yet what strikes the reader in retrospect is that how even in a more deferential age, the character which emerges is very much according to his own perspective, complete with all his own aphorisms and anecdotes.

In February 1954 Donald began a new assignment which lasted for the next twenty-six years and which featured over 500 articles. Contrary to what he wrote in his memoirs, the initiative for his participation in *Tribune*, the weekly socialist periodical founded in 1937, and essential reading for the Bevanite party activists in the constituencies, stemmed not from him but its editor, Michael Foot. Foot, who along with fellow columnists Dick Crossman and Tom Driberg, led the Bevanite ranks in the parliamentary party between 1951 and 1955, had long admired Donald since first hearing him speak in 1934. Keen to introduce someone of his erudition to *Tribune's* readership, he wrote to him expressing great interest at his remarks disassociating himself from statements made by other Free Church leaders about MRA, and wondering whether he might elaborate on them in several articles. Donald's reply was lukewarm, stressing that present commitments ruled out any such undertaking until the autumn. Undeterred by such a rebuff, Foot was nothing if not persistent and days later, he was back knocking at Donald's door with ever greater persuasiveness. "Just at the moment I think there is a feeling of apathy and acquiescence in the Labour Movement which you can help to remove. Of course I'll not disguise from you for a moment that we are also interested in the circulation aspect of such a series from our point of view ... I am sure that a series from you could give us a very good fillip at a critical moment, one on Buchman, the rest on other topics. I realise that your main difficulty is one of time, and you must be inundated with requests for articles and other work. I do hope that you will still consider doing such a series, if not now, at any rate a little later on. Naturally, the sooner we can have the articles, the better."[4]

His words clearly had their effect. Donald fired off 1,000 words on his concept of the social gospel which was very much to Foot's liking.

"Thank you very much indeed for the article. I think it absolutely first class and we could not have asked for anything better. It is exactly what we wanted, and I'm sure it will arouse widespread interest."[5] He was absolutely right. Beginning with that first explosive article on 19 February, Donald, his services free of charge, became one of *Tribune's* most prominent columnists, his words keeping the letters editor in business. Indeed, according to Richard Clements, editor 1959–82, they had the good fortune to publish what for many years was perhaps the most readable and stimulating column in the newspapers. "Agree with him or disagree with him," Clements later wrote in a moving tribute to his former employee, "Donald Soper maintained a standard that was incredible."[6] In fluent style which never needed correcting or editing, he turned his gaze to both national and international issues, as well as recording his impressions of countries he had recently visited. Understandably many of the injustices he properly highlighted were those associated with the evils of capitalism, nationalism, imperialism, totalitarianism and war, in the same way that the solutions he offered lay in the realm of Christian socialism and pacifism. For a crusading paper like *Tribune* with its radical left-wing agenda, Donald's independent, polemical style made ideal copy, not least because he was so controversial. His socialism was beyond question, but his Christian ideals often placed him at variance with the predominantly secular reader-ship, be it on abstinence, gambling or the Campaign for Nuclear Disarmament (CND). In those skilfully crafted sentences, Donald created an enduring memory for the causes he so passionately cherished, and it is certainly true that on some of them such as Suez, apartheid, Cyprus and Vietnam, his prophetic instincts served him well. Equally, for all his rhetorical flourishes, his insights and predictions on contemporary issues often owed more to wishful thinking than sound judgement.

In addition to *Tribune* and regular contributions to the *Methodist Recorder*, *Kingsway* and the *Hampstead and Highgate Express*, the Sopers' local news-paper in Hampstead, Donald could lay some claim to being an author. Between 1934 and 1937 he brought out five books with titles such as *Christ and Tower Hill*, *Question Time on Tower Hill* and *Christianity and Its Critics*. As the names suggest, they, for the most part, focus on his experiences at Tower Hill. He explained how it all began, the techniques of speaking in the open air and the kind of challenges he faced, and related some of the most memorable exchanges. He also talked about how the lives of certain people had been changed.

Behind the human story he outlined his familiar refrain that, far from Christianity having failed, it was the constant failure of the Church to act as an effective conduit between God and his people. Time after time he found himself sympathetic to many of the barbs directed against organised religion, hardly surprising given his own frustration at the passive attitude of so many of his colleagues towards community action. Yes, the Church as a place of worship could be cold and forbidding. Yes, ministers could be pompous and hypocritical. Yes, sermons could be tediously irrelevant and yes, their message of salvation for all could sound hollow in a world where wars were still common and poverty was rife. It was in this context of despair that Donald commended the human Jesus and his life of struggle, which made him a natural ally to those in trouble. Emphasising his Lord's genius at speaking home truths with great simplicity, Donald, in similar vein, depicted Jesus as a skilled pragmatist able to turn his vision into action. Building the kingdom in the world meant a political programme but although he rehearsed his familiar arguments for socialism, they remain secondary in his writings to things spir-itual. Having relayed the good news for both individuals and communities, Donald stressed that only a life of sustained prayer and obedience to Christ crucified could bring about the power needed to transform society. Such a task was the responsibility of the Church and Donald was unstinting in his support. For whatever their imperfections, churchgoing people were, in his experience, better endowed than outsiders in both faith and character.

Both in terms of sales and critical acclaim, Donald's books were highly regarded. Short and to the point they are readable, containing much that was useful, challenging and relevant, especially to the lay person. To highbrows by contrast, his reluctance to undertake extensive research meant his writing lacked freshness and theological profundity.

Post-war, a collection of his sermons and lectures formed the basis of books such as *Practical Christianity Today* (1947), *Singing Towards Bethlehem* (1954), *The Advocacy of the Gospel* (1961) and *Aflame with Faith* (1963). He also wrote about the roots of his Christian socialism and his attempts to marry Christianity with politics in a way that was thoughtful and provocative. By some way, his best book was his Lent devotional of 1957, *All His Grace*, when he expounded on Jesus' moral qualities such as courage, honesty and humility which were evident during his passion, before going on to commend the Eucharist as the means of meeting the risen Lord.

On leaving office as President in July 1954, Donald and Marie set off immediately on a tour to the Caribbean, one of Methodism's earliest mission fields, for what in many ways was the happiest of all their adventures since the sheer exuberance of the islanders to worship created a most congenial atmosphere. This wasn't entirely the case at the beginning since their first destination, British Guiana on the South American mainland, was in a state of some ferment as the united clamour for independence masked deep racial divisions between the Afro-Caribbean and Indian populations. Given this delicate situation, Donald acquitted himself with commendable discretion, but confronted with an explosive underclass teetering on the brink of starvation, he found the Methodist Church too steeped in a middle-class vestry mentality. More to his liking was Forbes Burnham, a socialist with a Methodist background, who later became Prime Minister then President of the newly independent state of Guyana, but was then joint leader of the multi-racial People's Progressive Party. When the following February Burnham split with Cheddi Jagan over his co-leader's support for international communism, and set up the rival People's National Congress, Donald urged the Labour movement back home to support him.

After British Guiana, the Sopers travelled northwards to Jamaica via Antigua, Trinidad and the Bahamas, winning plaudits as they went. Here in Jamaica the opulence of Montego Bay, home of the fashionable American trippers on the north coast, contrasted very starkly with the desolation of the slums in the capital, Kingston. Similar scenes had greeted them in Antigua, where they stayed in some style with the Governor-General and met the nation's elite. When they ventured out into the rural areas, the depth of poverty on display, especially the huts pasted up with newspapers, palpably shook them, as did the tales of moral degradation. Consequently on their return home, Marie started The Friends of Antigua Society from among young people at Kingsway to raise money for the islanders to build homes for the homeless.

From the West Indies, Donald travelled to the United States as a Methodist delegate to the Second Conference of the World Council of Churches at Evanston, Illinois. His visit was abruptly cut short by the news that his father had been taken dangerously ill. In the opinion of Eric Baker, it was always one of his regrets that Donald's enforced withdrawal deprived Evanston, and quite possibly the world ecumenical movement, of the benefits of his volcanic personality. David Mason thought otherwise. Because of his lack of gregariousness, coupled with his reluctance to do his homework, Donald, Mason asserted, was never truly happy at such events where earnest deliberation blended with bland socialising. Indeed Mason recalled that he was beside himself with boredom at Evanston until the opportunity for an early departure presented itself. The fact that he never attended anything similar again, despite his commitment to the ecumenical cause, lends substance to Mason's belief.

In November Donald was part of a delegation of churchmen to visit Russia. The origins of the visit came through a chance encounter between Charles Raven and Alec Horsley, a Yorkshire Quaker, at the University of Hull in June 1953. Horsley had been in Moscow in 1952 and had met the Metropolitan Nikolai who conveyed to him his disappointment that the only churchmen who had visited Russia since the war were Quakers. Once apprised of Raven's resolve to act, Horsley contacted the Russian Embassy in London to establish the prospects of arranging a visit of British churchmen. After more procrastination and uncertainty, Raven received an invitation from Alexis, Patriarch of Moscow and All Russia, to bring a six-man delegation which, besides Horsley, included Donald, Ebenezer Cunningham, a Congregationalist, and Archie Craig of the Church of Scotland. Having secured the permission of Archbishop Fisher, whose only stipulation was that if they went wearing the pacifist badge, they should do it in a personal capacity, Raven informed the Russians that their visit should be seen entirely in a religious context. He also managed to postpone the trip from April to November 1954 to accommodate Donald, since his Presidential commitments would have made him unavailable for the earlier date. When news of the trip became public, Donald was heckled by a large crowd in Nottingham as they recalled some of his recent remarks preaching benevolence towards the Russians. Asked by a reporter what he would do if they invaded Britain, he replied, "Welcome them with a cup of tea." Not surprisingly when they assembled at the airport it was Donald, much to Raven's chagrin, who received all the press attention as they learnt of their motives for going.

The trip, lasting two weeks, was based in Moscow, but also featured visits to Leningrad and Zagorski. During this time they met Russian Church leaders, attended many services, visited many familiar landmarks and were lavishly entertained by hosts bent on cultivating closer relations. But such an *entente* could not have included an agreement to send a Russian delegate to the World Council of Churches Conference at Evanston as Donald's autobiography alleged, because the Conference had already taken place earlier that year. Donald's address to the Moscow Baptist Church received a rapturous reception from the congregation of 2,000, not least his message of love from many Christian worshippers back home, but his request to broadcast and preach in Red Square was refused. When he asked why, he was told that there was no precedent for such meetings in Moscow. Not to be outdone Donald took from his pocket a photo of Lenin conducting a meeting in Red Square, to which the authorities then replied that the weather was too cold.

As they toured around, Donald detected far fewer churches and services than back home, but those in evidence were crowded, especially with older worshippers undeterred by the anti-religious propaganda still in vogue. He found the faces of Muscovites different but as happy as Londoners, and when he went to buy a fur hat in a big state department store, a crowd gathered round to help him choose it. On their final morning, the Patriarch's secretary placed an envelope on the plate of each of the delegation at breakfast. On opening it they discovered gifts and cash worth nearly £1,000, a bullish gesture from hosts not renowned for their wealth designed to convince them that Russia wasn't poverty-stricken. Tactfully they accepted their largesse and returned it via the collection plate.

Aside from their success in promoting relations with the Russian Churches, Donald returned home buoyed by the visit. Whilst disturbed by the loss of free thinking in every corner of normal life, not least in the Church itself where the priests had shown a sickening adherence to the party line, he had been entranced by the beauty of Russian Orthodox worship and inspired by the commitment of its rulers to eliminate social destitution. In an article for the *News Chronicle*, he described the experience of watching a thrilling advent of the human spirit which was already producing many of the characteristics of the good and, indeed, the Christian life. The idea, he concluded, of a sullen and frightened Russian people whispering their hopes of counter-revolution and pathetically awaiting the day of deliverance from the tyrants who oppressed them was just comic opera. Government in Russia was by consent.

This final observation he was rather to modify when talking to his congregation at Kingsway the following Sunday, as he was to modify his more contentious statements about Russia being a Christian country and their labour camps little different from any other prison. In his more sober moments, Donald recognised that the post-Stalinist era had brought some measure of civic relaxation, but in the age-old struggle between rendering to Caesar and God he found the former still very much predominant. "Outside it, [referring to the Church] the implacable Communist position is restated in all the old stale words that I heard thirty years ago and I thought had been decently forgotten. There is no compromise between the ideology of Stalin and Lenin and the ideology of the Christian Faith. It is only those people who are deluded by their own wishful thinking who think airily any more about an accommodation between dialectical materialism and the Christian Faith."[7] He concluded that there would be no religious revival until a Wesley-type prophet arose.

It was during the early 1950s that Donald forged closer ties with the Bevanite wing of the Labour Party as a sizeable body of MPs and constituency workers took issue with their leaders over foreign policy. Less committed to the NATO alliance than Attlee and Gaitskell, they wished to defuse the tension of the Cold War, so when in 1954 the rearmament of West Germany was on the agenda they were far from impressed. Fearing a remilitarised West Germany would unnecessarily exacerbate relations with the Soviet Union, they took their opposition to considerable lengths. In April Aneurin Bevan resigned from the Shadow Cabinet and in June he was joined by Michael Foot, Harold Wilson and Donald in petitioning Parliament to resist German rearmament. The impasse was finally resolved by the refusal of the French Assembly to counter any revival of German power but not before it had caused ripples at the Labour Conference that October. Donald, for his part, remained deeply suspicious of the right-wing Adenauer Government in West Germany. Sensing that the twin evils of militarism and nationalism hadn't been properly eradicated from the country's culture, he dismissed the substantial steps she had taken towards liberal democracy and European reconciliation as entirely spurious. He saw similar traits in the France of General de Gaulle, so that he would brand the historic Franco-German Treaty of Friendship of January 1963 as a return to the cynical power politics of an earlier era and "fraught with terrible possibilities"[8] as he envisaged a European crusade against Soviet communism. Perhaps it was his lack of experience of all things European which lay behind his failure to detect the winds of change blowing across the Continent. The ironic consequence of such a flawed analysis was that, as the surge for European unity began to gather pace, one of its leading pacifists turned his back on this great quest for peace.

Throughout the second part of 1954 Donald had kept up his pressure on the Government over the hydrogen bomb, with a large rally in August followed by meetings in Scarborough and Sheffield in the autumn. At Kingsway in December, a crowded meeting brought to a close the first stage of their campaign. Bevan, the leading socialist of his time and a hero in Donald's estimation, received an ecstatic ovation and in turn acknowledged his greatly enhanced admiration for Donald on hearing him speak for the first time. But for all their efforts, their target for a petition of one million signatures had fallen far short, and it was only some 375,000 which Donald, accompanied by the Labour MPs Tony Benn, Anthony Greenwood and Sydney Silverman, took to Downing Street on New Year's Eve. They also delivered a letter imploring the Prime Minister, Winston Churchill, to call high-level disarmament talks with the United States and the Soviet Union. Churchill, no great admirer of Donald, insisted in reply that he had already taken this initiative, and because this was true, it effectively spelt the end of the Hydrogen Bomb National Campaign as an organisation in its own right.

Undaunted, Donald returned to the attack with a challenge to the Labour Party to lead the country and the world in the direction of wholesale disarmament. Such a gesture, he assured his *Tribune* readers, would enable the party to win the forthcoming election hands down. On 11 February 1955 he supported Sir Richard Acland, the Labour MP who resigned his seat at Gravesend to fight a by-election on an anti-H-bomb platform, and savaged the Archbishop of York, Cyril Garbett, for his contrary views on this issue. Before the by-election could take place, Acland and Gravesend were overtaken by national events. On 5 April Churchill retired, aged eighty, to be succeeded by his heir apparent Anthony Eden. His first priority on taking over was to call a general election. Returning from a brief trip to Sweden where he detected a socialist malaise in a society increasingly exposed to secularism and drink, Donald saw similar dangers for Labour if it lacked conviction in its message. [9] "This general election ought to be won for Labour," he concluded. "With high hearts as well as clear heads it can be won."[10] The fact that the party was proposing the end of atomic tests, while not going far enough for his liking made them more Christian than Dr Garbett and the Conservatives who proposed doing nothing. As the campaign progressed, Donald was outspoken in his views, upsetting prominent Methodists in Mid-Bedfordshire when, in support of Tom Skeffington-Lodge, the Labour candidate there and a fellow Methodist, he claimed that Labour had a monopoly on Christian virtue. Clearly the electorate didn't think so, for on the back of rising affluence and divisions within the Opposition, the Conservatives increased their majority, their scalps including Acland's at Gravesend. "The uncommitted voter heard no clarion call from Labour to nobler deeds, and saw no solid reason for a change of government" was Donald's dissection of the result. He also felt that a little more courage from the cloth would have worked miracles on an apathetic turn-out, the upshot, he contended, of the recent Billy Graham campaigns. "'When Blessed Assurance' (their theme song) means a preoccupation with spiritual grace and favour which anaesthetizes its devotees against any intelligent awareness of earthly responsibilities and political duties – I find such a travesty of religion insufferable."[11]

His comments gave rise to a long-running spat that July with Lord Hailsham, a leading Conservative intellectual and jurist, about the ethical validity behind their opposing philosophies. The gist of Hailsham's argument in the *Spectator* in an article entitled "Is Dr Soper consistent with Christianity?" was that the Church should act as a unifying influence on issues on which Christians disagreed rather than follow a divisive one like Donald, who tended to fire broadsides at all and sundry. Having experienced unease about his contempt for individual piety, he then questioned Donald's theological contention that the kingdom of God must be sought by political means, arguing that the kingdom when it came was not of this world but within individuals. "It is not for a politician like myself to decry the value or importance of politics or political fervour. But it is surely somewhat strange to find a former titular head of the Methodist community in this country ready to bow down in manifest adoration before so obvious an idol as a political belief, and to claim that it has 'everything to offer to the Kingdom of God on earth'. It may be that he would do well to consider that the true role of Christianity in modern politics is to preach a largely forgotten Gospel to modern politicians, and not to endeavour to win over Christians to a partisan political creed."[12]

Two weeks later, Donald in *Tribune* dismissed the gibe about political parsons and Hailsham's definition of religion, as the inspiration of the voluntary, the service which is perfect freedom. "'My Kingdom is not of this world, else would my servants fight', is far from being a plea for withdrawing from earthly and political affairs. It is a tremendous statement that God's Kingdom, which cannot be brought about by violence for it is not that sort of Kingdom, will be reached by the path of suffering love, which path Jesus was about to take and which path he invited His disciples to take with him."

The kingdom that is said to be within them, continued Donald, wasn't one of spiritual detachment or future bliss, but present reality. The Sermon on the Mount wasn't between those seeking security and material prosperity, and those seeking the other-wordly kingdom. Rather Jesus was talking about one kingdom all the time, which was both the spiritual expression of the love of God, and a political expression of that love of justice and brotherhood.

"The more I think of this uncritical, unhistorical, unbiblical and unenforcable distinction between the world of piety and the world of human affairs," concluded Donald, "the more it seems to me that it is a defence mechanism, a non-mental attempt to justify a prejudice and maintain the *status quo*."[13]

Not surprisingly, Hailsham remained unmoved, and accused Donald in *Tribune* on 8 August not only of intellectual arrogance towards those disagreeing with him, but also the way he deprecated the practice of private piety. He also reproved him for the inadequacy of his doctrine of salvation. Parsons who entered the political arena, Hailsham concluded, rarely advanced the cause they espoused.

Donald's other spat that summer concerned the morality and use of the death penalty which had increasingly come under fire from liberal critics since 1945, when the Howard League for Penal Reform had vigorously lobbied the growing ranks of Labour abolitionists in Parliament.

Brian Frost wrote that it was the hanging in 1953 of Derek Bentley, an epileptic boy of nineteen for a crime which he allegedly didn't commit, that brought Donald into this public debate, since Bentley's father used to go to Hyde Park to enlist his support. He issued a statement when President of Conference, demanding the abolition of capital punishment. His overriding objection was an ethical one, seeing it as a savage piece of cowardice, the legacy of a less civilised age, an evasion of human responsibility and an act of vengeance contrary to the sanctity of life. His experiences as a prison chaplain only reinforced these views, since his discussions with convicted killers often revealed people of pathos rather than evil, unable to cope with the harsh hand life had dealt them. A second objection was more practical. He saw little evidence that capital punishment acted as a deterrent. In many other countries it had been abandoned with safety and without affecting the number of murders committed. It was the hanging of Ruth Ellis in July 1955 – the last woman in Britain to suffer this fate – for shooting her brutal lover which kept him hot on the trail as he tried unavailingly at Methodist Conference to stop her going to the gallows. Her execution at least galvanised efforts in informed circles to have done with this practice. The following month, Donald signed the Howard League Petition along with other luminaries such as Peggy Ashcroft, Michael Redgrave and E. M. Forster, urging the Home Secretary, Gwilym Lloyd George, to reconsider capital punishment. Donald was also a leading member of the National Campaign for the Abolition of Capital Punishment, led by Arthur Koestler and others. Their hopes were pinned on the Labour backbencher Sydney Silverman's Private Member's Bill. The Bill secured a Commons majority of 19 in June 1956, including support from some liberal Conservatives, but it fell two weeks later in the Lords where the Government whips were out in force. Donald took defeat badly, going as far as to predict a constitutional and moral crisis unless the Government bowed to the wishes of the Commons, but his rage engendered scant support as events moved quickly on.

He continued to speak out against the death penalty, lining up behind a number of those convicted, including a Kenyan hung in the Mau Mau disturbances against British rule in Africa. He also clashed with the Archbishop of Canterbury, Geoffrey Fisher, in February 1957, over his diametrically opposite stance to the Homicide Bill, which distinguished between two classes of murder, the more serious carrying the death penalty. What particularly riled Donald was Fisher's contention that there was no immorality attached to the death penalty. "The insufferable element in this statement," Donald wrote in *Tribune*, "is not that the Archbishop defends the death penalty on Christian grounds (though to me that would be bad enough) but that he asserts that the whole question of taking a man's life is not a matter for the laws of God or the doctrine of the Church, but a matter of expediency."[14] His sensitivities were also offended by Fisher's criticism of the Macmillan Government for holding a free vote on the issue since, to Donald, Christian justice would be better served by the exercise of conscience as opposed to the application of the whip. With the Bill passing, capital punishment survived albeit in a rather illogical form. It needed the return of a Labour Government and a Government-supported Private Member's Bill in 1965 before Donald could rest easy in the knowledge that one injustice had been laid to rest.

Now that Donald was past his fiftieth birthday, the physical toll of his various campaigns on top of his work at Kingsway was beginning to catch up with him. Even by his own standards, 1955 was a particularly demanding year with Marie's absence over Easter an added worry as she recovered from a hysterectomy. Although he gave of himself unremittingly during OCW week in Worcester in late August, it was clear to the likes of Renée Willgress, a colleague from the West London Mission, that he lacked his usual buoyancy as he struggled with his sleep pattern. There was to be no respite. In September 1955 Donald went to New Zealand, the first time that the Methodist Church there had brought out a visitor from England solely for its benefit. When Conference extended the invitation the President, C. O. Hailwood, told it to prepare for shocks. He clearly knew his man. Time and time again audiences were astonished not only by his willingness to answer questions of infinite variety but also the devastating honesty with which he replied, beginning with an interview he gave on arrival. One such answer which upset many fundamentalists both inside and outside the Methodist Church was his firm denial of the idea that Billy Graham had instigated a religious revival in Britain. Graham's audiences, he wrongly contended, were exclusively church-going people and hadn't drawn in the outsider. Furthermore, he opined, little of ultimate worth could eventuate from such a theology. Another answer which landed him in trouble was the vexed question of Sunday sport. Although Donald made clear his opposition to organised Sunday sport as a desecration of the Sabbath, his condoning of something less formal unleashed a torrent of fury from clergy and lay people alike. A Wellington Salvation Army officer thought his comments inconsistent in the light of his previous condemnation of the Duke of Edinburgh for playing polo on a Sunday. Then in a stinging public rebuke Reginald Owen, the Primate and Archbishop of New Zealand, claimed that he hadn't found one person who agreed with his proposals. The fact that his silence hitherto on the matter had been construed in certain quarters as approval of them had compelled Owen to speak out.

One of Donald's main engagements was to be principal speaker at the Industrial Relations Conference, a unique event in New Zealand church history, held at Wellington Boys' College. On three successive days he gave public lectures on the practical application of the Gospel into social and political terms. Recognising that industry had an increasing control over men's lives, as well as having the capacity to do wonderful things, he said it was the Church's responsibility to see that those riches were shared by one and all. Accepting that the workplace remained to be converted, he declared that evangelists had to deal with the problems uppermost in men's minds, not the ones they thought ought to be uppermost.

The final of the three lectures was the most political as he declared that only Christianity could provide peace, eradicate world poverty and achieve international co-operation. "The emergence of the nation state is unchristian and produces problems it cannot solve; we don't know what to do with Formosa or Cyprus. We are called in this twentieth century to a world family table. From 'Empire' to 'Commonwealth' was a great step forward. Jesus took a little child and said, in effect, 'If you want the kingdom of God, make a world fit for such to live in'."[15]

Donald's other role was to appear on a panel charged with answering the question "Need We Change the Economic System?" He maintained that there was no economic system in New Zealand. The fact that the country had enjoyed such affluence was due to the abundance of Nature. The Church's business was to look far ahead and adhere to basic principles. Some systems such as communism had had to depart from theirs. The welfare state, far from de-personalising people, was the nearest approach so far to the Christian family ideal which they all shared.

Aside from this conference, Donald spoke elsewhere in Wellington, including an open-air meeting in the Basin Reserve. It was after listening to him that Walter Nash, the leader of the New Zealand Labour Party, called him the greatest expositor he had ever heard. From Wellington to Auckland, and a surprise for those expecting mere fire and brimstone. In a sympathetic profile in the *New Zealand Methodist Times* their correspondent paid tribute to Donald's prophetic intensity and inner strength. "The impression that some will cherish most of this British churchman," he wrote, "will be his quiet, unobtrusive grace of personal presence. He was among us as one who desired to serve, never to dominate or declaim. The rough and tumble of open-air debate has not robbed him one whit of a fine sensitiveness of feeling and innate courtesy. His face is lined, not only with the gradual increase of years in an era of unexampled stress and strain, one suspects, but also because that which he most surely believes has become his through a spiritual pilgrimage that has known the wilderness, loneliness and the anguish of the Garden."[16]

Having made reference to his humour, courage and evangelistic breadth he went on, "Probably most Aucklanders waited for the domain open-air rally on the Sunday afternoon as the peak experience of Dr Soper's visit. If any went to see anything spectacular or expected to hear verbal fireworks, he was surely disappointed. The strength of the occasion lay in the speaker's quiet composure, the direct thrust of his answer, which in several instances left nothing more to be said and those who fain would have taken the matter further would have been wiser had they desisted. The orderliness of his mind and the ease with which he reached up to the right pigeon-hole of his knowledge and produced the answer with its ends all neatly tied up was a delight to watch."[17]

Having talked about the root of Donald's religion being both the Church in worship as well as the fellowship of the city square, and the writ of his Gospel running to the sinister results that emerge from the Nevada desert, he concluded magisterially, "He has done us this great service: he has sharply focused again the problem of the communication of the Gospel. How shall they believe in Him whom they have not heard? How shall they hear without a preacher? Dr Soper has raised these questions to the level of exceeding great urgency for us here in New Zealand. We are surely committed to the task of finding some answers worthy of the man who has come so far to raise such issues in our midst."[18]

Similar compliments were expressed about his visit to Christchurch with the local newspaper calling him one of the ablest religious orators the city had ever heard. After effortlessly seeing off the hecklers at the Edmonds Band Rotunda, Donald gave a stimulating address to 150 laymen and ministers at Durham Street School on Methodist witness. On the following evening at a youth rally in Durham Street Church he addressed the young about the modern world and encouraged them to get involved as Christians. Finally, on Sunday, despite feeling unwell, Donald talked in simple and moving terms about his own relationship with Christ – a testament so heartfelt that it totally disarmed a number of his critics. Others remained unreconciled. "Good audiences heard Dr Soper speak," the Revd Laurie Greenslade, Convener of the Spiritual Advance Committee of the New Zealand Methodist Church, was later to write in a letter to the *New Zealand Methodist Times.* "We feel that in many places they should have been larger but this was largely accounted for by the unwillingness of people of a fundamentalist line of thought to hear him. There can also be no doubt that if one's impressions of Dr Soper were gained from the public press, or from some religious periodicals they would be almost wrong. In this regard our visitor received much less than fair treatment,"[19] a view echoed by Donald himself in the same columns. "First, a feeling that such a one as myself was left rather naked and exposed to a press attack before he even had the chance of defending himself and, secondly, that the almost 100 per cent refusal of fundamentalist groups to attend my meetings created, superficially at least, unfortunate comparisons with other visiting clerics."[20]

The general reaction to his ministry was most positive. Conference formally thanked him for his outstanding service and E. S. Hoddinott, the Chairman of the Otago and Southland District, wrote that "... the visit of Dr Soper has been a vital and invigorating experience and will produce salutary results".[21]

Yet for all the undoubted impact that his presence created, Donald returned disappointed that socialism, as in Britain, was on the wane as prosperity and consensus prevailed. More important, his health continued to deteriorate. Apart from his serious illness in 1938, Donald had always been blessed with a robust physique, but the arduous schedule he kept and the adrenalin expended made him prone to insomnia, especially overseas when he was often afflicted by migraine. This was particularly the case in Australia in 1951 and the United States in 1952. Just before the latter trip, David Mason has recollections of Donald, by now President-elect, experiencing a slight crisis during OCW week with noises in his head and insomnia. For the first time Mason could recall, Donald came up to him seeking reassurance for his performance at various events he had presided over. He imagined that it was stress, and although there is no way of confirming his hunch, he was probably right. For all his debonair brilliance and imperious exterior, Donald combined a restless spirit for action alongside a raw sensitivity that could be easily pricked.

Never able to sit still for more than a few minutes except at the end of an exhausting day, he was essentially a workaholic who lived for the Church and causes arising out of it. On top of his busy schedule at Kingsway he found it difficult to refuse invitations to talk or preach elsewhere, so that often he would be returning to London in the early hours of the morning on the train from distant provincial outposts. Alternatively, if it was somewhere closer, he would take the car and, helped by his fast, erratic driving, which included the odd minor accident over the years, he would arrive at his destination way ahead of schedule. Once the formalities were over, he would yearn for a speedy release, so he could move on to his next assignment. A free afternoon on an overseas mission was all that he could bear, and even so-called relaxing holidays would be a mixed blessing, since well before the end he would be planning the future. Illness was the worst scenario, because instead of resting and getting better, he would use his enforced idleness to dream up new schemes – many impractical – which he would immediately relay to his subordinates by telephone. The burden of responsibility which he carried on his shoulders was enormous, and on occasions such as on missions overseas, he privately complained about his lot, but when his friends and family begged him to ease up a little, their pleas would be in vain. "The only time in my quarter of a century of friendship," wrote Leslie Weatherhead in July 1953, "when I have seen him annoyed was when Will Sangster and I got him on one side at a Christmas party and pleaded with him to make a New Year's resolution to do less. I won't write what he said."[22]

Such volcanic energy would have been fine if there was no price to be paid, but there was, often kept from view. Although Donald was a very courageous man who positively enjoyed the cut and thrust of public controversy, the setbacks and recriminations did upset him, not least abusive letters from which his secretary tried to shield him. He also, despite his martinet image, found disciplining a taxing business as Cliff Padgett, Senior Circuit Steward at Kingsway, once discovered. When the Warden of one of the hostels proved unequal to the task, Donald asked him to dismiss her because of his own reluctance to wield the axe. Even on the public stage he could display great sensitivity, not least on those few occasions when hecklers interrupted church services. Instead of losing his cool, Donald was decorum itself, quietly responding that this wasn't the occasion for such behaviour and that if they had a problem they could always see him afterwards. Denys Orchard recalled Keith Woollard holding an open-air debate in the middle of Salisbury in 1945 and losing control of proceedings thanks to the wrecking tactics of a soldier at the front. Suddenly Donald appeared from the crowd, and having excused himself to Woollard, forcibly corrected the soldier about his history. The soldier, humiliated by the experience, vanished only for Donald to set off in hot pursuit in an attempt to bind up the wounds. "I can't have him going away as an opponent," he said. Quite often, after some of his more heated exchanges in the open air, Donald would regret certain things he had said to people and would sometimes seek them out the next week to apologise. Indeed, from his penitential musings during his closing years a propensity to write people off was one of his faults which caused him most remorse.

Because of his frayed condition in New Zealand, Donald, once back from Margate where he had addressed a Labour Conference fringe meeting about the perils of German rearmament, reluctantly bowed to medical advice and cancelled his commitments outside London for the next three months. His capacity for making headlines, however, remained undiminished. On 28 October he used his column in *Tribune* to assail the atheistic beliefs of the eminent biologist Julian Huxley, in particular his recent announcement that in a hundred years time it would be impossible for an intelligent man to believe in God. "Were this periodical devoted first of all to the defence of Christian theology," Donald explained, "I should be at some pains to argue that there is a great deal more arrogance than erudition in Huxley's atheism – the arrogance, for instance, of claiming that the 'public knowledge' of the laboratory is infallible whereas the 'private knowledge' of the oratory is illusionary". He went on to acknowledge the priority of the classless society, "but I am equally sure that unless the classless society is the Kingdom of God, intended by God and made possible by God, then it is a forlorn waste of time to look for it."[23]

Not one to shirk a fight, Huxley replied that there was an increasing certainty of public knowledge gained by consistent method, as against the infallible claim for certain religious dogmas. Disbelief in God wasn't arrogance. "On the contrary, it is born of that mixture of humility, reverence and confidence needed for any human advance – humility in accepting the facts of reality (all the known facts), reverence in face of the facts (including the facts of our own nature), and confidence in the capacity of human minds collectively to discover more of the truth that can set us free."[24]

Next Donald turned his attention to the Royal Family as Princess Margaret bowed to political and religious pressure not to marry Group Captain Peter Townsend, on the grounds that his divorced status compromised the Crown's position as head of the Church of England. On 1 November he applauded Princess Margaret's decision, referring to it as "the act of a brave and good woman which would do everything to rehabilitate the esteem of the Royal Family in the eyes of many".[25] He had been uneasy about Townsend's marital past, but he was less rigid over the principle of divorce than a number of his colleagues, for while he conceded that an ailing marriage should be saved if at all possible, he also felt that society should exercise its power to provide a death certificate for a marriage which was effectively over. Many years later, when Princess Margaret divorced her husband the Earl of Snowdon, Donald reacted sympathetically. With divorce by then afflicting so many families, he felt it hypocritical to single out royalty for special indictment.

The Townsend affair, aside from its acute moral dilemmas, had again raised questions about the continuing desirability of such indissoluble constitutional links between Church and State. Donald for one thought not, as he disparaged the traditional means of Royal patronage in the Church of England. "It is theologically impudent," he wrote in *Tribune*, "that the crown should ever appoint the spiritual leaders of the Church, and it is preposterous that with the virtual extinction of those royal powers Church appointments should have fallen into the hands of the Prime Minister."[26] He called on the Church of England to demand from the Sovereign that she take the advice of a committee composed of its leading figures instead. While about it, he also criticised the exclusive Anglican composition of clerical representation in the House of Lords, an ironic statement given his later elevation to its ranks as its first Free Church minister.

All these spats did his profile no harm. The *Daily Sketch* voted him one of their Six Men of the Year – along with the Duke of Edinburgh and the actor John Mills – on account of his prophetic nature, devastating honesty and ability to challenge youthful minds in a way no ecclesiastic had done over the previous decade.

The year 1956 was a year in which Donald was preoccupied by foreign affairs as the Cold War entered a new and possibly more hopeful post-Stalinist phase, with the leadership of the Soviet Union passing to the more "liberal" Khrushchev. In January Donald denounced the profusion of US bases in Britain, calling her an occupied country.

In March he attacked British rule in Cyprus, where a nationalist revolt under the religious leader Archbishop Makarios was gaining ground. He called for the removal of the British army from the island and castigated the Government for deporting the Archbishop, since it was removing the one man with whom it could do business. Events were to prove the wisdom of his words. Makarios was released the following year and in time was regarded as the legitimate leader of an independent Cyprus.

Thereafter Donald turned his attention to the Soviet Union and the impending visit of Khrushchev and his colleague Bulganin to Britain in April. With the Cold War the overriding issue of British foreign policy, the communist bogy hung over London and Washington for the greater part of his time at Kingsway. As earlier stated, Donald was willing to be more open-minded towards the Soviet Union than most of his fellow countrymen, although within his broadly neutralist position there were some subtle fluctuations depending on circumstances. Out of a desire to ruffle a few feathers, not least in the open air, he wasn't averse to gilding the Soviet lily to act as a corrective to some of the wilder claims of the West. Yet alongside these seemingly pro-

Russian sentiments, there were some stinging rebuttals of the Moscow propaganda machine. One such outburst occurred in *Tribune* on 4 February 1955, ironically just at a time when Donald was upbraiding the West for their growing nuclear arsenal. The object of his vitriol was the World Peace Council and its attempt to exploit the Church in Britain for peace purposes. "I am quite satisfied that the World Peace Council and the British Peace Committee, which is its typical representative, are primarily organs of Russian propaganda. I would want to discourage peace lovers in England from allowing themselves to become the well-meaning but inevitable pawns of the Russian party line with its insistence that war is the 'original sin' of the Western powers and that peace is the 'immaculate conception' of the Soviet bloc."[27] In the first of a series of three sermons to mark their visit entitled "Christians and Friendship with Russia", he began on an optimistic note convinced that the prospects for world peace were better than they had ever been in his lifetime. Despite his unflattering reference to the Russian leaders as tyrants with hands stained with blood, he recognised that the West was just as culpable for the outbreak of the Cold War. He was also heartened by the first signs of green shoots of political reform in the post-Stalinist era and felt that the Eden Government should use this more favourable climate to build bridges by taking the lead in disarmament. As for the Church's part in the détente process, it should be at the forefront of encouraging sincere acts of unilateral goodwill towards old enemies but further than that its aim should be to win over the Russians to Christianity. To help further this process, he announced that he was writing to the Soviet leaders to invite them to worship at Kingsway. Their failure to respond somewhat miffed him, yet encouraged by the relatively favourable impression of the visit, he continued to give Khrushchev the benefit of the doubt in his troubled relations with the West.

In May Donald was invited by the Methodist Church in Poland, whose mother Church was the Methodist Church of America rather than the British Conference, for a ten-day tour, becoming the first British Methodist ever to visit that country, then under the grip of Soviet communism. Contrary to Douglas Thompson's account which had Donald arriving in pitch darkness to be met by a shadowy figure with an armed escort, purporting to be the new head of the Methodist Church there, he was, according to his own diary, warmly greeted in broad daylight by four leading Polish Methodists, three of whom spoke English.

After two frustrating days constantly checking in with the police, and listening to his hosts bickering with each other, not least over his itinerary, the relief of being able to address the English-speaking school without an inspector in attendance was all too palpable. He also enjoyed preaching in a crowded prefabricated wooden church sent over from America, and the Evangelical Reformed Church, which was little more than a room in the suburbs. Other early engagements included a meeting with the Minister for Religious Affairs, a tour of the Old City and the Palace of Culture in honour of Stalin – "all marble and ostentation" – and a visit to the Methodist orphanage. "Seeing the kids was almost too much for me," he wrote in his diary, "especially when one of them gave me a doll for Caroline"[28] [his youngest daughter].

Leaving Warsaw for the South, Donald travelled by train to Stalinograd, where he discussed the abject state of Polish Methodism with a local pastor into the small hours. Aside from its American style fundamentalism which wasn't to his liking, it came across as an aimless, faction-ridden rump, out of favour with the communist authorities, in contrast to the majority Catholic population, who were treated much more sympathetically. The next day in Katowice in the centre of the Silesian coalfield, which he compared to the Black Country, he spoke to a crowded congregation in what he called the first real Methodist service of the trip. Thereafter he was shown around Auschwitz in the company of a guide who had survived captivity there, including the experience of assembling in the execution yard every Sunday when one of his block was shot. Such trauma had led to his hair falling out. Donald in turn found simply visiting the death camp long after it had become a living monument to unparalleled barbarism the most traumatic experience he had ever lived through. The petrol syringes still lying on the tables in the extermination area, the rags of cloth everywhere, the ovens barely cool and the final messages of the condemned sprayed in graffiti, all told their grisly tale of undiluted horror. A viewing of the barn full of hair, the room full of children's toys and the photographs of the prisoners, all of whom looked alike with their shaved heads and emaciated appearances, only compounded the sense of shock. "Auschwitz, as nothing else in my experience except intolerable pain," he wrote in his autobiography, "has remained a constant reminder of the extent to which a human being can be depersonalized as to appear to make qualities such as dignity, forbearance and individuality nothing more than words from a dead language."[29]

With these disturbing thoughts fresh in his mind it was a relief to be met in Cracow, home of the future Pope John Paul II, by a crowd of Methodists who escorted him in triumphant procession to his hotel. On going out to dinner the sight of unruly carousing in the streets predictably drew strong words of disapproval. "This is the real Achilles heel of communism," he wrote, "drunkenness and teddy boys."[30] Another communist eyesore was revealed the next morning when he was shown around the new industrial city of Nova Huta, built without one church. Considering the place to be the epitome of secularism Donald subsequently wondered how many Our Fathers or Wesleyan hymns he would have needed to recite or sing to keep his faith alive. In contrast to the soullessness of Nova Huta, he was lost in admiration for the historic city of Cracow, comparing its ancient quarters to Nuremberg and revelling in its beauty and culture. After a large dinner at the Pastor's home his return to Warsaw on the train was spent locked in argument with a Polish officer *en route* to Moscow, an altercation which he found to be most enlightening. "People of Poland are not for the regime," he declared, "and would on a free vote kick it out tomorrow."[31] Later he was to write how in the new Warsaw born out of the destruction of war, he found the young with happy, carefree faces, healthy bodies and hope for the future living alongside an older generation, whose fearful, haunted eyes told of past suffering as well as present insecurity. For many of them this experience of suffering had brought degrading moral collapse, evident in the civilian administration where Marxist-Leninism was king. A marked exception to the intellectual inertia of the regime was the Foreign Minister whom he met on his penultimate day. Donald described him as the "best Communist I have met so far and well aware of what the position is".[32] The minister admitted that their biggest problem was not rebuilding cities but rebuilding people and giving them a sense of security. He told him that he wasn't interested in Methodism, but was interested in peace, and if Donald as a representative of British Methodism could help achieve this, then he was welcome back any time.

Aside from a united service at the Evangelical Reformed Church, where the Lutherans met as well (although Donald could detect few signs of ecumenism in the service), his final painful duty was a showdown with his hosts about the crisis in Polish Methodism. As ever in these circumstances Donald was candour personified and told two of the leaders that the days of their Church were numbered unless they resigned. Having said his bit he took his leave, but even the flight home revived uncomfortable memories, for when the man sitting next to him took off his jacket he saw displayed on his arm the number tattooed in a German concentration camp.

On his return Donald tried to put a positive gloss on his trip, but the reservations he had previously expressed were borne out weeks later when the Polish uprising at Poznan served as a grim reminder of the great chasm that had opened up between the people and their sovereign masters. On his instigation, Conference approved the sending of a telegram to Polish Methodists endorsing a forthcoming Methodist Conference there, but it never came to anything.

In the latter part of 1956 there arose a grave diplomatic-military crisis which split the country, and on this occasion Donald's pacifist instincts chimed more with the national mood than was often the case. Ever since the British invaded Egypt in 1882 to protect the Suez Canal, their presence there had inflamed nationalist passions which didn't diminish with time. Under pressure from their charismatic new leader, Colonel Nasser, the British withdrew their forces from the Canal Zone in 1954, although they remained the largest shareholder in the Suez Canal Company, a dangerous vacuum which couldn't last. The crisis erupted when Nasser, having failed to gain a vital loan from the United States to build the Aswan Dam on the Upper Nile to revolutionise the Egyptian economy, nationalised the Suez Canal Company on 26 July 1956 and used their assets to implement his project. This act of provocation caused great anguish in London and Paris. Anthony Eden, the British Prime Minister, viewed Nasser as an Islamic Hitler and was determined to topple him. As a Canal Users Association was convened in London for mid-September, military preparations went ahead, causing a major rift in the country over the legitimacy of force. Donald, not surprisingly, was categorically clear where he stood on the issue. On 15 August, addressing a series of overcrowded meetings at the Caxton Hall, alongside the Labour politicians Fenner Brockway and Barbara Castle and the historian A.J.P. Taylor in an event organised by the Movement for Colonial Freedom, he referred to the blatant idiocy of the Eden Government's actions. What particularly galled him was its duplicitous attitude towards the UN so that for all its commitment to it in public, its refusal to adhere to it in private had only enhanced the prospect for war. His views on the UN and his support for the legitimate nationalist aspirations of the Egyptian people were derided in the pro-Government periodical, the *Spectator*, but he wouldn't be deterred.

On the eve of the Canal Users Association meeting, Donald was in defiant mood. Recalling Dick Sheppard "that truly great man" and his cry of "War We Say No", he told his congregation that "if in five hundred churches the banners were being prepared and the people were heading out on to the streets to bear witness, what a transformation of the scene there might be by the morrow. It is to that witness that I call you."[33] His challenge was taken up by 500 of his congregation who, once the service was over, left Kingsway under his auspices to march through the West End. Many of them, like Donald, carried banners. His read "Stop Gunboat Diplomacy". Traffic was held up for some time on their march to Trafalgar Square and back. In his next article in *Tribune* he denounced Archbishop Fisher for his message that national unity was supremely desirable in time of war. Unity, he averred, was only desirable when it was the fruit of justice.

The Canal Users Association was unable to make much progress, and Nasser, correctly perceiving that Eisenhower, the American President, was unwilling to take action in election year, rejected all proposals. When similar demands were blocked at the UN by a Russian veto, Britain and France resolved to go it alone and, in collusion with Israel, attack Egypt. On 29 October Israel duly invaded and the following day Britain and France began hostilities, which culminated with the landing of their troops at Port Said on 5 November.

Ironically, in the middle of a series of five sermons, "The World can Live in Peace", to capacity congregations at Kingsway, Donald had stated the night before that for the first time in his life he felt ashamed of the country in which he was born and which he loved because it had betrayed its moral trust. By flouting the UN it had struck a mortal blow at the hope of the world. Having witnessed the Government betray its trust, he was compelled to ask himself as a professed Christian what action he should take. Neither constitutional opposition in Parliament, nor the current expressions of woe and grief in the Church were enough.

> I have to search my conscience and say to myself: What is my duty? – and remember that I speak myself as a Christian – what is my duty when I am convinced that a moral blunder has taken place, when I am convinced that the path we are now treading is a path which will lead to overwhelming disaster. The answer: I as an individual Christian must obey God rather than men; when I am satisfied that Jesus Christ demands a certain course of action from me, no constitutional or legal measures can stand in the way. I reconcile this stand with what Jesus said: 'The man who puts his hand to the plough and looks back is not fit for the Kingdom of God. The man who does not love Me more than his wife and child is not worthy of Me'.
>
> There is nothing sacrosanct about any State or any Government. True, it ought to be cherished as the corporate expression of our social life; it has demands which have to be met; it bestows blessings and expects duties in return. But there come situations when I must obey God, even if it means that I must disobey the Civil Magistrate. We have a glorious history of those who have, with simple consistency, challenged the laws of the land. We owe much to the Christian rebels of past generations. ... I stand before you tonight as one advocating for myself and my fellow Ministers an attitude of civil disobedience. That is not an easy thing to say, but as I think of the people of Hungary, of Egypt and Israel, and the people of this country, I am finally satisfied that until one community is prepared to base its policy on non-violent action, no real progress can be made.

He concluded with an appeal to support the UN. "Peace is not coming when we are clever enough. Peace will come when we obey God."[34]

After the service, he led his congregation towards 10 Downing Street with the intention of presenting a petition. He was however diverted by another group of marchers chanting "we want Soper" and addressed instead a meeting of several hundred Labour supporters off Charing Cross Road, where he was joined by members of PPU. At the end of the meeting, scuffles broke out between a group of young marchers and the police, who started breaking up the protesters into different groups, so that when Donald emerged he was hustled to the head of a ready-made procession of young students. As he set off with his new followers with mounted police in attendance, he met up again with his Kingsway congregation.

When the invasion duly took place, Donald called it a morally dirty crime. Addressing 800 people at Hornsey Town Hall for a protest meeting against Government policy on 8 November, he urged the young not to fight if their conscience told them not to. When a voice shouted, "Sedition", Donald replied that he wasn't inciting mutiny. No man, he said, whether in uniform or not, should be expected to carry out an order which his conscience considered to be wrong. For the sake of his immortal soul he should refuse to obey that order, eliciting loud applause for his defiance. "I believe," he added to more applause, "what is morally right can never be politically wrong."[35]

He expanded on this theme the next day in *Tribune* when he referred to the Nuremberg trials. Here men were hanged because by refusing to mutiny against the orders of their military superiors, they were deemed guilty of war crimes. Thankfully, it didn't have to come to this because sustained American pressure brought an ignominious climb-down, and by December the last of the Anglo-French troops had left the Canal Zone. It was the end of an era for British imperial power and might. "Liars and cheats" was Donald's final verdict on the Eden Government's conduct of Suez and certainly its connivance with France in the Israeli invasion of Egypt was one of the less glorious episodes in British diplomacy. Donald felt Eden should pay for his folly with the premiership and so, in private, did a lot of Conservatives. Within a matter of weeks hastened on his way by illness, Eden resigned, never to hold public office again.

While Donald stuck his oar into the Suez affair he was also casting aspersions on the ninth meeting of the World Methodist Council at Lake Junaluska, North Carolina. The content of its report he found so tempered with qualifications and platitudes that he defied anyone to define what it had affirmed. The failure, he felt, to identify the Gospel with any social and political programme encouraged the wrong people, edified no one and comforted the cynic. "I see no useful purpose in Methodism crossing the Atlantic to have its teeth drawn even under the most pleasant anaesthetist."[36] This broadside fuelled a pained response from the British representative on the body, Dr E.

Benson Perkins, who claimed somewhat unconvincingly that the programme was more precise than he imagined.

As Kingsway celebrated twenty-one years of Donald in 1957 a new symbol appeared above the entrance. Both he and Howard Wadman, a public relations adviser, had been concerned for some time about the unappealing aura which greeted visitors on their arrival. The dingy entrance gave few clues to there being a church in their midst. Consequently, Donald asked Wadman to discuss a new design with an architect. Wadman decided that they needed to light the place up and came up with the Dove of Peace released by a hand, and the hand pierced by the deep wound of Calvary. "Surely this couldn't be misunderstood," Wadman later wrote. "Peace released into the world through love to the uttermost. Hope born the very moment of apparent disaster. Suffering and victory in a single sign."[37] The idea commended itself to Donald, and within a day or so Wadman met Peter Lyon, the young designer who had made the sculptured figures in the famous Diaghileff exhibition of the year before. Lyon was intrigued by the project and produced a thirty-inch model of the dove in his studio at Chelsea. Donald was impressed enough to ask him to proceed with a ten-foot sculpture. After a seven-month interlude the plans were accepted by the LCC and once Lyon had created his ten-foot dove, Kingsway had a new symbol for a different age, appropriate for an institution which balanced the sacred and the secular.

The long-awaited unveiling at the entrance took place on 10 March. The congregation gathered in a semi-circle across half the street, in which the Church took precedence over traffic, for the dedication service. Two young girls in the Kingsway congregation, chosen to represent all the world's children, performed the unveiling ceremony, revealing the Dove of Peace standing out above the remodelled entrance. After various paeans to peace from four overseas members of the congregation, the service ended with Donald's great thematic hymn "Behold the Mountain of the Lord", announcing the coming of the day of peace. According to Kenneth Brown, the effect was immense. Now the entrance to Kingsway became attractive and its symbol signifying the essence of the mission ministry was undeniable.

That autumn Donald was invited to Japan to celebrate 100 years of Protestant missionary work by the Free Churches there. The horrors of war seemed a distant memory, with few memorials in evidence and little sign of contrition for the atrocities perpetrated by the imperial forces. He was struck by how quickly they had rebuilt Hiroshima and admired the magnificence of their new Roman Catholic cathedral, but otherwise thought little of the place since it lacked a new dynamic to take the place of the atomic bomb. Indeed, with the Christian legacy in decline, it was the forces of a secular society that appeared very much in the ascendancy, as modern new homes and industries arose with breathtaking speed from the ruins of the old.

Two particular memories stood out. The first involved a visit to a large prison on the island of Kyusho to address 400 prisoners, all dressed and groomed in the same manner. As the governor introduced him, they all arose and bowed, before listening intently to what he had to say. During the discussion afterwards, which contained a number of highly intelligent questions, Donald was somewhat flummoxed to be asked if the influence of the Marxist intellectual Kautsky on Lenin was sufficient to explain the dominance of the latter. He resorted to the trick of getting the questioner to tell him the answer.

The second was meeting a group of students on the island of Hokkaido who were largely unaware of Christian theology and culture. Speaking through an interpreter, Donald asked them to continue to listen to the Christian case, and although he expected few seeds to grow, he was heartened to hear later that a number had gradually come to Christ. After Japan it was the turn of Canada once again to host Donald. In Toronto he confidently rebutted a brash reporter who assured him that Britain was finished. Only as an imperial power, he replied, and that was no cause for regret. For the rest, despite his aversion to undue sentimentality from ex-patriots he encountered, especially in Australia, Donald remained a cultural imperialist in the sense that the British way of life to which he remained broadly sympathetic should act as a model for others. The fact that he still thought of Britain as a great power, explains his constant desire to see his country take the lead on weighty moral issues such as international disarmament and the destruction of apartheid. It also explains the huge personal capital he was prepared to invest in global travel despite the hardships it brought him, not least the homesickness. The following July Donald was again in foreign parts, this time at a World Peace Conference in East Berlin. He was well treated by his communist hosts but found the logistics of peacemaking a slow, frustrating business. Aside from the linguistic difficulties which hampered their deliberations, the ideological and military rivalries then afflicting the eastern and western blocs cast a pall over proceedings. After a week of fruitless dialogue, Donald left reconciled to a long, hard road ahead before the barriers of mistrust were overcome.

The years 1958–59 were very much devoted to CND, the LCC and the growing problems in Notting Hill (dealt with in the following pages). Two other issues concerned Donald in the summer of 1959. The first was the question of boxing, a sport that he had participated in at school with gusto and success. He had continued to follow it with interest, but now, having absorbed the growing medical opinion that the sport was liable to cause brain injury, imbecility and even death, he denounced the "capitalist" Boxing Board for its indifference to moral considerations. He also resolved to refrain from watching it ever again, a pledge he later admitted he adhered to more in the breach than in the observance.

The second issue concerned Northern Ireland, a part of the United Kingdom he had briefly visited twice before. In August Donald agreed to speak at one of Belfast's largest Methodist churches and at a couple of open-air meetings. He knew that by visiting a bastion of biblical fundamentalism he was entering enemy territory, but not even he quite anticipated the scale of the hostility awaiting him in the small market town of Ballymena, the stronghold of Ian Paisley, the Moderator of the Free Presbyterian Church, and a man as charismatic to his followers as Donald was to his. The meeting proved to be the stormiest held there for years, as Donald attempted to address a crowd of several hundred in the face of constant provocation by Paisley and his spiritual cohorts, who took great exception to his liberal theology. Even before the meeting had begun, feelings ran high as Paisley distributed leaflets and brandished placards carrying insulting slogans like "Soper is a communist". Then, once Donald stepped calmly up to the microphone, he was subjected to a stream of crude abuse which didn't relent until he later made a quick exit. According to Patrick Marrinan in his book *Paisley: Man of Wrath*, the whole disorderly performance was an obscene caricature of Christianity.

Sensitive to the hostile atmosphere, Donald began tactfully, saying that he had no interest in arousing denominational controversy as there was too much of it around already. What he wanted to do was to commend the Christian Gospel of love. Before he could proceed any further, a torrent of personal abuse came his way, much of it directed towards his "Roman" cassock, forcing him to plead with his tormentors that he be given a fair hearing. As he made his case, a Bible was flung from the crowd, striking a woman and fell to the ground in front of him, whereupon Donald picked it up, remarking that he had more regard for the book than some others. The stage was now set for Paisley to make his way to the edge of the platform and berate Donald in loud hectoring tones. He accused him of denying the virgin birth and bodily resurrection, to which Donald said that he had been acquitted by the High Court of the Methodist Church of the very charges raised against him. "I am entitled to hold the views I do," he said. "You are not a Methodist," continued Paisley. "Are you intellectual rabbits prepared to listen to an answer?" countered an increasingly exasperated Donald. "If you want one, why not hear it before you disagree?" Paisley retorted with a reference to the Roman cassock. "Sartorially I reckon I can stand up against you any day," declared Donald. "You don't look particularly decorative, nor do I," to laughter. Further exchanges followed until Paisley went for the jugular. "We would give you free speech if you came as an infidel, but not as a Christian minister." "My hecklers have now given themselves away," bellowed Donald. "In what way does this group differ from Fascists? A man, whatever his views, should be granted free speech."

As they continued to wrestle over religious issues, Donald accused Paisley of apparently being on the committee to decide whether or not a man was fit to get to heaven. If that was the case, he said, to much hilarity, he wondered if he wanted to go there.

Asked if he had been to Russia, Donald said he had and was promptly accused of being a communist, to which he replied: "In some ways the people of Russia are carrying out Christianity a darn sight better than you are. I am not a communist and I can prove it," he continued to further frivolity, "I have got an American visa." As the police in the crowd remained seated, indifferent to Donald's fate, he continued to grapple with the theological missiles directed at him. On the virgin birth he admitted that after much thought he had accepted the rational theory that the Christ Child was conceived in the normal way and received the sanctification of the spirit in the same way as John the Baptist. The final part of his answer was drowned out in a spate of boos and catcalls accompanied by cries of "communist" and "heretic". "What about Christ's bodily resurrection?" thundered Paisley, to the accompanying applause from his leading acolytes. Donald didn't flinch. Displaying great courage, he explained that he only believed in a spiritual resurrection, citing in his favour the fact that neither Mary Magdalene nor the disciples on the road to Emmaus recognised him in his risen guise.[38]

His words served only to inflame passions to new and dangerous heights, and it was only now with his safety under serious threat that the police finally moved in. As Donald was hustled away to a waiting car, the assembled reporters descended upon him to get his reaction to events. He told them that it was the most unpleasant meeting he had ever spoken at.

The next day when Donald arrived for Morning Service at Carlisle Memorial Methodist Church, one of Belfast's largest churches, a group moved forward carrying a banner on which was written "Dr Soper denies the virgin birth of Jesus". Paisley wasn't present but his deputy, the Revd John Wylie, produced a set of rosary beads, a symbol of his supposed Catholic sympathies, and dangled them in Donald's face. His attempts to place them on his shoulder failed as they fell to the pavement, at which point a plainclothes policeman moved in to restrain his assailant. Police sat in during the service as Donald pronounced upon the limits to evangelism, insisting that revivalism had to be accompanied by social actions. In the evening, at the same venue, Donald entered without incident and preached for over forty minutes on the lessons communism contained for Christianity.

His visit stirred reaction throughout the province as the debate raged for the next several weeks among press and public alike. "The insulting treatment he received outside church gates in Belfast and in the open air can scarcely be regarded with pride in the province,"[39] declared Ulster's evening paper, the *Belfast Telegraph*. A month after his visit, Paisley, Wylie and another minister were fined £5 in a crowded courtroom for disorderly behaviour. They refused to pay, deliberately courting imprisonment, until a sympathiser came to their rescue by paying the fines.

Not surprisingly Donald kept away from Northern Ireland thereafter, although when the troubles began in earnest a decade later, his pro-nationalist sentiments further inflamed his tetchy relationship with the Protestant community. In particular he remained an implacable opponent of Paisley, whose fervent anti-Catholic beliefs only moderated in old age. Having referred to him (somewhat provocatively) as an ecclesiastic fascist at Conference in 1966, he returned to the attack in the House of Lords two years later, calling him a rabble-rouser. There were to be other subsequent anti-Paisley tirades to ruffle the Lords' august ambience, suggesting that the scars of Ballymena took a long time to heal.

CHAPTER TEN

Red or Dead

Donald joined the Labour Party while at Cambridge, and first spoke for it
in 1926. Thereafter he was a committed if restless member as his
socialism developed through contact with such icons as George Lansbury and
Arthur Ponsonby in the peace movement, Lansbury in particular teaching
him that socialism and pacifism were part of the same inclusive concept.
Without the one it was impossible to have the other. By the mid-late 1950s he
was established enough to count a number of its leading lights such as Aneurin
Bevan, Frank Longford, Harold Wilson, Barbara Castle, Michael Foot and
Tony Benn as trusted friends, some of the best he had in public life. His views
also assumed a greater importance, what with his column in *Tribune*, his
membership of the LCC from 1958, his chairmanship of the Christian Socialist
Movement [CSM] in 1960 and his appointment to the House of Lords in
1965.

Yet for all his prominence, Donald, partly by choice, remained something
of an outsider, so that his influence on actual policy-making was minimal. To
understand this paradox, several factors need to be borne in mind. First,
Donald's politics were very much on the left, separated from mainstream
thinking for, although Labour had always had its colourful socialist fringe, it
wasn't essentially a socialist party. Aside from economic doubts about the efficiency of a centrally controlled economy, the electorate, it appeared, wouldn't
stand for it. If this wasn't bad enough, the left as a grouping lacked cohesion.
Even the much fabled Bevanites where Donald's soul resided during the early-
1950s, were less united than perception would warrant, as Bevan himself
hovered between rebellion and conformity. Then, for all the feverish opposition generated by Hugh Gaitskell's leadership 1955–63, there were basic
differences within it, not least over nuclear weapons and the American alliance. Many of Donald's closest associates, for instance, weren't pacifist, and
their bonds were further eroded when a number of them, such as Barbara
Castle and Tony Benn, joined the Wilson Government in 1964. In time, a
newer, more extreme form of socialism arose from the grassroots during the

1970s, but such people weren't natural soul mates of Donald, whose influence by then had in any case further diminished. Part of this was down to age and part to changing times. In an era when many in the Labour Party were less in thrall to the Nonconformist conscience of his youth, his puritanism grated with libertarians who associated socialism with individual rights and pleasure.

His puritanism helped highlight another trait generally detrimental to those entering the political arena, namely his dislike of socialising. Clubs, bars and restaurants, scheming, speculation and gossip, the staple diet of so many politicians' lives, were totally alien to his lifestyle. Consequently he missed out on the opportunity to make contacts, especially among the trade unions who controlled the bloc vote at Labour Party Conferences, which could help build the coalitions he needed. Even when he gave a rousing tribute to Aneurin Bevan, one of his heroes, on a Welsh hillside in 1960, he slipped away straight after the ceremony without staying to mingle with friends. This aloofness was also a question of priorities. He had, of course, a strong sense of duty to the Church and although he firmly believed that politics was part of his ministry, it was secondary to his spiritual mission. In that sense he wasn't a political parson as some chose to see him. "My place in the Labour Party," he said in November 1992, "has been as an exalter rather than as a participator."[1] Finally, Donald's qualities as a Christian could be deemed defects as a politician. His idealistic view of the world, his firmly-held convictions, his reluctance to compromise and his brutal honesty didn't always endear him to his frontbench superiors to whom politics was the art of the possible. For a man used to getting his own way at the West London Mission, or as a consummate performer in the open air, he disliked taking orders from others, especially from those he held in low esteem. Hugh Gaitskell, Bertrand Russell and John Collins were among those with whom he fell out, which in the case of the last two (President and Chairman of CND respectively) is one reason why his influence on the anti-nuclear movement was less pronounced than it might have been. Had he had his time again he might have concluded that a little more time invested in exchanging ideas with Labour's leaders rather than simply railing at them in *Tribune* or at a fringe rally, could have paid rich dividends, especially since Gaitskell, on a personal level, admired him, and Wilson liked him more than most. The fact that he wasn't prepared to compromise or adapt his core beliefs seemed strange given his cheerful contention that Jesus could act in such a fashion, and also his awareness of developing social trends. Such discernment, which informed his approach to countless moral and religious issues (although by no means all), sometimes eluded him in the political field despite the fact that many of Labour's most fertile minds were on its reformist wing.

After Gaitskell succeeded Attlee as leader in November 1955, Donald wrote in *Tribune*, "I think I speak for a great multitude of radically minded citizens when I say that we have great expectations of the new leader of the Labour Movement. We want to feel the throb of a new impulse towards real socialism, and want to be led out of uncertainty into action, and out of diffidence into enthusiasm."[2] His words must have been written more in hope than expectation, for Gaitskell, with his pro-American multilateralist views, was very much on the right of the party, out of sympathy with the style as well as the substance of Donald's politics. At first an uneasy calm prevailed, helped by Gaitskell's uncompromising opposition to Suez, and Donald's desire to see unity restored to Labour's battered ranks. By 1958 the party's failure to show any urgency in moving in a socialist and pacifist direction was causing him some disquiet, but he couched his reservations in fairly restrained language. In March 1959 he even appealed to fellow unilateralists within the nuclear movement who were threatening to withhold their vote from Labour on the grounds that it wasn't fully signed up to their creed, to think again. Compromises were the staple diet of political parties, he reminded them, and for all the frustrations this entailed, only Labour could deliver the final victory they sought. The fact that Labour proved less than amenable to the unilateralist argument as the election approached, caused him to vent these frustrations in *Tribune* that July. He denounced the party's nuclear policy as morally empty and unrelated to the socialist faith, but thanks to the efforts of Tony Benn, a leading member of Labour's general election committee, Donald was to the fore during the campaign that October. Not only did he take part in a political broadcast along with Gaitskell and Bevan, the party chairman, he spoke for Michael Foot in Devonport, Barbara Castle in Blackburn and Arthur Henderson, his Circuit Steward, in Rowley Regis and Tipton. His comments upset the latter's Tory opponent who accused him of saying horrible things about Conservatism, and certainly his platform style was not for the fainthearted. "Little man, you've had a busy day," he told a heckler who was barracking the Labour candidate in Bromley. "Can a man be a Christian in a capitalist world?" he was then asked. "Of course," he replied, "just as a teetotaller can work in a pub." His presence in the campaign, along with other left-wing clerics such as Trevor Huddleston, John Collins and Mervyn Stockwood, the Bishop of Southwark, was featured in the *Daily Sketch*, one of whose columnists called for a ban on pink parsons. He need not have worried. Divine providence didn't shine on the Labour Party as the Conservatives increased their majority once again, leaving Donald to conclude in *Tribune* that Labour had lost because it lacked socialist conviction. His assessment – totally at odds with Gaitskell who now began his ill-fated campaign to abandon the party's long-standing commitment to nationalisation – found support among fellow Christians on the left.

Ever since the formation of the Christian Social Union by Henry Scott Holland and Bishop Charles Gore in 1889, there had been a number of different Christian socialist groups, the most recent of which had been the Socialist Christian League, established in 1932. The following year Donald had spoken at one of its fringe meetings at the Methodist Conference alongside S. E. Keeble, the eminent Methodist minister, and thereafter played an increasingly prominent role in its deliberations throughout the decade with his discourses on pacifism. After the war his role seems to have been a more passive one, becoming a vice-president in 1954, and the initiative for a new grouping came from a maverick left-wing MP very much his antithesis in character. Tom Driberg was a flamboyant High-Church homosexual whose socialism, according to his biographer, Francis Wheen, had always had a distinctly religious flavour to it. This became more conspicuous during the 1950s in the shadow of the Cold War. Unable to accept his party's support for the hydrogen bomb in April 1955, he resolved to restore an ethical basis to left-wing politics which he felt had been lacking for some time. Consequently, under his auspices, a group of prominent Christian socialists met every few weeks at the Lamb, a cosy old pub in Bloomsbury, between 1956 and 1959 to put together a cogent case for Christian socialism. The result was a pamphlet, *Papers from the Lamb*, calling for international peace, common ownership, racial equality and closer relations with the Soviet Churches. Donald, who signed the pamphlet, hadn't attended any of the meetings (not surprising because of its location) and much of the text was the work of Driberg. He was, however, the driving force behind CSM, and the ideal candidate as leader because of the universal respect he commanded, even though his puritanism sat uneasily alongside sybaritic Anglo-Catholic priests such as Stanley Evans and John Groser. On January 22/23 1960 he called a two-day meeting at Kingsway, at which 600 attended, including Donald's hero R. H. Tawney, the first time, ironically, that they had ever met, in what was to be one of the latter's last public appearances.

The event opened with Donald saying prayers for the terminally ill Aneurin Bevan. He then explained that the meeting was a continuation of the activities of the group responsible for *Papers from the Lamb*. The declared aim of the new organisation was twofold. First, to amalgamate the existing Christian socialist bodies, the Socialist Christian League and Society of Socialist Clergy and Ministers, and second, to invest the Labour movement with a greater Christian social ethic. A draft constitution was drawn up which pledged members to work for Christianity, the redistribution of wealth and international reconciliation. An executive committee of twenty-four, comprising the two groups, was also established and Donald elected chairman, a position he held until his retirement in 1975, when he became president.

The executive met monthly in Donald's office at Kingsway on Tuesday evening. He would sit at his desk with his secretary next to him with pencil and notepad at the ready while his colleagues sat round the room in a semi-circle. He would greet them on arrival and see them out after a meeting which he chaired in his usual brisk fashion, leaving little room for discussion, as David Hallam, a member of the executive, discovered in 1968. Feeling that Christianity was out of touch with young people, he wanted to foment closer links between the CSM and the burgeoning student movement. He suggested a conference, but Donald simply dismissed the idea as nonsensical. Under his roof the movement was something of a one-man band, hardly a recipe for inclusiveness, and even among his deferential followers faint stirrings were heard. On one occasion someone had written in to complain about Donald's chairmanship and he went around the whole executive seeking reassurance, but whatever private reservations they might have had, they kept them to themselves. In the view of Peter Dawe, sometime Chairman of CSM, the movement remained something of a fledgling body, reluctant to emerge from its master's shadow. This was borne out by the fact that the executive continued to meet at Kingsway for some time after Donald's retirement as chairman. Only by 1983 had it begun to display some independence and by 1986, after its affiliation to the Labour Party, did CSM attain a greater prominence as more MPs joined its ranks.

Away from the LCC and the Labour Party, there was plenty to keep Donald preoccupied, not least the anti-apartheid movement, to which he had gradually become more committed, partly as a result of his links with Trevor Huddleston, the illustrious Anglican priest whose strong opposition to apartheid had seen him exiled from South Africa in 1956. That same year in February, Donald, along with other leading clerics and Harold Wilson, had been party to a letter sent to *The Times* by a new group, Christian Action, launched to help finance the defence of leading opponents of apartheid in South Africa charged with treason. In March 1960 he criticised the British Government over its failure to condemn the Sharpeville massacre when sixty-nine black demonstrators were killed and nearly 200 wounded. In April he crossed the Atlantic for a tour of the United States, Canada and the Caribbean, primarily to deliver the Lyman-Beecher Lectures on Preaching at Yale Divinity School, a task he accomplished to much acclaim. As usual Donald spoke without notes, a fact which escaped the Dean who, as they entered the hall for the first of the six lectures, informed him that he had forgotten the script. "Yes," said Donald. "So I have." He took some blank sheets of foolscap from his briefcase, rolled them up under his arm, strode to the podium and delivered himself faultlessly for an hour on the chosen theme. Afterwards, the Dean congratulated him on a marvellous performance and asked him for a copy of his script, to which Donald replied, "I'm afraid you can't have one. You see, it wouldn't be fair to you. I departed from the printed text at so many points."

It was at Yale that Donald met the eminent theologian Reinhold Niebuhr for the first and only time. He was most impressed, but although willing to acknowledge in private the trouble that Niebuhr's views had caused him, in the open air, there was no meeting of minds over pacifism. He also appreciated the courtesy and intelligence of the students. Having started his trip in high spirits, the rest of the American leg, comprising Hartford, Connecticut, adult home of Mark Twain, and thereafter Denver and Boston – "very English" – was lacklustre in comparison. Confronted with an unusually light itinerary he became bored and disillusioned by being left to his own devices. An exception to this state of affairs was a visit to *My Fair Lady* in New York since he thought this a wonderful show.

In contrast to his penchant for domestic entertainment back home in front of the television, Donald was more inclined to venture out when in America for a night on the town. On a previous visit he went to see *South Pacific* in Chicago, describing it as "crude but powerful", and visits to the movies weren't unknown, especially to see one of his favourite actresses, Ingrid Bergman. Westerns were a particular favourite, an ironic choice for a pacifist until we recall his thirst for action and adventure. As a lover of jazz and blues, in particular Fats Waller and Jelly Roll Morton, and Negro spirituals, he empathised with much of American culture. Once when it was under attack at Tower Hill, Donald launched a spontaneous ten-minute defence of its literature, which, according to David Mason, was breathtaking.

But despite his appreciation of many things American, he felt that the average denizen, obsessed with things material, lacked the sophistication and breadth of his European counterpart. Television there he found particularly excruciating with its shallow insularity, not least the subsequent growth of televangelists since they seemed to pander to the most nauseous elements in religious financial exploitation. As a devotee of the work ethos, he admired much of American ingenuity and efficiency which characterised their civilisation. Unlike Britain which continued to be mired in class consciousness, this ingenuity in a more open society enabled many to make good. However, rank inequalities remained and to Donald the treatment of many trade unions, African-Americans and inner-city poor was nothing short of monstrous. The fact that these casualties of the capitalist system were a low priority for many churchgoers, as was the growing danger of their burgeoning war-machine, only added to his disillusionment. As far as he was concerned, the United States was as much responsible for the origins of the Cold War as the Soviet Union and as the clash between the superpowers became ever more protracted, he appeared to become more vociferous in his criticism of the former. In 1952 he attacked them for their needless fear of communism, as expressed through the McCarthyite purges, and in 1956 he dubbed Britain an occupied country in reference to the profusion of US bases there. Later during the 1960s as their space programme became ever more advanced, he contrasted the enormous funds associated with this project to the paltry amounts relieving poverty in large cities such as New York and Chicago.

All these reservations about the United States might lead the neutral observer (if there were any) to the view that given the choice Donald appeared to favour Soviet values in comparison to American ones. At Preston in July 1952, he informed his MSF audience that the Americans were as peculiar a people as the Russians and the following year he raised eyebrows by calling the latter quite decent fellows. Yet perhaps a more accurate comparison had come on another occasion that year when asked which of the two superpowers he preferred. The Americans, he answered, because a rotter there could read improved books whereas in Russia a rotter would either be liquidated or made to read prescribed texts. Whatever the exact comparisons, his ambivalence towards the country he visited ten times remained to the very end. After his final trip there in 1982, he alluded to the vast gulf in standards and lifestyle there among its people. The best were the cream of the earth, the worst simply awful.

After the tedium of the United States it was a relief to find Ottawa more stimulating with its plush churches and responsive audiences. A highly successful return to Glebe High School was offset by a fractious meeting at the United Church, a tense encounter with "very pious right-wingers" at the House of Commons and a row with the Mayoress of Ottawa at dinner. At issue was Donald's consternation at the country's general ignorance of communism, especially in light of renewed Cold War tension caused by Eisenhower's U-2 spy plane fiasco. After a brief visit to the industrial city of Detroit where he received a standing ovation from the trade unions and visited the automobile entrepreneur Henry Ford's house ("what the capitalists do with their money"), he headed for Trinidad via Prince Edward Island. He found the former bustling with life and progress, compared to his visit six years earlier, thanks to the oil boom. While he was there he attended a party at the Governor-General's, and met the charismatic Prime Minister, Dr Eric

Williams, whose blend of African-Indian socialism greatly impressed him. He left full of hope, a feeling not applicable to his final destination, British Guiana, which, with its ailing sugar industry and volatile ethnic mix, looked backward in comparison. Under attack from mosquitoes, he was more than happy to depart. On his return via America, Donald, clad in his cassock, bearing a lush orchid from the Caribbean for Marie, approached Customs diffidently because of their strict entry regulations over insect pesticide. "I hope you don't mind," Donald explained, "but I want to give this to my wife." The customs officer, looking at the cassock and thinking he was a Catholic, replied. "Well, Father, I've no legal objection but the moral problem is one for you."

Donald's next duty was the poignant one of conducting Aneurin Bevan's memorial service in South Wales, where 5,000 of his own people bade him farewell on a windswept mountain above his birthplace at Tredegar. As his widow Jennie Lee wept, Donald saluted a man who "was good in the essential sense of the word and whose goodness was no narrow piety but a bountiful charity".[3] Having implored his audience to see through his life's work to completion, he then led his widow to the microphone where she gave a heart-felt eulogy to her late husband, her brave words greeted by thunderous applause. The service, rich with socialist symbolism, ended with a hearty rendition of "The Red Flag" and "Land of My Fathers".

Despite the affairs of Notting Hill and CND preoccupying him at the Methodist Conference and keeping him busy thereafter, his campaigning zeal didn't stop there. He had the Home Secretary, R. A. Butler, in his sights for his failure to decriminalise private homosexual practices between consenting adults, despite the recommendations of the 1957 Wolfenden Committee.

Butler proved more accommodating to the liberal conscience when he helped Roy Jenkins, an up-and-coming Labour backbencher, to pilot his Obscene Publications Bill through the Commons, a parliamentary triumph which led to a sensational court case involving *Lady Chatterley's Lover*.

From its publication in 1928 in Italy, *Lady Chatterley's Lover*, D. H. Lawrence's explicit account of marital infidelity between a sexually un-fulfilled upper-class woman and her paralysed husband's game-keeper, Mellors, attracted great obloquy for the crudity of its language and its erotic content, despite Lawrence's attempt to purify sexual relationships. By the mid-1950s the law on censorship in Britain had become hopelessly obsolete as five established works of literature were separately prosecuted for alleged obscenity, leading to two convictions and three acquittals, and the movement for reform gathered pace. Helped by A. P. Herbert, the former MP for Oxford University, and Butler, Jenkins's Obscene Publications Bill became law in 1959 with the crucial provision of allowing expert evidence in future prosecutions to prove literary merit. Whether *Lady Chatterley* merited the accolade or not was a matter of some conjecture, but when its publishers, Penguin Books, one of the most reputable in the business, were prosecuted for publishing an unexpurgated version, they exercised their right under the 1959 Act to opt for trial by jury rather than by a magistrate. They accordingly instructed their solicitors, Rubinstein, Nash and Co., to approach a collection of potentially sympathetic luminaries willing to testify on their behalf. Donald wasn't on their initial lists, but after mulling over the first round of replies, the solicitors, realising that their witnesses were too redolent of academia, decided to canvass wider support by sounding out allies from within the Church and legal profession. Contrary to an editorial in the *Methodist Recorder* which denounced *Lady Chatterley* as dirty and dangerous, Donald, while deploring the fact that many read it for the wrong reasons, defended it as excellent literature. Thus when approached by Penguin's solicitor, Michael Rubinstein, in September 1960, he, unlike Leslie Weatherhead, had no hesitation in accepting, although a pending trip to the United States delayed the preparation of his statement supporting publication, out of which counsel would prepare a draft Proof of Evidence. When he asked Rubinstein whether his evidence should be slanted towards any particular angle, Rubinstein was specific in his reply. He wanted Donald first to outline the Methodist attitude towards relations between the sexes and second towards the need for education about the sexual problems of its younger members. On the latter point Rubinstein confessed to very real difficulty in gathering evidence since marriage guidance counsellors who normally talked to youth clubs were governed by strict rules of confidentiality. Consequently, these people were growing up in a prurient society which had restricted their opportunity to discuss sexual problems without shame or embarrassment. It had been Lawrence's intention, Rubinstein told Donald, to try to free the words referring to sexual organs and their natural functions from obscene connotations, and in this spirit of greater openness he hoped that Donald would be able to say something positive about *Lady Chatterley*. Rubinstein also asked him to confirm that it wasn't obscene in the sense that it wouldn't tend to corrupt or deprave.

After Donald had sent him the requested information, referring in particular to the Revd D. Alan Keighley, a Methodist working for the British Council of Churches, Rubinstein replied the next day enclosing a draft copy of the draft Proof of Evidence.

"In particular you may not wish to refer to the Declaration of the Methodist Church on the Christian view of Marriage and the Family.

The Revd D. Alan Keighley's letter to you on 10 October quotes the view of the Christian Citizens' Department of the British Council of Churches in a report on the Obscene Publications Bill. The reference to the Bill in the extract from the report is not at all helpful to our case since it suggests that 'well-produced obscenity' may be more harmful in its effects than matter which is badly written and shoddy in appearance, and some might well regard *Lady Chatterley's Lover* as in this sense 'well-produced obscenity'. On the other hand if the Department had had to apply itself to a consideration of this book it might very well have shared your view that the book is not obscene, so the Department's views on the Bill are to this extent not really relevant.

"The quotation from Ken Greet's book is more relevant but I do not know whether or not you would wish to use it."[4]

Donald duly returned his draft Proof of Evidence suitably amended. Having given his particulars, it read as follows:

> I have written eight books chiefly about Christian faith and practice in the world today. Together with Christians of all denominations and therefore including Methodists, and in particular Christian ministers of religion, I have to be concerned with sex in the modern world, and in particular the divine purpose in the institution of marriage and the family. A declaration of the Methodist Church on the Christian view of marriage and the family was published on adoption by Conference in 1939, and is still the official statement of our Church.
>
> I first read *Lady Chatterley's Lover* when I found it in a house I occupied in 1943. I have read it again recently and favour its publication, and believe that its publication by Penguin is for the public good.
>
> My grounds for this belief are as follows:
>
> Firstly, it is fundamentally a serious, indeed solemn work which bears out what Lawrence himself wrote of his intention to make sex 'valid and precious instead of shameful'. I would think that it approximates to the Matthew Arnold definition of a true work of art – 'a high criticism of life'.
>
> This conviction of mine is not impaired by the fact that I disagree profoundly with many of the assertions about sex, and Lawrence's general convictions about sexual relations.
>
> Secondly, I believe, on balance, the absolute clarity and frankness with which the whole realm of sex, as well as the realm of sexual relations are couched, has on the whole, an antiseptic, rather than a pornographic effect.
>
> The antiseptic effect is needed more now, at a time when the snigger and the perversions and obscene connotations which are attached to every sex symbol do nothing but degrade.
>
> Thirdly, the book has obvious merit, though not in my view outstanding literary merit. In my estimation not the least part of its merit is the

acknowledgement of the social and psychological impacts of a predominantly 'laissez-faire' society.

Finally, as to whether any piece of literature tends to corrupt and degrade people can only be answered by the twofold experience, (a) the nature of the literary work itself, and (b) the motive and expectation of the reader.

Any book from the Bible to a manual on 'Feeding the Baby' can be a means of corrupting and depraving those who read such documents in order to satisfy or stimulate lustful desires.

I believe *Lady Chatterley's Lover* comes into this category of books which can be read for the wrong reasons rather than into the category of literature which itself sets out to provide such satisfaction and stimulus.

In view of my opinions about the book I would, of course, have no objection to any of my daughters reading it, being satisfied that they would only attempt to do so when able to understand and therefore absorb something of Lawrence's uplifting attitude to sex in relations between a man and woman in love.

Concluded.[5]

When the trial opened to much public interest at the Old Bailey on 20 October a number of eminent witnesses appeared for the defence, including Roy Jenkins and the writers Rebecca West and E. M. Forster, their cause aided by the Crown's failure to subject them to rigorous cross-examination. A more controversial witness was John Robinson, the radical Bishop of Woolwich, who argued that Lawrence had portrayed sexual intercourse in a real sense as an act of Holy Communion, comments which earned him a public rebuke from the Archbishop of Canterbury for what appeared to be a defence of adultery.

Despite being considered a top-flight performer by Rubinstein and his defence team, Donald was one of thirty-six witnesses not to be called. With the Crown failing to present a persuasive case, most notably the prosecution counsel's notorious remark, "Would you want your wife, your children or your servants to read this book?", reinforcing the image of a class-based censorship, Penguin won the right to publish the book in its entirety. Their sweeping victory not only guaranteed them massive sales of two million in a year, outselling even the Bible, it unleashed an avalanche of permissiveness in writings and pictorial displays. Donald, welcoming the verdict of the court, told his audience at Speakers' Corner the following Sunday that *Lady Chatterley*, in addition to being an attack on class prejudice, had been a sincere attempt by the author to present one side of married life. His stand, however, led to yet another batch of vituperative correspondence, causing him to ponder the sheer vindictiveness of practising Christians whenever their beliefs were threatened.

Donald began 1961 with a visit to Canada for a series of lectures. The weather was excruciatingly cold, especially in Montreal, where he was leading a mission at McGill University. To Stanley Frost, by then a resident in Canada, the pleasure of listening to him in Christ Church Cathedral brought back happy memories of the South London Mission. He hadn't heard him for well over twenty years, but felt that he spoke with the same calm eloquence, the same persuasive reasonableness and the same quality of intellectual integrity that he had once heard in his youth.[6] Always rather dubious about the spiritual commitment of Canadians, Donald now observed a distinct falling-off in the crowds compared to former times. However, those who did turn out left inspired, leading him to the satisfying conclusion that for all his time in French-speaking Canada, the English-speaking peoples of the world still looked to the mother country for leadership.

In March Donald, Barbara Castle and Anthony Greenwood, a fellow left-winger whom he much admired, joined a large crowd in Trafalgar Square to face South Africa House in silent protest against apartheid. By the end of the year South Africa had left the Commonwealth, and apartheid there remained a running sore. It would need further sustained pressure over the course of the next thirty years to bring about genuine multi-racial rule, and while Donald wasn't one of the leaders in this campaign, he was always a willing foot soldier. More important, he was to the fore in the attempt to build a multi-ethnic society at home in the face of bitter reaction. In the aftermath of the 1958 Notting Hill riots, the pressure was building on the Conservative Government to curb the flow of immigration which had been steadily increasing for the past decade. Its response was an Immigration Bill discriminating against entrants from the Black Commonwealth, which offended liberal opinion. On 3 November 1961 at a meeting of the Movement for Colonial Freedom in St Pancras Town Hall to protest against the Bill, hecklers shouting "keep Britain white" surged onto the platform turning over tables as they went. In the melée that followed, Donald and Fenner Brockway were threatened before they wriggled clear. After five minutes, twenty hecklers were ejected by the stewards and the meeting continued, but the Bill, much to Donald's consternation, became law.

Before Christmas, Donald briefly visited Spain in a private capacity, having vigorously opposed the visit of her foreign minister to Britain the previous year on account of his Falangist past. He was struck by the palatial splendour of the capital, Madrid, and the dire poverty elsewhere. With the Roman Catholic Church in close alliance with the Falangist Government of General Franco, he felt that unless the country experienced a kind of Protestant reformation that Britain underwent in the sixteenth century, it would be ripe for revolution, a prediction which fell well wide of the mark.

In the New Year Donald was embroiled in a couple of legal wrangles. In February the Press Council upheld his contention as Chairman of CSM that the editor of the *Catholic Times*, having published a letter which attacked the movement for being tainted with communism, should also have published the official reply. Then in April a libel action he, John Collins and Sydney Silverman issued against the periodical *Encounter*, the mouthpiece of moderate Labour, which had alleged that their support for CND was based on personal gain, was dropped after the editor apologised. That month, Donald's father died aged ninety-one, after enduring years of frail health. He had never been as close to him as he had to his mother, but he always acknowledged his essential goodness and the great influence he had on his subsequent development. As to his passing, Donald wasn't haunted or distressed about any speculations regarding his father's future destiny, especially given his strong and vibrant faith. "He has gone to God," he told his congregation days later, "and there I will leave him."

Throughout his career Donald had inherited from his father the traditional Methodist aversion to gambling which he thought was yet another seamy side of capitalism, since it gave much to the few at the expense of the many through the element of chance. It also helped exacerbate destitution by providing a superficial outlet through which the more reckless members of the working class could squander their hard-won earnings. So rigid was his attitude that in 1952 he showed scant sympathy for the suicide of the Methodist choirmaster from Nottinghamshire who, having won £700 on the pools, had been told to resign by his minister. "Let us clear our minds of sentimentality," Donald declared at Tower Hill. "The fact that the man committed suicide only adds an emotional touch to the story, but does not invalidate it, or corroborate the main factors from the Christian point of view ... In my judgement, gambling for the Christian is impermissible."

"Let Dr Soper be reminded that even if gambling were a sin against Christianity," countered the *Daily Express*, "there is another sin that is greater by far. The sin of intolerance."[7] "I would describe that as a harsh, almost bitterly correct speech," declared Cassandra in the *Daily Mirror*, "made all the more intolerant coming, as it does, from a brave, and deeply religious man."[8]

In 1956 Donald felt bound to support the establishment of betting shops as the best way to avoid the perceived hypocrisy of the status quo where the authorities turned a blind eye to the abuse, a decision he later came to regret. When Harold Macmillan, the Chancellor of the Exchequer, introduced premium bonds the same year, Donald was quick to condemn this innovation as spiritually indefensible and politically bankrupt, comparing it to the politics of Monaco. He reserved his most trenchant assault, however, for one of his own at the Methodist Conference in 1962, when he accused the Treasurer of the Christian Citizenship Department of delinquency. The spat, which attracted much press comment, had a long history behind it centred around the figure of J. Arthur Rank, a cinema magnate who developed his interest in films as a way of propagating the Methodist cause, and like his father, Joseph Rank, a generous patron of the Central Halls movement. Although Donald admired Rank's positive contribution to the British film industry, he had little time for his simplistic Christian faith, free-market philosophy and the methods by which he made his wealth. They had first clashed during Donald's Islington days when going in search of munificence from the Rank Fund for his cash-strapped Central Hall, Donald found that his concept of the social gospel drew a dismissive response from this most committed of capitalists. Another altercation arose when, following repeated criticism of Rank's methods at Tower Hill from his audience, Donald decided to get to the bottom of the allegations and acquaint himself with the true facts. It was in this spirit that he wrote to Rank requesting an interview with him to discuss his business practices. Rank, who according to his biographer Michael Hamelin, talked despairingly about Donald's unworldliness and his opposition to his business philosophy, wasn't forthcoming, fobbing him off with one of his representatives. When the British cinema began to lose some of its post-war lustre, Rank had no compunction about trying to recoup his losses by introducing bingo. Although such a move appeared to challenge the strictures of his Church, he saw no conflict, especially since bingo in his eyes was a harmless social activity which brought much pleasure to many of life's disadvantaged. This wasn't the view of many Methodists and when his plans became public, there was an outcry that one of their leading lights favoured such an abhorrent activity. With Conference gearing up to impose retribution, Rank found solace in Edward Rogers, the Secretary of the Christian Citizenship Department. His report offering qualified support for his treasurer, helped persuade Conference to take an emollient line, (opportunism may also have had something to do with it since Methodism needed Rank's money).

Despite Conference agreeing that the cinema magnate was mistaken in his judgement, it refused to criticise him, accepting that he had a right to act according to his conscience. Once again, in a more permissive age, Donald's obsessive puritanism seemed marooned, especially since bingo was thriving most in the old Methodist strongholds of the Midlands and North. And although thereafter he continued to stick resolutely to his principles, another part of his Methodist heritage was history by the time of his death. For not only had the gaming industry's tentacles extended into the realm of spread-betting and the National Lottery, London under New Labour with its deregulatory ethos, was fast becoming the casino centre of the world.

The winter of 1962–63 was a particularly severe one, reducing Donald's audiences in the open air to a mere handful. With no let-up by mid-February, he was relieved to escape the chilly blasts for a five-week tour of the United States and Canada. His prime commitment was to give the Earl Lectures at Berkeley, California, alongside the celebrated theologian Paul Tillich, whose towering intellect didn't allow for contrary views, as Donald, much to his displeasure, was soon to discover. For when they were discussing the concept of God, Tillich described the divinity in phraseology so abstruse that Donald was left totally bemused as to his train of thought. He proceeded via Fresno and Holywood to Canada where he preached in the main cities for FOR. Again, as on previous visits, he was confronted with the sheer affluence of the lifestyle in California, and the boast of one of his hosts that they had more cadillacs per square yard than anywhere else in America. This affluence troubled him, since he felt it fostered in the large church congregations and the universities, a spiritual complacency which made them unresponsive to the concept of social responsibility. This was especially so in matters of race, an issue festering beneath the surface, and soon to explode into unseemly mass riots in the major cities.

Back home as his disillusionment with the extra-parliamentary tactics of CND became ever clearer, Donald entered the domestic fray as the increasingly tarnished Macmillan Government became weighed down by scandal. The main one involved the Secretary of State for War, John Profumo, who was forced to resign in June after lying to Parliament over a relationship he had with a lady of several lovers, who also happened to be enjoying the favours of the Russian defence attaché in London. To Donald the Profumo affair indicated that the country was becoming more decadent and it was time the Church said so. If man was sexually dirty he wouldn't remain politically clean. "This does not necessarily mean that he will practise the same deceit in a lobby as in a bedroom, but it means inexorably that his politics will reflect the same low and selfish ambitions as his amours."[9] The apparent obsession over security caused by Profumo's liaison, however, passed him by since to him the real security risk was having a Minister of War at all. He wanted the security services abolished.

Donald's vehemence over Profumo contrasted with his usual inclination towards lenience whenever a crime or misdemeanour occurred. For instance, the following April he was one of sixteen public figures to press for the reduction of the thirty-year sentence imposed on three of the Great Train Robbers, including Ronald Biggs. He called the sentences dreadful and unchristian and compared it to the extreme leniency shown to those perpetrators of cruelty to children.

With the resignation of Macmillan in October 1963 because of illness, the

Conservatives caused surprise and disillusionment alike with their choice of Lord Home, the Foreign Secretary, as his successor since Home was an aristocrat seemingly at odds with the spirit of the age. He was, however, a man of great integrity and a practising Christian, qualities which earned him a public accolade from the new Archbishop of Canterbury, Michael Ramsey, who described him as a man of humility. His tribute brought a blistering riposte from Donald, on behalf of CSM, who saw Home as the enemy. He castigated his policies on defence as clinically insane and with an election pending, placed himself on a war footing.

After a brief rest he was soon back in the news. On 5 March he launched a tirade in the *Methodist Recorder* about Britain's new sensation, the Beatles, warning that their rootless subculture was no substitute for the full life of the kingdom of God. Having dismissed their music as completely trivial and evanescent, he went on, "If this is western society, then with all their faults give me the Soviets. They at least believe that all aspects of life must be related to their overriding political beliefs."[10] While Donald's views once again caused much disquiet, the question was whether he really believed this? Although the brutal Soviet invasion of Hungary in November 1956 had provoked him into a stinging denunciation of communism for producing more scoundrels to the square yard than any other system of government, he also described the great adventure of the human spirit which had been implemented under its watch. Such achievements had in his estimation, stamped it with immortality. Thereafter, as he detected a thaw in democratic centralism under Khrushchev, he resented the bleak and barren landscape depicted by western propaganda of life in the Soviet Union. For his part he admired the drive and vitality of a society that produced many outstanding scientists, technicians and sportsmen, and applauded their continued attempts to build the alternative society.

"Despite the fallacies and ferocities of the communist system," he wrote in *Tribune* on 16 January 1959, "it has demonstrated this vital truth – that the power to make people change their physical and moral habits so that they begin to lead a new and better life is generated in a particular kind of community – the sort of society that is emerging in China and in Russia."[11] Unless non-Marxist socialism could produce a comparative powerhouse, he felt that there was no answer to this challenge. Seven years later he was again commending these countries for their sense of moral responsibility shown by their youth in the field of sexual morals in comparison to the West. "If they have rejected the Christian's heaven they have accepted a Marxist *community* life which is not very different in this regard from the Kingdom of Heaven – and for its sake have worked out a sexual pattern which may vary from the traditional Christian one, but is at least responsible."[12] Ironically, he felt that the main threat to these nascent societies was the growth of western materialism and all that it entailed for purposeless lives.

If one thing epitomised this new obsession for greed, it was, according to Donald, the advertising industry, since he felt it to be sleazy, dishonest and destructive, especially when applied to tobacco, alcohol and cars. The fact that modern man was increasingly susceptible to these products as well as gambling and drugs meant that shallow self-gratification rather than communal responsibility became the prevailing ethic. The fact that this cult of modernity was broadly reflected in Beatlemania and Liverpool becoming the new Jerusalem, accounted for much of his spleen towards the sound of the Mersey beat. Nothing that subsequently occurred in Britain, not least the growth of football hooliganism and organised crime, convinced him that the good society was any closer to completion, but equally his return to the Soviet Union in 1970 disabused him of some of his more optimistic assumptions about communism.

In May Donald and Marie led a party of forty-two, half of whom were from Kingsway, to Israel. Their tour began in Galilee, where in those tranquil surroundings encompassing the lake, he felt closest to the spirit of the Gospel, and proceeded to Jerusalem, visiting the holy sites. The experience proved a moving one, especially walking and praying in the Garden of Gethsemane with its rich sense of wonder. Although disenchanted by the commercialisation of Bethlehem, a poor contrast to Nazareth, he found that by seeing so many of the places in the flesh, it gave the Bible story an added meaning, as well as rein-forcing his view of the human Jesus. On a more political level, he felt that the replacement of religion by nationalism in the Middle East and the spawning of the nation state had created the conditions for its own destruction, a percep-tive enough view with war once again around the corner.

In the summer of 1964 the final preparations were drawn up for the October election. After their heated differences over defence and nationalisa-tion, Donald appeared back in harness with Labour now that Harold Wilson had replaced Gaitskell as leader, following the latter's sudden death in January 1963. Wilson was a close neighbour of the Sopers in Hampstead Garden Suburb where he and his wife worshipped at the Free Church, and he lavished affection on Donald in a way he did to few others. From the very start he proved an effective leader of the Opposition, contrasting his vision of a modern, meritocratic Britain with a tired and dated Conservative Party. Particularly edifying was his speech at the Labour Party Conference that autumn which extolled the importance of science in the new technological age. Donald was one of the many both within and outside the Labour Party to be deeply impressed by the speech. He commended it for its vitality and message of opportunity for all in this new age. The Conservatives, however, weren't giving up their lease on Downing Street without a fight. Throughout the summer, with the onset of a consumer boom, they closed the gap on Labour until the two parties stood neck and neck in the polls.

During the campaign Donald's talents as a speaker were again in demand, not least in Smethwick where the Conservatives won a vicious campaign on the back of racial prejudice, and in Wembley North for Illtyd Harrington where he drew the largest crowd. Harrington, a London councillor on the left of the party, had originally been selected to fight Dover, but after an internal dispute motivated by the right, he was unseated and forbidden from appealing to the Party Conference. He later recalled how Donald was the first man to spring to his defence, believing that he had every right to promote his views. His readiness to stand shoulder to shoulder with the victim of discrimination was one of his most endearing traits. His defence of conscientious objectors throughout the Second World War has already been noted, and in the face of a raging storm, he defended the right of Margaret Knight, an agnostic, to broadcast in a series of talks critical of Christianity in 1955. Pauline Webb, later a leading figure in the Methodist Missionary Society, recalled how in 1957 Donald was the one person to console her following the opprobrium heaped upon her at Conference for an uncompromising speech in which she had urged the Church to be more militant in tackling poverty. His soothing words that there was nothing better than being a fool for Christ's sake, and his entreaties that she continue the fight, meant a lot to a young woman temporarily devoid of friends. Finally in 1963 there was his support for Donald Chesworth, the Labour councillor in Notting Hill (who incurred unpopularity with the right wing for his anti-racist sentiments) by personally canvassing for him in the multi-ethnic Golborne Ward. This was a substantial gesture on Donald's part since temperamentally he didn't enjoy face to face canvassing with its propensity for small-talk and soliciting of electoral favours.

Overall, the 1964 result was watertight, but Labour with the smallest of overall majorities was able to return to power for the first time in thirteen years. By way of a novelty, Wilson, a practising Congregationalist, inaugurated a service in the Crypt Chapel of the House of Commons for the Government, at which he read the lesson, Donald said the prayers and Mervyn Stockwood preached. The service closed with "Jerusalem", although any hopes of a radical programme would be stymied by their tiny majority. Appreciating the constraints under which the Government operated, Donald kept his powder dry during its honeymoon period, other than to criticise it for supporting the US war operation in Vietnam at a rally in Trafalgar Square in April 1965. In any case he was too busy causing offence closer to home.

Donald's 1965 New Year resolution was anything but happy for many Christians, when he used the pages of the *Methodist Recorder* to advocate a moratorium on reading the Bible for a year. Recalling his well-known aphorism that the Bible was a marvellous servant but an intolerable master, he felt that the scriptures represented an intellectual incubus that couldn't be removed until the Church approached this controversial collection of books in an entirely fresh way. For good measure he also called for a ban on revivalist sermons which looked to immediate conversion. His refrain was a familiar one to those who knew him, but his readership wasn't amused, accusing him of all kinds of heretical beliefs. Few rallied to his defence in what even his friends concluded was one of his sillier statements, but Donald being Donald was unrepentant. Weeks later, adhering to his familiar ruse of overstating a case in order to keep it in the public eye, he was telling his congregation at Kingsway that neither the reading of the Bible nor Sunday observance were part of the original pattern of worship. He argued that the most important thing about the early Christians was their awareness that they were no longer bound by the old customs as much as by the love and will of God. Instead, the first day of the week became not a day of regulations but a day of love and rejoicing. Relating this to the present, Donald said that the first characteristic of Christian living must be in the way one lived. "The Christian is the one who, loving freely, is free in every other part of life as well. The emphasis is not upon 11.00 and 6.30; it is not upon kneeling at our bedside before we go to bed, or upon saying grace before meat. The emphasis is that, for our very soul's sake, we remember our Lord and rejoice in his triumph, and at regular intervals – pre-eminently perhaps on Sunday mornings – we remember his Resurrection, we pay our tribute to his love, and we ask that we may be joined with him in his work."[13] It was a theme he was to return to again and again.

Aside from his support for the underdog, Donald was unswervingly loyal to friends and colleagues. It was in this spirit that he often traversed the country in some discomfort (especially as he could never sleep on trains) to speak in humble surroundings, as well as more salubrious ones, regardless of whether he was paid expenses. In January 1965 at short notice he acceded to a request from Harry Morton, then in charge of Central and East African Affairs at the Overseas Mission Department, to preside over the new United Church of Zambia. This Church had been created out of seven Churches including the Methodist District's eleven circuits, the Church of Barotseland and the United Church of Central Africa – the latter under the Presidency of Colin Morris, one of the prime movers behind union as the new state of Zambia celebrated its independence from Britain. These differences were referred to by the new President, Kenneth Kaunda, an occasional worshipper at Kingsway on visits to London, at the great inaugural service at Mindolo, when he stressed the need for unity. It was in this spirit that the United Synod of the new Church elected Morris as its first President, and he had the honour of having the presidential scarf adorned with two silver eagles, bestowed upon him by Donald. Morris recalled how during Donald's brief stay, he invigorated his audiences with some typically insightful speeches on nation-building, which mixed the secular with the profound.

At an inaugural thanksgiving service in Lusaka, Kaunda warned the minister in charge that he would have to leave prematurely for a Cabinet meeting, but reminded of this during Donald's impassioned address, he decided on second thoughts to stay. The Cabinet could wait. After a hectic round of mission churches and university campuses in the capital, Donald, despite his bad leg and little sleep, undertook a whirlwind tour of the Zambesi Valley to see for himself the state of the Church in the outlying areas. He returned exhausted but heartened by what he saw, not least the expression of the country's socio-economic infrastructure and the sincerity of its new President.

During the years 1958–65 when Donald was at the height of his political activity, three particular causes consumed his time. The first related to his life-long concern for pacifism, the other two to improving the social conditions in London through the good offices of both Church and State. As ever, his courage and commitment couldn't be doubted as he waded into dangerous currents of controversy and if his hopes weren't realised over nuclear disarmament, his work in Notting Hill and municipal government brought real progress.

The Suez crisis helped to foment the anti-nuclear movement, since it precipitated a reassessment of Britain's defence policy, which now gave a higher priority to nuclear rather than conventional capability. In practice this meant even closer associations with the Americans, although the logic of a British nuclear deterrent presumed the possibility of independent action. The Macmillan Government's Defence White Paper of 1957 drew attention to the future role of nuclear weapons in defence policy, and that April Britain exploded her first hydrogen bomb on Christmas Island at a time when her independent nuclear deterrent was in its embryonic stages. At the annual FOR Council meeting in May, Donald stressed the moral rather than the political and scientific issues involved in the manufacturing of the bomb. He accepted that conventional weaponry was just as repellent as the hydrogen bomb, but saw no reason why FOR shouldn't mobilise against the latter. "Let us keep our eyes on the supreme objective," he said, "while we complain and campaign against this beastly thing."[14] And by campaigning, Donald didn't just mean leafleting and public meetings. "There is a kind of direct action which, I believe, can have profitable results," he told *Peace News*. "I am sure we must get out on to the streets more often."[15]

Already the National Committee for the Abolition of Nuclear Weapon Tests had been set up in February 1957 to which Donald became a Sponsor. That May 2,000 demonstrators called on the Government to halt or postpone the planning tests in order to give a moral lead. The Methodist Conference passed a resolution declaring that the Government had an obligation to discontinue the further testing of nuclear weapons, and in November the Direct Action Committee[DAC] was launched in protest at Britain's hydrogen bomb testing in the Pacific.

Prior to this, Donald, along with seven MPs, had tabled a resolution on unarmed defence for the 1957 Labour Conference, claiming that mass action could prevent suicide. This set the scene for a highly divisive week at Brighton as the defence question dominated proceedings, especially the spectacular volte-face by the great tribune of the left, Aneurin Bevan, a unilateralist hitherto. His assertion that a Labour Foreign Secretary couldn't be sent naked into the conference chamber shocked his followers, as much as his strident denunciations of their desire to ditch the British bomb incensed them. His speech, effectively abandoning unilateral disarmament, not only caused further rifts in the party – it brought considerable disillusionment to Donald. Because his trip to Japan had caused him to miss Conference, his public reaction in *Tribune* didn't appear until 13 December. The fact that he employed reasonably restrained language in no way diminished the force of his message. "For long enough there have been all too obvious signs in the Labour movement generally of a dearth of strong moral principles and the lack of a big enough philosophy to sustain its activities. Perhaps that is why the attitude of Aneurin Bevan at the Labour Conference towards the manufacture of the H-bomb and the rejection there of the proposals for the unilateral abandonment of the bomb, not only knocked the stuffing out of many of his ardent supporters, but took the heart out of many more who looked to him for the convictions they did not possess themselves. Whatever his motives (and I do not for a moment impugn either his courage or his sincerity) he has temporarily turned the Labour movement from a crusade into just an alternative bunch of politicians to those who now sit in office."[16] It was in this spirit that CND was formed.

The inspiration came from a vitriolic anti-nuclear article by J. B. Priestley, the eminent playwright and broadcaster, in the *New Statesman* that November, which attracted a groundswell of support. A meeting of leading anti-nuclear campaigners at the home of John Collins proved the prelude to a public meeting at Caxton Hall, Westminster, on 17 February 1958. On the night, 5,000 turned up, forcing the use of several adjoining halls. A new pressure group was born. Most of its self-appointed executive were well-known radicals such as Priestley, Kingsley Martin, editor of the *New Statesman,* A. J. P. Taylor, Michael Foot, Bertrand Russell who became president, and John Collins who acted as chairman. A whole series of public meetings were instituted, but what really brought the movement national prominence was its participation in the Easter Aldermaston march, organised by the DAC. On the wettest Easter holiday for fifty-eight years, 9,000 set off from Trafalgar Square to Aldermaston, the Atomic Weapons Research Department in Berkshire, students joining with public sector workers, trade unionists and churchmen in an upbeat mood. On the second day, in teeming rain, Donald led the march and found it a very moving experience, not least the unexpected thrill of finding Marie and his daughters having made their own separate arrangements to accompany it. He was also taken by the way that members of the Hayes Council in Middlesex stood for hours by the roadside to pay their respects for a cause they ardently supported. The march ended with a long oration, in the dank fields at Aldermaston, from Martin Niemöller, the celebrated Lutheran pastor who had been one of the prime movers behind the German resistance to Hitler.

The impact of CND, which, despite Donald, John Collins and some other clerics, was largely a middle-class, secular organisation, was given added meaning by renewed concern about the safety of nuclear testing and talk of American planes patrolling over Britain with hydrogen bombs on board. In May 1958 Donald joined others to lay a wreath at the Cenotaph and the following month addressed 6,000 in Trafalgar Square with John Collins and Michael Foot. A great orator himself, Foot derived a particular pleasure from hearing Donald's own distinctive style expressed with such authority and goodwill. Of all the speakers he ever heard, he felt that Donald was second only to his great idol, Bevan, especially in the way he could develop an idea in perfectly shaped grammatical sentences, and demolish the weak point of an opponent's case. He also never saw him beaten in argument and felt that he put the pacifist case better than anyone else.

At Mansfield, Donald told his FOR audience that no one ever told the truth about armaments and that the first casualty of war was truth. The British people probably lacked the freedom to get the Americans out of Britain but they had the power to put an end "to this miserable and fatal process of experimenting with hydrogen bomb weapons". In *Peace News* on 6 June he was clearer as to what this power consisted of. "All who oppose nuclear weapons," he declared, "can stand together and can share equally in the risks and the penalties. I hope that I shall find the courage to practise 'passive resistance' – the kind of non-violent and unhateful opposition to law and order that Gandhi raised to a fine art and made a tremendous weapon."[17]

Following the success of the Aldermaston march, CND wanted to keep up the momentum. A week's vigil outside the factory was followed by a nine-week picket beginning on 20 July, designed to confront those most directly involved in the testing and manufacturing of the weapons in as direct a way as possible. The climax to this protest came with a sit-down demonstration outside the Aldermaston gates following the refusal of Sir William Penney, the Director of the Atomic Weapons Research Establishment, to meet the delegation. In torrential rain and without food, Donald, with Pat Arrowsmith, a prominent member of DAC, led twenty-five other leading activists in an all-day vigil, spending his time discussing infant baptism with an Anglican priest. At that point police asked them to move on as they were on private property. On their refusal, names were taken including Donald's, but, despite several exchanges of letters throughout the day with the management, their protest failed to rouse either them or the workforce into action.

For the 1959 Aldermaston march the route was reversed so that by finishing in the capital, the emphasis would be on pressurising politicians, not nuclear workers. A crowd of 20,000 turned out and Donald was among the speakers at Trafalgar Square on Easter Monday. He worked the crowd into a frenzy as he berated the press for deliberately underestimating CND's appeal, a claim later politely questioned by John Collins, and extolled Khrushchev's latest moves towards peace. "... looking at the vast crowd as they chanted 'Ban the Bomb'," he later wrote in *Tribune*, "... I felt more convinced than ever that in this tremendous demonstration the voice of God was being heard in the voice of the people."[18] He spent time that summer at various rallies and fortified by a resolution at the Methodist Conference condemning nuclear weapons outright, he raised the nuclear scare during the election that October, but the truth was that it had relatively little bearing on the result as the Conservatives again increased their majority.

In April the following year Donald took issue with a British Council of Churches Report entitled "Christians and Atomic War" on two counts. First, the tendency to place all the blame for the nuclear arms race on the Soviet Union and second, the acceptance of the need to live with the bomb. He condemned such rationale as indefensible.

For two years CND and DAC had maintained an uneasy truce over the nature of their tactics since the latter's inclination to take the path of civil disobedience caused anxiety with the former. Their tactics were made clear at a demonstration at Harrington on 2 January 1960, when six leading members were arrested and charged with incitement to breaking the law, and two ended up going to prison. Collins was publicly forced to disassociate CND from this violence, while applauding their overall objectives. The tension didn't end there, as DAC-inspired demonstrations continued at arms manufacturers with a view to halting production. At Siddeley Engineering in Bristol in August, 100 out of the 500 workforce deliberately extended their lunch hour to listen to Donald preach pacifism, but again coaxing the management into lending a sympathetic ear proved beyond them.

That Easter 100,000 had participated in the Aldermaston march and when the Government replaced Blue Streak, the land-based rocket, first with Skybolt and then the Polaris nuclear submarine, thereby relying on the Americans to supply the missiles, CND grew both in numbers and credibility. But what really boosted their campaign was the changing attitude of the Labour Party. The party had always been home to a pacifist, anti-militarist minority and once the 1959 election was over, unilateralist supporters, encouraged by the wavering of some of the larger unions, stepped up their pressure for change – not just for pacifism but also for socialism. It is important to stress this point because as Frank Parkin wrote in his book *Middle Class Radicalism*, post-October 1959, the dispute over nuclear warfare became incorporated into the more general and deep-seated disagreement over the future direction of the party under its abrasive leader, Gaitskell. On 24 June 1960 Donald had made his feelings clear in *Tribune*. "... it is the Right-wing which is essentially divisive, and if, indeed, it prevails will rend the Labour movement in two, whereas the unilateral Clause Four Socialist Left-wing provides the only conceivable platform upon which all members of the Labour movement could finally stand together."[19]

What had upset Donald and others was Gaitskell's desire to ditch Clause IV, the commitment to nationalisation, which Gaitskell now felt redundant to an increasingly affluent society. This, along with his rigidly pro-American instincts, helped account for the extraordinary sight of 5,000 supporters packing the fashionable Yorkshire resort of Scarborough on the eve of Conference, chanting "Gaitskell must go" as party bosses deliberated on their resolutions for the week ahead. Given that the majority of the big unions, following the lead of Frank Cousins, the Secretary of the Transport and General Workers Union, had switched to a unilateralist stance, victory for them seemed a mere formality. But if this was the case, and it was, Gaitskell wasn't going to take it lying down. In a fiercely uncompromising speech he promised to "fight and fight and fight again" to retain sanity within the party, thereby placing his leadership on the line.

Not surprisingly his words left Donald cold. "No one wants a leader who is going to lie down – but what is he going to fight?" he declared in *Tribune* – "not first of all the enemy, but his own side – and that is a bit peculiar ... it is surely farcical to entrust the leadership to a member of the party who represents the minority view."[20] In the ensuing dogfight, when Gaitskell was challenged by Harold Wilson for the leadership, Donald supported the latter, placing CSM four-square behind his candidacy. With the right rallying to his cause, Gaitskell saw off Wilson fairly easily and began his spirited fightback to regain control of the party agenda. Meanwhile, Donald in contrast to the 1930s when the peace movement had been independent of party, began to push for the incorporation of CND into the Labour Party, believing that pacifism could only thrive within a socialist system. These views made little impression on the CND executive, who, Foot aside, weren't conventional party types. They saw themselves primarily engaged in a great moral crusade untarnished by sordid political machinations, which for all its undoubted attractions, prevented them from turning headlines into tangible political achievements. Their reluctance to engage in radical street politics also placed them in conflict with DAC, which under the abrasive influence of Ralph Schoenman, an American postgraduate and radical member of Youth CND, was stepping up its campaign of mass civil disobedience. In October 1960 the Committee of 100 was formed comprising a galaxy of public figures under the tempestuous leadership of Bertrand Russell, who resigned as CND's president, and for the next twelve months they became the cutting edge of the peace campaign. Their tactics placed Donald in something of a quandary. As a Sponsor of DAC he had supported mass protest as a way of raising public awareness of the nuclear peril, but had been troubled by the illegal trespassing of the US Thor rocket bases in East Anglia as far back as 1958. Now with non-co-operation being taken to new heights, he gave on 3 March 1961 his starkest warning yet about the direction in which DAC was heading. Civil disobedience was only justifiable when political action was otherwise impossible. Further militancy would only exacerbate the growing divisions within the movement and detract from the imperative of securing its aims through constitutional means.

A month later he was more specific. "It should be crystal clear to all, except those who are wilfully blind, that the Labour movement must be the political instrument for the achievement of nuclear disarmament,"[21] he cautioned in *Tribune*. Consequently, although he continued to campaign with gusto, especially that year's Easter march in which 150,000 participated, and a Pacifist Fortnight campaign in September, he turned his back on the more extreme protests. These reached their culmination in Trafalgar Square that September when at an organised sit-in of 12,000 protesters, over 1,300 were arrested, including the nonagenarian Russell, the highest ever in Britain in one day. While once again registering his opposition to this form of civil disobedience, he also felt bound to applaud the "sincere and sacrificial actions as exhibited by those who have gone to prison for conscience sake".[22] Such dedication, he told the *Methodist Recorder*, shamed the average Christian who, apart from a greedy private interest in salvation, seemed apathetic if not cowardly in comparison. This last statement was partly a swipe at his own Church, since although the Methodists had gone further than any other Church in deploring nuclear weapons, support for the peace movement among the rank and file was at best ambiguous. Not surprisingly in this context many took umbrage at his comments, as they did over his later claim that it was the non-pacifists within Methodism who were now the heretics. Writing in the February 1963 edition of *Reconciliation*, his views were nothing if not forthright. "Especially in the realm of what we call reason, the cult of violence, expressed in the nuclear deterrent, is turning men, and particular politicians, into blithering idiots even before it turns them into incinerated corpses."[23]

As the civil unrest continued, Donald again reiterated the priority of preaching the pacifist case within the Labour Party, but the problem was that the high-watermark of pacifism had passed. In deference to Gaitskell's insistence that multilateralism be reinstated, the trade unions, craving party solidarity, reversed that stance at Blackpool in September 1961 and gave their leader the votes he needed to re-establish his authority. Undaunted, Donald continued to pursue his goal as the Committee of 100 remained bent on a collision course with the State through a series of mass demonstrations at key military installations. These culminated in a planned mass showdown at Wethersfield US Airforce base in Essex on 9 December, (which in the process turned out to be something of a damp squib). Sensing the political gravity of such a challenge, Special Branch raided the homes of leading activists of the Committee of 100 and arrested six of them on charges of conspiracy under the Official Secrets Act. One of the accused had converted to pacifism after listening to Donald in Hyde Park, but neither he nor the general public were overtly supportive come their trial in February 1962. Despite a number of uncomfortable questions being posed, the judge showed no mercy to the accused and handed out heavy custodial sentences.

With the authorities now on the offensive, public support on the wane and racked by internal division, CND looked a shadow of its former self. This decline also owed something to the Cuban Missile Crisis in October 1962, which showed Britain's role in a superpower age to be minimal, and the Nuclear Test Ban Treaty in June 1963, which relieved some of the tension between East and West. As the gulf widened within the peace movement, Donald became more contemptuous of the extremists, not least their unseemly tactics on the Easter Aldermaston march in 1963. In a savage article soon afterwards in *Tribune* entitled "CND Must Grow Up or Shut Up", he called on the ailing pressure group to cast aside its childish gestures in favour of acting responsibly through the Labour Party, especially since the latter was becoming more unilateralist, a claim which didn't square with reality. His outburst unleashed a torrent of correspondence, taking issue with his contention that constitutional rectitude was the right road to travel down. One letter read: "If Dr Soper who calls himself a pacifist wishes to call for support for the Labour Party, let me suggest that something more than a smear campaign is necessary, and that he would do well to find an alternative to direct action that can be seen to lead towards unilateralism."[24]

For all his prominence on marches and platforms, Donald hadn't been at the heart of CND decision-making. At first sight this seems rather surprising, given his wealth of experience and commitment to the cause, allied to his attractive personality which Pat Arrowsmith thought shone in comparison to some of the others. Part of the answer is down to strategy. While applauding the general drift of its policy, the movement's inclusive nature didn't conform to Donald's fundamentalist position on the disarmament of all weapons, or slightly paradoxically, his desire to integrate CND within the confines of the Labour Party. More important, perhaps, was his distaste for committee work and his alienation from both Bertrand Russell, the President until his resignation in 1960, and John Collins, the Chairman, whom he considered to be vain and cantankerous. Colin Pritchard and Robert Taylor in their book *The Protest Makers* related how Ralph Schoenman approached Donald at one stage to see if he would be at all interested in standing for the leadership of CND. Donald refused to consider the matter. "With hindsight," wrote the authors, "it is interesting to speculate what might have ensued had Soper become Chairman of CND: he was certainly more acceptable to both wings of the Movement than Collins."[25]

As for Donald, he considered the early Aldermaston marches to be one of the noblest crusades he was ever associated with, for a cause which in his estimation surpassed all others in importance. Once again, as with PPU, he felt that the true relationship between disarmament and the political and economic conditions within which it was being advocated, was never pressed as it should have been. To him the economy and the nation state were both dependent upon the arms industry, the main reason he felt behind CND's failure since it didn't marry its intention to get rid of weapons with an equal resolve to get rid of the system which required them. This wasn't necessarily the analysis with which all his fellow campaigners would have concurred (he also, to be fair, accepted that lack of numbers, especially among the working class, was an impediment), but there is no doubting the fact that it was a conviction from which he never wavered.

On the domestic front Donald was grappling with problems of utmost gravity at the same time as he was highly committed to CND. The area of Notting Hill/North Kensington had long been blighted by dilapidated housing, inadequate facilities and juvenile delinquency. In this combustible atmosphere, Irish people resided uneasily with recently arrived immigrants from West Africa and the Caribbean, and egged on by right-wing extremists, tension spilled over into race riots in August 1958. Shocked by these developments, Donald began to immerse himself in local affairs and became fully acquainted with the social ills prevalent in that environment. In a letter to *The Times* on 23 May 1959 and in an article in his *Tribune* column two weeks later, he condemned the evil power of landlords to extort excessive rents for rotten accommodation from frightened tenants, many of them black people. He also responded vigorously to the call for a radical new Christian initiative from Donald Chesworth, the Labour councillor for that area, and a major influence behind Donald's nomination to the LCC as an alderman.

At the Methodist Conference in Bristol weeks later, Donald, in response to the report on London Mission Affairs, highlighted the poverty and inaction of the Church in that area. The answer he felt lay in community centres run on secular lines by a team of Methodist ministers and helpers shorn of traditional piety which could reach out to all parts of the community. To help his vision become reality, he was prepared to take financial and pastoral responsibility for it. Galvanised by this challenge, David Mason, together with Geoffrey Ainger who had worked in East Harlem, New York, and Norwyn Denny, an outstanding Circuit Minister, quickly got to work. They sent him a memorandum on Group Ministry as the panacea for inner-city renewal, complete with an enquiry as to whether it was the type of thing he was looking for. No sooner had he received it than Donald was on the phone to Mason to confirm that it was, and asking when he could start.

Such audacity, however, would be hard to accomplish in an era when there was a relative shortage of personnel, alongside a prejudice against anything outwith the normal Circuit ministry. It required a series of special meetings to which Donald was very much privy, to see whether the Lancaster Road Church, situated in a run-down multi-racial area of North Kensington under the auspices of the Bayswater Circuit, could be incorporated into the West London Mission. The Superintendent Minister of the Circuit, the Revd Eric Elliott, in charge for the previous eight years, was strongly in favour and his support, according to Mason, was absolutely crucial.

In July 1960 Donald won Conference approval for his proposals. That autumn Mason, with his wife Ann, took up residence, to be joined in 1961 by

Norwyn Denny, and the following year by Geoffrey Ainger. From the very beginning there was an air of intense activity as the church premises were given a facelift, congregations escalated and pastoral visiting was made a priority. In time there were experiments in worship, an expansion of youth work and the formation of a Housing Trust to help provide cheap and decent rents. Over twenty nationalities worshipped, worked and learnt together, providing a model for the Church at work in the community. Given the fact that there was no funding within Methodism for this kind of enterprise, Notting Hill owed much to Donald's courage and financial backing, ensuring that the new ministers were provided with generous facilities. He made a point, too, of visiting frequently and chairing a conference at the church of eminent people to lend credibility to the new project. When difficulties arose from jealous Methodist ministers elsewhere in the capital, or from the right-wing clique of the local Labour Party, Donald, in addition to soothing ruffled feathers, remained unwavering in his support. In this context it isn't surprising that he was a trifle disappointed when Norwyn Denny requested autonomy for Notting Hill in 1967, but accepted with good grace. The decision to sever links, although a shade premature, was justified in the long term, since the present Notting Hill with its flourishing church and more salubrious environment is a far cry from the wilderness of the 1950s. When Donald, looking back on his life, considered this experiment to be one of the best things he ever did, his words lacked nothing in conviction.

Donald's special knowledge of social work at the West London Mission led to his surprising nomination as one of twenty aldermen to the LCC by the ruling Labour group in 1958, especially since he had no previous links with the Council. He accepted the nomination to some consternation from a number of his colleagues who opposed his more radical views, on the understanding that he would abide by the party whip, provided it didn't conflict with a matter of conscience.

That conscience was soon offended over a question of freedom of speech. When the Labour Party, under its formidable chairman Sir Isaac Hayward, rather clumsily tried to suppress any kind of public dissension on pain of the whip being withdrawn, Donald took his concerns to Michael Foot. Foot told him that the standing orders of the LCC went much further than anything ever attempted in the Parliamentary Labour Party. He could see no reason for such stringency, especially when no effort had been made to debate the general principles of a particular case within the confines of the LCC Labour group. Armed with Foot's support, Donald launched a blistering broadside on his leader in *Tribune* on 30 January 1959. He called his decision impudent and insufferable. "... I publicly criticise, attack, repudiate, denounce, execrate and abominate it,"[26] he fulminated. Claiming that he would never have joined the Labour Party if such a ban was typical of its practices, he called it an egregious and impudent innovation. Having thrown down the gauntlet, Donald found that his words appeared to carry weight with sympathetic colleagues, for when the group met there was no word of rebuke. When a Conservative member asked the Chairman of the Establishments Committee, R. E. Goodwin, why a copy of *Tribune* containing the offending article was missing from the Members' Reading Room, Goodwin said that this was a matter of speculation. There were to be other spats in 1960. First, over civil defence, when Donald successfully carried an amendment, going well beyond party policy, calling on the Government to support unilateral disarmament through international agreement. Second, his public criticism of the Labour group for their unimaginative brand of socialism as he drew public attention to the limitations of municipal government. In general, however, his contributions were constructive, if rather undemonstrative, especially during his first two and a half years when he voted on only 16 divisions out of 107 – a statistic which caused some murmurings among his colleagues. The reason for this chequered record lay in the fact that most of the more important divisions took place later in the day between 7 p.m. and midnight after long and tedious debates. Such arrangements held out little appeal to Donald, since the need to hang around and socialise would have been at the expense of precious time at home.

At Labour group meetings, Donald would sit at the back and volunteer opinions which were both forthright and amusing. He was also receptive to the views of the younger, less established members, and to the smaller authorities in the capital. According to Illtyd Harrington, a borough councillor in Paddington and then a colleague on the Greater London Council [GLC], he discharged his duties very efficiently by the standards of the left. Compared to his colleagues, he never had a document in front of him and having understood the politics of any situation, he expected others to do the same. In committee, without compromising his own views, he never stifled debate unless it descended into verbosity. In the tussle over defence shelters, he brushed aside bureaucratic interference because it was preventing something beneficial from happening. Not surprisingly, he was particularly effective in those areas in which he was familiar.

In the 1960s the big question affecting London was the plight of the homeless and whether the Council could come up with solutions. Donald, in Harrington's opinion, was of profound influence here when serving on the Housing Committee, especially in the need to find space and keep families together. The power of his intellect and the rapidity of his response to changing circumstances based on his experiences at Kingsway were ready assets, such as his willingness to support, in November 1964, the Health Committee's recommendation that family planning should be advocated for unmarried people. He also supported the cutting of the levy made on Sunday cinemas in 1965 in the name of enjoyment. What he wouldn't stomach was the persecution of minorities, which explained his motion in January 1960, supported by the Conservatives, deploring the rise of Nazism and anti-semitic activity in London, and his participation in a high-profile march to highlight the concern.

Donald undertook valuable service on the Health Committee for two years and the Children's Committee for five, not least in terms of his expertise on the relationship between voluntary and statutory institutions. He was a strong supporter of replacing large-scale units for young women in need with self-contained bed-sits, and when he also became Chairman of Mayford Approved School, he found it to be an illuminating experience. Aside from supervising the rebuilding of the chapel, one of his responsibilities as chairman was to examine the boys after a period of time to see if they had improved enough to be released. He discovered that for so many of them there was no way of appealing to their better nature, since they lacked a distinct understanding of the difference between right and wrong, leading him to ponder the devastating consequences of a godless society.

When the GLC replaced the LCC in 1963, Donald was one of Labour's first aldermen to be selected, a tribute to his audacity which shone in the company of more cautious colleagues. In Harrington's opinion, Donald won great respect as an alderman and his work in local government helped him on his way to higher and greater things.

CHAPTER ELEVEN

The Red Baron

When Labour returned to power in 1964 after its years in the wilderness, partisan supporters like Donald looked forward to an era of fundamental change in which Britain finally shook off the relics of her aristocratic constitution. The fact that this never really happened was epitomised by Labour's cautious approach to the House of Lords and to the monarchy. The old Tory gibe about one half of the party wanting to abolish the Lords and the other half to enter it contained more than a kernel of truth, as subsequent events were to prove.

For years Donald had been a scourge of the establishment, his egalitarian views allowing no room for the existence of either the monarchy or the Lords, the latter "the natural extension of this immoral class consciousness, into the realm of political and economic practice".[1] The imposition of the Life Peerages Act in 1958, designed to diversify its aristocratic composition, did little to appease him, so that when his name featured among eleven new life peers in May 1965, it created a minor sensation. His allies on the left were bemused and dismayed in equal measure, fearing lest he had sold his soul for a mess of pottage. Even his good friend, Michael Foot, then still a radical backbencher, felt moved to chide him gently in an affectionate missive.

> Dear Donald,
> I am sure you don't expect a letter of congratulations from me. I merely send you my affection and assurance of my continual devotion and admiration. However, I warned you when you became an alderman that it might go to your head – and now see what happens. I think at some point I will have to take your spirituality in hand.
> In the meantime, I send you my love and good wishes.
> > Yours ever,
> > > Michael[2]

His critics at Hyde Park had a field day, and one who roasted him at length was dismissed as a miserable little twit. Later, the Revd Henry Edwards, Vicar of St Michael's Highgate, wrote in his church magazine, "The Revd Donald Soper is now Lord Soper, and this seems to me a pity. He was always a rebel in favour of the underdog, agin the Government, but now it feels as though he has left us just for a riband to stick in his coat – a thing one thought he would have rejected with scorn."[3]

Others, in contrast, took a more charitable view. "Mr Wilson," the *Northern Despatch* declared, "has brought a new spirit of imagination to the job of staffing the House of Lords. The choice of Donald Soper, a critic of the Government's Vietnam policy, shows how far these new Labour peers are from being dependable yes-men."[4] The *Sun* proclaimed him the most colourful figure of the new peers. The *Daily Mirror* described him as one of Labour's most forceful speakers, predicting that his lively Nonconformist radicalism would make a fascinating contrast to the restraining style usually associated with Church of England bishops. The *Methodist Recorder* was similarly effusive."Dr Soper is the first Methodist minister to receive such an honour, and this tribute to his vigorous and uninhibited ministry is one which will be welcomed in the warmest possible way by his fellow Methodists all over the world."[5] It wasn't just the Methodists. The Archbishop of Canterbury, Michael Ramsey, whom Donald later considered to be a very great man, wrote to express his immense pleasure at his coming to the Lords. He had long been hoping to see some ministers of religion other than those of the establishment brought into the second chamber and he thought it excellent that Donald would be bringing his gifts of religion and concern for right.[6]

Ramsey's comments about Donald and the Free Churches seemed rather at odds with his predecessor. John Travell, in his biography of Leslie Weatherhead, related how when the New Year Honours List for 1960 was being drawn up, Geoffrey Fisher wrote to Kenneth Slack, the General Secretary of the British Council of Churches, to say that he was struggling to think of an outstanding Methodist to nominate and could he help put him right. Slack nominated Sangster, Weatherhead and Donald, to which Fisher replied that Sangster was too ill, Weatherhead too tinged with theological controversy and Donald too political. In the end Weatherhead was awarded the CBE, the first Methodist minister to be so honoured, and not before time. "By any standards of greatness, Weatherhead was a great man"[7] was Donald's verdict in the *Methodist Recorder*, on his friend's death in January 1976.

From the Government's perspective, Donald's elevation to the peerage was an inspired choice. Not only would his personality add a weighty presence to the Upper House, his Methodist colours, his admirable social work at the West London Mission and international renown as a popular evangelist was very much the type of breadth envisaged by the Life Peerages Act. When

Wilson first apprised Donald of his intentions by telephone, he appeared surprisingly chuffed by the offer, given his known antipathy to the Lords. David Mason has recollections of Donald confiding in him as to what he should do, but his procrastination didn't last for long. Moreover, it was a decision which he subsequently never regretted, even though the hereditary peerage narrowly outlasted him. When taxed about this, he cheerfully admitted it was a compromise, adding that his friend Fenner Brockway, a left-wing peer, told him that it was an opportunity not to be missed. And this to Donald was the crucial point. For a cleric fascinated with politics and power, the Lords was the ideal forum for him to propagate his views, especially since the laxity of the whip system there compared to the Commons wouldn't compromise his independence. The fact that the Lords was close to Kingsway also meant that he could attend frequently without relinquishing any of his other spiritual commitments. On top of this there was the personal kudos that membership of the Lords conferred on him and his family, whom he wasn't averse to introducing by their titles. For all his iconoclasm Donald, as his time at school and university showed, was very much at home with the establishment, revelling in the company of brilliant people. Always a model of decorum when away from the platform or soapbox, he was well respected on the Tory benches, as evident by the number who turned out to listen to him, and even when they profoundly disagreed with some proposition he ventilated, they often couched their opposition in mellifluous tones.

In some ways the Lords' sedate atmosphere militated against Donald's style of speaking, and he used to claim that he missed the hecklers. His reservations were understandable. George MacLeod, for all his brilliance in the pulpit, never shone there as Lord MacLeod of Fuinary, mainly because of his tendency to lecture, nor did Mervyn Stockwood, an equally charismatic preacher. Stockwood always felt that the sheer vastness of the auditorium made it alien territory for orators. Despite this he agreed with Michael Ramsey's observation that Donald was an outstanding success, because he was brief, factual and possessed an attractive voice. His humour, too, was appreciated, a fact apparent in his maiden speech when speaking as the first Methodist minister there he felt that he should consult its founder about the House. "And, trawling through John Wesley's immortal Journal, I find that there is only one reference ... He says on January 25, in his diary of 1785, 'I spent two or three hours in the House of Lords. What is a lord but a sinner born to die?'"[8]

Certainly Donald, whatever his views about the Lords and his quip about them being evidence of life after death, didn't underestimate the place. He recognised that whenever he spoke, there was bound to be someone present who had more expertise on the subject in question than he did, and in contrast to normal practice fretted over his research. Over the years he addressed them on some 250 occasions on a wide number of topics, as ever without notes, finding that on practical matters his personal experience in social work formed a basis on which to express theological truths. The fact that Donald didn't just confine himself to spiritual matters was welcomed by his fellow peers, since they didn't like clerics to speak exclusively on religion. How effective these contributions were, given the Lords' limited power, is a matter of some conjecture. Donald certainly felt that he would never achieve more as a politician, always claiming that after initiating a three-hour debate on alcohol before a packed house, he was able to lay on the equivalent of a Royal Commission on Alcohol. Barbara Castle reckoned that he was right to breach enemy territory to put the socialist case there, a view belatedly supported by Michael Foot who, in retrospect, recognised that Donald had used his time there to good effect.

Although a regular attender of the meetings of the Labour peers every Thursday for twenty-five years, and content to be guided by the whips when unsure how to vote, Donald naturally, as a free spirit, liked the independence associated with an unelected house. Indeed, he increasingly saw this independence and expertise as vital to the constitutional process, since matters of high complexity could be properly considered, rather than merely left to partisan whim in the other place. Consequently, for all his talk about the need to abolish the Upper House, he recognised that it worked, and that if abolished, something else of an advisory capacity unbeholden to Prime Ministerial patronage would need to be put in its place which didn't usurp the superiority of the Commons. Confronted with this dilemma, he ruled out an elected second chamber and, as time went on, quietly dropped his calls for complete abolition, settling instead for removal of the hereditary peerage. Even this measure was hardly a priority, for when, during the final year of his life, the Blair Government announced its intentions to do precisely this as the first stage of an undisclosed plan for Lords' reform, Donald wasn't exactly euphoric at the prospect. In public he supported the proposals but in private harboured deep reservations about the precise nature of the alternatives, reservations he doubtless would have developed had he lived.

All this was for the future. Having taken the title of Baron Soper of Kingsway in the London borough of Camden, and been appointed to the Lords as the first Methodist minister (although it was his good works at Kingsway rather than his denomination which gained him his elevation) the question was what he should wear. The traditional Anglican surplice worn by the bishops would be inappropriate for a Methodist minister. When he turned up in his usual attire of the well-cut cassock, he incurred the wrath of his old enemy Ian Paisley. Inevitably the problem was put to a commission of inquiry and it eventually decreed that the cassock he had worn for years was a perfectly acceptable costume for the Lords.

Early sorties into this new chamber concentrated on long-standing concerns of his, such as homosexuality, alcohol and racial unrest. He also became preoccupied with the impending crisis in Southern Rhodesia, where the main debate was on how to respond to the declaration of independence by the white Government of Ian Smith which was implacably opposed to black majority rule. After a year of sterile negotiations, Wilson, according to his biographer Ben Pimlott, made the cardinal error in October 1965 of declaring that while Rhodesia (now Zimbabwe) might be punished with economic sanctions, there would be no question of using military force. Fortified in the knowledge that his country wouldn't be subjected to a military invasion, Smith duly went ahead on 11 November with his declaration of independence. His effrontery posed the British a dilemma of how they should respond. Some like Archbishop Ramsey advocated the use of force to coerce Rhodesia if need be into protecting the rights of the majority. His belligerence offended Donald's pacifist inclinations. On 25 November in the Lords he supported the Southern Rhodesia Bill which passed through both Houses in one day. It reaffirmed Britain's control over Southern Rhodesia and imposed economic sanctions on her errant colony.

In his review of the Government's first year Donald's verdict was, like the curate's egg, good in parts. He heartily endorsed the re-nationalisation of the steel industry, the end of capital punishment and a better deal for pensioners, but called their foreign policy flaccid, if not perverse. He also bitterly opposed its Immigration White Paper which substantially reduced primary immigration, not least for dependant relatives. "Naturally if this Government had been intrinsically pacifist and socialist," he wrote in *Tribune*, "I should have expected results much different from these,"[9] but went on to admit that if they had professed such creeds in their election campaign they would not be in office at all. Soon he had fresh cause for hope. A significant swing to Labour at the Hull North by-election in January 1966 convinced Wilson that the time was now ripe to dissolve Parliament and seek a fresh mandate. During the March campaign, Donald spoke as far north as Carlisle in support of Labour candidates, and caused embarrassment in Saffron Walden when he said that he found it impossible to reconcile toryism with Christianity. His views upset the Rector of Little Sampford who disapproved of what he saw as partisan politics from the pulpit. When he pressed Donald about his inference that a Conservative couldn't be a sincere Christian, Donald did concede that his remarks had been somewhat frivolous, but pointed out that this was a public meeting not a church service. His partial recantation failed to quell the outrage. The Conservative candidate, Peter Kirk, called him arrogant and unchristian and his Labour opponent, Stephen Haseler, disassociated himself from his remarks. Two weeks later Labour swept back to power with a majority of 97 and Wilson repeated his 1964 innovation of a service in the Crypt Chapel. Donald again conducted it and, as was his wont, composed such an eloquent prayer of dedication that Wilson chose to use it as his peroration to his speech at the Party Conference that autumn. He also seconded the Graceful Address of Thanks to the Queen's Speech in the Lords, remarking that its content – devoid of radical redistributive measures – reminded him of the phrase in St Paul's Epistle to the Hebrews "about faith being the substance of things hoped for, the evidence of things not seen". It wasn't long before his disenchantment with the Government was to grow, beginning with its tax on charities, but as the problems piled up, there were pleasant distractions of a more personal kind. First, there was an appearance on *Desert Island Discs,* introduced by Roy Plomley, when his choice of music ranged from Bach's *Brandenburg Concerto in F Major* to the overture to *The Pirates of Penzance* and "Spring Cleaning" by Fats Waller. Second, there was a Greek cruise, when Donald emulated St Paul by preaching on Mars Hill, contrasting the birth-place of democracy on that spot two and a half thousand years previously with its current strangulation as the army waited menacingly in the wings. The following year they overthrew the Parliament, then the monarchy of King Constantine and imposed a military junta on the country. Their action prompted Donald to appeal to all British holidaymakers to boycott Greece by way of protest. Few obliged.

At the Methodist Conference Donald was very much to the fore, moving a motion of extreme urgency calling on the Government to disassociate itself completely from American policy in Vietnam where the stakes were rising all the time. He excoriated the American bombing of Hanoi as indescribably wicked, warning that the world was nearing a nuclear holocaust. His other leading role came in the debate on abortion, one of a number of moral issues which had moved centre stage in a more permissive era.

In the great debate between conformity and liberty, worldliness and piety, the Cavalier in Donald marched side by side with the Roundhead. Eschewing the austerity of many holy people, Donald's vivacity and charm could lighten even the most solemn of occasions without in any way impairing its dignity. Dismissive of the idea that levity could never infiltrate the walls of worship, his sermons were often spiced with humour in exactly the same way that his wise words in the House of Lords could be leavened with wit. Such character-istics invariably helped to defuse tension at both public and private ceremonies. When officiating at the wedding of one relative, the large wink he gave the bride at the beginning of the service so amused her that her nerves quickly evaporated.

According to Colin Morris, he had that indefinable quality, style, so that in appearance more Olivier than Isaiah, he could make even a routine sentence sound like the Gettysburg Address. And when this great orator occasionally found his authority under threat in the open air, his response was invariably to the manner born. The eminent musician Ronnie Scott heard him hold court at Speakers' Corner when a heckler made a derogatory reference to jazz. "I fear you are referring to ordinary dance music," Donald retorted, "and not that of Louis Armstrong, Bix Beiderbecke or Jelly Roll Morton." On another occasion he outsmarted a female heckler who had upset proceedings with a vicious harangue of a fellow heckler followed by a raucous rendition of "Roll Out the Barrel" by not only completing the song for her, but continuing with a flawless performance of "Bless 'em All". The crowd loved it and soon they were back in his palm.

A great admirer of elegance in everything around him, Donald relished the beauty of holiness in worship, the unspoilt grandeur of the Cornish coastline, the exquisite décor which adorned his home and the glamour of his wife and daughters. On this latter score Colin Morris recalled that his family life was a matter for animated discussion in theological college circles in the 1950s, and Donald would acknowledge with a twinkle that his following among unmarried ministerial students wasn't entirely explained by his great gifts of leadership. Thus in background, depth of talent and breadth of interests, it would be difficult to meet a more rounded extrovert personality with a capacity to entertain, not least on the piano or the tin whistle. But coupled with such charismatic flamboyance which any man of the world would pine for, there was an inbred self-control which turned its back on the dazzling sights and tempting sounds of the world ever near.

In compliance with his strict Methodist upbringing, Donald was in many ways the arch-puritan, out of sympathy with the *zeitgeist* of the 1960s, when long hair, rock music and marijuana were all the rage. He had always abhorred drinking and gambling and after a brief dalliance with smoking in his youth had hardened his line here too, so that by 1962 he was exhorting all ministers to give up, after the publication of a medical report linking cigarettes with cancer. Since 1947 he had in principle embraced vegetarianism, and was, for the most part, strait-laced on sex. Pornography, despite *Lady Chatterley*, he rigidly opposed, deeming it as unworthy and inadequate because of its inferior quality of life. In 1971 he became a member of the Longford Committee into pornography, when only illness prevented him from playing a more active role, and that same year he supported the conviction of three editors of the underground magazine, *Oz*, for publishing obscene articles. As far as he was concerned, their attitude to sex had been unduly frivolous, even though he did regard their sentences of fifteen, twelve and nine months respectively as totally unjust. Impropriety among his staff was another matter he considered of the utmost gravity, so much so that on one occasion he instantly dismissed a leading employee for infidelity after his wife had revealed all. Even more innocent liaisons with the opposite sex could make him feel uncomfortable. David Mason recounted how often on a Sunday when working at University College Hospital, he worshipped at Kingsway accompanied by a young nurse. Donald duly took note and after a few weeks had passed he growled, "David, I don't mind you falling asleep in my sermons, which you regularly do, but I do object to you bringing a different young woman every Sunday for six or seven weeks in a row." When Mason protested that it was a kind of evangelism, Donald retorted sharply, "I don't think Mr Wesley would approve of that kind of evangelism."

Yet for all his commitment to family values, his liberal theology and experience in his social work combined to ensure that his practical tolerance grew more pronounced as the years passed by. With the former he recognised that scientific developments in sex had far outrun theological teaching on a subject on which Jesus (in Donald's eyes) had little to say, although he would have approved of his pardon of the woman condemned for adultery. Thus on moral questions such as contraception, abortion and artificial insemination he was prepared to adopt an undogmatic position, so that charity rather than judgmentalism became his priority, especially when dealing with the outcasts of London's mean streets. Accepting that prostitutes and single mothers were as much the victims of a society that lived by different rules as authors of their own fate, he realised that practical help and education were the best remedies to prevent further trouble.

Donald's tolerance extended to the mainstream majority when the sexual revolution of the 1960s caused consternation in many a middle-class household. Recognising that teenagers were reaching puberty at an earlier age than hitherto, he opposed a law prohibiting sexual intercourse below the age of sixteen, supporting instead a more educational approach which persuaded teenagers not to have sex until they were physically or mentally old enough. He was also prepared in the name of unwanted pregnancies (not least in the underdeveloped world where widespread starvation was caused by growing populations) to countenance contraception and the provision of family planning by local authorities. When tackled by *The News of the World* in June 1966 about the growth of sexual promiscuity, he felt that comparisons with earlier times were a futile exercise. "In any case, I'm always suspicious of those who relate decadence to the height of a girl's skirt,"[10] he replied. To him the true means of a moral society was one which strove for peace and social justice for all, as opposed to one which stressed personal values.

Donald's view on contraception and homosexuality broadly corresponded with official Methodist thinking which tended to be more progressive than the Anglican, not to mention the Roman Catholic Church. The same was the case with abortion, which proved more contentious when it came before Parliament between 1965 and 1967. The background to David Steel's Bill lay in the growing chorus of opinion, much of it emanating from the medical profession, committed to overhauling Britain's notoriously harsh abortion laws unreformed since Victorian times, despite a number of attempts since 1953 to change them. Aside from the efforts of the Abortion Law Reform Association, the influential Church of England Board for Social Responsibility had published a weighty report which accepted that the interests of the mother were less well served by the law. Having acknowledged that there was no certainty of its being able to verify the exact relationship between the soul and the embryo, or the precise moment or stage at which the relationship began to exist, it tried to balance the claims of both mother and foetus. It concluded that abortion should be permissible when either the life or well-being of the mother was under threat.

Such findings were similar to Donald's own position when the House of Lords discussed the Labour peer Lord Silkin's Abortion Bill, which was introduced on 30 November 1965, the beginning of a two-year haul through Parliament. Drawing on the traumatic experiences of pregnant teenagers at a couple of his hostels when contemplating the thought of giving birth, and the sleazy, dreadful conditions under which backstreet abortions were carried out, his sympathy lay very much with the mother. Rejecting the premise that abortion was the product of a sexually promiscuous culture, he claimed that 80 per cent of all cases arose from married women with large families, alarmed about the social as well as the psychological prospects of yet another child. This latter point pitted him against the Archbishop of Canterbury when he, Donald, opposed Baroness Wootton's amendment to the Bill in February 1966, which removed the physical and mental inadequacy of the mother as a ground for abortion. He also locked horns with the Bishop of Exeter over his references to the sanctity of human life of the foetus, calling them semantic nonsense, since the foetus couldn't be compared in value to a fully grown person. The only sort of life that he, as a professing Christian, deemed to be sacred was that which had acquired self-consciousness.

He enlarged on these views in a lively correspondence in *The Times* later that year. In reply to the Abbot of Downside's contention that, since there was no point between conception and birth when killing of the embryo was justified, there was no determining point other than conception at which life began, Donald had this to say: "There is no convenient dividing line in human development at which the embryo instantly acquires a special worth. There is invariably a continuous slow development. It is therefore irrational to equate abortion with murder, as some opponents of the Bill have done. Those who recognize development as a continuous process in no way diminish the worth of a new born child, and are as far removed from practising infanticide, as those who hold a more arbitrary view of the status of the egg and embryo."[11]

The Anglican Archbishop of Wales found the logic of his argument obscure. "I cannot believe that Lord Soper holds that abortion is never murder,"[12] he wrote. He agreed that therapeutic abortion when the embryo could be sacrificed to save the life of the mother wasn't murder, but drew the line at the inability of the mother to cope, especially when adoption wasn't an available alternative. The flurry of correspondence which followed included a letter from Professor Glanville Williams, Professor of English Law at Cambridge 1968–72, and at the time President of the Abortion Law Reform Association. He supported Donald's argument that during the early months of pregnancy, the embryo, by not being fully formed, was incapable of pain and totally unrecognisable as a human being. The debate was brought to a magisterial conclusion by Lord Fisher, former Archbishop of Canterbury, who saw birth as the moment when the embryo acquired a special worth.

The House of Lords had passed Silkin's Bill unopposed in March 1966, but because Parliament had been dissolved soon afterwards for the election, it couldn't proceed to the Commons. Another almost identical Bill was soon passed when Parliament reconvened, whereupon the baton was taken up as a Private Member's Bill in the Commons by a young Liberal backbencher, David Steel, later leader of the party. Thanks to Government support, especially from the reforming Home Secretary, Roy Jenkins, the Bill gained a second reading in July just when Donald was teaming up with Pauline Webb at Conference to bring Methodism in to the forefront of the abortion movement. His amendment enabling a woman, whose physical and mental health would be endangered by a continuing pregnancy, to have an abortion was carried by a massive majority. He and Pauline Webb dominated Conference, according to the *Guardian*, getting a liberal resolution made even more liberal so that it resembled the actual Bill passed the next year. They also triumphed on a motion approving in principle the ordination of women clergy. As far back as 1938 at Conference, Donald had supported a similar motion believing the idea that God could only work through the ministry of men preposterous. If women were of a similar quality to men, he argued, they should achieve the same status. He remained committed to their cause thereafter but never spoke a lot in favour, because to do so might well have delayed the cause of Anglican-Methodist reunion, given that the Church of England was more conservative on the issue compared to the Free Churches. It was, ironically, only after the breakdown in negotiations that Methodism went ahead and ordained women in 1974. The fact that Kathleen Lee, one of his deaconesses at Kingsway, was one of the first to be received into the ministry naturally afforded him much pleasure.

In August 1966 Donald left for a lecture tour of Canada and the United States. In the former he compared the industrial malaise then gripping the country as similar to the situation in Britain, where the seamen's union were engaged in a long drawn-out acrimonious dispute with the Government over pay. During his stay he twice appeared on *Speak Your Mind*, the exceedingly popular late-night chat show, and was bombarded with questions about Vietnam. He found himself at one with most of his listeners in his well-rehearsed line that America should cease fighting and return home. If Britain were to withdraw its moral support for the war, he continued, that would be a positive step forward in the quest for peace. At St Mark's Methodist Church, Harlem, New York, he found the singing of "Let us break bread together on our Knees" at Communion by the 1,000 strong multi-racial congregation the most direct emotional experience he ever remembered, a quite colossal expression of devotion to Jesus. He witnessed some progress in the status of the African-American in the South, most notably in Durham, North Carolina, a centre for genuine multi-racial progress in housing and education. Yet even here, the first stirrings of the Ku Klux Klan, the staunchly white racist society in the southern states, told of the limits to genuine racial integration. More important, he returned more than ever convinced that the war in Vietnam was a lost cause for the USA, a line he consistently peddled at the Labour Party Conference in Brighton. The continuing intensity of American bombing there served only to inflame passions, and even before the Conference proper had begun, anti-war-in-Vietnam demonstrations disrupted the Sunday Morning Service at the local Methodist Church as the Prime Minister was reading the lesson. The outburst led to eight people being charged with inde-cent behaviour. At their trial two months later, Donald was a surprise witness for the defence, his appearance a closely guarded secret. While accepting that their words were provocative, he contemptuously dismissed the idea that their interruptions were indecent or illegal since interruptions had a long history in the Methodist Church. Rather bizzarely, he went on to say that the majority of those present weren't members of the regular congregation, but delegates attending the Party Conference. If they were distressed in any way, it probably did them good to listen to the sincerity of the protests. His intervention gave rise to much press publicity, and although the ringleaders were convicted and imprisoned for two months, the sentence could have been even harsher.

With disillusionment having set in because of economic stagnation and government-trade union differences over wage control, there was little triumphalism in evidence among the rank and file at Conference. Wilson gave a mundane speech, although his attempt to rally the faithful by quoting Donald's prayer of dedication which he used at the service a few months earlier, caused a few ripples. "Considering that Jim Callaghan, Barbara and I who were all sitting beside the P.M., are fervent atheists," confided Dick Crossman to his diary, "it was a little tough to be told by our leader about how the Cabinet was dedicated to God in the Chapel of St Mary-under-Croft in Westminster."[13]

One other matter attracted Donald's attention that year. As he had realised for some time, the traditional Sunday was under attack and he recognised that the Church couldn't expect to impose a ban on a community which wished to engage in various forms of sport and recreation. In this spirit, he was willing to support Lord Willis's attempts to scrap the Sunday entertainment laws, but opposed Lord Chesham's subsequent amendment to allow sport at 12.30 rather than 2.00, arguing that the fellowship of Sunday lunch was worth preserving. Increasingly this became a minority view as the unity of the family declined even further. Gradually the quest for the secular Sunday became ever more pronounced and in 1993 a Bill legalising Sunday trading was passed. Donald had his reservations. He accepted that in a changing world there was a case for easing the previous restrictions but expressed concern that too few safeguards were in place for those who adopted the Christian view and wished to rest. He also wanted to ensure that those obliged to work on a Sunday had a statutory day-off in the week.

In January 1967 Donald was one of twelve eminent public signatories of a letter supporting the Abortion Bill, dismissing the idea that the embryo could be given special legal and ethical status. After Steel's Bill had finally passed the Commons that July, it moved to the Lords a few days later, where in a major speech, Donald rehearsed his well-worn arguments accepting abortion. Having attributed the sanctity of foetal life to a medieval philosophy of instant life unrelated to modern theology, he found it hypocritical that such a philosophy could be sanctioned by the Christianity which was consigning millions of human beings of adult stature to mutual massacre in war.

Although not relishing the thought of the termination of a pregnancy, least of all for convenience, he accepted that making a choice was a compromise between the well-being of a potential life and the well-being of those who had already acquired a certain stature in human behaviour. He finished with the following peroration: "... that at this juncture of time in the search for the kingdom of God, which is the first consideration of a practising Christian, it is the well-being of little children already born, the well-being of mothers already mothers, the well-being of a family already a family; indeed the well-being of society as a whole, which invite us to subscribe to this measure".[14]

Donald made one final intervention at the Report stage of the Bill that October when he supported an amendment which didn't place restrictions upon the type of doctor to see the patient, since to impose further delays on the mother only added to her burden. His reaction to the Bill's final completion days later was to call it a triumph of mercy and love over legalism and, in many cases, over a pseudo-scientific view of the sacrosanctity of the foetus. When in 1971 Sir John Peel, President of the Medical Association, alleged that the majority of abortions were for social and economic rather than medical reasons, Donald said that this was far from the case. The number of abuses, he contended, was small, compared to the amount of pain and misery spared. Thereafter he continued in the company of many churchmen and liberal-leaning politicians, to defy numerous attempts to turn the clock back on abortion, most notably the Corrie Bill of 1980 which decreed that it should be illegal after twenty weeks instead of twenty-eight. The moral case for revision was simply not clear-cut enough in either his view or that of many in the Church.

One issue which had taxed Donald since his year as President was the vexed question of homosexuality, especially since he found little to guide him on the issue from biblical sources which he respected. The result was a stance that amounted to a tortured compromise, since for all his laudable attempts to root out prejudice, he never felt entirely comfortable defending a practice which ultimately he thought unnatural. In line with mainstream Christian thinking, he considered the prostitution of the body, either in heterosexual or homosexual practice to be wrong, and in an ideal world it wouldn't exist, a position reflected in one of his more outlandish statements.

"My personal view," he wrote in 1957, "is that the root of perversion is violence. I believe that a disarmed world would be a world in which homosexuality would die out. I believe that if we could get rid of power politics and conscription we should get rid of sexual perversion."[15]

That said, he accepted that certain homosexual expressions such as innocently holding hands weren't harmful. Above all he recognised the difficulty of legislating against sin. This rationale formed the basis of his support for the Wolfenden Committee's recommendation that private homosexual practice between consenting adults over the age of twenty-one be decriminalised.

"We do not think that it is proper," Wolfenden had concluded, "for the law to concern itself with what a man does in private unless it can be shown that it is contrary to the public good and that the law ought to intervene in its function as the guardian of the public good."[16]

Whilst accepting that the remedy to homosexuality, like prostitution, could only be partially met by legislation, Donald still hoped that the State would take the lead in cherishing the dignity of the individual by promoting a personal faith, the family life and economic security. The failure of R. A. Butler, the Home Secretary, to act on Wolfenden led Donald (who had seen the Methodist Conference the previous year vote in favour of decriminalisation, at the age of twenty-one) to join forces with others to press for action. In March 1959 he signed a letter to *The Times* along with a host of luminaries, including Clement Attlee and Bertrand Russell, calling on the Government to legislate, arguing that it was the responsibility of those in authority to lead public opinion rather than follow it. In June 1965 in one of his earliest speeches in the House of Lords, he branded the existing law on homosexuality as both unrealistic and illogical. Christian principles dictated change, he declared. And so did the spirit of the age, according to the Home Secretary, Roy Jenkins. It was his initiative which led to the Wilson Government sponsoring Lord Arran's 1967 Private Member's Bill which broadly implemented Wolfenden. While raising some reservations, most notably the failure to draw a line between acceptable and unacceptable levels of consenting homosexual behaviour, Donald supported it on behalf of the Free Churches (something he rarely did).

"To pass this Bill," he declared, "will remove a great deal of the terror, the fear, the unnatural hazards that affront so many good and decent homosexuals." He hoped that it would be the prelude to subsequent legislation whereby "the recovery of such people to what we call a normal pattern of life may be made easier".[17] His ambivalence to the subject remained with him thereafter. When the question of whether Methodist homosexual ministers should be barred from the ministry was debated at Conference in 1993, he unfailingly supported their retention, and in April 1994 attended a meeting of the Methodist Caucus of the Lesbian and Gay Christian Movement. In his welcome address, however, he stressed that his presence should be seen as a symbol of solidarity in honouring Conference's resolution the previous year of giving dignity to people whatever their sex, as opposed to conferring respectability.

In March 1967 Donald and Marie visited Malta at the behest of the Superintendent Minister of the main Methodist Church there. They were entertained to lunch by the Governor-General and received with great kindness by the island establishment, although their happiest time was spent talking to children. While he took issue with the power of the Roman Catholic Church, symbolised by the sheer size and scale of so many churches on the island, not least in its reactionary right-wing prejudices, he formed a high opinion of Dom Mintoff, the leader of the Opposition. Here he felt was a man capable of putting Malta back on its feet with his socialist vision.

Throughout the year, beginning with his participation in a march to St Paul's Cathedral in February, Donald continued to campaign against American action in Vietnam. Ironically, in April, Wilson had been guest of honour at Kingsway for the CSM Annual General Meeting, when anti-Vietnam war demonstrators had to be forcibly cleared from the entrance. In June Donald addressed a large rally in Trafalgar Square, and in August there was even talk of him accompanying three MPs to North Vietnam to help bring peace. While happy to support the efforts of others, Donald was reluctant to go there himself. He continued to keep up the pressure on the Government. In November he took a petition to Downing Street, deploring the continuation of the war and urged America to take the initiative to end it by stopping the bombing. The Prime Minister was nominally sympathetic but it had little effect.

Another foreign entanglement which embroiled Donald in conflict with the Government was the Civil War in Nigeria and Biafra. Back in October 1963 he had conducted a week-long mission at Ibadan University in Lagos from which he derived considerable pleasure, not least the renewing of links with Fela Sowande. He returned full of hope. Africa, he informed his *Tribune* readers, had come of age, a stupendous achievement in the art of growing fellowship, and was now leading the fight against apartheid in South Africa.

His enthusiasm for Nigeria, however, didn't last. When the country descended into bloody conflict in 1967 following the secession of Biafra, the relatively affluent eastern region, Donald was outspoken in his opposition to General Gowon's regime. Repelled by the treatment meted out to the Biafrans, he joined the chorus on the Labour left demanding a ban on arms to Nigeria. In March 1968 he became the first chairman of the British-Biafra Association but with little effect. For the Wilson Government – much to his fury – fearing Russian intervention if a void was created, continued with arms sales. They helped to crush Biafra by January 1970.

Amidst his busy lifestyle, Donald managed three weeks in East Africa with Marie in June 1967, where they visited their daughter Judith who was out in Uganda. Amongst the pleasure, there was some business as he gave away the prizes at Kaptagat Prep School and its sister school The Banda School, Nairobi. In August Donald's mother died, aged ninety, leaving £11,748 net, the bulk going to Donald and his sister Millicent. That November Marie was slightly injured in a car crash in Streatham, when her mini was in collision with a post office van. It could have been much worse.

The beginning of 1968 found Donald in pessimistic mood as he pondered the future of the Church on the BBC programme *Meeting Point.* No longer seeing it as the centre of community life, he questioned its continual monopoly of ultimate truth and ability to establish acceptable patterns of social behaviour. Admitting that many people had parted company with institutional religion without any apparent ill effects, he felt that it was heading for irrelevance unless Christianity could be expressed in new ways. The broadcast caused a minor furore, but Donald was unrepentant in the *Methodist Recorder* the following week, convinced that the situation was desperate enough to provoke debate. It was a theme he was to keep on pressing, and with good reason, for although his views were far too unorthodox for many, he was at least confronting the future head-on, a point acknowledged by the eminent Canadian writer and broadcaster Pierre Berton in *The Cool, Crazy, Committed World of the Sixties.*

> He is as far removed from the mitred archbishops in their ivyed chapels as he is from the stereotyped vicars in their smug parishes. Seeing this vastly amusing and thoroughly dedicated churchman tower above his audience, his cheeks glowing russet in the biting cold, his voice cutting like the wind itself above the babble around him, I could not help but think 'This is a man'. This is also the Church of the sixties in its most vital form, pushing out beyond the Gothic buttresses, coming to people, unafraid of challenging controversial or impolitic postures. Soper the political activist, the ex-alderman, the Christian socialist, the weekly columnist, the broadcaster, television star and authority is human proof that the Church when it wishes, can be a vital, meaningful and communicative force in a secular world.[18]

And yet, ironically, there were those within Methodism who were beginning to view Donald's churchmanship as rather dated, not least one of his closest disciples, John Vincent, the then Superintendent Minister of the Rochdale Mission. The occasion for his critique was a series of articles Donald had written in the *Methodist Recorder* in March and April 1967, in which he placed sacramentalism, evangelism, socialism and pacifism within the context of the Christian life both in thought and action. In his reply in the same journal, Vincent commended his mentor for his radical beliefs which he had imbibed in his youth, before going on to advocate a more contemporary definition of these core beliefs to maintain the Church's relevance in a changing world.

As regards sacramentalism, Vincent no longer saw the debate as about sacraments or experience as ways of receiving Christ, but rather about the nature of the Christ and the Christianity to be received. In place of the Eucharistic offering as "the means of grace and the core of fellowship", Vincent advocated looking at the living Lord eating with his modern disciples, alongside publicans and sinners.

On evangelism, witness must go beyond words to deeds, be it giving Christmas presents to Moslem families, or running a play-centre for the use of mothers shopping. Vincent longed to see some movement in Methodism resembling the communal life of the Iona Community.

On pacifism, the old debates had become sterile and meaningless to peacemaking. Now something more dynamic and realistic was required to deal with the modern world where war was so total that personal attitudes were unlikely to make much difference. Instead of withdrawing from the world, pacifists needed to make their voices heard by getting politically involved.

On socialism, Vincent felt that while its Christian version had strong associations with much of the New Testament, its depiction as the kingdom of God on earth seemed simple. Perceiving socialism to be a lost cause to the radical movement because of Labour's compromising ethos in government, with the mixed economy and its dependence on class-based support, he looked to new alignments emerging through which a radical church could serve the needs of secular man.

Observing that the greatest sin of Methodism since the war had been its failure to permit the younger generation a proper voice, Vincent ended with a plea for fresh analysis to discover the new priorities of the moment.

"To ask these questions is, for me, to concede willingly and wholeheartedly the brilliance, coherence and relevance of the older positions. But we cannot go on worshipping the past, even when the past has such outstanding exemplars. Each generation must find its own feet, and find its own radical forms of obedience."[19]

Clearly rattled by Vincent's alternative vision, Donald's apologia a month later in the *Recorder* was nothing if not withering. "I simply cannot understand what he is getting at most of the time," he wrote. He castigated his claim that Eucharistic worship concentrated spiritual attention upon the Cross, instead of making a bid for the total mystery of Jesus Christ. "This is a travesty," he fulminated, "and Dr Vincent ought to know it." Turning to pacifism, Donald likened his protégé's impulsiveness to a budding cricketer who, by neglecting the art of a straight bat in the pursuit of adventure, had laid himself open to the first straight ball. He didn't doubt his principled stand, but suggested, a little patronisingly, that he was trying to deliver some quite edible hay without bailing it first. "Let me end by trying to find common ground with him. The language in which socialism, pacifism, evangelism and sacra-mentalism is communicated needs constantly to be examined to see that the substance is not obscured by the verbiage. A rigid attachment to formulae and a parrot-like repetition of slogans may well persuade the forward-looking Christian to dismiss these basic ideas as outworn because the jargon in which they are presented is moth-eaten and outmoded. Very well then, let us agree that we have outgrown the language patterns of forty years ago, but let me strenuously insist once again that far from outgrowing the principles and ideas which they sought to express – they still beckon us forward, as goals not yet reached, but still as pre-emptory as ever they were."[20]

At Easter 1968 the Sopers were in Rome with thirty other companions on a week's pilgrimage, the highlight of which for Donald was a private audience with Pope Paul VI and a front row seat for the traditional Easter blessing in St Peter's Square. As he surveyed the scene, he was struck less by the spirituality of the occasion, as compared to the exuberance of the pilgrims and the continued power of the Papacy with its vast entourage of cardinals and prelates. At a time when Donald was looking for greater unity between all the Churches, he had been encouraged by the ecumenical leanings of the previous Pope, John XXIII, whose kindness and humility had won the hearts of all. "Here was an unmistak-ably good man who took his faith seriously and practised it continuously," wrote Donald on 7 June 1963 shortly after the Pope's death. "In the fields of reunion and peace it is no exaggeration to say that John 23 has ushered in a new era ... The hope of an undivided body of Christ is still remote, but it is not now unreason-able."[21] In this spirit of greater openness, Donald, a frequent preacher at the neighbouring Catholic church in Kingsway, had invited Cardinal Heenan, the Roman Catholic Archbishop of Westminster, and an old friend from the days when they used to speak at youth gatherings together, to contribute an article on Christian Unity to the *Kingsway* magazine the previous year. Now as Church and State in Britain took their first faltering steps towards a more liberal posi-tion on such vexed issues as contraception and abortion, Donald looked to similar signs emerging from the Vatican. He looked in vain. Despite reforming tendencies at the start of his papacy, Paul VI was increasingly beholden to his conservative curia, and his continued adherence to strict doctrinal orthodoxy, not least on questions such as abortion or the virgin birth, was one reason why Donald could never become a Roman Catholic. His disappointment turned to outright dismay following the publication on 29 July 1968 of the Papal encyc-lical, *Humanae Vitae*, reaffirming the Vatican's total opposition to artificial birth control. Accusing the Roman Catholic Church of recommitting itself to a concept of life which was medieval, he deplored its neglect of the burgeoning population explosion and the worldwide suffering of women in repeated childbirth. "The facts are that unless man controls the reproduction of his own species he may well destroy not only human welfare, but his future existence on this planet ... The papal announcement raises in inescapable form the prime question as to whether a celibate religious hierarchy is not finally guilty of insufferable impudence in asserting its authority in an arena of human experience as intimate and complex as that of the procreation of children, and moreover one in which professionally it has no experience whatsoever. Is not this encyclical a piece of masculine arrogance masquerading not only as spiritual insight but as divine authority?"[22]

Donald's distaste for religious dogma – Roman Catholic and Protestant alike – was again in evidence as the simmering discontent in Northern Ireland boiled over into open confrontation between the two communities. He fully recognised that much of the momentum behind the nationalist Civil Rights Movement lay in the realm of economic injustice and political discrimination, but such grievances were accentuated by religious bigotry. "The confrontation in Ulster," he wrote in *Tribune* on 10 January 1969, "is between a Roman Catholic church which has asserted the infallible authority of the Papacy, and a Protestant church which has asserted the infallible authority of the Bible."[23] They were the ultimate barriers to any future progress, he opined, until such time as both sides renounced the concept of religious totalitarianism. This remained his position although the prime cause of his ire was the province's Protestant majority, particularly that faction affiliated to the Democratic Unionist Party under Ian Paisley.

It was while in Rome that Donald heard of the furore breaking back home surrounding Enoch Powell's infamous "Rivers of Blood" speech in Birmingham, which painted a lurid vision of Britain's future, unless the current rates of immigration were seriously curtailed. The previous year Donald had warned the Lords about the growing racial tension in Hyde Park, where non-white people had become much more prominent in both the crowd and on their soapboxes. In March 1968 he had voted against the Government's tough new Immigration Bill restricting foreign entry to Britain, claiming "it added fuel to a furnace already brightly lit", and now on his return from Rome he was thrust into the controversy. He happened to be at Tower Hill when his words were drowned out by the second of the dockers' marches in favour of Powell, who had been dismissed from the Shadow Cabinet by Ted Heath, the Conservative leader. The rumpus provided promising material for debate and argument in Hyde Park. When asked how he would cure Powellism, Donald raised a laugh by saying, "Our friend is asking 'How do you deal with sin?'" He remained wedded to his belief that rather than pander to racial prejudice, Britain should be doing its best to create a genuinely multi-racial society by withdrawing the controversial Nationality Acts and supporting legislation outlawing racial discrimination. Not everyone, however, proved so enlightened, as questions of race continued to flare up intermittently over the years.

That June Donald and the social work of the West London Mission featured in a BBC documentary called *Kingdom Come*. He also, as President of the International Order of Good Templars – an organisation committed to abstinence – in their centenary year, preached the centenary sermon in Canterbury Cathedral. He reiterated his earlier contention that all ministers should be total abstainers and called for the creation of a climate of good. For only by establishing a Christian society would one eliminate alcoholism and other evils equated with it. At the Methodist Conference in July, all but one delegate supported UN sanctions against Rhodesia. Donald declared that the object was not to bring Rhodesia to her knees but to her senses. In addition his motion calling on the Government to end any arrangements by which the production of the chemical defences at Porton Down was available to nations which refused to sign the Geneva Protocol, gained unanimous backing.

After Conference, Donald, having ignored medical advice for some time, eventually had to bow to reality and have an operation on his shoulder which incapacitated him for the rest of the summer. His return to the fray coincided with the Party Conference season, an appropriate time to pass judgement on a Labour Government which, because of its failure to measure up socially and economically, had suffered a series of major by-election reverses. Compared to his treatment of several other Labour leaders, Donald was always rather more circumspect about criticising Wilson. Nevertheless, his disillusionment with his government's lack of vision was plain for all to see. The previous year he had spoken for many when he wrote: "They have publicly failed to harness their various legislative wagons to a theological or ideological star. They appear as pragmatists rather than prophets."[24] Now his reservations remained the same. "What has happened," he wrote in *Tribune*, "is that the opportunity [as yet] has been squandered of turning a mood of tolerant expectation, which it widely enjoyed four years ago, into one of real credibility."[25] He went on to say that the sort of creed which Labour needed now was justification by faith, which to him could only mean socialism. Not surprisingly, he was to be disappointed, but despite the travails of the Government throughout 1969 when it failed in its great design to bring the trade union movement to heel, Donald was unusually coy. By October 1969 he consoled himself with the fact that the economy was beginning to pick up and that the Government's chances of being re-elected were better than even. His confidence was even greater the following June. He informed his *Tribune* readership that Labour's manifesto lacked novelty, but applauded its record on health, welfare and penal reform,

and, denigrating the Conservative Opposition on every score, keenly anticipated another Wilson triumph. His views were commonplace. Heath's victory
against all expectations not only made a mockery of informed opinion, it
added to his disillusionment. In the subsequent inquest Donald rather predictably felt that the panacea for Labour lay in a genuinely socialist vision, an
aspiration which gained some credence as the party moved broadly leftward
during the 1970s.

One issue which Donald continued to hold dear was the cause of Anglican-
Methodist reunion and while never party to the formal negotiations between
the two Churches, he had plenty to say from the sidelines. Reflecting the views
of John Wesley himself who had wished to remain within its confines, the
Methodists of all the Free Churches were historically and spiritually closest to
the Church of England. Doctrinally, there was no major division and on the
question of hierarchies most Methodist Churches in the world had bishops.
Even in Britain the restructuring of the Chairmen of the Districts, giving
them greater responsibilities over even larger districts, was, according to
Adrian Hastings, a process of moderate episcopacy bringing Methodists ever
closer to the Anglican way of restructuring the ministry. At the same time the
process of sacramental worship permeating the Free Churches, and symbolised by Donald's presidency of MSF, was another step on the road to
reconciliation.

For Donald, brought up on the Anglican prayerbook and a budding
ecumenist since SCM days at Cambridge, this process couldn't come a
moment too soon. Apart from the brickbats he had witnessed over the years at
Tower Hill in the clash between Catholic and Protestant fundamentalists, he
believed that schism was the mortal sin of the Church because it meant a
community without power. He bitterly regretted the failure of the European
Churches to come together in 1914 and 1939 to stop the general drift towards
war, because had they done so, he felt, catastrophe would have been averted.
Accepting that the Churches could never subscribe to a uniformity of doctrine
or a common form of worship, he nevertheless believed that they could
demonstrate fellowship in action towards the world's dispossessed.

As far back as 31 December 1931, on the eve of a reunion between the
three branches of the Methodist Church, Donald had been a staunch advocate
of Church unity when he wrote, "I want the wider Methodism to constitute
itself a religious order within the Holy Catholic Church. I want it to proclaim
that the Church is one and universal, a fellowship of pilgrims walking in the
steps of Jesus Christ."[26] Five years later he supported Leslie Weatherhead's call
for Methodism and Congregationalism to unite, figuring that "such a proposal
ought to commend itself to everybody who has the kingdom of God at heart".

This ecumenism was enhanced by the fulfilment he gained from preaching in Anglican establishments and his work with other denominations through his political activities and OCW, not to mention his growing sacramentalism.This latter point is a theme which Donald expanded upon in an article called "Towards Church Unity" in the October 1946 edition of *Kingsway*. Decrying the grievous condition of organised Christianity in the world, he rested his hope for the unity he craved on the act of Eucharistic worship. "Intercommunion is not a delightful gesture of goodwill, an occasional show of divine grace; it is the bonding of unity. Under the symbolism of bread and wine is the broken yet perfect body of Christ. Those who meet in penitence and faith at the Lord's Table have one in Him who is their common Lord. Methodism is so blasphemously casual in our loyalty to his expressed command, 'Do this in remembrance of me' … . The Methodist Church member who refrains stands condemned of the sin of disobedience first and then of schism … . Looking back, I realise that I have come under this indictment. How many more in every Church are similarly condemned. The unity of Christians must be the one body of Christ and the step that we can all take towards that unity is the step that brings us to the Communion ourselves."[27]

"Remove a few minor idiosyncracies," wrote the ex-Roman Catholic priest Adrian Hastings, "and Soper's Methodism, in its wide social and sacramental character, fits very much within the mainstream of modern English religion, just as the evangelicalism of Billy Graham does not."[28]

Against a backdrop of growing ecumenical co-operation caused mainly by the war and reflected in the formation of the British Council of Churches in 1942 to promote greater Christian unity, and William Temple's new social order, it was Archbishop Fisher who launched a historic initiative. In November 1946, in a speech in Cambridge, he reopened the question of Protestant unity by inviting the Free Churches to establish intercommunion (not union) with the Church of England by taking episcopacy into their system. Despite Donald's disillusionment with the *Methodist Recorder* for its negative reaction to the speech, only the Methodists agreed to exploratory conversations, helped by his efforts when President. They began in 1955 and gradually the sense of a single Christian communion began to take hold, especially in academic circles. An Interim Report published in 1958 rejected Fisher's concept of partial communion between the two Churches, opting instead for full union, with the Methodists accepting episcopacy. The Full Report, proposing a two-stage method of achieving organic union, appeared in 1963, signed by all twelve Anglicans on the Commission but rejected by a significant minority of Methodists who feared that the proposals signified the surrender of their Church to Anglicanism. As the negotiations became mired in technical detail, Donald continued to look to the wider picture. "The broken and divided Body of Christ must be re-united,"[29] he wrote in the 1964 spring edition of *Kingsway*. What's more, he was willing to go the extra mile to achieve this, dismissing Methodist resistance to Anglican use of alcoholic wine at Communion as a matter of secondary importance. On the bigger issue he was not only prepared to abandon all Methodist forms of worship and conform to the Book of Common Prayer, he was also prepared to see Methodist ministers reordained, himself included. On the latter point the Methodist historian G. Thompson Brake related how Harold Goodwin, a journalist turned ordained lecturer attached to St Giles-in-the-Fields, tried on an unspecified date to advance the cause of Anglican-Methodist reunion by getting a prominent Methodist such as Donald to be ordained into the Church of England as a deacon and priest on the same day. When taxed about his feelings over such a proposal, Donald was more than accommodating and Goodwin then approached the Bishop of London, Robert Stopford, who promptly dismissed it, much to Donald's disappointment. "Possibly one or, at the most two, other people knew of this attempt to give impetus to the cause of Christian unity," Brake wrote. "Had this been generally known there is no doubt that it would have seriously affected the course of the Conversations. Some Anglicans would have shared the Bishop of London's misgivings about an attempt to jump the gun, while some Methodists would have resented a cavalier manner in which the bishop had dealt with a genuine and serious attempt to advance the cause of Christian Unity, by a distinguished and respected Methodist minister whose commitment to that cause was well known."[30]

This is slightly to digress. Conference accepted in 1965 the 1963 Anglican-Methodist Report, although some ministers felt that they couldn't participate in the Service of Reconciliation. There now followed three more years of laboured discussion, which included a deferred publication of the final report in 1967 for another year, a decision which disgusted Donald. "I am tempted to say to hell with these theologians,"[31] he fulminated. He felt that as the negotiations became more protracted, people on both sides became increasingly tired of the issue, while all the time church pews were emptying. It was only by concentrating on Jesus the Son of Man, and religion as a way of life, as opposed to metaphysical dogma could the Church in his estimation rehabilitate itself.

The final scheme for a two-stage reunification was published in 1968. This allowed for a conditional reordination of the Methodist clergy through a Service of Reconciliation, on the condition that they effectively accepted episcopal denomination. It was agreed that the decision would be made on the same day by both Churches, and that each Church would sanction a required 75 per cent majority. Donald, while expressing concern about some of the ambiguity in the Service of Reconciliation, nevertheless urged acceptance. On 8 July 1969 Conference at Birmingham approved by 78 per cent, but, on the same day, despite the support of Archbishop Ramsey, the broad theological divisions of the Church of England were laid bare in the Anglican Convocations. A combination of evangelicals and of Anglo-Catholics more interested in union with the Roman Catholic Church, expressed staunch opposition, ensuring that the combined vote reached only 69 per cent. When a similar scheme was put to both Churches again in May 1972, the result was almost identical to the previous one. It was greeted with dismay in Methodist circles, not least by Donald, who always hoped and assumed that he would end his days in a Church of England pulpit. "No one with any political, let alone spiritual sense," he wrote days later, "can ignore the hole that is left in the social timber when and if the ecclesiastical nail falls out. It is precisely because this particular failure of Christians to come together contains in microcosm essential elements in the religious and social set-up generally that it deserves the closest attention." Why, he wondered, did the General Synod (the new governing body of the Church of England) if jealous of the *de jure* rights of the episcopacy to be its apostolically appointed governors, repudiate the almost unanimous vote of the bishops in favour of the scheme of union? Why did some Methodists forget John Wesley lived and died within the Anglican communion? "The melancholy answer is that, to a calamitous degree, Christians regard their churches as 'for themselves' rather than 'for others' and this introspection produces a religious conservatism in which the genuinely revolutionary elements in the Christian faith tend to get muffled if not stifled."[32] He continued to follow his own star in this direction but sadly for him he never reached the promised land. It was to be the greatest ecclesiastical regret of his life.

Donald's passion for Anglican-Methodist reunion was genuine enough, but it also needs to be seen in the context of changing patterns of worship and the onset of the consumer society. "If further proof is needed of Dr Soper's personal appeal," wrote Derek Walker, editor of *Kingsway*, in the *British Weekly* in March 1957, "the decline in attendance on the many occasions when he had to be absent during his Presidential Year might be cited … . This is the twenty-first year of Dr Soper's ministry in Kingsway Hall. It is, perhaps, pertinent to ask what would happen to the congregation of this church, situated, as it is, in a largely non-residential area, and off the 'tourist track', if the influence of his personality were removed. That is a question which the West London Mission hopes will not have to be answered for many years to come."[33] As Walker frankly acknowledged, Kingsway was living to some degree on borrowed time, thanks to Donald's inspirational leadership in an era when congregations continued to flock to the three great shrines of London Methodism. By 1960, however, the wheel was beginning to turn, as the age of the celebrity preacher in Britain became a thing of the past. Sangster and Weatherhead had moved on, leaving Donald to hold the fort alone. Despite mounting a brave rearguard action, it became an unequal struggle as the tight-knit Kingsway community forged by the war-time experience began to break up as people died off or moved elsewhere, inhibited in part by the escalating costs of public transport.

With brilliant foresight, Donald had been warning for years not only about the decline of Methodism, but also the slow death of Central London as a place of worship in the face of the flight to the suburbs. This analysis had partially explained his desire for a Methodist cathedral in West London back in 1944. Now, seeing which way the wind was blowing, he felt bound to warn Conference again in 1964 about the withering of Methodism's roots in the inner cities, unless more experiments of the Notting Hill type were tried. In 1965 he came up with the radical suggestion of closing Kingsway and merging with Central Hall, Westminster, believing that Methodism needed only one large assembly hall in Central-West London. A committee was set up to consider the proposition but they rejected it the following year on the grounds that the two congregations were very different.

Frustrated by Conference, Donald opened other lines of attack. As far back as 1963 he had established close relations with St Martin-in-the-Fields for occasional hymn-singing and prayers. In January 1965 the latter had joined Kingsway for its annual mission, but any scheme for yet further union ultimately foundered on the back of two exceedingly strong characters in charge in Donald and the Revd Austen Williams. Now in 1966, he instituted a semi-merger with the local Anglican Church, Holy Trinity, whereby the two churches would play host to each other for Sunday services once a month. This was the first step towards "church sharing" which Donald felt was consistent with their denominational hopes. The plan to worship at Holy Trinity on Sunday evenings took time to unfold, but in September 1969, in the shadow of an appeal by the Archbishop of Canterbury for the closest co-operation between Anglicans and Methodists, it eventually began. Donald acknowledged that there were those with reservations, a point borne out by the first time Holy Communion was held at Holy Trinity for the Harvest Festival, since some Methodists not used to an alcoholic communion wine, objected to the one used. From then on there were two types.

In light of Anglican-Methodist steps towards reunion, as well as his own aesthetic dislike for mission halls, Donald felt that the big hall at Kingsway was no longer conducive to continuing worship. These sentiments were brought home in dramatic circumstances when a large section of the hall caved in one Sunday in January 1969, minutes after the conclusion of Evening Service. Fortunately, no one was injured, but with the cost of repair likely to be exorbitant, it convinced Donald that Kingsway should close with the revenues from its sale going to preserve the social work of the West London Mission. Discussions thus began with Holy Trinity for a proposed share agreement, which was brought to the notice of its Parochial Church Council. Despite the support of its vicar, the Revd O. T. Fuljames, and the Area Pastoral Committee of the London Diocese, who felt that Holy Trinity would have little difficulty in adapting, the Parochial Church Council rejected the proposal in 1971. They felt that Kingsway hadn't given adequate financial guarantees for the future upkeep of their church. Again, it was another defeat that left scars, leaving Donald to regret thereafter his failure to sell his vision of a Kingsway-Trinity merger with greater clarity. Perhaps on this issue, as with Church unity in general, he was too far ahead of his time.

CHAPTER TWELVE

Against the Tide

When Donald was sixty-five, his staff bought him a pensioner's ticket to the theatre. It was a well-meaning gesture which backfired. David Smith recalled how it was the only time he ever saw him moved to anger. He might now have reached retirement age, but Donald had still far too much to accomplish to opt for a sedentary lifestyle, writing his memoirs. His figure might have been slightly frailer and his arthritic limp more pronounced, but otherwise the large, aggressive head, the ruddy, tanned complexion, and the smooth flat hair, albeit with a white tinge, had hardly changed his appearance. What's more, his firm, cultured voice, his penetrating humour and meticulous self-discipline were as much in evidence as they ever were. He did admit to making the odd concession to age by slightly reducing his commitments, most notably his overseas missions, but in addition to his manifold responsibilities at Kingsway, the lure of the march, the platform and the broadcasting studio remained as enticing as ever.

As the 1960s gave way to the 70s, the issue of apartheid remained at the forefront of the national consciousness. This was especially the case following the cancellation of the MCC cricket tour to South Africa in 1968 because of the South African Government's opposition to the inclusion of Basil D'Oliveira, a Cape-coloured all-rounder. From now on the anti-apartheid movement would increasingly use the weapon of sports boycott as an effective means of bringing pressure to bear on South Africa.

Consequently the Springboks' rugby tour to Britain in 1969–70 took place against a background of considerable unrest, with the pitch itself becoming the focus for the more extreme protests. Donald was against anything which smacked of disorder, but when England hosted the Springboks at Twickenham in December, he was there with Mervyn Stockwood and others to register his disapproval, prompting the usual complaints about Church interference in politics. The tour was successfully completed, but a proposed one by South Africa's cricketers the following summer wasn't so fortunate. In the weeks before it was due to begin, the arguments for and against gained much coverage in the media, including Radio 4's *Any Questions* in which Donald squared up to a rising Conservative politician called Margaret Thatcher who, as a fellow Methodist, was fully acquainted with his preaching. Despite his love of cricket and the opportunity of watching one of the great sides, Donald placed this as secondary to his hatred of apartheid. Mrs Thatcher retorted that politics shouldn't intervene in sport and pointed out that no restrictions were imposed on cultural and sporting relations with the Soviet Union, despite persecution there. There was to be no meeting of minds. Donald, however, had the satisfaction of seeing the tour called off because of fears about public order and the safety of the players. With the unanimous support of the Methodist Conference at his back, he kept the pressure on the new Conservative Government by marching to Downing Street in July with Trevor Huddleston, Bishop of Stepney, demanding a total arms embargo against South Africa. What he wasn't prepared to do, however, was to countenance the donation of funds by the World Council of Churches to liberation fighters in South Africa and elsewhere, on the grounds that it was sanctifying violence contrary to Jesus' injunction in the Sermon on the Mount of overcoming evil with good. His stance placed him at odds with old friends such as Pauline Webb and Colin Morris, who both believed that to do nothing was merely to give succour to the State-sponsored violence of the apartheid regime. The dispute erupted at Conference in Bristol in 1974 when Morris, on behalf of the Missionary Society, found himself fending off a motion which opposed support to any fund that could be held to support violence. In a combative speech he informed Conference that the Overseas Division wouldn't allow itself to be subjected to blackmail through a withdrawal of financial support if it didn't act according to wishes. In a passionate reply, Donald called the demand moral and spiritual dynamite and it needed a compromise from Harry Morton to still the waters. In future the Overseas Division should only accept donations specifically earmarked to curb racism and only donations earmarked as such should be submitted to the programme.

In August 1970 Donald and Marie led an ecumenical group to Russia, much enjoyed by all those who made the trip. In Leningrad they fell for the marvels of the Hermitage Art Museum, but Donald, to his distress, saw more drunks on the streets there in three nights than in London in three months. At Sochi, on the Black Sea, they attended a Russian Orthodox service in an Orthodox cathedral filled to capacity. They stood for two hours and were elevated by the experience. Having been enthused by his previous visit there back in 1954, Donald was intrigued to see whether Soviet attempts to build the new earthly paradise had been realised. In a more measured assessment than his starry-eyed account of sixteen years earlier, he was careful not to confuse social and economic progress with a new moral order. Thus the explosion of public housing he dubbed a concrete Esperanto, as rootless and conventional as in any European conurbation, except that the suburbs were cleaner and litter free. He also detected little movement spiritually, so that while the people had gravitated towards western style tastes in clothes and fashion, they were still subjected to the all-powerful, all-pervading mantras of the State, which left little room for genuine Christian belief. In short, the so-called new Soviet man seemed as suggestible and gullible as his pre-revolutionary forbear. Weighing up the impact of his visit in *Tribune*, he found himself caught between two conflicting thoughts. "The one is that the promotion of general welfare in the Soviet Union is a stupendous achievement. The other is that the Soviet claim (advanced again and again by Lenin) to be creating a new sort of human being cannot be sustained by the evidence. There is no necessary permanence in their New Jerusalem, for the 'new' man who will cherish it and maintain it is yet to be born."[1] Donald's assessment of the Soviet experiment was certainly more downbeat than hitherto, but never in his dreams could he have imagined that within two decades it would be consigned to history, a victim of its own contradictions. He had been more sympathetic than most, yet come its collapse, he shed few tears for the demise of an ideology he consistently decried as imperfect and devoid of godliness and respect for humanity. The Soviet persecution of the Jews particularly angered him.

In the 1970s there was a blossoming of Donald's links with the Jewish community which he had cultivated since the 1950s through contributions to the *Jewish Chronicle*, and which had survived his condemnation of the execution of the Nazi war criminal, Adolf Eichmann, in 1962. To understand this slightly unusual position for a mid-twentieth-century socialist without any Jewish links, we need to consider several factors. First, Donald was a man who hated persecution of any type. Despite one or two insensitive comments about the Holocaust, which related to his pacifism, the murder of six million people left an indelible mark on his conscience, enhanced by his visit to Auschwitz in 1956. He always prefaced any statement or answers on the Jewish question by apologising on behalf of the Christian Church for the persecution of Jews by Christians over the centuries, especially for the Roman Catholic doctrine that they had inherited the guilt of such Jews as had connived at the death of Jesus. Second, the fact that he lived in Hampstead Garden Suburb and belonged to the Hampstead Golf Club, both of which contained a sizeable Jewish contingent, helped account for his many Jewish friends and admirers. A number of them were regulars in the open air and one of them, Louis Carrier, a heckler at Tower Hill for over forty years, loved him for his sense of justice. Donald always pointed out what a remarkable people they were and the outstanding contribution they had made to science and culture. As far as he was concerned, they had a right to stay in Israel, as they had been granted a homeland there by the British Government in the Balfour Declaration of 1917. When the continuing desire of the neighbouring Arab powers to destroy this new state culminated in the Six Day War of 1967, Donald, although fiercely opposed to the war itself, found his sympathies lay very much with Israel as underdog. The fact that its governments of this era inclined very much to the left only enhanced these sympathies.

Back in 1959 he highlighted the plight of Jews in Romania and thereafter that of their counterparts in the Soviet Union. In March 1971 he boycotted the Red Army Ensemble from Kiev in protest against their continuing harsh treatment and two months later he attended a rally in support of Soviet Jews in Trafalgar Square. There was no good condemning apartheid in South Africa, he said, and ignoring it in other parts of the world. When thirteen Israelis were gunned down in September 1972 by Palestinian guerrillas during the Olympic Games in Munich, Donald was quick to register his protest. He was to the fore again in 1973 when the Arab nations, led by Egypt, attacked Israel, calling for complete disarmament in the Middle East. On 13 December he led a group of church leaders to the Syrian Embassy to urge its government to provide the International Red Cross with the names of Israeli prisoners of war captured during the recent fighting on the Golan Heights. The Ambassador refused to meet them. His efforts hadn't gone unnoticed, however, and in 1976, on behalf of an all-party parliamentary delegation, he opened a high-powered conference in Brussels under the chairmanship of Golda Meir, the former Israeli Prime Minister, to discuss ways of enabling Soviet Jews to migrate to the West. He remained committed to the Israeli cause even as its government, reflecting a surge to the right, adopted a more aggressive stance. When Lord Carrington, the Foreign Secretary, made overtures towards the Palestine Liberation Organisation (PLO) in 1980, Donald remained unconvinced. More remarkable was his reaction in 1982 to Israeli motives in the escalating tension in Lebanon. At the Methodist Conference in Plymouth, David Mason moved an emergency motion, deploring the Israeli attack to eradicate the PLO by military means. He was flabbergasted by the stinging rebuttal he received from Donald who defended Israeli interests, before urging a note of caution. He couldn't see any final resolution of the Middle East crisis until other countries such as Britain set an example to all by disarming. His words shocked others but the speech was never mentioned again to Mason. For all his support of Judaism, there were limits as to how far he was prepared to go. During his final few years he became embroiled in a local controversy about whether a eruv (a special Jewish area) should be created in a 65-square-mile area of Barnet, including Hampstead Garden Suburb, to give orthodox Jews certain benefits on the Sabbath. The rabbis were all in favour, but many of the more enlightened Jews had reservations. When a public inquiry was established, opponents to the eruv sought out Donald's support. He obliged, providing a statement in December 1993 in which he deplored this expression of a ghetto mentality which would simply act as a ploy for Jews to circumvent their own Sabbath laws. They would be encouraged into the area and it would lose its multi-ethnic complexion. "As to the idea of eruvs and their purpose – the whole concept is a retrograde step," he wrote, "looking to a world in which we can be separated and have a right to a private domain rather than a corporate community. It is understandable but regrettable: an attempt to find a way out of a dilemma by an attitude of self-satisfaction. It is never good religious observance to maintain the letter of the law in circumstances which make it inherently hostile to the well-being of the wider community."[2] His words were in vain. After years of argument, the eruv was finally granted by Barnet Council come the millennium.

In January 1971, as part of the week of prayer for Christian Unity, Donald became the first Methodist to preach at Sandringham in front of the Royal Family. Although a republican by inclination who disliked the National Anthem being sung at the Methodist Conference, Donald's sermon on love was non-controversial, but despite being on his best behaviour, he felt ignored by the Queen.

In February Donald once again crossed the Atlantic to address a Methodist gathering in Western Ohio. It gave him the opportunity to study the two branches of Methodism. First, he detected a more classless form of Methodism in the United States, compared to its lower-middle-class roots in Britain. Second, the Church there was more hierarchical with its system of bishops and third, it displayed a kind of pioneering spirit absent in British Methodism. It was one of his more upbeat assessments of a country about which he continued to harbour many reservations, not least its extremes of wealth and the Vietnam war still in progress. On his return he defended an American Air Force officer, Thomas Culver, court-martialled for organising an anti-war demonstration at Speakers' Corner near the American Embassy, arguing that this shrine to free speech was the obvious place to voice such sentiments. The following year he spoke out in favour of Pauline Jones, a young twenty-two- year-old from Essex, sentenced to twenty-one months imprisonment for abducting a baby, calling her sentence barbaric. Prison was not the way to treat her, he professed. His concern was understandable but it riled the local MP Norman Tebbit, who had helped transfer his constituent to an open prison. He, like Donald, felt that the sentence had been too severe, but vigorously defended the Home Secretary, Reginald Maudling, for upholding the verdict of the Appeal Court, which had cut her original sentence from three years to twenty-one months. As a vociferous critic at Tower Hill in his youth and a trenchant free-marketer in the Conservative Governments of the 1980s, Tebbit wasn't Donald's natural soul mate and when he came to write his autobiography he was unsparing in his judgement of him. "Sadly a group of Labour MPs and Lord Soper, who had always appeared to me the epitome of sanctimonious ill-judgement, leapt upon the Pauline Jones bandwagon, turning a sad human case into a political weapon against the Home Secretary and the judiciary whilst she quietly served out her sentence, less remission."[3] To be fair, as an inveterate campaigner against injustice, Donald was often at his most magisterial when confronting the quirks of the legal system as it then stood. Equally, there were occasions when his sympathy for the underdog could blind his sense of perspective and goad him into counsels for the defence which bordered on the bizarre. There was the occasion when he made a special journey to court to defend a Methodist minister fined £75 for gross indecency in a private lavatory. As far as Donald was concerned, the incident could well enrich the minister's mind and make him a more understanding person. His comments inflamed the Tory tabloids as did his partial defence of shoplifting from supermarkets in March 1997 on the grounds that the capitalist system was based on theft.

In October 1971 Donald joined battle on the great issue which confronted Britain that autumn – whether or not to join the European Economic Community (EEC) some fourteen years after its inception. Originally he had been in favour of the concept of a Europe sharing economic and political power, such was his abhorrence of the nation state, which he saw as a willing accomplice of those other evils, capitalism and war. In the early 1960s, however, he began to have second thoughts when the Macmillan Government expressed an interest in joining. Not only did he dislike the capitalist connotations of Europe, he now saw it developing, with American encouragement, into a superpower against communism, thereby impairing his vision of world government through the UN. In one of the very few volte-faces he ever made, Donald's aversion to the EEC grew with every passing year as the issue continued to cause as much division within parties as between them. On 27 October he relayed his reservations to the House of Lords when both Houses debated the Heath Government's terms for entry. Beginning with the claim that public opinion was against entry, he correctly ascertained that, contrary to official denials, there were far-reaching constitutional implications about joining. "No one is going to tell me that economic unity is not the bell-wether of political unity," he said, highlighting what he saw as a major flaw, for contrary to the views of the majority, he depicted political union as a kind of nation state which he branded as predatory, nasty and violent. "I do not want to see the nation's state coagulated into a series of super-States," he continued. "This seems to me a very real and definite prospect."[4] A European superstate in his estimation was unlikely to serve the cause of peace and the well-being of the dispossessed, since it would represent the failures of the past, little appreciating the genuine desire of countries such as Germany and Italy to begin anew.

Despite these reservations, which to some degree reflected those of the socialist left and nationalist right, the European Communities Bill comfortably passed both Houses and Britain joined on 1 January 1973. A new chapter in the country's history had begun, but Donald remained unconvinced. When the Wilson Government held a referendum in June 1975 on whether Britain should remain in Europe, he condemned the community as a capitalist club. To stay in, he argued, would be felony, especially as few benefits had accrued so far. He wasn't alone in his thinking, but sensing a bleak future in isolation, the British people swallowed their doubts and voted to stay in by a two-to-one margin. Calling the whole referendum process a genuine if clumsy exercise in democracy, Donald remained unreconciled to the European idea for the rest of his days, even though the Labour Party in time became much more enthusiastic about its benefits.

In 1971 the first biography of Donald, written by Douglas Thompson, a stalwart of the Methodist Missionary Society, was published, followed the next year by *Portrait of Soper* by William Purcell, Canon Residentiary of Worcester Cathedral. Neither could offer a final verdict. For besides saying little about Donald's relationship with his colleagues and his overseas trips, they ignored some of the hidden depths of his personality which his public role rarely revealed. Both gave a suitably flattering assessment of their subject, but were rather too deferential to ask the pertinent questions which need to be asked about any major public figure with a flair for controversy.

In the spring of 1972 Donald and Marie led a brief trip to Egypt, which included a tour of the pyramids. He was impressed by the growing importance of the vast Aswan Dam, and felt that there were prospects for future prosperity, but remained justifiably alarmed about the festering tension with Egypt's great rival, Israel. Within less than eighteen months they were at war again. At Conference in July he was full of foreboding for the Church's future as congregations at Kingsway continued to fall away in line with national trends. He told his colleagues that he saw little future for Methodism unless it stressed moral and ethical principles rather than a number of credal statements. His words received a lukewarm reception, as did his expressed disquiet about an appeal to help Britain's unemployed orchestrated by the British Council of Churches, which he felt far too timid. His frustration boiled over in a forthright interview in the *Methodist Recorder*, when he slated the conservatism of Conference with its endless procrastination and called for a radical overhaul of the archaic method of presenting reports, so that important matters could be elevated to the exclusion of the trivial. He dubbed denominationalism "as dead as mutton" and called for the death of Methodism as a separate entity, so that it could be resurrected as a preaching order within the Church of England. His parting shot was his familiar plea for the Churches to become more Jesus-centred in their approach, taking their lead from the best-selling rock opera *Jesus Christ Superstar*, then at the height of its fame. His words made fresh headlines, causing the usual dissension within Methodist ranks, unhappy with his apocalyptic views about the future, but the *Methodist Recorder*, without sharing his profound pessimism, supported the broad thrust of his message. And it wasn't hard to see why, as the dramatic decline in Methodist congregations during the 1960s, especially in the North, caused the closure of 493 churches between 1971 and 1974, as well as of three prominent Methodist theological colleges, including Richmond.

Donald also plunged headlong into battle with Conference over its attempts to moderate its forty-one-year-old commitment to total abstinence, with college and other residential premises exempted from the ban on the supply, sale and use of alcohol. He remained adamantly opposed to concessions, prompting the question why a person so given to progressive causes remained unbending over alcohol. The answer appears to lie in Donald's background and experience. Ever since earliest times the curse of drink had been roundly drummed into him. It had afflicted both his parents' families and the trauma this had caused the young Ernest Soper helped account for his militant stance on temperance. His views were in any case prevalent in certain sections of the Free Churches, especially those with links to the industrial cities of the North, where alcoholic excess was common, as well as in the Labour and Liberal Parties. Donald had a more sunny temperament than Ernest and was well disposed to enjoying himself, but the respect that he had for his father, the depth of his faith and his own experiences in the South London Mission, where he saw families going hungry because the menfolk had dissipated their savings in the pub, kept him resolute to the strictures of his youth. There was, however, a subtle shift in his justification for abstinence as the basis of his faith widened.

Instead of simply slamming drink as intrinsically evil and medically dangerous, he opposed it on the grounds that its mere existence constituted a profound menace to the kingdom of God. This could be due to the exacerbation of poverty, the promotion of prostitution, the threat to family life or the cause of road fatalities. His belief that such opposition should be supported by practical displays of abstinence may help explain the extremes to which he would go, including his call to close every pub in Britain, and his aspersions on fellow Christians who thought otherwise. Denys Orchard recalled that the only time he crossed swords with Donald came during the war when working with an Anglican unit from St Martin-in-the-Fields to help the homeless. Donald felt it intolerable that people witnessing for the Gospel should be seen in the pub at lunchtime. Orchard stood his ground, arguing that it was the only place where they could get a decent lunch, but although Donald was forced to back down, he did so reluctantly. Certainly, with dismissal not unknown, his staff didn't drink when he was around, and even at weddings when they might sample a glass of sherry, he was less than ecstatic. In common with Methodist standing orders at the time, there was no drink at home. To please him, Marie, until his retirement from Kingsway, didn't drink, and no alcohol was available at the wedding receptions of his two eldest daughters. Such stringency even caught Donald out on one occasion. David Smith, when Assistant Minister at Kingsway, has recollections of a bottle of Harrods' sherry being presented to Donald as a Christmas present and being the fortunate recipient of a gift shunned by his superintendent. The problem arose when Marie, unhappy about his reckless generosity, asked Donald to get it back again, only for Smith to confess that he had drunk it. He did, however, offer to take Donald to Harrods to get another one, whereupon London SW7 was treated to the extraordinary sight of Donald hurtling into the world famous department store in his cassock to purchase alcohol before anyone seemed the wiser. Although the Methodist Conference had never made total abstinence a condition of membership, it had recommended since 1933 that all ministers accept it as a better way. Even this stipulation wasn't good enough for Donald, who had tried unsuccessfully at Conference in 1949 to get members individually to accept the pledge. He continued to stand his ground as the hardliners within Methodism's ranks on this emotive issue gradually began to subside.

At Conference in 1971 a Commission had been appointed by the Christian Citizenship Department to study the feasibility of total abstinence in light of changing attitudes, not least by younger Methodists. The Commission accepted the more liberal climate towards drink and recommended to the 1972 Conference at Nottingham that drinkers shouldn't be treated as second-class citizens. These findings predictably drew Donald's ire. He argued that the case for temperance was greater than it had ever been, given the growing preponderance of women to drink to excess. He felt himself called, and he thought the Methodist people were called for the sake of their care of other people, to have nothing to do with alcohol. In the event, Conference agreed to suspend consideration of the appropriate standing order until the declaration of total abstinence had been revised. When the issue re-emerged at Bristol in 1974 the recommendation of the Christian Citizenship Department was to change, so that in future personal conscience, not Conference, would guide the drinking habits of the individual. In an impassioned plea, Donald, seconding the motion to reinstate total abstinence, linked the growth in violence with that of intoxication. "I would suspect," he continued rather bizzarely, "that if alcohol were taken out of the situation in Northern Ireland, a great many of the savageries which stain that unhappy land could to some extent be removed."[5] He ended with a plea for continued abstinence in the name of the kingdom of God. It was all to no avail. Determined to face reality and avoid hypocrisy, Conference voted by a massive majority for change.

That wasn't all. Weeks earlier the National Council on Alcoholism had upset Donald, who was one of their patrons, by suggesting that the young should be taught at home to drink wisely. He retorted that they should never start. In time Donald became slightly less implacable in his resistance, wryly admitting that Jesus hadn't outlawed drink and that light wines might be served in the kingdom of heaven. He not only served alcohol at the weddings of his two youngest daughters as well as at his Diamond Wedding, he was even known on occasions to buy a drink for a friend such as Ron Watts, a member of the West London Mission. He continued, however, to desist himself and to use the House of Lords as a platform to highlight the dangers of alcohol as well as proposing practical measures to alleviate its baleful effects, such as prohibiting advertising in any form. Sadly, for all his effort, not least the exemplary lead given by the West London Mission, it proved a forlorn struggle as rising affluence hastened the spread of alcohol-related diseases, especially among women.

The year 1972 ended on an acrimonious note. During the later 1960s the sectarian tensions in Northern Ireland between the Unionist majority and the Nationalist minority had deteriorated to such an extent that British troops had been sent to the province in 1969 to keep the peace. Although welcomed at first, their presence ultimately came to inflame matters, and soon they became embroiled in some poisonous spats with the paramilitaries, especially the Provisional IRA. In February 1972 a civil rights march in Londonderry had spiralled out of control leading to the "Bloody Sunday" massacre when thirteen Catholic civilians were killed. The outrage caused a national furore, not least with Donald who announced that he was seething with anger. He became all the more convinced that an essential precondition for peace was the withdrawal of British troops. Later in the year when he used the *Methodist Recorder* to advocate a "Vigil for Derry" in Londonderry to commemorate Bloody Sunday on the first anniversary, he upset many Methodists by his apparent hostility towards the troops and the Unionist community. So much so, that he felt compelled on 28 December to clarify his commitment to reconciliation, not provocation, and apologise for unwittingly making things more difficult. He continued, however, to campaign for the withdrawal of the troops, and a united socialist Ireland offering justice for all which he saw as the real panacea for lasting peace. Furthermore, in June 1974 in a House of Lords' debate on Ulster, he denounced his old foe Ian Paisley as a "loud-mouthed mob orator with an unfortunate mind, a capacity to arouse emotions, and a savagery which I believe precludes him from any inclusion in what I would call a servant of the Lord Jesus Christ".[6] By no means everyone in Methodism approved of this outburst.

Away from the public gaze, Kingway's future was being decided against a background of declining morale, as it appeared to be living on borrowed time. For years, as the advertising boards at London Underground stations made plain, Donald's name had been its prime asset, but his own dynamic leadership had been balanced by a wise and experienced team of Mission staff which brought a collective feel to proceedings. Now, with that generation departed, and declining resources preventing adequate replacements, Donald was more than ever the oracle to whom people looked for inspiration when advancing years and multifarious commitments made him less able to move mountains. In 1981 Harry Morton publicly denounced him for staying on too long at Kingsway, a charge that Donald reluctantly accepted, confessing that as one of Mr Wesley's travelling preachers he had been a bit sluggish. Conversely, in the opinion of Olive Delves, one of the Kingsway faithful, it was only someone of Donald's stature who enabled the Mission to flourish as long as it did. The spark and vitality which he injected into the place was visibly lacking when he was absent, while the doleful looks on the faces of the congregation when they discovered he wasn't preaching, told their own simple story.

After negotiations with Holy Trinity had broken down in 1970, Donald conceived the idea of sharing with St Mary-le-Strand, an historic church in the heart of the City fighting closure. This would operate through an agreement under the Sharing of Church Buildings Act of 1969, whereby the Methodists would contribute £80,000, and the parish £20,000 to create a basement hall by lowering the crypt floor. Concerned about the reaction of the local authorities to the plans for the hall, a working party was set up to examine the proposals. They reported back to the Pastoral Committee on 18 May 1971, who decided that St Mary's wasn't suitable for sharing, especially since alternative accommodation was available at Holy Trinity. Even had this decision gone his way, Donald would have had trouble selling his proposals to his congregation. They had been kept in the dark about the planned merger and when news leaked out, they didn't like what they heard. Not only was St Mary's "High" Church, with a plaque to Charles II at its front, which many felt quite inappropriate for the Methodists, it was disadvantaged by its remote location. Kath Humphreys recalled how after Evensong at Holy Trinity one Sunday, the Kingsway congregation held a meeting in the church to hear out the plans. Some were in favour but the majority were steadfastly against, and in the face of their unexpectedly strong reaction, led by Sister Kathleen Lee, one of the deaconesses, Donald, so used to getting his own way, was forced to concede defeat. The following Sunday he stopped Kath Humphreys as she was leaving church and with a baleful look on his face said, "Now, I'll have to go cap in hand to Holy Trinity and see if we can stay on there." Such a prospect failed to excite his flock who had been dragged there reluctantly for Evensong in the first place. They didn't like its inadequate heating, poor acoustics and its evangelistic tradition, with the result that a number left Kingsway. A Church Neighbours Group was formed, but this did little to improve the size of the congregation because many of the locals were Irish and Italian working-class.

Frustrated twice and unwilling to countenance a possible successor to himself at Kingsway, Donald now instituted negotiations with Hinde Street, a church which had been part of the West London Mission Circuit until 1957. Its Superintendent, Brian Duckworth, agreed in 1971 that a merger would be to the mutual benefit of both. A special joint Quarterly Meeting of the two Circuits endorsed it in February 1972, as did Methodist Conference that summer, just as Kingsway was about to be sold off to British Land for £2.5 million, although the Mission would rent back part of the premises for ten years. During the Kingsway-Hinde Street negotiations that followed, chaired, for the most part, by Donald, the question of redeveloping the latter loomed large. The process of conducting feasibility studies, architectural plans and planning appeals all took time, as did the need to consult the Kingsway congregation more fully than hitherto. In 1977 the plans for redevelopment were approved and work began three years later. They were completed in 1982, after which vastly expanded facilities costing nearly £800,000 came into force at 19, Thayer Street, next to Hinde Street Church. These facilities would safeguard the social work of the Mission, Donald's cardinal concern, which had continued to operate effectively within a more professional ethos. Although some projects had been wound up, others were taken on, such as the West London Mission Day Centre for the Homeless and Rootless, first in the basement at Kingsway then at 136, Seymour Place. The moving spirit behind the latter was Derek White, its Co-ordinator. He recalled how the unstinting support he received from Donald helped overcome resistance from some of the Management Committee as they fretted about the cost of the venture. The result was London's first purpose-built homeless centre which provided food, medical care and housing advice for some of the capital's rootless thousands.

There were also the continued acts of personal kindness, including the inspirational story of Saul Cantor, a Canadian Jew, who had won fame in the boxing ring on both sides of the Atlantic in the post-war years but had fallen on hard times. Prone to dark thoughts about his Jewish background and his sinfulness, he found nobody he could talk to about his experiences, until he stumbled across Kingsway by chance one Sunday in 1974. Having been welcomed by Donald personally and shown to his seat, he was entranced by his Lenten sermon, as his words about the light of Christ reached into his subconscious, where, prior to this, the angel of darkness had resided. He couldn't wait to get back to listen to him again. After regular attendance at church, and continued personal discussions with Donald, at which he gently drew out his thoughts, Cantor, much to Donald's astonishment, elected to be baptised. He became his Cross-bearer and to this day ranks Donald the greatest friend he has ever had.

There were others who also worshipped him, but in a manner which caused him distress and embarrassment. Because of its political complexion, Kingsway attracted more men than women, but Donald, in his pastoral duties, related more to the latter since he felt more relaxed in their company. They, in turn, warmed to his alluring good looks and arresting personality, and a number took their admiration to obsessive lengths, such as hiding in his garden and ringing him at all times of the night. A particularly serious case arose during his final years at Kingsway when one young woman followed him everywhere, creating a scene during worship and throwing herself in front of his car. So alarming did the situation become that Denys Orchard, as Senior Circuit Steward, had to accompany him to his car when Donald left Kingsway and run to the nearby traffic lights to restrain her when the lights were red. Throughout this upsetting episode, Donald, although rather at a loss as to how to handle such behaviour, remained a model of tolerance, but there were limits to what even he could endure. With great reluctance he asked a High Court judge for legal protection and in February 1979 the woman was threatened with imprisonment if she continued to pester him. Only then was he safe.

Throughout the rest of the 1970s, Donald continued to play a leading role in pressure group politics, euthanasia, blood sports and the homeless being his priorities. February 1974 was an exceptionally busy month as the Heath Government, after weeks of industrial strife, called an early election on the slogan of "Who Governs Britain?" As ever, Donald spoke in support of his friends such as Will Sheaf in Epping Forest and Tim Rhodes in Sutton and Cheam in addition to assuming new responsibilities as Chairman of Shelter, the pressure group for the homeless. Although the intricacies of its programmes sometimes remained beyond his grasp because he lacked the time to master the detail, his years in charge of a variety of hostels at the West London Mission gave him an invaluable insight into the plight of all types of vulnerable groups. For some time Donald felt that housing had ranked a poor third behind food and clothing as basic rights for the destitute. His concerns had been exacerbated by the remorseless rise in homelessness, which had come about for a variety of reasons, chief among them the decline of the nuclear family and a shortage of public accommodation.

In 1974 the outgoing Conservative Government made the provision of housing for the homeless the responsibility of local authorities rather than the social services. Then in 1977 the Callaghan Government provided legislative teeth to that circular, especially in light of the failure of many authorities to adhere to it. The fact that it had taken Labour three years to get to grips with the problem frustrated Donald, especially since local authority stringency had facilitated the rise in homelessness from 33,000 to 50,000 during that period. Having denounced the housing authorities for their deplorable response to homelessness in June 1975, he expressed his shock at the total absence of any reference to remedial measures to the problem the following year in the Queen's Speech, especially when there were promises to prosecute squatters.

When the Housing Bill appeared in 1977 with its intention to accommodate the homeless, Donald welcomed its general principle but pinpointed the failure to give priority to the young homeless as a major flaw, especially given the threat to increased social alienation and delinquency. "What scares me almost as much – I say this with considerable hesitation and after long thought" – Donald confided to the Lords, "is that I believe there is a moral deterioration in a great many young people today. One of the causes producing that situation, lamentable as it is, is their lack of any sense of belonging, and one cannot belong unless one has somewhere to live."[7] As far as he was concerned, the young homeless were the group most unable to adapt to the world. In order to rectify this situation he wanted more cash for voluntary hostels and short term stock – a better prospect than sleazy bed and breakfasts – as well as an end to the discriminatory system whereby youngsters were given priority treatment only.

His hopes were in vain. Economic stringency saw to that, but at least Shelter under his leadership between 1974 and 1978, had made some progress compared to what was to happen during the 1980s when mass unemployment and Tory housing policies resulted in an escalation in the number of homeless, especially among the young.

In April 1974 Donald and Marie went to Turkey for the last of their pilgrimages. He was much taken with the beautiful plains of Anatolia, the impressive tourist facilities, the affability of the locals and the new sense of community in a country which had experienced its fair share of ructions hitherto. What vexed him was the still prominent role of the army and police in a society caught between its theocratic past and its future as a modern western democracy. Another finale came two years later when Donald, in 1976, made the last of his ten trips to Canada. He found it mired in the same kind of economic difficulties all too familiar back home.

In 1975, as well as becoming President Emeritus of MSF, Donald exchanged the chairmanship of CSM for the less demanding one of President. He continued, however, to hold court on the contemporary scene, calling for more socialism to cure unemployment and more rigorous legislation against the use of knives and firearms to curb the rise in violence. He remained active in the House of Lords, speaking on such topics as penal reform (the parole policy was too timid), alcohol (he was against the relaxation of late night drinking laws) and pornography (he was in favour of tougher laws). He also raised a few eyebrows at the Methodist Conference in Preston in 1976 by suggesting that communism could be included in the curriculum for religious education in schools, since it was in its own way a religious faith.

A similar line on inclusiveness appeared evident in Donald's contribution to the political debate about entryism into the Labour Party by extreme left-wing groups, which was endemic in the mid-1970s. While he abhorred the intolerance and intimidation of such minority cliques which he had seen become ever more conspicuous in the open air, he supported the broad thrust of their programme, which in essence was little different from what he had been advocating for years. When Wilson retired as Prime Minister and leader of the Labour Party in April 1976, Donald supported Michael Foot as his successor, and although disappointed that he lost to Jim Callaghan, his friend's strong showing gave him a pivotal role in the new Government. Indeed, Foot's own enforced moderation in the face of severe economic and political buffetings might well have helped account for Donald's relative quiescence as the Government took a decisive turn to the right.

The year 1977 was a year of celebration, not just the Queen's Silver Jubilee but also the fortieth anniversary of *Tribune* when Donald joined a rally of the entire left in Central Hall, Westminster. He also celebrated fifty years on Tower Hill, his spirit undaunted by the weekly challenge which inevitably placed a greater toll on him now that he was over seventy. In March he led a group of British churchmen to the Soviet Embassy to inquire about believers imprisoned for their faith. The delegation was told that those complaining of persecution probably belonged to a distinct minority of the population who didn't approve of the Soviet lifestyle. The Embassy expressed surprise that the British Churches appeared so concerned with the Soviet Union, set against the many problems they faced at home. Another country which he continued to turn his fire on was South Africa. In May when in Vienna, he managed to listen to its hardline Prime Minister, John Vorster, give a talk to businessmen about his country's essential role as a bulwark against global communism. He returned full of foreboding. Despite hopes of change he insisted that the apartheid regime survived in all its depravity and that any talk of Vorster as a reformer was claptrap.

That September Donald took on new responsibilities, becoming closely involved with the Voluntary Euthanasia Society (Exit), an organisation formed in 1935 to secure legal endorsement of euthanasia. This was no easy matter as the medical profession was reluctant to depart from its long-standing professional ethos of saving life as opposed to terminating it, while the world's association with Nazi atrocities towards the mentally handicapped, euphemistically called "euthanasia", did little to advance the cause post-war. It needed the 1960s with its more liberal climate to shift opinion, particularly as advances in modern medicine such as the respirator raised important ethical questions about the artificial prolongation of life for the terminally ill.

Donald was a great rarity within the Church in that he had never accepted the traditional Christian view that suicide was a sin, citing the numerous examples when it was associated with self-sacrifice. These included his childhood hero, Captain Oates, on Scott's expedition to the Antartic, despite the fact that Oates didn't commit suicide. He simply gave his colleagues his share of food and shelter and means of further transport.

Donald felt that the terminally ill, enduring great pain, should have the right to die with dignity through the withholding of life prolongation drugs, thus sparing themselves and their relatives as much distress as possible, especially since to him Christian death wasn't the end but the gateway to eternity. He spoke here with some feeling, remembering his father's dismay at the way he was kept alive during his final unpleasant illness.

These convictions formed the basis of his speech in the House of Lords in March 1969 on Lord Raglan's Bill, which provided for the painless inducement of death in patients suffering from irredeemable conditions. "From a professively Christian point of view, I am perfectly well persuaded that there are innumerable instances in the dark places of the hospital wards of animate yet not sentient creatures living an entirely vegetable existence – if, indeed, one can say they are living at all. This is a problem upon which much greater research and careful analysis has to be made, but surely it is rather silly to talk as if any organism which shows the outward and visible signs or sense reaction or of mechanical stimulation should be regarded as of sacred value."

He went on: "If I reached a sub-terminal or terminal condition in which I was in great and inconsolable pain, in which I was in such a condition as to be irreparable, and a cause of great sorrow and suffering to those who had to care for me, when they might be caring for somebody else, I hope that I should have the courage and the intelligence in such circumstances to opt to give my life; and if I did, I believe that I have a right to ask the medical profession to stand back and let me die."

Despite his support in principle for Lord Raglan's Bill, he voted against it on the grounds that it confused the direct action of bringing somebody's life to an end (which he opposed) and the indirect one of being an accessory to suicide. "I believe," he opined, "that in certain circumstances to be an accessory to that process of exercising one's right to opt out of life, under conditions which will benefit others and will be of no final benefit to the one who opts out, is a reasonable and a Christian demand."[8] The Bill was defeated. When Baroness Wootton introduced the Incurable Patients Bill in 1976 Donald, despite continuing to harbour a number of reservations about its wording, lent his support, employing many of the arguments he had used seven years earlier. In particular, he supported the 1974 Methodist Conference Declaration that doctors should have the support and protection of law in circumstances whereby they chose to discontinue the prescription of drugs merely to preserve life in artificial form. "... I believe that we are moving into a world in which something of this kind will sooner or later be inevitable. It is the right way to do it; not to turn our backs upon it and say that this is some process to which we should give no assent, but rather to believe that the ministries of science, and particularly of medicine, can not only conduce to the benefactions of this world, but can usher us into, first, a better concept of, and then a deeper enjoyment of, that life which follows."[9]

Despite a growing acceptance of the case for euthanasia, the Bill suffered a similar fate to previous ones on the same subject. Hence Donald's challenge the next year when becoming attached to Exit, and one he remained committed to for the rest of his life, in principle if not always in practice. At a conference in Oxford in September 1980, he lambasted a booklet published by Exit called *A Guide to Self-Deliverance* outlining various methods of painless suicide through lethal overdose. His remarks followed advice that the society could be prosecuted under the Suicide Act of 1961 for aiding and abetting. He resigned as a formal supporter but later returned in 1985 to become Vice-President.

Away from the front line, events closer to home were conspiring to force Donald into some hard thinking about retiring, a word which filled him with dread. With the West London Mission about to move to Hinde Street, this seemed the appropriate moment for a change at the helm, especially given the fact that he was now seventy-five and less appreciated by some than hitherto. It is true that he didn't look and act his age, a point emphasised by Brian Breed in the *Methodist Recorder* who detected remarkably little change in his appearance over the previous thirty years, not least the absence of cracks in that marvellously modulated voice. All the same, he couldn't go on for ever. After some gentle "persuasion", allied to a generous retirement settlement which provided him with a room at Kingsway and Hinde Street respectively, continuing occupation of his home and financial support, he reluctantly took the plunge. His congregation was summoned to a meeting by the Revd John Richardson who announced that Donald Soper would be retiring at the end of July and that his successor would be Dr John Newton, Principal of Wesley College, Bristol. Although Donald reassured his congregation that his retirement in no way applied to Tower Hill or Hyde Park, he did offer that June to relinquish the presidency of OCW to a younger man. The executive wouldn't hear of it and unanimously made him Life President, but though he continued to be their leading attraction on the set piece occasion, even he couldn't entice the young to join up. The allurements of the modern world put paid to that and despite the dogged perseverance of the executive to arrest the decline, the final years of OCW were a pale shadow of the heady days of the late 1940s and early 50s.

At the Bradford Conference in 1978 Donald was his usual crusading self as he seconded a motion asking Methodists to withdraw accounts from Barclay's Bank because of its involvement in loans to South Africa. He raised a laugh by introducing himself as Soper-Midland Bank, but for all the power of his anti-apartheid sentiments, Conference wasn't convinced. It did, however, react in the appropriate fashion as Donald officially took his leave after fifty-two years service in the Methodist Church. Although capable of searing criticism of individuals both in public and private, Donald could also be extremely charming and when hosting visiting speakers, his votes of thanks were models of finesse. The same was true of his encomia towards colleagues and friends, none more so than his *tour de force* at Conference in 1970 to mark the retirement of Eric Baker as Secretary. Speaking as ever extempore, his words were expressed with such powerful eloquence that he all but moved his old friend to tears. Now, as he came to take his final bow it was left to others to sound the trumpet on his behalf. "He has gifts so dazzling as to defy description … ," declared Gordon Wakefield, the Chairman of the Manchester and Stockport District. "The Church which has not always been unanimous in agreement or understanding is now one in its love and pride, and seeks to put on record, though imperfectly, its sense that here in this man is one of God's greatest gifts to us in all our history."[10] And then as Donald approached the tribune, Conference rose both in respect and affection to give him a heartfelt ovation. In his reply, he intimated that the one joy which had sustained him lay in the knowledge that he was one of John Wesley's travelling preachers, a member of a preaching order within the Holy Catholic Church.

Weeks later, the farewells were repeated at Kingsway, when his congregation past and present gathered on a sultry afternoon to honour his forty-two years as Superintendent. After tea in the hall, 1,000 lusty voices, including George Thomas, the Speaker of the House of Commons, sang his favourite hymns and gave thanks for a great churchman. Michael Foot, in bringing greetings from the Labour Party, recalled how his mother, a staunch Methodist, had introduced him to Donald in the mid-1930s to rekindle his faith. "He has not made me a better Christian," he confessed, "but has made me a better socialist."

A more apprehensive Donald than usual spoke on the message behind the hymns they had sung, neatly encapsulated in the vision offered in "Behold the Mountain of the Lord" which inspired his pacifism, socialism and open-air preaching. Then when it was over he was off to Australia with Marie for a working holiday at Alan Walker's church in Sydney, his first visit there in twenty-eight years. He found that rising affluence had gone to its head and that it had become unduly self-satisfied. While he was there, there was time for reflection, now that a major chapter in his life had closed, but never a man to sit still for long, he began also to look to the future, determined that his work would go on. Retirement was never really an option.

CHAPTER THIRTEEN

Christian and Hopeful

"When I leave Kingsway, I want to go to heaven" had been one of Donald's favourite sayings. After forty-two years there it was an understandable reaction, but with his health holding up well he would have some time to wait. He had, of course, suffered a thrombosis at the age of thirty-five and another clot in his fifties, which necessitated monthly blood tests thereafter and a regular dose of morphine. He had been operated on for a frozen shoulder in his mid-sixties, and had metal plates in an arthritic hip in his late seventies, a condition aggravated by continuing rounds of golf, contrary to medical instructions. So aggrieved was Donald's surgeon by this wilful display of abandon that he castigated him for his disobedience in a manner to which he was totally unaccustomed. On top of this were his painful bouts of arthritis, but despite these various ailments he had an excellent heart and lung system, and the toughest of physiques, exemplified by a capacity to swim in all temperatures, swollen leg and all. It was this kind of physical and mental resilience that had kept John Wesley active until the last, aged eighty-eight, and now two centuries later his foremost disciple was living out his twilight years to the full, a towering example to a more complacent generation. It was in accordance with this spirit that Pauline Webb recalled seeing Donald, then approaching ninety, preaching to a sparse lunchtime audience in Newcastle upon Tyne in the rain during Conference. When some younger ministers deigned to have some fun at his expense, she rebuked them for lacking the courage to follow in his footsteps.

Donald's retirement from the West London Mission after so many years in charge, posed a challenging inheritance for his successor, Dr John Newton, not least the completion of the merger with Hinde Street. Hinde Street, situated close to Oxford Street in the West End, was classically built in 1887, its two-storey portico and small dome reminiscent of St Paul's, stained-glass windows and huge pulpit behind the altar giving it a distinct Anglican feel. Originally part of the West London Mission, it had become a separate circuit in 1957, whereupon its influx of students from London University, and professional residents, had given it a more conservative, middle-class aura than Kingsway. The disparity helped account for reservations among the latter about joining the former.

Before John Newton went to the West London Mission, he was assured that there was general agreement in the circuit about the development scheme. In particular they should cease to rent part of the Kingsway Hall complex and form a united society at Hinde Street, the more thriving church of the two, as well as refurbishing its premises to make them suitable to serve as the head-quarters of the West London Mission.

At the first Circuit Meeting which Newton chaired, however, the Kingsway people expressed strong disagreement, claiming that they hadn't been prop-erly consulted. The new superintendent therefore thought it right to go back to square one and hold special consultations on the issue at General Church Meeting (all members), Church Council (Kingsway) and Circuit Meetings. At each stage, when the issue was fully debated, they had decisive majorities in favour of the development plan and were able to proceed accordingly.

While this consulting phase was in process, a few Kingsway stalwarts went behind their superintendent's back to ask Donald if he would openly support a plan to buy back the whole of the Kingsway property from British Land. "To his great credit," wrote Newton, "his response was: 'Now look here. This is nothing to do with me, I'm retired; but if anyone should ask my opinion, for what it is worth, you may tell them that, in my considered judgement, the future of the West London Mission lies at Hinde Street!' This was enormously helpful, both to me as new Superintendent, and for the future of the scheme."[1]

Newton had cause to be grateful to Donald in other ways, since he sat quietly at the back of the 11 a.m. service and always disappeared before the Benediction so that he wouldn't be the centre of attention at the end of the service. He also stayed away from committee meetings, and, whatever his own personal views, didn't interfere in the life of the circuit. In return, Newton was receptive to Donald's request to take the 10 a.m. Communion Service at Hinde Street once Kingsway finally closed in May 1982. Not only did he administer the sacraments, he also played the piano, and delivered a brief homily, normally on the Epistle or Gospel for the day. In addition, he preached occasionally at the 11 a.m. service when, because of his presence, the size of the congregation would increase. At Christmas, as people went up to take Communion, he read, as of old, the opening of St John's Gospel, his favourite biblical passage. Most precious of all, he continued to play a major part in the traditional Three Hour Good Friday Service, the one which always meant more to him than any other, (Eastertide was his favourite time of the year), and the one where his words left their greatest mark on his congregation. Although never feeling entirely comfortable at Hinde Street, not least the frustration of no longer being in charge, the superintendent and congregation were very accommodating to him, giving him his own office, where he continued his pastoral work either on the phone or in person.

Aside from his concern for things close to home, Donald continued to view the world as his parish, not least his weekly sorties to Tower Hill and Hyde Park. In September 1979 he was speaking at the former as usual one Wednesday when a young policeman, unaware of his identity, came up to him and requested that he get down from the wall. When asked the reason why, he was told that he was obstructing the Tower of London. On refusing to comply, he was helped down and arrested. It needed the arrival of one of the officer's superiors to sort out matters and restore calm to the crowd who, seeing the act as a flagrant injustice, rounded on the hapless young officer. The arrest made headlines, so that when the Duke of Gloucester came to open the West London Mission's new Day Centre shortly afterwards, he turned to Donald and said, "I'm glad to see you're not inside."

His retirement in 1978 coincided with the travails of the Callaghan Labour Government. Its battle to bring down inflation through wage restraint had his full support not least because he saw no practical alternative, as the Tories in his estimation were approaching their demise. On 23 September 1977 he told his *Tribune* readers he was willing to bet his cassock that Labour would win the next election, prompting a witty rejoinder from Norman Lamont, a future Conservative Chancellor of the Exchequer. "No wonder the Methodist Church is opposed to all forms of gambling if its senior clerics are so recklessly naïve,"[2] he wrote. Certainly Jim Callaghan, the Prime Minister, wasn't as optimistic about Labour's electoral prospects as Donald was. His decision to postpone a general election in October 1978 and struggle on through another winter was always fraught with risks, as trade unions queued up to flex their industrial muscle in a bitter battle with their political masters over pay. In a particularly ice-bound start to 1979, the sight of roads going ungritted, rubbish uncollected and in some cases the dead not being buried, brought to a head simmering public anger against overbearing union power. As Britain seethed, Donald was one of the few public figures to defend the rash of strikes. He told the readers of the *Methodist Recorder* that they shouldn't overreact to the industrial crisis. He said that it was merely the labour pains in the birth of the only society which could succeed in the modern world, a socialist society. As far as he was concerned, the union pay demands were justified, and he blamed the media for using the crisis as a means of soiling their reputation. His view remained a minority one, and as the strikes increasingly paralysed the country, support for Mrs Thatcher's Conservative Opposition grew dramatically. Their victory in the May election proved a defining moment, signalling the end of the old post-war consensus built around Keynesian economics and the welfare reforms of the Attlee Government.

Needless to say, the new Prime Minister, with her free-market philosophy and social authoritarianism, left Donald distinctly unimpressed. "There is nothing worse than a lapsed Methodist," he used to say, alluding to Mrs Thatcher's transition from Methodism to Anglicanism at the time of her marriage, "the higher you go the further you fall." Soon he was using his platform in the House of Lords to wage war against rising unemployment, homelessness and cuts in the public services, as well as joining forces with his old friend Lord Longford to draw attention to the pressures under which the probation service was labouring. His words were in vain, but in 1980 he combined with R. A. Butler, the Duke of Norfolk and the Bishop of London, Gerald Ellison, in a cross-party coalition to oppose a clause of the Government's Education Act which would have imposed charges on school transport. Denouncing it as a piece of class legislation, he believed that the Government had erred through a lack of understanding of the lot of poor people, "... or they are so besotted with the need, as they see it, for the reduction of expenditure in the public sector that they are prepared to impoverish even that area which I would regard as sacrosanct – the area of education particularly for those who are least capable of providing it for themselves..."[3] His words struck home. The Government was heavily defeated and felt honour bound to withdraw its proposals. Such a curb on executive power spelt a considerable triumph for the Upper House and, coming at a time when the Labour Party in the Commons was too riddled with division to lend effective opposition, it gave credence to Donald's conviction that the Lords still had its constitutional uses.

As Mrs Thatcher embarked on her course to change Britain, Donald, who always underestimated her, was confidently predicting in June 1980 that she would be gone within six months as the cracks in her party became more exposed. The irony was that it was his own party which was then prone to deep-seated schism, as the left wing, under Tony Benn, pressed hard for genuine socialism. They managed to force through a number of constitutional changes which helped them on their way. Then, under the leadership of Michael Foot who succeeded Callaghan in November 1980, they embraced unilateral disarmament, withdrawal from Europe and a centrally planned economy. This lurch to the extremes proved too much for many moderates, and in March 1981 a new party, the SDP, was born. This rift within Labour ranks was catastrophic, the inevitable result, according to Donald, of a party which had never fully spelt out what it stood for. He thought it bizarre that people were castigating Benn for advocating proper socialism, yet at the same time he found it difficult to be too antagonistic towards the leading defectors. Shirley Williams, daughter of his old friend Vera Brittain, he was particularly attached to, and the others he referred to as sincere, intelligent people, if wrong. His views were laid out on the pages of the *Methodist Recorder*, but his explanation drew a somewhat pained rebuttal from David Mason. He felt his old mentor was underestimating the damaging effect of these changes, especially withdrawal from Europe. He too joined the SDP, much to Donald's distress, although their friendship remained very much intact.

As Labour lurched from one crisis to another, Donald continued to believe that its predicament had nothing to do with its policies, and everything to do with its public image. He attributed its trouncing at the 1983 election, at a time when three million lay unemployed, to political ineptitude and in-built divisions. Consequently he saw no reason to join the rush to move the party back towards the centre, which began once Neil Kinnock replaced Foot as leader in October 1983.

In 1981 Donald was active on other fronts. Following another approach from Harold Goodwin, on 31 August, he met him and confirmed that he was still prepared to be ordained into the Church of England, provided that the function for which he was being ordained was made perfectly clear. It was agreed that Goodwin would put out feelers to the new Bishop of London, Graham Leonard, to ascertain his views. Several weeks later, Goodwin wrote downcast to say that there was little point in him, Goodwin, putting Donald's generous offer to the Bishop. This was because Leonard, an Anglo-Catholic, would accept nothing less than re-ordination with all that this entailed in its acceptance of episcopacy as the essence of the Church. It was the end of Donald's own repeated hopes and expectations to finish his life in the Church of England, quite possibly as a bishop, although he never ceased trumpeting the cause of ecumenism right to the very end.

A happier event occurred that October when Donald received the World Methodist Peace Award, first established in 1978, and whose previous winners included President Sadat of Egypt, at a reception in London. Part of the citation read by Bishop William Canon, Chairman of the World Methodist Council, included the following words.

"Your role has been and still is that of the messenger described by Isaiah, the prophet, and our response to your message is now what it was to his in the long ago. 'How beautiful under the mountain are the feet of him that bringeth good tidings, that publisheth peace'."[4]

His award, ironically, was to come at a time when the chill winds of the Cold War seemed to be depositing their icy blasts the world over, as the Carter and Reagan administrations in the United States set out to undermine the

Soviet military superiority of the 1970s. Their decision to build Cruise missiles sparked off a revival of the anti-nuclear movement all over Europe, not least in Britain, where many of the missiles were to be stationed, and where the Thatcher Government was all set to buy Trident submarines, an independent nuclear deterrent costing £5 billion. In October 1980 60,000 demonstrators in Britain took to the streets. Thereafter, from December 1982, protests concentrated upon the US Air Force bases at Greenham Common in Berkshire and Molesworth, near Cambridge, where the Cruise missiles were to be installed, and at Faslane on the Clyde, home to the nuclear-powered submarines.

As the mood darkened once again, Donald returned to the front line to proclaim his witness to pacifism, opposing Trident and taking part in the final day of the year-long World Disarmament Campaign peace vigil in June 1982. For the previous few weeks he had vehemently opposed the Falklands War, when the Thatcher Government used military force to reclaim British sovereign territory in the South Atlantic, invaded by the Argentine junta weeks earlier. Rather than threaten lasting peace and bad relations with the Argentine people, he thought a £1 million compensation for each islander in the Falklands to settle elsewhere would have been a more sensible way to end the dispute. Now, with CND back in business, Donald played his part both in the House of Lords and on the streets, as well as speaking at rallies. Their leader, Bruce Kent, thought of him as a great intellectual icon and good friend, but accepted that his type of absolute pacifism could only be achieved by a new social order. Donald, for his part, found the mood much more apocalyptic and unilateralist compared to two decades earlier, in that they were fast waking up to the fact that Britain couldn't remain part of an alliance whose main policy was the nuclear deterrent. He felt that mutual deterrence – the idea of massive nuclear arsenals deterring East and West from attacking each other – increasingly invalid as massive rearmament and mutual suspicion became even greater. These fears were given voice at the special Queen and Country debate staged by the Oxford Union on 9 February 1983 to commemorate its famous predecessor fifty years earlier, when pacifism was all the rage. A regular performer at the Union over the years, Donald partnered the socialist polemicist Tariq Ali and the Greenham Common activist Helen John against the Lords Home and Beloff and the Conservative MP Douglas Hogg. His gloomy prognostications about the effects of increased armaments were to no avail as in a debate covered by ITN, the motion "That this House will in no circumstances fight for Queen and Country" was substantially defeated.

Donald's view incidentally towards the Greenham Common women, many of whom set up semi-permanent homes in makeshift tents around the perimeter fences, was decidedly mixed. He admired them for their spirit of valour and personal sacrifice, but felt unable to support their more robust antics of pulling down fences on the perimeter of the base and blocking access to its entrance, not least for the bad publicity this generated. Again, he found himself invoking Gandhi and his outright policy of passive resistance which thwarted any attempt, except by downright lies, to sully his campaign for justice through personal suffering. "So, almost with reluctance," he wrote in *Calling for Action*, "I find the various activities and the mixed reception accorded to the brave women of Greenham Common, a further confirmation that nothing short of pacifism which opposes violence with a total repudiation in so far as any individual in this war-soaked human climate is a free agent, will finally work."[5] These were views he continued to adhere to with great conviction, but with the thawing of relations with the Soviet Union in the Gorbachev era, the unilateral seeds of most of his compatriots withered as quickly as they had sprung up in the first place.

In January 1983 Donald celebrated his eightieth birthday with style as the media interest in his life and work was extensive. He admitted to feeling increasingly clumsy when it came to dropping things and that his Sunday exertions exhausted him more than hitherto, but otherwise didn't feel his age. After preaching to 500 at Hinde Street the day before, and braving the elements in Hyde Park where the Salvation Army played "Happy Birthday", the actual day was marked by a celebratory tea at the West London Mission's Seymour Place Day Centre. Friends, family and politicians mingled with the homeless to enjoy a birthday tea of *petit fours* and Donald's favourite jellies. Before giving a tune on his new tin whistle, presented to him by the Day Centre, he told the assembled company that they all looked well enough to come back to his ninetieth birthday celebrations. That evening he was the special guest at the annual dinner of the Methodist members of Parliament, hosted by the Speaker of the House of Commons, George Thomas, in the banqueting room of Speaker's Palace. In his address, the Speaker, himself a prominent Methodist, spoke of the debt that all present owed him.

He was less charitable the next year when Donald, according to form, spoke out against the impending mission of Billy Graham and his fellow evangelist Luis Palau. In a front page article in the *Methodist Recorder* on 1 March, entitled "Why I'm bothered about these campaigns", Donald ploughed over familiar terrain in expressing his opposition. "To frighten men into the acceptance of the Gospel by the fear of Hell is now properly regarded as a totally unworthy 'means' of grace, and to comfort them into acceptance of the Gospel by offering an infallible substitute for doubt is just as insufferable as an evangelical agent."[6] In reply, Thomas, now Viscount Tonypandy, as the Honourable Chairman of Mission England, was uncompromisingly trenchant.

"Lord Soper's idiosyncracies sometimes get me down. He seems to have an obsessive dislike of everything represented by Dr Billy Graham who is probably the greatest evangelist of our generation. [a stinging rebuke to Donald] Lord Soper's objection to the Christian mission makes strange reading in a generation when worship is so sadly neglected."[7]

Tonypandy felt Billy Graham was God's link with people who the Church had failed to reach and hoped that the Methodist family could unite around the success of Mission England. Donald once again unleashed passions on this most emotive of issues. Letters poured in with opinion roughly divided, but for all his serious reservations, Mission England's three-month, six-city tour, despite having less impact than the great campaigns of the 1950s, was deemed a success by the tour organisers.

Later that year Donald participated in the deliberations into the Warnock Report on human fertilisation and embryology, which provoked fierce opposition from many Christian and pro-life groups. The committee under Baroness Warnock, a distinguished Oxford moral philosopher, had concluded that certain special forms of infertility treatment, including artificial insemination by donor and *in vitro* fertilisation, were ethically acceptable subject to regulation by an independent authority, but recommended that surrogate motherhood organised by commercial agencies should be banned.

In the Lords, Donald broadly accepted the findings of the Warnock Committee. He found no ethical problem with AIH (artificial insemination) as a means of assisting people medically to bear children. On the question of AID, he could support it to help bring joy to people who otherwise couldn't have children and to preserve the principle of the family. As regards surrogacy, he had the greatest of difficulties: "If there is the slightest taint of commercialism about it, I want nothing to do with it."[8] In conclusion he endorsed the document on the premise that if scientific discovery could be married to compassion within the general parameter of the family, then it could be reconciled with the Christian faith.

Legislation to ban commercial surrogacy agencies was passed in 1985 and when in 1990 the Human Fertilisation and Embryology Act implemented the main recommendations of the Warnock Committee, Donald was again supportive. Of the view that it was impossible to find a moral judgement which was perfect and immaculate, he felt it better to conduct research even where the effectiveness of that research might be flawed. The Bill comfortably passed on a free vote in both Houses and authorised centres to provide certain infertility treatments, as well as undertaking human embryo research.

In May 1982, days after he had preached at Kingsway for the final time, Donald set off for San Diego in California to debate with the Creationists and their emphasis on Bible-based doctrines of creation, which he felt to be flawed. The visit was both enjoyable and successful as he gave as good as he got in the kind of free exchange of views he rarely expressed in America. Then in 1985 Donald was invited to go to New Zealand to be reunited with one of his former Kingsway protégés, David Lange, recently elected Prime Minister, after an absence of seventeen years. It was an appropriate time to visit, since Lange, who derived great inspiration from Donald's visit, was facing his toughest test yet. As his country was a signatory of the ANZUS defensive treaty with the United States and Australia, he was under pressure from the Americans to disown his electoral pledge of banning nuclear warships from visiting New Zealand. Donald, as was his wont, stuck to his well-rehearsed line that one couldn't baptise some arms, but Lange, while accepting his mentor's position in theory, felt that he couldn't implement it in practice. Apart from the electoral consequences, he accepted the need for some form of national security. He refused, however, to cave in to the Americans over ANZUS, giving Donald some grounds for comfort on what turned out to be his last overseas trip.

The year 1986 in a sense was the end of an era as Donald and Marie left their home in Willifield Way after thirty-seven years for something smaller in neighbouring Bigwood Road. It was also the year when Donald, much to his embarrassment, became engulfed in a controversy not of his own making, by virtue of his presidency of the League Against Cruel Sports. His opposition to bloodsports which developed over the years, stemmed from his fervent pacifism. To him, shooting, stalking and hare-coursing weren't only cruel and barbaric towards animals. By demonstrating an enjoyment of violence, they revealed a degradation of human behaviour and an unhealthy attitude of mind. In 1947 he was so repelled by the smell at an Australian slaughterhouse at which he was preaching, and the chilling sight of the animals awaiting their fate, that he vowed to become a vegetarian, a pledge he kept till 1963 when, on doctors' advice, he began eating some white meat to increase his protein levels. As more literature came to light exposing the cruelty animals were subjected to, Donald became more uncompromising in their defence. He opposed the staging of the Grand National, Britain's premier steeplechase, because of the grievous – sometimes mortal – injuries sustained by some of the horses due to the challenging nature of the jumps. Then at Christmas 1955, he incurred unpopularity with his children by denying them their annual trip to the circus because of his contention that performing animals were made to suffer unnecessary pain. He even began to wear plastic shoes, after being criticised at Tower Hill for wearing leather ones, at variance with his vegetarianism.

In 1967, after many years of protest against bloodsports, Donald succeeded the socialist Lord Listowel as President of the League Against Cruel Sports, a pressure group dating back to 1925. At the Annual General Meeting, in a speech which elicited thunderous applause, he called the cult of cruelty the outstanding evil of modern life. The sad fact was that the law enabled people to indulge in this kind of incipient cruelty as far as animals were concerned. Many who learnt this cruelty in the animal world went on to exploit it in the human one. On Boxing Day that year, Donald spoke at a rally against hare-coursing. In 1968 he supported the Conservation of Seals Bill, in 1972 he argued unavailingly for a ban on hare-coursing and in 1980 he publicly denounced members of the Royal Family for their active participation in fox-hunting.

For all his years as President, Donald never missed a meeting. He made inspirational addresses each year and was adept at handling these meetings, especially the stormy ones of the mid-1970s, forcing him to conclude that the activists appeared to love animals more than they did each other. He also liaised with Lord Houghton in the Lords to further the League's interests and readily allowed his name to be used in various campaigns which helped give them credibility.

This credibility was stretched to breaking point in October 1986, when a prominent member of the League attacked the Duke of Edinburgh in the League's winter edition of *Wildlife Guardian* for involving himself with the bloodsports lobby and for slaughtering wildlife. The strongly worded article and the ensuing uproar caused Donald much embarrassment and he seriously contemplated resignation as President. Eventually, after much discussion with the League, he relented, but felt honour bound to write to the Duke to apologise for the article and explain that he had not been consulted about it, apologies which the Duke graciously accepted.

In 1984 Donald's autobiography *Calling for Action* appeared. Based on the methods of Marcel Proust in *A la Recherche du Temps Perdu*, he related some of the defining moments of his life to the development of his core convictions, from which he reached certain conclusions. Above all, that the Christian call was a call for action and that obedience to that call yielded the increasing certainty of its eternal truth and power. Intellectually, it was a powerful read, but it shed little further light into his personality and his relationship with others. Such reticence was very much in character and although the relaxed bonhomie of accomplished interviewers such as Cliff Michelmore and Colin Morris managed to coax more out of him when reminiscing about his career, it was more or less the same story on radio. Programmes such as *Lord Soper at 80*, *Home on Sunday* and *Soper's Corner*, revealed a man of great charm and stature who had undoubtedly left his mark on history. But this was history as discerned through his eyes. Hence the familiar stories and emphasis on the great causes of his life with a more than passing regret about their diminishing importance. Again, what these programmes rarely addressed was the paradox of how such a gentle, humble man in private transformed into something more fractious and intransigent in public, so that even within Methodism and the Labour Party he wasn't a unifying figure. The exception to this rule rather inadvertently was Harry Morton's brutal dissection of his character, most notably his incorrigible egotism, on the *Friendship* programme already referred to. The fact that Morton's youthful adulation of Donald, which extended to dressing and speaking like him, had clearly waned, exposed the difficulty Donald had in maintaining a close relationship, especially when his leadership was under scrutiny. It is perhaps no coincidence that the clerics he reserved the most respect for, such as Eric Baker, J. E. Rattenbury, Leslie Weatherhead, Dick Sheppard, William Temple, George MacLeod, Michael Ramsey and Cardinal Basil Hume, the Roman Catholic Archbishop of Westminster at the time of his death, were all, Baker, Rattenbury and Weatherhead aside, members of other denominations.

In 1988 Donald was greatly chuffed to be made a Freeman of the Haberdashers' Company and of the City of London and to receive an honorary doctorate from Cambridge University, twenty-two years after he was made a Fellow of his old college, St Catharine's. The citation concluded: "His ministry is wider than any Church and engages with the temporal no less than the spiritual and does not shun the unpopular fight. As the true heir to John Wesley who carried his message into the streets and marketplaces and into every corner of the land so he, by his books, his journalism, his broadcasts and his travels, has become a living legend and has touched the hearts and minds and stirred the conscience of a whole nation."[9] The next year there was cause for more celebrations as Donald and Marie marked their Diamond Wedding with a telegram from the Queen and a party at the House of Lords. Light wines were served and 100 of their friends attended, including three Labour leaders, Harold Wilson, now a shadow of his former self, Jim Callaghan and Michael Foot.

As Donald aged, his friends noticed a mellowing in his character, so that while there was no diminution in his proselytising instincts, he did become more relaxed in company. Indeed, at times he positively sought it and could hold an audience spellbound as he gladly reminisced about aspects of his life and times. David Mullins, who first encountered Donald as a young probationer at Kingsway, has recollections of him visiting Hull in 1985 and being a very easy guest. Having spoken to 200 in his church, one of the audience at question time afterwards accused him of living in cloud-cuckoo-land. "I take it from your question," Donald replied to great mirth, "that you don't entirely agree with me. First let me deal with your biggest mistake." Although more inclined to seek reassurance for his performances than hitherto, the intellect, sparkle and wit showed no sign of diminishing, which helped explain why his presence as a guest speaker continued to fill any church or hall, many of whose attendees would be staunch Tories. Paul Hulme, Superintendent Minister of Wesley's Chapel 1988–96, recalled him as one of his favourite interviewees for his Thursday lunchtime conversations as he always had a fresh angle on any subject. Even the unexpected rarely fazed him, such as the two occasions during his final decade when trouble on the roads caused the very thing he loathed most, a late arrival. Martin Lawrence, Donald's nephew, has recollections of Marie and him getting lost when coming to preach at his church at Fleet in Hampshire as part of an Easter trilogy of sermons. When they eventually arrived, Lawrence, to his horror, discovered that, because of a misunderstanding, Donald was unaware that he was due to be speaking on love. "Don't worry," he replied, "that's right up my street," and for half an hour spoke with great fluency. Afterwards over dinner, he turned to Marie and remarked that one word of what he had uttered wasn't quite right.

The other occasion occurred several years later when Donald was guest speaker at Kingswood School's annual Founder's Day service in Bath Abbey to commemorate John Wesley, the founder of the school. Gary Best, the headmaster, recalled that as the dignitaries were assembling in his study, word reached him that Donald had been delayed on the M4 and was likely to miss the service. The onus was now on the headmaster to fill the breach at the eleventh hour, a prospect which didn't appeal. It was thus with great relief that soon after the service had started, Donald with stick in hand, limped purposefully down the aisle to deliver a masterly oration. To the end he remained committed to the cause of youth. William Smith recalled how at an anniversary service at North Shore Methodist Church in Blackpool in May 1993, two school brass bands were in attendance, situated below the choir. Their presence was a source of fascination for Donald as he leaned over the pulpit rail for most of the meeting, mesmerised by this show of youthful vitality and enthusiasm. Later, when he came to speak, he declared that he would direct his views to the young. In a powerful voice he spoke movingly of the challenges and opportunities that lay before them, as well as some of the hardships that he had seen at Cambridge when some of his contemporaries had had to give up university because of financial hardship. His challenge and appeal was heard almost in silence as the sincerity of his words struck home. Unexpectedly, once the rally was over, he insisted on meeting the congregation and stayed for at least half an hour surrounded by teenagers.

Donald's prowess continued unabated on radio or television, as he remained in great demand, especially since his proficiency for the kind of quick thinking demanded by instant commentary compared favourably to a younger generation of clerics. When taxed about the general decline of preaching, he recognised that the demands of the sound-bite era in the modern media spelt problems for the preacher keen to develop an argument as of yore. At the same time, he regretted the lack of confidence and enjoyment associated with his successors, not least their reluctance to engage in the open air. While many dismissed this form of evangelism as an anomaly in an age of mass communication, to him the lure of the great outdoors remained as intoxicating as ever. Jean Anderson remembered the occasion when Donald in old age visited her home town of Rainham in Kent to preach. When few people showed up at church, he opted for an outdoor meeting instead. "Clap your hands," he instructed her in a manner reminiscent of his baptism on Tower Hill, and in no time a healthy crowd had formed.

Despite relinquishing his *Tribune* column in 1980, he continued to write his monthly column for the *Methodist Recorder* now entitled "Personally Speaking", adopting a more contemplative tone in his dotage than hitherto. In an article coinciding with his eightieth birthday he looked back over his life and wondered whether it had conformed to one overall meaning amidst its multifarious parts. Drawing on his reading of Hans Kung's *Does God Exist?*, he answered in the affirmative in the sense that without a divine purpose behind creation his life, good or bad, would be meaningless.

Turning more specifically to his own experiences, not least his first visit to Tower Hill and his decision to stand on the wall, he couldn't help feeling in retrospect that it had been divinely ordained.

> This reflection prompts me to see my ministry as a whole in terms of guidance. I write this with a sense of real unworthiness but I am sure that I took 'holy orders' because I was already under orders. To believe that I have been called by the God who is the ground of all being, is the skein which runs through my eighty years. It by no means answers all the problems of free will and determinism, but it in no way destroys the reality of personal responsibility.
>
> This genuineness of personal freedom is the other thread in the skein of recollection, because the choice is a moral one. I have lived my life in a moral universe, of that I am convinced, despite the many difficulties that such a venture of faith presents. Morality, like meaning itself, depends on God for he is also the source of goodness.
>
> Looking back over the pastoral, political and ethical complex that has gone to make up my ministry, I can honestly aver that in Jesus Christ is the manifestation

of God's good nature. This demands my allegiance, and sets my life in terms like fatherhood, and sonship, and God's kingdom of heaven.[10]

In June 1990 the House of Lords locked horns with the Commons in a lengthy skirmish over the Thatcher Government's Nazi War Crimes Bill, facilitating Crown prosecutions of Nazi war criminals. The Bill had passed the Commons, but the Lords, concerned about the fairness and appropriateness of the measure, chose to reject it. In a crowded chamber, Donald was one of many peers who expressed opposition primarily from a Christian perspective. Having placed these crimes of total depravity in the context of war which in itself was criminal, he questioned whether perfect justice could be attained in this wicked world. This made him hostile to the Bill because it was impossible to conceive of the Christian answer to evil without recognising that in a world governed by a heavenly Father, only he could act as the dispenser of final and absolute justice. "Therefore, those who are indignant that we should allow bygones to be bygones with regard to past enormities by Nazis and others should reflect that it is not a question of letting bygones be bygones but rather a question of letting God be God. That is a faith which I would almost hesitate to intrude upon this argument unless I profoundly believed it." He went on to link justice with compassion and forgiveness, although he stressed that this forgiveness wasn't unconditional. "Forgiveness is the offering of the hand of re-creation but it is not forgiveness until the response has been made by those who look to that hand as a way of redemption." Penitence had to accompany this compassion.

He concluded: "I must admit that if I am not guilty of total depravity, I am part of the realm of original sin. In that realm, a humble attitude of compassion is probably the way to open far more doors than the attempt to discover an absolute standard of justice, which evades us. To plod on in the hope of compassion working the miracles which justice cannot fully attain is part of the obligation and opportunity of this debate."[11] The Lords were persuaded by such arguments to hold out against the Commons, but the Government was nothing if not determined, and won through in the end by resorting to the Parliament Act of 1949, which gave the Commons the power automatically to ride roughshod over a House of Lords veto, once a full year had elapsed.

No sooner had this internal drama been played out than attention turned to events in the Middle East where the oil-rich state of Kuwait was invaded by its much larger neighbour, Iraq. As the West prepared to come to the aid of Kuwait, Donald led a delegation from FOR to Downing Street in August to hand in a statement, urging a non-military solution to the Gulf. Readily conceding that the Iraqi leader, Saddam Hussain, should be punished, he was all for economic sanctions, but when these failed to dislodge him from Kuwait and war broke out in January 1991, he resolutely opposed it. The fact that Kuwait was liberated with minimal Allied casualties made little difference to his thinking, since the overall destruction to the Iraqi forces simply revealed the new, more terrifying power of modern weaponry.

Staying on a similar theme, Donald voiced opposition the next year to the Queen Mother, whom he privately rather admired, unveiling a new statue to Air Marshal Sir Arthur Harris in the Strand, since Harris had masterminded the punitive bombing of German cities in the Second World War. The resultant fatalities had outraged Vera Brittain at the time, and in December 1993 Donald gave a commemorative address to mark the centenary of her birth at a packed service at St Martin-in-the-Fields. He was the only one of the original Sponsors of the PPU still alive. He also denounced the escalating civil war in Yugoslavia, as that multi-ethnic state imploded, and criticised the Chief Rabbi for advocating armed intervention in Bosnia. Even at his advanced age he remained as committed as ever to his basic premise that wars weren't only morally wrong, they rarely brought practical solutions. In the year in which he celebrated his ninetieth birthday, he had the satisfaction, as President of CSM, of giving a vote of thanks to the new leader of the Labour Party, John Smith, after he had given the annual Tawney Lecture. (Donald himself had delivered it in 1980.) Claiming that he had heard once again the clarity and precision of Tawney and Temple, those two champions of the faith, he saluted Smith as the true voice of Christian socialism for that era. His confident prediction, however, that in time he would prove to be an excellent Prime Minister could never be affirmed, as within little more than a year Smith was dead, victim of a fatal heart attack.

In 1987 Donald celebrated sixty years on Tower Hill and, in 1992, fifty years in Hyde Park. An inner compulsion throughout this time had driven him to both venues each week in all kinds of weather, and at times in poor health when wiser counsels pleaded with him to stay at home. His resolution could be partially explained by the pleasure he continued to derive from the ritual, and partly by his conviction that the open air was the true location for a real conversion. "Here I stand [quoting the great Luther] I can do no other," he used to say, and when taxed about the decline of Christianity, the dwindling crowds and the onset of greed, he would respond that obedience, not results, was his priority. "I sow the seed, the harvest isn't my responsibility, though I may be able to deal with the weeds." Certainly his audiences had declined drastically from his heyday, particularly the ones at Tower Hill where the docks had long since closed. By the 1990s, they rarely numbered more than a couple of dozen compared to Hyde Park, which still managed in excess of 100, including the tourists who sought out Donald as part of their London experience.

The subjects for discussion had changed too, with ideology, especially communism, largely overtaken by an unhealthy preoccupation with tabloid morality. If somebody asked a question in Hyde Park on sex, Donald used to quip, you doubled the size of the crowd and halved the quality of the argument. But beyond that there was something more sinister, as the good-humoured, intelligent hecklers of old had increasingly given way to an intolerant assortment of morons and fundamentalists whose blend of churlish interruptions and crude profanities made an unedifying spectacle. Sadly, with the smaller crowds now in evidence, the easier it was for these types to prevail, especially since Donald's voice had lost its power of old. He continued to respond to them with his old-fashioned tolerance and humour, shot through with occasional flashes of exasperation, betraying a sensitivity altogether clearer in private. For the cynics had drawn blood. Not only did their personal invective hurt, it annoyed him that the abuse turned away potential listeners, a reflection, he thought, of the growing violence and irresponsibility in society.

A number of these issues were the subject of some debate, as Donald's ninetieth birthday was the occasion for copious features on his life and work. Justin Cartwright in the *Daily Mail* called him "the human photograph of a more idealistic age ... a national treasure", having seen him ply his trade in atrocious weather. "There is in Soper's life," he wrote, "so much of an England which is lost or half-forgotten: Joseph Rank's Methodist Central Halls, outdoor meetings, pacifism, ethical socialism, passionate discussion of issues, working men's missions, and a belief in the perfectibility of man in society."[12]

On the day, Hinde Street was overflowing at both the 10 o'clock and 11 o'clock services, as friends and family joined the regular congregation in worship. On Donald's entry for the main service, they rose to applaud before sitting back to listen to him pronounce upon the Pauline virtues of faith, hope and love. His words found favour with Tony Benn, who called it a marvellous address. "It was wise and his voice was clear and strong. He really is one of the great speakers of our time ... . That man has kept alive a tradition of the improvement of mankind over so many years. It's really an inspiration; he offers much more to the public than any archbishop or cardinal in Britain, or any political leader."[13] At the buffet lunch which followed, children from the Sunday School gave him red roses, MPF a beautiful copy of the *Companion to Hymns and Psalms* and Michael Foot a copy of a booklet, written by his father Sir Isaac Foot, on the comparison between Oliver Cromwell and Abraham

Lincoln. In one of several tributes, Foot, who claimed to have known Donald longer than anyone else, referred to him as the supreme preacher.

Then it was on to Hyde Park, accompanied by a media scrum, for the traditional Sunday afternoon meeting. As he clambered painfully onto his shaky platform, an extra large crowd of 500 sang two choruses of "Happy Birthday". Later he was clearly embarrassed when a cluster of brightly coloured metallic balloons, emblazoned with anniversary messages, was thrust into his hand. In the interim, it was business as usual as he dealt with many themes from the evils of capitalism to the centrality of the life and teachings of Jesus. The hecklers played their part, and not always with grace or decorum. One who spoke ill of the Church was told to "just go away, you silly old man". Others were seen off with little sweat.

"What is your greatest achievement?" one questioner asked. "Putting up with people like you," he countered to loud guffaws. Only once was he worsted when a pugnacious character in a leather-jacket asked him about reincarnation. "Well, the last thing I would want is to be reincarnated in an environment where I should encounter you all the time," Donald replied wearily. Reincarnation he explained was so much stuff and nonsense. "Come off it, Donald," the man shot back, "You said that in your last life."

Having given a virtuoso performance, Donald was back at Hinde Street for a live BBC *Songs of Praise* in his honour – an honour tinged with irony given his enforced exile from the national airwaves during the war. In the programme, another capacity congregation sang seven of his favourite hymns, most of which were the great theological statements of Charles Wesley and Isaac Watts interspersed with recorded tributes about his life and work. As his wife and daughters recalled the devoted family man so very different from the fiery prophetic figure on his soapbox, fellow clerics commended him for his deep spirituality. Robert Runcie, the former Archbishop of Canterbury, talked about his confidence born out of a hidden life in prayer, while Cardinal Basil Hume called him a great servant of the Gospel. The tributes in words and music were splendiferous as they were heartfelt. A man rarely given to outward displays of emotion, the enormity of the occasion seemed to overwhelm him as, with faltering voice, Donald gave the blessing. Recovering the next day from all the celebrations, he admitted to having found the whole experience both humbling and exhilarating. He was greatly touched by the hundreds of cards, the presence of so many familiar faces and the profusion of memories which marked every stage of his ministry. An agreeable letter from Pam Rhodes, the presenter of *Songs of Praise*, expressing her pleasure at the way the evening had gone, proved a welcome additional fillip. And there was one other birthday honour. Following an initiative from his secretary, Kath Humphreys, who obtained the necessary permission from all the appropriate authorities, a commemorative plaque was erected on Tower Hill in recognition of his accomplishments there. It read, "Donald Soper, Methodist minister spoke weekly on Tower Hill for over 65 years. Celebrated his 90th birthday January 31 1993".[14] Was this the moment, people wondered, when he would finally retire? Certainly it was the wish of his family that he should give up, especially Marie, who felt it all rather undignified as his physical powers began to wane.

Throughout most of his eighties, Donald, despite growing arthritis which slowed his mobility, was still able to lead a fairly normal life, not least the playing of an erratic round of golf with the help of a trolley. While Sunday remained the centre-piece of his week, he attended the House of Lords regularly, speaking on a number of important occasions, and participated in much pressure group activity, not least the peace movement. He also remained a media favourite, appearing on the BBC's *Wogan* an unprecedented three times in 1986–87, and a popular visiting preacher. To help him cope with transport to Tower Hill and more distant locations, he increasingly relied on Peter Terry, a Methodist lay preacher and London taxi driver, who on his retirement in 1986 was at his service to ferry him around. The relationship which began as one of mutual admiration, developed into one of close friendship, as Terry treasured the wisdom of his conversation while Donald found Terry his essential prop in his links with the wider world. As they discoursed, Terry discovered that Donald rarely harked back to the past, and certainly didn't talk about regrets, but kept his eyes firmly fixed on the future – a trait helped by his continued interest in current affairs. In Terry's estimation, he'd never met anyone with so much stamina, a quality he displayed to the full on his ninetieth birthday, when physically he still seemed in good fettle for a man of his age. Yet for all his redoubtable temperament, winter was drawing in fast as the ravages of old age were finally catching up with him. Aside from minor ailments such as a slight loss of memory, he suffered from carpal tunnel syndrome, a wasting away of the muscles in his fingers which prevented him from playing the piano, as well as making writing and distributing the bread at Communion a more taxing business. More serious, there was the sharply deteriorating arthritis, especially in his knees, so that clambering up the steps at Hinde Street became an increasing impediment, as did getting up to greet a lady entering a room.

And then there was Marie. Although a very athletic figure who had played golf to a high standard, she had been frail for some time with a succession of dislocated hips and a heart attack in 1987. Displaying great courage and determination, she rallied for a while, but during her final two years her decline became much more marked, leaving Donald nursing his own infirmities somewhat at a loss as to how to cope with her predicament. One answer was to have continual care in the house, especially overnight, a considerable drain on the resources of a family whose status was comfortable, rather than wealthy, middle-class. In September 1993 Marie developed Parkinson's Disease and then on 2 January 1994 she died of heart failure. The large chapel at Golders Green Crematorium was crowded for her funeral, taken at Donald's request by David Cruise, the Superintendent at Hinde Street. In her obituary in the *Methodist Recorder* Cruise wrote of her outstanding contribution as a wife and mother, and her great gift for getting along with people. Donald was stoical in his grief but, alone after sixty-five years, he felt his loss keenly, so much so that he moved to her favourite chair by the phone since he couldn't bear to look at it empty. Conversation became more laboured and while he was able to talk about Marie, his memories were tinged with regret. On Tower Hill he stated that his wish was to meet her again and apologise for his foolish behaviour when they were together. His loneliness was compounded by the death of many of his contemporaries, [his sister Millicent had died in 1991] and physical decline, which cut him off from the centre of events. Not only did his impaired hearing restrict his visits to the House of Lords, and his declining mobility to his office at Hinde Street, he found that the press, to his consternation, were less inclined to seek out his opinions.

Donald's increasingly passive state gave him much time for reflection. Although not weighed down by a series of personal disappointments, he saw before him a more godless, less caring world where responsibility was at a premium. He also feared for the future of institutional Christianity unless it showed greater flexibility to worship, and took its message out on to the streets in language that people could understand. In his desire to shut out present anxieties, he found that he was always on the look-out for happiness, so he retreated into the past for sublime memories such as family holidays when the sun always seemed to shine. As he pondered the meaning of pain, it not only enhanced his sympathy for his fellow sufferers, it gave him some comfort to witness the way Jesus endured similar tribulations in his passing. "I don't pretend to be very profound on this matter," Donald said in an interview with the *Methodist Recorder* in January 1998, "but Jesus showed us that the way of suffering itself can be a power, it can be an instrument, it can be a divine energy whereby that which resists all other kinds of authority and power can be overcome."[15]

Above all, as he neared the end of his journey Donald became more obsessed by death and what lay beyond that final frontier. Throughout his ministry he had never paid too much attention to the concept of heaven, other than to say that he didn't know much about it, and was always suspicious of those who claimed they did. In one sense, he admitted in an article in *Seasons of Life* in 1997, he couldn't believe in a worthwhile life after death as he could in a sunrise the following morning; in another he found it profoundly significant and he wanted to believe. Over the years the conviction had deepened that man was made for God and was restless till he rested in his eternity. He couldn't prove such an assumption, but he could reasonably hope for it. "As an old man, I am satisfied that this cultivation of hope is a healing process, and that it is found in the middle of faith and love, as St Paul says. There are impediments to faith. There are peaks of love which in all honesty we know we cannot climb, but there is no bar to hope. To say that I will hope in the face of apparent contradiction is an infinitely worthwhile determination. Arguments about death can stop us in our tracks, but nothing can prevent me from deciding that I will go on hoping. This is the supreme blessing. It can give the elderly like me the wages of going on 'when faith grows dim' and love seems hard to find."[16]

Such thoughts might form the basis of his conversation with old friends such as Kay Calton, Ann Bird and Mary Hicks, whose visits afforded him much pleasure. Peter Terry was on call whenever required and he was blessed by the kindness of his Filipino night-nurses, one of whom loved him enough to call him "darling". Above all he had the companionship of the supremely loyal Kath Humphreys, who had done his cooking and secretarial work since 1985, and after Marie's death had gone to live with him. When she was off duty, there was always at least one of the family to rally round to ensure that his needs weren't neglected. As declining eyesight and hearing diminished the pleasure he derived from reading or watching television, the family and their concerns continued to be paramount. In particular there were his nine grandchildren and eight great-grandchildren to whom he was always someone very special as he reminisced with humour or lent a sympathetic ear to those in trouble. And there still remained his holidays.

In 1994 and 1995 Kath escorted him to Cornwall to stay with Betty Tredinnick, an old friend of his from Kingsway. She was very kind, gladly reminiscing about the great days of Methodism, and driving him to all his old haunts. Kath recalled one occasion at Padstow harbour when he was sitting attired in baseball cap and sunglasses to disguise his identity. It was to no avail, since the old man sitting next to him said, "I know you. You're Donald Soper." When travelling to Cornwall by train became too difficult, his daughter Judith and son-in-law Alan took him by car the following two years. Only during his final summer when infirmity finally defeated him did he go without his holiday.

In June 1994 Donald, to great acclamation, put in his usual appearance in the open air when Conference took to the streets of Leeds. According to John Singleton in the *Methodist Recorder*, "... Lord Soper slowly mounted the stand looking every inch a prophet. Strands of silvery hair whipped across his face in the breeze and the sun glinted on the golden rim of his glasses. When he spoke, the years seemed to fall away and you couldn't really believe that he was ninety-two."[17] The difficulties came later. In the two minutes it took him to get down from the stand he said, to sympathetic laughter, "I wish to God the Church could do something about arthritis."

In February 1995 Donald attended a concert in Central Hall, Westminster, by Trinity College of Music and was presented with an Honorary Fellowship by the Duke of Kent. David Cruise recalled the contrast between the physically frail nonagenarian who literally had to be carried to the rostrum to speak, and the mentally alert performer who suddenly came to life as he discoursed as of old. The next month he was present at the opening of the Museum of Methodism at Wesley's Chapel, by the Duchess of Kent. Later he donated to it his speaker's stand which he used at Hyde Park. Come May, he spoke to a capacity VE Day commemoration rally in Central Hall, Westminster, against the glorification of war, and continued thereafter to appear intermittently on the public stage. One such event occurred in December when he chaired a stormy meeting of the League Against Cruel Sports in Union Street. Unable to paper over the cracks between moderates and extremists, he decided to resign, but was subsequently persuaded to resume his presidency. Apart from the genuine esteem in which they held him, the executive was conscious of the prestige his name brought their organisation and especially keen that he "front" their seventy-fifth anniversary in 1999.

As he found walking an increasing liability, Donald transferred from one stick to two and finally with the greatest of reluctance he accepted the need for a wheelchair. Locally, it had its advantages, as Kath would wheel him around Hampstead Garden Suburb and park him outside Waitrose, where he would pay court to all and sundry, since even in old age people wanted to meet him. Fulfilling public engagements, however, was a different matter.

Even the briefest of journeys by car could be a major logistical difficulty. He was fortunate to have his faithful army of helpers to keep him going. Every Sunday morning he would telephone Judith and Alan at 8.10 a.m. and say, "You haven't forgotten me have you?" When they arrived at his home to take him to Hinde Street, he would be sitting there expectant in his cassock. On Wednesday mornings, Peter Terry would get him to Tower Hill early so that he could prepare his thoughts in All Hallows Church nearby. The most tortured assignment was to transport him to Hyde Park on Sunday afternoon.

Donald would scream with pain as Kath and Eddie Anderson struggled to get him out of the taxi into his wheelchair. By the time the process had been repeated on the return journey, they arrived home exhausted. When he asked Kath whether he should give up, he was shocked to hear her say yes. Others said the same, but he couldn't turn his back on the habits of a lifetime. At least once he was in a wheelchair, most hecklers took pity on him and gave him an easier time than hitherto at Hyde Park, while at Tower Hill the meeting assumed the air of a university seminar.

On his ninety-third birthday on 31 January 1996, after the crowd had sung "Happy Birthday", Donald, looking back on his life there, still felt that Christianity had little to offer unless it was placed in the context of the real world. The greatness of Jesus Christ began where people were, not where he wanted them to be. He found that in the turbulence of a meeting in which doubts were discussed, it was possible to find peace of mind through the satisfaction of a problem.

As the questions flooded in, Donald warmed to his theme, fairly brimming with sparkle and wit. On being asked whether the Millennium Dome should be in London or Birmingham, he replied that if there were more people present from Birmingham, he would say Birmingham. To a more profound question about whether there was any purpose in growing old, he replied that one could use the opportunity to prepare for the world beyond death. That world was a fulfilment of God's purpose, since he was quite satisfied that it didn't occur before death.

That January Brian Frost's biography of him aptly called *Goodwill on Fire* was published. His notes for the book, along with a collection of Donald's writings, tapes and newspaper cuttings were to form the basis of the Donald Soper Archive at the John Rylands Library, the University of Manchester. In March, following the appalling massacre of sixteen children and their teacher at a primary school in the Scottish town of Dunblane, Donald criticised the Queen in a radio interview for an intolerable lack of feeling. The comments which upset him came at the opening of the Royal Armouries Museum in Leeds, when she remarked that the weapons of war could be as beautiful as they were terrible.

In June he was back in Bristol to preach and plant a tree at the rededication to mark the restoration of Hanham Mount, the open-air forum where John Wesley first preached in the open air in 1739. In miserable conditions, he was pushed by Leslie Griffiths in his wheelchair over the muddy field to the platform. Appropriately, the rain stopped as Donald, contrary to expectation, stood up to preach. John Newton recalled that in order to help him cope with the rain, South Gloucestershire Council had given him a golfing umbrella with the Castlemaine Four-X logo on it, thinking that he wouldn't notice, but ever alert, he did and referred to it. In September he opened the FOR headquarters at Clapton in Northamptonshire and the following month delivered the Gandhi Lecture in the Moses Room in the House of Lords. Days later, on an occasion suffused with nostalgia, he preached at the OCW Thanksgiving Service at Hinde Street to mark the official termination of the organisation, recalling the central tenets which had distinguished its proud history.

Another link with the past was commemorated in January 1997 when Donald, surrounded by his family, unveiled a plaque and portrait of his wife in Wandsworth to mark the opening of the Marie Soper Project for mothers who misused alcohol and for their children. The Project was set up by the West London Mission in partnership with the National Children's Home, although much of its finance was dependent on local authority resources. Here lay the sting. The cash-strapped councils had so many other demands placed upon them that the residential costs proved beyond them, and with the Mission unable to finance it itself, the Project had to close. It said much for Donald's equanimity that he bore this embarrassing setback with understanding fortitude. He continued to give his support to a number of well-deserving causes, speaking at an asylum seekers' demonstration in Hyde Park in March, and at a Christian Aid meeting there in April. In June he attended his last Methodist Conference in London and spoke with John Vincent at the Conference open-air meeting on Tower Hill. On holiday in Cornwall, he attended a CSM meeting at St Agnes and when preaching at Crantock Church near Newquay, he very aptly presented a fifty-year service local preacher's certificate to Betty Tredinnick. For it was Donald who had seen her on her way with warm words of encouragement when she first spoke on a public platform back in 1945 during the Salisbury campaign.

In September Donald recorded for Radio 4's *With Great Pleasure* a number of his favourite books and poems. In reflective mood, he chose *Three Men in a Boat, 1066 and All That* and stressed the vital importance of Charles Wesley's hymns. In his quest to understand the meaning of life, he had leaned very heavily on Blaise Pascal's the *Pensées* with his curiosity to discover whether scientific knowledge was compatible with religious belief. Pascal's conclusion that rigorous loyalty to the former didn't destroy the latter because the heart had its reasons that reason couldn't reach, provided him with great comfort. He also drew comfort from Marcel Proust's contention that things past generated the confidence in things yet to be and found in Dostoevsky's *The Idiot* the stark truth of the possible return of Jesus Christ.

As he approached his ninety-fifth birthday, Donald was inundated with requests for interviews. In one for Radio 2's *Good Morning Sunday* he confessed to being troubled by old age, with aspects of it pretty grim. He was grateful for small mercies such as the recent occasion at Tower Hill when a businessman who had been in his audience over thirty years previously was astonished, on a brief journey back from New Zealand, to find him still there. The fact that he was full of compliments for the positive effect that Donald had had upon his life gave him an added incentive to keep going with his work and mission. In what was a broad restatement of his core beliefs, Donald reiterated the need for Methodism to go on adapting to the needs of the time as Christianity battled to stay afloat in a society seduced by alternative attractions. He wanted its end as a Church and its beginnings as one of the great societies of Christian behaviour similar to the Jesuits or the Dominicans. He ended with a blast against outdated Christian doctrines on sex, which didn't marry with the lifestyles of the overwhelming majority of young people in the contemporary world. Thus while he remained committed to fidelity in marriage, he felt that this could only be achieved through an enlarged Christian concept of love.

In a special birthday tribute in the House of Lords, Lord Longford spoke of Donald as a hero. Having known him for many years, he had come to recognise him as unique, so that when he made his final crossing it would be the end of an era. No one could possibly follow him.

On the Sunday after his birthday, friends and family gathered at Hinde Street as they had done five years earlier for his ninetieth celebrations. Having conducted the 10 a.m. Communion in a voice as powerful as ever, Donald preached at the 11 a.m. service on a well-rehearsed theme: how the kingdom of God was the prime concern of the Christian Church and how Jesus in his life and death represented the essential programme of that kingdom. These thoughts were amplified in a long interview he gave to Avril Bottoms in the *Methodist Recorder* which touched on a host of matters past, present and future. First, he turned to politics. Despite four successive election defeats for the Labour Party, Donald had remained resolutely opposed to any moves to embrace the capitalist system, since such a system to him continued to possess few redeeming features. Consequently he harboured considerable doubts over "New Labour", the creation of its new, young leader Tony Blair, especially the abandonment in 1995 of Clause IV. In the immediate aftermath of Labour's great triumph at the 1997 election, Donald sensed an unparalleled opportunity for the new Government to make a real difference, but his hopes soon turned to disillusionment. In his estimation, its fundamental error, aside from its obsession with news-management, lay in its reluctance to increase taxation significantly to help redress the grosser inequalities of the Tory years. Warming to his theme, he felt that the current culture of selfishness was society's failure to cultivate penitence, symbolised by the abandonment of the traditional Sunday. He found that in his dotage there had come a more powerful sense of penitence, since with age he could no longer rectify all his deficiencies. "I'm much more likely to be penitent now when I remember what a fool I was as a young man and how easily I took that foolishness as a part of my dignity."[18] He also berated himself for his lack of humility, which had never come easily to him, and hoped that in the long run people would judge him kindly since his ultimate desire was always to serve God. He concluded with some further thoughts about heaven which was on the horizon and whose mysteries continued to transfix him, not least what people would talk about and how they would recognise each other. Ultimately as he continued to peer through the glass darkly, he placed his faith in the hope that if he loved God here on earth on Good Friday, he would be able to rise with him on Easter Sunday.

Ten days after his birthday, Donald spoke at a memorial meeting at the House of Lords for Lady Llewellyn-Davies, the former Labour Chief Whip. On Sunday 1 March he returned to the fray on the day the Countryside Alliance came to town in a massive display of force against a proposed parliamentary ban on fox-hunting. When the marchers descended on Speakers' Corner, Donald, seated in his wheelchair in the bitter cold, his frail body covered from the neck downwards by a tartan rug and black hat, chided them for their lack of compassion towards animals. After his session in Hyde Park had finished, he and Kath Humphreys had to endure the freezing conditions for an hour as they waited for a taxi back into Central London.

On 10 April Donald participated in the Three Hour Good Friday Service at Hinde Street, speaking on three of the "Seven Words from the Cross". In June he attended a reception of Labour peers at 10 Downing Street with his daughter Judith, managing a brief word with Tony Blair. The occasion didn't in any way compromise him for on 23 August he condemned the Government's support of American bombing in Sudan and Afghanistan, both countries which allegedly had links with the Saudi millionaire, Osama bin Laden. Whether a brief return to the spotlight helped galvanise his spirits is a matter of pure conjecture, but certainly he was in ebullient form when, days later, he, Judith and Alan were guests of Martin and Patricia Lawrence. The following morning he rang Martin to say that nothing had given him greater pleasure since Marie died. On 10 October he, along with Lord Murray of Epping Forest, the former Secretary of the TUC and himself a Methodist local preacher, supported Baroness Richardson, a former deaconess at the

West London Mission, on her introduction to the House of Lords. In the same week he welcomed debate on reform of the Upper House and supported the Government's avowed intention to abolish the hereditary peerage, but cautioned against embarking on a reformist road without being clear of the final destination. Six days later, on 25 November, he attended the House of Lords for the last time, although he didn't speak. The following Sunday he took Holy Communion as usual at Hinde Street. When reading the lesson, he became distracted by the entry of Colin Morris, the preacher for the 11 a.m. service, and losing his train of thought, he began to read the wrong Gospel before Kath Humphreys put him right. It was only the second time that this had ever happened.

On Wednesday 2 December, dressed in a hat and scarf with a rug over his legs to protect him from the perishing cold, Donald braved Tower Hill for the last time, nearly seventy-two years after his first appearance. On seeing one of his faithful followers, Ted Edwards, he expressed his thanks to him and his wife for all the support they had given him over the years. His exposure to the elements proved too much. Donald caught a chill which he was unable to shake off and during the early hours of 4 December began coughing. The nurse felt Donald was confused and rang the doctor. The doctor, finding he had pains in his chest, in turn called an ambulance and when it arrived, the medical team started doing tests. As well as diagnosing a chest infection, they found the oxygen in his blood to be very low and not penetrating the brain. The Royal Free Hospital, Hampstead, declared that he was anaemic and kept him in to carry out further tests. Their decision upset Donald. Under great duress, he lost his appetite and began to be sick, something he'd never suffered from previously. While he was there, he received a steady stream of well-wishers, including Martin Lawrence, who, on thanking him for everything, received a grasp of the hand, a wink and a reassuring "you'll be all right". When David Cruise visited, he took him by the hand and said, "Well, David, I'm a bit of a coward." Finally, on his penultimate day, Peter Terry took the unusual step of kissing him on his forehead and told him to do as he was told. Deep down he felt that he wouldn't see him again.

The next day, Wednesday 22 December, Donald after clamouring to go home was, much to his relief, granted his wish. An ambulance was at the ready for the short journey. On arrival the ambulancemen took him inside and there in the presence of his family, they placed him in his favourite chair. As Kath Humphreys bent down to adjust his oxygen mask, she noticed that he wasn't breathing. The ambulanceman felt his pulse and realised that he had passed peacefully away. One of the century's great Christian leaders was no more. While the ambulancemen lifted him on to the bed which had been prepared downstairs Kath phoned David Cruise. He came round and said a prayer for him as she and the family gathered around in silent homage.

Despite it coinciding with a serious ministerial scandal and the resignation of Peter Mandelson, a leading confidant of the Prime Minister, the death of Donald Soper was a major story in its own right as tributes flowed in from all quarters. George Carey, the Archbishop of Canterbury, praised his immense contribution to British Christianity. "As a teacher, prophet, evangelist and social reformer Donald stood firmly in the Methodist tradition but his gifts have enriched us all." To Tony Blair, the Prime Minister: "Lord Soper was a fine Christian and a man of great integrity and principle. He always spoke with passion and conviction and won the respect of many, many people, even those who did not always agree with what he had to say". To his friend Tony Benn, he was "an outstanding figure – a Christian, a genuine prophet, a socialist, a pacifist, scholar, preacher, activist. What a man. He will leave an indelible mark on his period in history".

In easily the best of the obituaries, Colin Morris in the *Independent* wrote, "Arguably the most influential Methodist leader of the twentieth century, his unique ministry touched the life of church and nation at many points, and he discharged his ordination vows not just with utter faithfulness, but with that indefinable quality, style. His was a gallant debonair faith, yet under all the layers of sophistication he was at heart a simple believer. Jesus was his master and friend right up to the end."[19]

On Thursday 30 December Donald's funeral, complete with all his favourite hymns, was held at Hinde Street. (He was later cremated at Golders Green.) The sight of a number of his Hyde Park regulars in the congregation, and one of the hecklers in the front row, added a poignant touch, as did the laying of some flowers in his memory in the Park by an unknown well-wisher. In his tribute, Dr Kenneth Greet talked about one "whose life and ministry have been like a star in my firmament, bright as the one which led the magi to the manger bed". On 31 January at Wesley's Chapel, at the first of two Services of Thanksgiving (this one being a family occasion), Leslie Griffiths in a thought-provoking sermon declared that the challenge to be vulnerable and take risks was Donald Soper's legacy. Finding the lonely and lost and telling them that they were loved was his achievement. A month later, on 3 March, all the diverse causes and interests which Donald supported crowded Westminster Abbey, alongside the might of the religious and political establishment, rather more Old than New Labour, for the official Service of Thanksgiving. His granddaughter, Catherine Jenkins, and Shirley Williams read the lessons, Tony Benn read one of his articles from *Tribune* and Colin Welland recited some of Donald's most well-known aphorisms. In his Tribute, the Revd

Professor Peter Stephens, President of Conference, declared that as a sign-post not a weathervane he inspired many. In his Sermon, Colin Morris referred to his commitment to truth, justice, attractiveness and excellence. "What G.K. Chesterton did for the Christian faith in print and C.S. Lewis on the radio, Donald Soper achieved in face to face encounter. He was one of the great apologists of our day." Morris went on to speak for the many who considered themselves disciples of this venerable man. "In a sense, Donald acted as a bench-mark for the rest of us. So long as he was there, there was no danger of our getting above ourselves. Plato based his whole argument for immortality on the conviction that a world without his teacher and friend Socrates was unthinkable. That's how many of us felt about Donald, and now he is gone."[20]

After the rousing sounds of Charles Wesley's "Love Divine" to Blaenwern, the congregation spilled out into the early spring sunshine, as the bells of Westminster rang out across Parliament Square in celebration of a life well lived. Although not a man to stand on undue ceremony, the sight of Methodists and Anglicans coming together in the stronghold of Anglicanism to pay him their final respects would have touched this great apologist for Church unity. A few months later on 14 October, in Wesley's Chapel, Tony Benn, in front of Donald's family, unveiled a beautiful bust of his old friend by the sculptor Ian Walters.[21] It was an appropriate choice, since for well over forty years they had been crusading comrades in arms, their friendship cemented by the wood of platform. All this was now for the memory. For the present the thought persisted that with the twentieth century drawing rapidly to a close, you had the poignant spectacle not only of one leading Christian socialist bidding farewell to another, but also to the dream that sustained them.

The Last Wesleyan

Of all the great Christians of the twentieth century, Donald Soper was unique, both in the duration of his ministry and the burning intensity with which he espoused a myriad of causes. Such was the breadth of these causes, that no party could claim him for their own, a fact which was both his strength and his weakness in a life grounded in paradox. An authoritarian figure among his own, a rebel when challenging others; an ecumenist who stirred up factionalism wherever he went; a socialist at home in the House of Lords; a puritan who tolerated sexual deviancy; a man some depicted as a communist, yet who did more than many to expose its limitations; an uncompromising controversialist in public, a gentle soul in private; a prophetic figure over many issues, but ultra-conservative over others such as the curse of alcohol and gambling.

In assessing such a rich and eclectic life, the starting point should be Donald's churchmanship. Although not a great writer or theologian, he was an outstanding evangelist, pastor and sacramentalist, greatly loved by many who came under his guidance. A man of Franciscan simplicity and deep piety himself, his conduct of worship was always dignified and his sermons invariably profound, as he married spiritual truth to practical reality. Although a sceptic about so much biblical orthodoxy, his iron rations of faith were extremely conventional, not least in his devotion to the risen Christ as his Lord and Saviour. Whatever the political fall-out arising from his interpretation of the kingdom of God, his life was shaped by a firmly-held vision which gave added meaning to his work on the streets. For over fifty years he fought to rectify some of the ills of the nation's capital in the three Missions over which he presided, with the pioneering efforts of the West London Mission being a model of its kind. Many of society's outcasts had every reason to be grateful to Donald for giving them a second chance. The fact that by no means all of them took it, in no way belittles his achievement. Indeed, ever the realist in social matters, Donald was the first to appreciate that man often was but the unwilling victim of his environment, making him all the more determined to combat the evils of poverty and unemployment. If that meant entering the political arena, so be it, and although some of his campaigns were unduly partisan he was surely right to do so, especially when giving voice to those injustices still deemed unworthy of reform.

For someone whose star shone brightest in the Methodist firmament, it was perhaps inevitable that his relationship with lesser lights, whom he was prone to disparage, could be somewhat fraught. Apart from substantial theological and political differences, Donald found the wheels of Methodism very slow in turning, especially amongst the surfeit of committees which discussed but rarely decided. Consequently he rarely appeared on such bodies, leaving one with the irony that the most famous Methodist throughout the country and the voice of Methodism to many, was something of an outsider amongst his own kin, constantly isolated on such issues as pacifism and abstinence.

Despite that, Donald was by no means a general without an army. Through his leadership of the West London Mission, OCW, MPF and MSF, he became a role model to many, not only in the fullness of his message but the means by which it was communicated. Here at least was a generation of churchmen who realised the need of the Church to see the world as its parish and to offer a light to the most vulnerable by catering to their basic needs. Had others joined them in this Wesleyan enterprise it is quite conceivable that the sudden descent into a secular society could have been halted, as it has been in the United States and large parts of Africa, Asia and South America.

In time, helped by a certain mellowing in his character, others came to acknowledge the full measure of Donald's achievement, so that during his closing years he won near universal acclaim as the Grand Old Man of Methodism, not least at Conference which hadn't always been persuaded by his powerful rhetoric. Perhaps this growing recognition, while tinged with a kind of British nostalgia for a repentant sinner, was also a lament for a lost age, when the Church was a force to be reckoned with. It says much for Donald's genius that he held out longer than most, but in the end, for all his heroic endeavours, he was unable to resist the tide beating at Methodism's door. With the death of Donald Soper, wrote John Travell in his biography of Leslie Weatherhead, there was no longer a single Free Church personality recognisable to the general public.

If Donald died disappointed with the ailing health of Methodism, not least its failure to reunite with the Church of England, he would have entertained similar thoughts about the other great passions of his life, socialism and pacifism. Because his intense commitment to both was the product of his moral fervour, his consistency was admired by friend and foe alike, but increasingly this consistency undermined his effectiveness, since ideas formed in the 1920s needed adapting in a fast changing world. The fact that Donald continued to champion the virtues of a planned economy and nationalisation throughout the 1980s and 90s, when there was clear evidence to the contrary that they weren't the necessary panaceas for Britain or the Labour Party, exposed his limitations as a politician. Compared to his pragmatism so evident in matters spiritual, especially his realisation at an early stage that institutional religion was becoming increasingly outdated in a more secular society, his constant pronouncements on the demise of capitalism betray a certain näivety.

Despite his acceptance that politics was the art of the possible, not least in his membership of the House of Lords, he was something of a waning asset to the Labour Party just when his influence was at its peak. Had he and his friends on the left been rather more open to new ideas during the Gaitskell-Wilson era, the party might well have been spared some of its tribulations during later decades as Thatcherism took root.

Over pacifism, Donald's Christian convictions shone through with admirable sincerity, as did his courage, but his logic was rather undermined by the events of the 1930s. A glance back at history proves that he was unduly optimistic about the nature of totalitarian dictatorships and their receptiveness to western olive branches. Equally, his interpretation of the Holocaust as the direct product of war was flawed given the intense Nazi hatred of the Jews and the willingness to countenance extreme violence against them and other minorities in the years leading up to the war. When CND was at its height in the early 1960s, Donald remained adamant that the best way towards peace was through the Labour Party, as opposed to campaigns of civil disobedience advocated by the more militant wing. For one brief moment in October 1960, it looked as if his hopes had finally been realised, but even had the party stuck with its unilateralist line, there is little evidence to suggest that it would have won power on that basis. To most Britons, however irrationally, surrendering their nuclear defences was a risk too far, especially at the height of the Cold War when co-operation with the Soviet Union seemed a tall order. When CND briefly re-emerged as a force during the early 1980s, it was up against similar obstacles. In a fallen world, Donald never effectively confronted the Niebuhrian argument of how one resisted those elements of evil or aggression, that were immune to reason. According to Alan Wilkinson, his pacifism, like his socialism, was marred by his platform facility for the clever phrase at the expense of reasoned debate. Yet equally, the case for war and nuclear weapons was never cast-iron, as their advocates would have us believe. Donald's diatribes divested his opponents' arguments of some of their moral force, so that the Churches, as they demonstrated over the Iraq War of 2003, now hold a much more sceptical, less romantic view of war than hitherto.

Donald's dislike of violence extended to many areas of domestic life, which, alongside his abhorrence of discrimination and injustice, formed the background to much of his pressure group activity. For many years he was the unfashionable voice of enlightened tolerance against the unbending moral and judicial consensus, which offered little hope to those who had fallen foul of society's conventions. Gradually, however, the walls of prejudice began to crack. The 1960s saw the relaxation in censorship and divorce, the abolition of capital punishment and legalisation of homosexuality and abortion; the 1970s a greater commitment to animal rights and racial and sexual equality, which in turn has paved the way for the ordination of women in most denominations. On few of these issues has the last word been uttered, and not every step forward has been to the betterment of all, but, in a more permissive age, there is little chance of turning the clock back. Here then in terms of practical results was the lasting legacy of someone such as Donald Soper who had championed the cause of the underdog for well over seventy years. It was an enviable record of unswerving Christian discipleship throughout life's changing scenes, richly deserving of the ultimate accolade; "Well done, good and faithful servant;—enter thou into the joy of thy Lord".

Bibliography

Newspapers
Adelaide Advertiser
Belfast Telegraph
Christchurch Star-Sun
Daily Express
Daily Herald
Daily Mail
Daily Mirror
Daily Sketch
Daily Telegraph
Daily Worker
Evening News
Evening Standard
Guardian
Hampstead and Highgate Express
Independent
Manchester Guardian
News Chronicle
News of the World
North Devon Journal
Northern Despatch
Oxford Mail
South Eastern Herald
South Wales Echo and Evening Express
Sunday Times
Sydney Morning Herald
The Age[Melbourne]
The Times
Western Herald
Yorkshire Post

Periodicals and Journals.
Baptist Times
British Weekly
Care of the Elderly
Christian World
Church Times
Crusade for Christ News Sheet 1952
Free Churchman
*Hansard House of Lords parliamentary
    debates 1965–92*
Jewish Chronicle
Kingsway
Kingsway Messenger
Listener
Methodist [Australia]
Methodist Recorder
Methodist Times
New Statesman
New Zealand Methodist
Peace News
PPU Journal
Reconciliation
St Catharine's Society Magazine
Socialist Commentary
Socialist Leader
Spectator
The Askean
The Oldie
Tribune
Wesley House Minute Book volume 1

Other publications

Glass, Paul, The Origins of Wesley House, *Proceedings of the Wesley Historical Society*, volume 49, May 1993

Hatcham Tercentenary

OCW Yearbook 1960

St John's Hill Church 1864–1964 Centenary Celebrations

Seasons of Life. The 1997 Methodist Companion, Methodist Publishing House, 1996

Wilkinson, Alan, *Donald Soper in Oxford DNB*, volume 51, Oxford University Press, 2004

Bibliography

Bagwell, P., *Outcast London, A Christian Response?*, Epworth Press, 1987

Barclay, Oliver R., and Horn, Robert M., *From Cambridge to the World: 125 years of Student Witness*, Inter Varsity Press, 2002

Bardsley Brash, W., *The Story of our Colleges 1835–1935*, Epworth, 1935

Beasley, John D., *The Bitter Cry Heard and Heeded: The Story of the South London Mission 1889–1988*, SLM, 1990

Bebbington, David, *Evangelism in Modern Britain: A History from the 1730s to the 1980s*, London Unwin/ Hyman, 1989

Benn, Tony, *Free At Last, Diaries 1991–2001*, edited by Ruth Winstone, Arrow Books, 2003

Berry, Paul and Bostridge, Mark, *Vera Brittain: A Life*, Chatto and Windus, 1995

Berton, Pierre, *The Cool, Crazy, Committed World of the Sixties*, McClelland and Stewart, 1966

Bridger, Francis [ed], *The Cross and the Bomb*, Mowbrays, 1983

Briggs, Asa, *War of Words: The History of Broadcasting in the United Kingdom*, volume 3, Oxford University Press, 1970

Brittain, Vera, *Chronicle of Friendship. Diary of the Thirties 1932–1939*, edited by Alan Bishop, Gollancz, 1986

Brittain, Vera, *Wartime Chronicle. Diary 1939–1945*, edited by Alan Bishop and Y. Aleksandra Bennett, Gollancz, 1989

Brockway, F. (ed), *Bermondsey Story: The Life of Alfred Salter*, Allen and Unwin, 1951

Bryant, Chris, *Reclaiming the Ground: Christianity and Socialism*, Hodder and Stoughton, 1993

Bryant, Chris, *Possible Dreams: A Personal History of the British Christian Socialists*, Hodder and Stoughton, 1996

Calder, Angus, *The People's War*, Granada, 1971

Ceadel, Martin, *Pacifism in Britain 1914–45: The Defining of a Faith*, Oxford: Clarendon, 1980

Chadwick, Owen, *Michael Ramsey*, Oxford: Clarendon, 1990

Charlton, Leslie, *Spark in the Stubble: Colin Morris of Zambia*, London: Epworth, 1969

Cock, Douglas J., *Every Inch a Methodist*, London: Epworth, 1987

Cort, John C., *Christian Socialism: An Informal History*, Orbis Books, 1988

Crossman, Richard, *The Diary of a Cabinet Minister*, volume 2, Hamish Hamilton and Jonathan Cape, 1976

Dale, Graham, *God's Politicians: The Christian Contribution to 100 Years of Labour*, Harper Collins, 2000

Davies, A.J., *To Build A New Jerusalem. The British Labour Movement from the 1880s to the 1990s*, Michael Joseph: London, 1992

Davies, Rupert E., *Methodism*, Epworth Press, 1963

De-la-Noy, Michael, *Michael Ramsey: A Portrait*, Fount Paperbacks, 1991

De-la-Noy, Michael, *Mervyn Stockwood: A Lonely Life*, Mowbray, 1996

Dillistone, F.W., *Charles Raven: Naturalist, Historian, Theologian*, Hodder and Stoughton, 1975

Dinwiddie, Melville, *Religion by Radio, Its Place in British Broadcasting*, Allen and Unwin, 1968

Driver, Christopher, *The Disarmers: A Study in Protest*, Hodder and Stoughton, 1964

Duff, Peggy, *Left, Left, Left*, London: Allison and Busby, 1971

Ferguson, Ronald, *George MacLeod: Founder of the Iona Community*, Fount, 1990

Fletcher, Sheila, *Maude Royden: A Life*, Basil Blackwell, 1989

Frost, Brian, *Goodwill on Fire: Donald Soper's Life and Mission*, Hodder and Stoughton, 1996

Frost, Brian[ed], *A Vintage Soper: God, Faith and Socialism*, Hodder and Stoughton, 1997

Glass, Paul, *A History of Wesley House*, PHD Thesis, University of Leeds, 1993 [unpublished]

Harris, Jeffrey, *Going Places: The Review of the Methodist Church*, London Mission, 1985

Hastings, Adrian, *A History of English Christianity 1920–1990*, SCM Press, 1985

Hayes, Denis, *Challenge of Conscience. The Story of the Conscientious Objectors of 1939–45*, George Allen and Unwin, 1949

Henderson, Harold, *Reach for the World. The Alan Walker Story*, Disciple Resources Nashville, 1981

Hill, Douglas [ed], *Tribune 40: The First Forty Years of a Socialist Newspaper*, Quartet Books, 1977

Hinton, James, *Protests and Visions: Peace Politics in Twentieth-Century Britain*, London: Hutchinson Radius, 1989

Holden, Andrew, *Makers and Manners. Politics and Morality in Post-War Britain*, Politicos, 2004

Holman, Bob, *Good Old George-The Life of George Lansbury*, Lion, 1990

Hunter, George, *Evangelistic Rhetoric in Secular Britain: The Theory and Speaking of Donald Soper and Bryan Green*, Evanston, Illinois, 1972 [unpublished thesis]

Ingarfield, L.E., and Alexander, M.B., *A Short History of Haberdashers' Aske's, Hatcham Boys' School*, The Worshipful Company of Haberdashers, 1985

Iremonger, F.A., *William Temple*, Oxford University Press, 1948

Jones, Raymond, *Arthur Ponsonby*, Christian Helm, 1989

Lange, David, *My Life*, Viking, 2005

Marrinan, Patrick, *Paisley: Man of Wrath*, Tralee Anvil Books, 1973

Martin, David and Mullen, Peter [ed], *Unholy Warfare: The Church and the Bomb*, Blackwells, 1983

Mason, David, Ainger, Geoffrey and Denny Norwen, *News from Notting Hill*, Epworth Press, 1967

Matthews, Charles H.S., *Dick Sheppard: Man of Peace*, James Clark and Co, 1948

Moorehead, Caroline, *Troublesome People: Enemies of War 1918–86*, Hamish Hamilton, 1987

Morrison, Sybil, *I Renounce War: The Story of the Peace Pledge Union*, Sheppard Press, 1962

Murphy, Terence and Perin, Roberto [ed] *A Concise History of Christianity in Canada*, Oxford University Press, 1996

Parkin, Frank, *Middle Class Radicalism*, Manchester University Press, 1968

Pimlott, Ben, *Harold Wilson*, Harper Collins, 1992

Pollock, John, *Billy Graham: The Authorised Biography*, Hodder and Stoughton, London, 1966

Purcell, William, *Portrait of Soper*, Mowbrays, 1972

Robertson, Edwin, George: *A Biography of Viscount Tonypandy*, Marshall Pickering, 1992

Rodaway, Angela, *A London Childhood*, Virago Press, 1985

Sangster, Paul, *Dr Sangster*, Epworth Press, 1962

Sangster, Paul, *A History of the Free Churches*, London: Heinemann, 1983

Shepherd, John, *George Lansbury: At the Heart of Old Labour*, Oxford University Press, 1992

Soper, Donald, *Christ and Tower Hill*, Hodder and Stoughton, 1934

Soper, Donald, *Question Time on Tower Hill*, Hodder and Stoughton, 1935

Soper, Donald, *Answer Time on Tower Hill*, Hodder and Stoughton, 1936

Soper, Donald, *Christianity and Its Critics*, Hodder and Stoughton, 1937

Soper, Donald, *Popular Fallacies about the Christian Faith*, Hodder and Stoughton, 1937

Soper, Donald, *Practical Christianity Today*, Ken-Pax, 1947, republished Epworth Press, 1954

Soper, Donald, *All His Grace*, Epworth Press, 1957

Soper, Donald, *The Advocacy of the Gospel*, Hodder and Stoughton, 1961

Soper, Donald, *Tower Hill, 12.30*, Epworth Press, 1963

Soper, Donald, *Aflame with Faith*, Epworth Press, 1963

Soper, Donald, *Calling for Action*, Robson Books, 1984

Stammer, Neil, *Civil Liberties in Britain During the Second World War*, Croom Helm, 1983

Stockwood, Mervyn, *Chanctonbury Ring: An Autobiography*, Hodder and Stoughton, 1988

Stott, Caroline, *Dick Sheppard: A Biography*, Hodder and Stoughton, 1977

Taylor, Richard and Pritchard, Colin, *The Protest Makers: The British Nuclear Disarmament Movement of 1958–65*, Oxford: Pergamon, 1980

Taylor, Richard, *Against the Bomb: The British Peace Movement 1858–1965*, Oxford: Clarendon, 1988

Tebbit, Norman, *Upwardly Mobile: An Autobiography*, Weidenfeld and Nicholson, 1988

Thomas, George, *George Thomas, Mr Speaker: The Memoirs of Viscount Tonypandy*, Century, 1985

Thompson, Douglas, *Donald Soper: A Biography*, Denholm Press, 1971

Thompson Brake, G., *Policy and Politics in British Methodism 1932–82*, Edsall, 1984

Travell, John, *Director of Souls: A Biography of Dr Leslie Dixon Weatherhead*, Lutterworth Press, Cambridge, 1999

Trudeau, Pierre E. [ed], *The Asbestos Strike 1949*, James Lewis and Samuel, Toronto, 1974

Turberfield, Alan, *John Scott Lidgett. Archbishop of Methodism?* Peterborough: Epworth, 2003

Turner, J.M., *Modern Methodism in England 1932–98*, London: Epworth, 1999

Valentine, Simon, Ross, *W.E. Sangster*, Peterborough Foundery Press, 1998

Vickers, John (ed), A Dictionary of Methodism in Britain and Ireland, Peterborough: Epworth, 2000

Vincent, John, *Christ and Methodism*, Epworth Press, 1965

Vincent, John, *Here I Stand: The Faith of a Radical*, Epworth Press, 1967

Wakefield, Gordon, *Methodist Spirituality*, Peterborough: Epworth, 1999

Wakelin, Michael, J.A. Rank: *The Man behind the Gong*, Lion Publishing PLC, 1996

Wallis, Jill, *Valiant for Peace: A History of the Fellowship of Reconciliation*, London Fellowship of Reconciliation, 1991

Wallis, Jill, *Mother of Peace. The Life of Muriel Lester*, Hisarlik Press, 1993

Weatherhead, Kingsley, *Leslie Weatherhead. A Personal Portrait*, Hodder and Stoughton, 1973

Welsby, Paul, *A History of the Church of England*, Oxford University Press, 1984

Wheen, Francis, *Tom Driberg: His Life and Indiscretions*, Chatto and Windus, 1990

Wilkinson, Alan, *Dissent or Conform? War, Peace and the English Churches 1900–45*, SCM Press, 1986

Wilkinson, Alan, *Christian Socialism: Scott Holland to Tony Blair*, SCM Press, 1998

Wolfe, Kenneth M., *The Churches and the British Broadcasting Corporation 1922–56*, SCM Press, 1984

Wright, Don and Clancy, Eric, *A History of Methodism in New South Wales*, Allen and Unwin, 1993

Wright, Don, *Alan Walker. Conscience of a Nation*, Open Book Publishers, 1997

Wright, Vernon, *David Lange. Prime Minister*, Wellington and Unwin, 1984

TV and Radio

Donald Soper to David Franklin, BBC, *Cambridge Revisited*, recorded 22 July 1968, BBCT33217, British Library, National Sound Archive, T11047 WR

The Time of My Life, [1921–26], 5 January 1969, British Library, National Sound Archive, BBC P317 R

"Under Bow Bells": Donald Soper in dialogue with Joan Bakewell, BBC, 4 April 1976

At Home with the Sopers. Woman's Hour, BBC, 22 February 1981

Friendship: Donald Soper and Harry Morton with Colin Morris, BBC, 15 March 1981

"Soper at 80". Donald Soper with Ronald Eyre, BBC, 1 February 1983

Home on Sunday, with Cliff Michelmore, BBCTV, 22 July 1984

Prime Minister with the Preacher, BBC Everyman, 3 November 1985

The Power of the Preachers, with Eric Lord, BBC, 1 June 1986

Wesley Day: Donald Soper with Roger Royle, BBC, 24 May 1987

"When I get to Heaven". Donald Soper in conversation with Richard Holloway, BBC, 17 May 1987

Matter of Conscience, with Simon Rae, BBC, 14 May 1992

Songs of Praise, BBC, 31 January 1993

Soper's Corner. Donald Soper in conversation with Colin Morris, BBC, July 1994

Good Morning Sunday, BBC, 28 January 1998

With Great Pleasure. Donald Soper in conversation with Margaret Sharpe, BBC, 31 January 1998

Tapes

Face to Face. Donald Soper in conversation with the Revd Len Barnett, Central Methodist Church, Bromley, October 1978

Vote of Thanks to the Rt Hon John Smith MP, Bloomsbury Baptist Church, 20 March 1993

Thanksgiving Service for the Life of Donald Soper, 31 January 1999

Various recordings of Donald Soper at Hyde Park and Tower Hill

Notes

Prologue
Alan Wilkinson, *Christian Socialism: From Scott Holland to Tony Blair*, p.187.

Chapter 1
1   Greta Reynolds to Brian Frost, 23 March 1993.
2   Testimonial from the Headmistress of Swaffield Road Primary School, Wandsworth, 3 June 1914. [family collection]
3   Testimonial from the Managers of Stillness Road School, 18 September 1919. [family collection]
4   Testimonial from the Chairman of the Managers of Morden Terrace Girls' School, 8 November 1922. [family collection]
5   *Soper's Corner, No 5, Militant for Faith;* Donald Soper in conversation with the Revd Dr Colin Morris, July 1994.
6   Donald Soper to Brian Frost, 21 May 1992.
7   Donald Soper quoted in *"A London Childhood: Lord Soper"*, interview with Judy Goodkin, *The Times* Saturday Review, 23 March 1991.
8   Ibid.
9   Headmaster's Reports, Aske's School. [Kept in the London Borough of Lewisham Manor House Library.]
10 Ibid.
11 Ibid.
12 Ibid.
13 Ibid.
14 Ibid.
15 *South Eastern Herald*, 22 December 1916.
16 *The Askean*, July 1920.
17 Ibid.
18 *"Childhood: Lord Soper"*.
19 *The Askean*, December 1920.
20 BBC programme "Frankly Speaking" (29.7.1965) quoted in William Purcell, *Portrait of Soper*, p.46.
21 *"A Childhood: Lord Soper"*.
22 *Portrait of Soper*, p.49.
23 *The Askean*, July 1924.
24 Donald Soper, *Calling for Action*, p.129.

25 *Soper's Corner, No 2, Socialism,* July 1994.
26 *Calling for Action,* p.76.
27 Ibid.
28 *Calling for Action,* p.26.
29 Ibid.
30 Wesley House College Minute Book, vol 1.

Chapter 2
1 Donald Soper, *Aflame with Faith,* p.125.
2 Donald Soper, *Calling for Action,* p.152.
3 Ibid.
4 Donald Soper, *Popular Fallacies about the Christian Faith,* p.30.
5 Rt Revd Lord Sheppard to the author, 7 July 00.
6 Donald Soper, *Tower Hill 12.30,* p.151.
7 *Peace News,* 25 April 1947.
8 *Kingsway,* autumn 1958.
9 Donald Soper in *Portrait of Soper,* p.63.
10 Rt Hon Lord Callaghan to the author, 22 June 00.
11 *British Weekly,* 17 August 1936.
12 The Revd George Dolbey to Brian Frost, 13 January 1993.

Chapter 3
1 Donald Soper quoted in Purcell, p39.
2 Angela Rodaway, *A London Childhood,* p.125.
3 Donald Soper to George Irons, 2 February 1930.
4 *A London Childhood,* p.60.
5 Donald Soper in conversation with Brian Frost, November 1992.
6 The Revd Dr Colin Morris, sermon preached at Service of Thanksgiving for the Life and Work of Donald Soper, 3 March 1999.
7 *Christ and Tower Hill,* p.89.
8 The Revd F.A. Iremonger to Donald Soper, 18 February 1935, BBC Written Archives Centre, Caversham, Donald Soper file.
9 The Revd F.A.Iremonger to Donald Soper, 30 December 1936.
10 The Revd F.A.Iremonger to Donald Soper, 18 October 1937.
11 The Revd F.A.Iremonger to Donald Soper, 19 November 1937.

Chapter 4
1 *Western Evening Herald,* 10 April 1937.
2 *British Weekly,* 10 February 1938.
3 Harold Henderson, *Reach for the World,* p.23.
4 *Reconciliation,* May 1936.
5 *Reconciliation,* June 1936.
6 Adrian Hastings, *A History of English Christianity 1920–90,* p.333.

7 Donald Soper in *Portrait of Soper*, p.124.
8 *Methodist Recorder*, 2 February 1939.
9 *North Devon Journal*, 25 May 1939.
10 *Peace News*, 15 December 1944.
11 *Calling for Action*, p.36–7.
12 Ibid., p.37.
13 Donald Soper quoted in Purcell, p.136.
14 Ulrich Simon quoted in *The Cross and the Bomb*, p.99.

Chapter 5
1 *Kingsway Messenger*, April 1942.
2 Leslie Gore to Brian Frost, 31 March 1993.
3 Paul Berry and Mark Bostridge, *Vera Brittain: A Life*, p.399.
4 The Revd David Mason, letter to the author, 4 February 02.
5 Leslie Weatherhead, *Methodist Recorder*, 14 January 1943.
6 Donald Soper, sermon at Kingsway Hall, 4 February 1940.
7 Ibid., 12 May 1940.
8 Ibid., 26 May 1940.
9 Donald Soper, sermon at St John's Methodist Church, Southampton, 1 June 1942.
10 *Methodist Recorder*, 28 September 1944.
11 *Peace News*, 15 December 1944.

Chapter 6
1 Peggy Dring to Brian Frost, 16 May 1993.
2 Clifford Austin to Brian Frost, 11 February 1993.
3 The Revd Len Barnett in *The Power of the Preachers,* 1 June 1986.
4 *Methodist Recorder*, 11 February 1993.
5 *Kingdom Come: The story of a film, Kingsway*, summer 1968.
6 Douglas Cock, *Methodist Recorder*, 3 September 1953.
7 *OCW Yearbook*, 1960.

Chapter 7
1 Basil Jackson to the Secretary of the Methodist Missionary Society, 12 August 1947. [The letter is in the archives of the Methodist Missionary Society.]
2 Donald Soper, Ceylon Travel Diary [unpublished], 16 September 1947.
3 Ibid., 14 October 1947.
4 Basil Jackson, 21 October 1947. Reflections on Donald Soper's visit to Ceylon in Basil Jackson's official correspondence in the archives of the Methodist Missionary Society.
5 Australian Travel Diary [unpublished], 23 October 1947.
6 Ibid., 27 October 1947.
7 Meeting at Albert Hall, Brisbane, 27 October 1947.
8 *Methodist*, 15 November 1947.

9 Australian Travel Diary, 10 November 1947.

10 Ibid., 13 November 1947.

11 Ibid., 19 November 1947.

12 Ibid., 30 November 1947.

13 Canadian Travel Diary [unpublished], 9 November 1949.

14 Ibid., 11 November 1949.

15 Ibid.

16 Ibid.

17 Ibid., 16 November 1949.

18 *PPU Journal*, August 1947.

19 Donald Soper, *Christ and Tower Hill*, p.50.

20 Speech to Methodist Conference, Bradford, 12 July 1950.

21 *Daily Mirror*, 20 July 1950.

22 Speech to MPF at Bradford, 24 July 1950.

23 *Socialist Leader*, 29 July 1950.

24 *British Weekly* editorial, 27 July 1950.

25 Purcell, p.92.

26 Revd Dr John Newton, obituary to Donald Soper, *Methodist Recorder*, 31 December 1998.

27 Letter in *Methodist Recorder*, 29 March 1951.

28 Letter in *Methodist Recorder*, 5 April 1951.

29 Donald Soper in interview with Avril Bottoms, *Methodist Recorder*, 29 January 1998.

30 American Travel Diary[unpublished], 5 September 1951.

31 Ibid., 7 September 1951.

32 Press Conference, Sydney, 15 September 1951.

33 Meeting at the Domain, Sydney, 16 September 1951.

34 Speech at Rivoli Hall, Hurtsville, 18 September 1951.

35 Australian Travel Diary [unpublished], 19 September 1951.

36 Ibid.

37 Ibid., 25 September 1951.

38 The Revd David Mason to the author, 19 November 04.

39 Australian Travel Diary, 27 September 1951.

40 *Methodist*, 29 September 1951.

41 Letter in *Methodist*, 29 September 1951.

42 *Methodist,* 13 October 1951.

43 Speech at Armidale, 3 October 1951.

44 Australian Travel Diary, 5 October 1951.

45 Methodist Church Australia *Crusade for Christ News Sheet*, February 1952.

46 Australian Travel Diary, 7 December 1951.

47 *Crusade for Christ News Sheet*, February 1952.

48 *Methodist Recorder*, 28 February 1952.

49 The Revd David Mason to the author, 4 February 02.

Chapter 8

1 Presidential Address, 10 July 1953.
2 Ibid.
3 *British Weekly*, 6 May 1954.
4 Donald Soper, sermon at Moseley Road Church, 13 July 1953.
5 *British Weekly*, 23 July 1953.
6 Sermon at Donald Soper's funeral, 30 December 1998.
7 Speech at Deansgate, Manchester, 16 November 1953.
8 *British Weekly*, 26 November 1953.
9 *South Wales Echo and Evening Express*, 23 November 1953.
10 *Methodist Recorder*, 26 November 1953.
11 J.E.Rattenbury to Donald Soper, 25 November 1953.
12 Ibid., 10 December 1953.
13 Harold Roberts to Donald Soper, 22 December 1953.
14 Speech at Plymouth, 30 January 1954.
15 Douglas Cock, *Methodist Recorder*, 11 February 1954.
16 Keith Woollard, letter to Donald Soper, 27 January 1954.
17 *Tribune*, 26 February 1954.
18 Donald Soper, sermon at Kingsway Hall, 4 April 1954.
19 Donald Soper, sermon at Kingsway Hall, 16 May 1954.
20 J.E Rattenbury, *British Weekly*, 6 May 1954.

Chapter 9

1 Kenneth Grayston to R.A.Rendall, 17 March 1947, BBC Written Archives Centre, Caversham, Reading, Lord Soper file 1b, Talks 1940–52.
2 R.A.Rendall to Kenneth Grayston, 18 March 1947.
3 *Methodist Recorder*, 1 December 1955.
4 Michael Foot to Donald Soper, 1 February 1954. (In presidential papers for 1953–54, Methodist Archive, John Rylands Library, University of Manchester.)
5 Ibid., 11 February 1954.
6 Tribute to Donald Soper, *Tribune*, 15 January 1999.
7 Sermon at Kingsway Hall, 6 December 1954.
8 *Tribune*, 1 February 1963.
9 Ibid., 29 April 1955.
10 Ibid.
11 Ibid., 3 June 1955.
12 *Spectator*, 8 July 1955.
13 *Tribune*, 22 July 1955.
14 *Tribune*, 1 March 1957.
15 *New Zealand Methodist Times*, 15 October 1955.
16 *New Zealand Methodist Times*, 1 October 1955.
17 Ibid.

18 Ibid.
19 The Revd Laurie Greenslade, letter in *New Zealand Methodist Times*, 4 February 1956.
20 Donald Soper, letter in *New Zealand Methodist Times*, 4 February 1956.
21 *Methodist Recorder*, 13 October 1955.
22 Ibid., 9 July 1953.
23 *Tribune*, 28 October 1955.
24 Ibid., 18 November 1955.
25 As quoted in the press, 1 November 1955.
26 *Tribune*, 2 December 1955.
27 Ibid., 4 February 1955.
28 Polish Travel Diary [unpublished], 28 May 1956.
29 *Calling for Action*, p.47.
30 Polish Travel Diary, 31 May 1956.
31 Ibid., 1 June 1956.
32 Ibid., 2 June 1956.
33 Sermon at Kingsway Hall, 16 September 1956.
34 Sermon at Kingsway Hall, 4 November 1956.
35 Donald Soper, reply at Hornsey Town Hall, 8 November 1956.
36 *Methodist Recorder*, 11 October 1956.
37 *Kingsway*, spring 1957.
38 Patrick Marrinan, *Paisley: Man of Wrath*, p.55–60 and other sources.
39 *Belfast Telegraph*, 3 August 1959.

Chapter 10
1   Donald Soper in conversation with Brian Frost, November 1992.
2   *Tribune*, 16 December 1955.
3   Tribute to Aneurin Bevan, Tredegar, 15 July 1960.
4   Michael Rubinstein to Donald Soper, 14 October 1960.[Papers donated by Michael Rubinstein, the solicitor for Penguin Books Ltd at the time of the trial, to the University of Bristol Library Department of Manuscripts.]
5   Donald Soper, draft Proof of Evidence, October 1960.
6   Stanley Frost to Brian Frost, 12 April 1993.
7   *Daily Express*, 19 September 1952.
8   *Daily Mirror*, 19 September 1952.
9   *Tribune*, 14 June 1963.
10 *Methodist Recorder*, 5 March 1964.
11 *Tribune*, 16 January 1959.
12 Ibid., 15 April 1966.
13 *Kingsway*, spring 1965.
14 Donald Soper quoted in Jill Wallis, *Valiant for Peace: A History of the Fellowship of Reconciliation*, p.166.
15 *Peace News*, 18 January 1957.

16 *Tribune,* 13 December 1957.
17 *Peace News,* 6 June 1958.
18 *Tribune,* 10 April 1959.
19 Ibid., 24 June 1960.
20 *Tribune,* 14 October 1960.
21 Ibid., 7 April 1961.
22 *Methodist Recorder,* 21 September 1961.
23 *Reconciliation,* February 1963 editorial.
24 *Tribune,* 31 May 1963.
25 *Protest Makers,* p.102. Note 108.
26 *Tribune,* 30 January 1959.

Chapter 11
1   *Tribune,* 2 December 1960.
2   Michael Foot to Donald Soper, May 1965 (family collection)
3   *St Michael's Highgate Parish Magazine,* 30 July 1965.
4   *Northern Despatch,* 3 May 1965.
5   *Methodist Recorder,* 6 May 1965.
6   Michael Ramsey to Donald Soper, May 1965 (family collection)
7   *Methodist Recorder,* 15 January 1976.
8   Hansard, *H.L,* 15 June 1965, vol 267, col 43.
9   *Tribune,* 15 October 1965.
10 *News of the World,* 5 June 1966.
11 *The Times,* 26 November 1966.
12 Ibid., 29 November 1966.
13 Richard Crossman, *The Diaries of a Cabinet Minister,* vol 2, p.63.
14 *Hansard, H.L.,* 19 July 1967, vol 285, col 301.
15 Quoted in Purcell, *Portrait of Soper,* p.99.
16 *Tribune,* 13 September 1957.
17 *Hansard, H.L,* 13 July 1967, vol 284, col 1309.
18 *The Cool, Crazy, Committed World of the Sixties,* p.44.
19 *Methodist Recorder,* 11 May 1967.
20 Ibid., 1 June 1967.
21 *Tribune,* 7 June 1963.
22 Ibid., 2 August 1968.
23 Ibid., 10 January 1969.
24 Ibid., 29 September 1967.
25 Ibid., 4 October 1968.
26 *Methodist Times,* 31 December 1931.
27 *Kingsway Messenger,* October 1946.
28 Adrian Hastings, *A History of English Christianity 1920–90,* p.464.
29 *Kingsway,* spring 1964.

30   G.T. Brake, *Policy and Politics in British Methodism*, p.113.
31   *Methodist Recorder*, 3 August 1967.
32   *Tribune*, 12 May 1972.
33   *British Weekly*, 28 March 1957.

Chapter 12
1   *Tribune*, 28 August, 1970.
2   Evidence submitted to Barnet Eruv Objectors Group, December 1993.
3   Norman Tebbit, *Upwardly Mobile*, p.109.
4   *Hansard, H.L.*, 27 October 1971, vol 324, cols 697–702.
5   Speech to Methodist Conference, 1 July 1974.
6   *Hansard, H.L*, 4 June 1974, vol 352, col 146.
7   *Hansard, H.L.*, 8 March 1977, vol 380, col 986.
8   *Ibid.*, 25 March 1969, vol 300, cols 1195–98.
9   *Ibid.*, 12 February 1976, vol 368, cols 260–63.
10   *Methodist Recorder*, 29 June 1978.

Chapter 13
1   The Revd Dr John Newton to the author, 12 July 02.
2   *Tribune*, 30 September 1977.
3   *Hansard, H.L.*, 25 February 1980, vol 405, col 1094.
4   William Cannon, Chairman of the Executive Committee, World Methodist
     Council, Citation in Presentation of the Peace Award, 2 October 1981.
5   *Calling for Action*, p.65.
6   *Methodist Recorder*, 1 March 1984.
7   Ibid., 8 March 1984.
8   *Hansard, H.L.*, 31 October 1984, vol 456, cols 547–48.
9   Citation for Hon DD Cambridge University, 10 June 1988.
10   *Methodist Recorder*, 27 January 1983.
11   *Hansard, H.L*, 4 June 1990, vol 519, cols 1162–65.
12   *Daily Mail*, 30 January 1993.
13   Tony Benn, *Free at Last*, p.161.
14   The plaque was replaced by another one in 2007 which read, "Lord Donald Soper
     Christian socialist and pacifist preached here for over 70 years". The original
     plaque has been given to Hinde St Church.
15   *Methodist Recorder*, 29 January 1998.
16   Donald Soper in *Seasons of Life*, p.172–73.
17   *Methodist Recorder*, 7 July 1994.
18   *Methodist Recorder*, 29 January 1998.
19   *Independent*, 23 December 1998.
20   Sermon at The Service of Thanksgiving for the Life and Work of Donald Soper at
     Westminster Abbey, 3 March 1999.
21   Ian Walters's sculpture of Donald Soper won him the Tussaud's Studios
     Millennium Prize for Portraiture.

Index

Donald's parents at the time of their Golden Wedding in 1950. Their staunch Christian values were to play an important part in the life and work of their elder son.

Donald, left, aged fourteen, with his sister Millicent and brother Meredith Ross known to the family as "Sos". All three were talented musicians and athletes.

Donald (third from the left, middle row) captaining the Aske's cricket XI.
Work commitments curtailed his cricketing opportunities after university, but for the
rest of his life he remained devoted to this most English of games and often alluded to
it in his sermons.

Donald operating a projector at Islington Central Hall. A master of all forms of communication, he was an early pioneer of the Children's Cinema, paying particular concern to the content.
Methodist Recorder

Opposite "The Probationer"
Donald at Oakley Place off the Old Kent Road in the heart of South London.
West London Mission.

For a Methodist minister and his wife, Donald and Marie Soper cut a very glamorous couple, not least on their overseas trips.

"Before the Lights Went Out"
As Europe edged ever closer to war, Donald (right) enjoys a rare week's relaxation with
a Christian Cruise Party on board the SS *Montrose* – visiting Gibraltar, Naples and
Algiers – summer 1939.
Below Marie on board the RMS *Beregaria*.

"The Entertainer" – Donald enlivened many a religious and social gathering with his skill on the piano, playing anything from the hymns of Charles Wesley to Fats Waller.
Methodist Recorder

Donald and members of OCW at Huddersfield, August 1947. One of his proudest achievements was the foundation of this Order to promote open-air preaching, especially among the young, and many a talented Methodist minister learnt his craft on these trips to all parts of the country.
Renée Willgress

Relaxing on his day-off – Donald on OCW,
August 1947.
Renée Willgress

Donald with students at Ibadan University, Nigeria, 1963.

Opposite Donald at home with Marie to mark his retirement from the West London Mission, aged seventy-five, although retirement in the normal sense of the word was never an option.
Methodist Recorder

Marie at home with the family, June 1970.
(from left to right) Bridget, Caroline, Ann and Judith. *Photocraft[Hampstead] Ltd*

Donald, as visiting speaker, being presented with a cup in stainless steel in Hillsborough Trinity Methodist Church, Sheffield, September 1980. As a speaker and controversialist, he was capable of filling any hall or church in the land until well into his eighties.

Norman Cooper

Donald celebrating his eightieth birthday with his tin whistle presented to him by the West London Mission Seymour Place Day Centre. With him is his good friend Michael Foot, the leader of the Labour Party. *Methodist Recorder*

The "Fellowship of Controversy"
Donald, aged 91, still in control at Speakers' Corner. Note the number of young people in the audience. *Kath Humphreys*

"No Museum Piece"
Donald maintained his passionate convictions and combative style till the very end.
Kath Humphreys

"The Faithful Few"
During his last couple of years, Donald, by now confined to a wheelchair, was inevitably less of a force than hitherto, but he still retained his admiring circle at both Tower Hill and Hyde Park.
Kath Humphreys